Islam and Muslim Politics in Africa

Edited by

Benjamin F. Soares
and
René Otayek

palgrav
macmillan

First published in 2007 by
PALGRAVE MACMILLAN™
175 Fifth Avenue, New York, N.Y. 10010 and
Houndmills, Basingstoke, Hampshire, England RG21 6XS
Companies and representatives throughout the world.

PALGRAVE MACMILLAN is the global academic imprint of the Palgrave Macmillan division of St. Martin's Press, LLC and of Palgrave Macmillan Ltd. Macmillan® is a registered trademark in the United States, United Kingdom and other countries. Palgrave is a registered trademark in the European Union and other countries.

ISBN-13: 978–1–4039–7963–6 (hardcover)
ISBN-10: 1–4039–7963–4 (hardcover)
ISBN-13: 978–1–4039–7964–3 (paperback)
ISBN-10: 1–4039–7964–2 (paperback)

Library of Congress Cataloging-in-Publication Data

Islam and Muslim politics in Africa / edited by Benjamin F. Soares and René Otayek.
p. cm.
Includes bibliographical references and index.
ISBN 1–4039–7963–4 (alk. paper)—ISBN 1–4039–7964–2 (alk. paper)
1. Islam and state—Africa. 2. Islam and politics—Africa. I. Soares, Benjamin F. II. Otayek, René.

BP64.A1I835 2007
322'.1096—dc22   2006103220

A catalogue record for this book is available from the British Library.

Design by Newgen Imaging Systems (P) Ltd., Chennai, India.

First edition: October 2007

10 9 8 7 6 5 4 3 2 1

Printed in the United States of America.

Islam and Muslim Politics in Africa

CONTENTS

Part III   New Ways of Being Muslim

ACKNOWLEDGMENTS

This book began as part of a collaborative research project entitled "Islam, Disengagement of the State, and Globalization in Africa" between the African Studies Centre (ASC) in Leiden and the Centre d'Études d'Afrique Noire (CEAN) in Bordeaux that the Netherlands Ministry of Foreign Affairs generously funded. The project culminated in an international conference ("Islam, Désengagement de l'État et Globalisation en Afrique Subsaharienne") held at UNESCO in Paris on May 12–13, 2005, during which versions of the papers in this volume were presented. The French Ministry of Foreign Affairs provided additional support for the conference.

We are grateful to the Netherlands Ministry of Foreign Affairs for the funding that made this project and publication possible and for allowing the academic researchers to retain control of the actual content of the project and the definition of its themes. We owe special thanks to Norbert Braakhuis of the Netherlands Ministry of Foreign Affairs, who was the driving force behind this project. We also thank Yvette Daoud of the Netherlands Ministry of Foreign Affairs and François-Xavier Léger of the French Ministry of Foreign Affairs for their support. We are grateful to Gerti Hesseling for her contributions to the project from its earliest stages and to Leo de Haan for his support. Jean-Michel Dolbeau, Joop Nijssen, Paul Schrijver, Elizabeth Vignati, and Marieke van Winden provided much-needed organizational support, and they helped to ensure the project ran smoothly.

We thank the individual chapter authors, as well as John Chesworth, Carolyn Fluehr-Lobban, Éric Morier-Genoud, Hassan Mwakimako, Fabienne Samson, and Abdoulaye Sounaye, who also participated in the project. Although Rüdiger Seesemann did not participate in the conference, we are pleased to include his paper in this volume. Abdullahi An-Na'im was the invited keynote speaker at the conference, and we are grateful to him for sharing his work with us and for his suggestions about how to improve the volume. As discussants during the conference, Christian Coulon, Stephen Ellis, David Robinson, and Leonardo Villalón provided stimulating commentary that has helped to improve the individual papers and the volume as a whole. In a roundtable discussion at the conference, Abdullahi An-Na'im, Penda Mbow, Sanusi Lamido Sanusi, Abdulkader Tayob, and Mahmoud Zouber debated some of the conference themes, helping us to sharpen our own views. Dale Eickelman, Rosalind I. J. Hackett, Roman Loimeier, Rüdiger Seesemann, and Leonardo Villalón provided valuable assistance to us in the preparation of the volume. Robert Launay did an excellent job translating the chapters written in French into English. Finally, we owe special thanks to Shoshanna Green for her editorial acumen and most judicious copyediting.

Some of the material presented here has been previously published. Parts of the introduction have appeared earlier in French as "Religion et globalisation: l'islam subsaharien à la conquête de nouveaux territoires," *La Revue internationale et stratégique*, n° 52, hiver 2003–2004, pp. 51–65, and are used here with permission. An earlier version of Chapter 11, "Islam in Mali in the neoliberal era," by Soares, appeared in *African Affairs*, vol. 105, pp. 77–95, and it is reprinted here by permission of the Royal African Society. Parts of the Introduction and Chapters 1, 5, 6, 10, and 12 have been translated from the French.

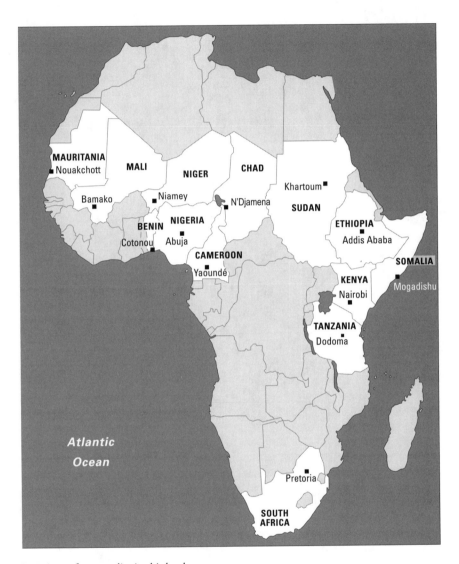

Locations of case studies in this book.

Introduction: Islam and Muslim Politics in Africa

René Otayek and Benjamin F. Soares

During the decade and a half since the end of the cold war, Africa has seen momentous changes. Indeed, since the early 1990s, economic and political reform and liberalization, the weakening of the state (or even in some cases its collapse), and increased global interconnections have all had dramatic impacts on the continent. Such processes have also influenced Muslim societies and the practice of Islam in Africa in ways that are still not well understood. The contributors to this collection explore the intersecting dynamics of Islam, society, and the state in sub-Saharan Africa. They address the gap in our understanding of contemporary Africa and also challenge us to rethink many of our assumptions about Islam and Muslim societies in Africa and elsewhere in the world.

In this Introduction, we have two main objectives. First, we consider conventional ways of understanding Muslim societies and Islam in contemporary Africa, along with their limitations, especially in the post–September 11, 2001, world in which knowledge of Muslims in Africa is so inadequate. Second, we reassess the understanding of politics in Muslim Africa and offer some new terms of analysis and styles of interpretation. Our main focus is on *politics*. Moving beyond a narrow conception of the political, we attempt a better understanding of what Dale Eickelman and James Piscatori (1996) have called Muslim politics (see also Hefner 2005). That is, we explore here how politics have played out in the lives of Muslims in Africa. Our understanding of politics is thus, and intentionally, quite broad. It includes the formal politics of political parties, elections, and governing, as well as everyday politics "from below" (see, e.g., Bayart, Mbembe, and Toulabor 1992). However, it goes beyond such formal and informal arenas of political action to encompass the new spaces and opportunities for debate in the public sphere, which has expanded considerably in many African countries since the 1990s. In addition, we foreground the complex and changing global interconnections between Africa and the wider world that have influenced politics in Africa. In this way, the studies that follow draw attention to Muslims from across the African continent who have been involved in different ways in Muslim politics. These range from seasoned politicians and civil servants to young Muslim activists, students, scholars, preachers, and social service providers whose activities have flourished in the era of political and economic liberalization. Focusing on the recent challenges and predicaments that Africans, and African Muslims in particular, have faced, we reflect upon how the practice of Islam is changing in an increasingly globalized world.

Islam in Africa

According to recent estimates, as many as one-fifth of the world's Muslims currently live on the African continent. Estimated at more than 200 million today, the number of Muslims living in sub-Saharan Africa has grown considerably over the past few decades.[1] Islam has been present in Africa for at least a millennium, and countries such as Somalia and Djibouti, along with Mauritania, have long been nearly entirely Muslim. However, it was only in the twentieth century that Islam spread into many new areas and among many different groups of people. Today, Muslims constitute a clear majority in most of the countries in the Sahel in West Africa, including Senegal, Mauritania, Mali, and Niger. In Sudan, Chad, and Tanzania, Muslims are the largest religious group. With a population of more than 120 million inhabitants, Nigeria is Africa's most populous country, and approximately half of all Nigerians are Muslims (the other half are Christians). Although Muslims are only a very small minority in South Africa, they make up sizeable minorities in Kenya and Uganda, as well as in such countries as Malawi and Mozambique. Even where Muslims are a minority in sub-Saharan Africa, they sometimes constitute large majorities in certain regions of their countries, as for example in northern Benin, Cameroon, and Ghana and in highland Ethiopia and coastal Kenya.

The fact that so many Muslims and Christians live in close proximity in sub-Saharan Africa makes the continent different from some other places in the Muslim world. For example, Muslims are the overwhelming majority in all the countries of the Middle East and North Africa, with the obvious exception of Israel and possibly also Lebanon, where Muslims may nonetheless constitute as much as 60 percent of the population. That Muslims constitute significant minorities in several countries in Africa where Christians are in the majority has sometimes helped to make the relative numbers of Muslims and Christians a politically sensitive and contentious issue. There are, however, simply no reliable enumerations of Muslims and Christians available for most countries in Africa. The numbers of Muslims and Christians have occasionally featured prominently in longstanding and ongoing conflicts in countries such as Côte d'Ivoire, Kenya, Nigeria, and Sudan. Given the extent to which such statistics have become politicized in so many places, most governments in Africa would be reluctant to release such figures even if they were available.

Over the past few decades, scholars have produced an enormous body of literature on religion in sub-Saharan Africa. A substantial amount of that research has focused on so-called African traditional religions and Christianity, including the recent waves of Pentecostalism and Charismatic Christianity in Africa. Although there has also been considerable research into the history of Islam in Africa (see Levtzion and Pouwels 2000), our knowledge about Islam in contemporary Africa is much more limited.

Much of the existing research on religion in Africa suggests that religious pluralism is the norm in sub-Saharan Africa. In fact, one can find practitioners of African religions, Christianity, and Islam side by side or in close proximity in a great many places. The ways in which different confessional groups—Muslims, Christians, and practitioners of African traditional religions—in Africa have interacted with each other and engaged with the state and politics have been both multifaceted and changeable.[2] It is clear that there is considerable diversity among Muslims in Africa, both within and across countries. While some are Shia, the vast majority of African Muslims have historically been and remain Sunni, like the vast majority of Muslims in the world. In sub-Saharan Africa, secularism or *laïcité*, which was inherited from the British, French, and Portuguese colonial states, has been more or less the rule. Notable exceptions are Sudan and Mauritania, with the latter being officially an Islamic republic.

Although many commentators acknowledge the diversity of African Muslims, the conventional wisdom is that there are basically two variants or traditions of Islam in Africa: "African Islam" and Islamic reform. First, there is the so-called traditional Islam of Africa, which many refer to as "African Islam" in its historical and contemporary manifestations.[3] In this way of thinking, "African Islam" is associated with the Sufi orders (Arabic *turuq*, singular *tariqa*) or brotherhoods and the mystical traditions in Islam. In this tradition of Islam, Muslims treat certain charismatic persons, living or deceased religious leaders, saints or *marabouts* (to use the French colonial lexicon) as intermediaries between ordinary Muslims and God. Such charismatic Muslim religious leaders, their descendants, and their followers are organized into Sufi orders, which became one of the main organizational forms for the practice of Islam in some parts of the Muslim world.

Historians have convincingly demonstrated that Sufi orders have been present in sub-Saharan Africa since at least the eighteenth century.[4] In the nineteenth and twentieth centuries, the Sufi tradition gained in importance in Africa and Sufi orders have played important roles throughout the continent. In many places, leaders of Sufi orders have been involved in Islamic scholarship, as well as long-distance trade, state and empire building, jihad, conversion, and resistance to colonial conquest. Sufi leaders have had various kinds of working relationships with the state in colonial and postcolonial Africa, involving what some have called an "exchange of services."

As this suggests, the considerable attention devoted to Sufism and Sufi orders in Africa does indeed have a solid empirical base. However, it is important to note that the conventional understanding of Islam in Africa as fundamentally Sufi in orientation is both limited and distorting. In fact, the origin of the notion of "African Islam" is intimately tied to the history of nineteenth- and twentieth-century European modes of apprehending Islam in Africa. It derives from European colonial attempts both to identify and to cultivate tractable Muslim subjects in their African colonies.[5] European colonial administrators saw Islam, Muslims, and pan-Islamic movements, particularly from the Middle East and North Africa, as potential challenges and threats to their authority. For this reason, they focused on the organized Sufi orders, which were corporate groups with ostensibly identifiable leaders. Thus, the British and French sought out the leaders of Sufi orders in their colonies and relied on them to act as intermediaries between the colonial administration and ordinary Muslims. After independence, postcolonial states have frequently continued such efforts to cultivate tractable Muslim citizens.

Many observers have assumed that Sufism and its associated practices, including saint veneration, pilgrimages to tombs, elaborate rituals, and the economic activities associated with these, have an organic connection to African societies and their cultures. Indeed, one finds such an attitude not only in much of the anthropological research on Islam in local contexts but also in some recent comparative studies. For example, in their study of Islam in five countries in sub-Saharan Africa, Charlotte Quinn and Frederick Quinn assert that "Sufism is still the strongest Islamic force in most of sub-Saharan Africa, despite the higher press profile of reformers" (2003, 14). Moreover, many commentators give this allegedly ubiquitous "force," "African Islam," a particularly positive valuation. In the words of political scientist William Miles, African Islam is "famously syncretistic, tolerant, and assimilationist" in nature (Miles 2004, 111). The general assumption that usually follows is that African Muslims practicing so-called African Islam are on the whole politically quiescent. However, "African Islam" has not always had such a positive valuation, nor has it always been assumed to be peaceful. Indeed, colonial observers of Islam were keenly aware that some of the fiercest opposition to colonial conquest came from Muslims affiliated to Sufi orders. In addition, it is important to note that some of the practices said to be central to "African Islam," such as saint veneration and tomb visitation, are in fact widespread throughout the Muslim world, from Morocco to Indonesia. It is thus difficult to insist that such practices are somehow inherently African. Moreover, it is equally questionable to assert that other ways of being Muslim in Africa, which might have little to do with Sufism, are any less African or lack an organic connection to African societies.

According to the conventional wisdom, the second variant or tradition of Islam in Africa (as elsewhere) is so-called Islamic reform or reformist Islam. Some point to what they call "Wahhabism" or "Wahhabi" interpretations of Islam, usually referring to eighteenth-century Arabia and the ideology of the modern state of Saudi Arabia, which are often assumed to be connected in one unbroken thread. Others point to Salafis and the Salafiyya, thereby making reference to twentieth-century North Africa, where some modernist Muslims invoked "the pious ancestors" (Arabic *al-salaf*) as their preferred models for Muslims and their societies. When discussing African Muslims' efforts to change their own societies, many point to Islamic fundamentalism, Islamism, or political Islam, especially when an objective is to take control of the state and to Islamize society. But certain commentators tend to lump such categories as Wahhabi, Salafi, reformist, "orthodox," Islamist, and "fundamentalist" together and sometimes even use the terms interchangeably.[6]

As many have noted, so-called Islamic reform in Africa has frequently entailed attempts to change the way Islam has long been practiced there, or, in other words, to reform "African Islam" (read "Sufism").[7] In some rather simplistic readings, Islamic reform is reduced to so-called Wahhabi interpretations, which, in turn, are assumed to be vehemently anti-Sufi. According to Donal Cruise O'Brien, "The proponents of Islamic reform . . . are part of a movement towards the emulation of current Muslim belief and practice in the Arab or Iranian world" (2003, 185). Although certain would-be Muslim reformists in Africa have indeed sometimes looked beyond sub-Saharan Africa, often to the Arab Middle East—that is, the presumed Islamic heartland—for models for their own societies, in our view that which might be labeled Islamic reform is certainly more complex and varied than mere emulation.

It is true that some Muslims in Africa have taken inspiration from various contemporary Muslim thinkers in the Middle East, North Africa, and beyond. In the twentieth century, some African Muslims looked to such Muslim reformists and modernists as the Egyptian Muhammad 'Abduh (d. 1905), the Syrian Rashid Rida (d. 1935), and later Hasan al-Banna (d. 1949), the founder of the Muslim Brotherhood (al-Ikhwan al-Muslimin) in Egypt, for ideas, models, and inspiration. Some also looked to pan-Arab nationalists (such as Gamal Abdel Nasser in Egypt), pan-Africanists, and other Third World anticolonial nationalists. More recently, some have looked to the works and ideas of such radical Islamists as Sayyid Qutb (d. 1966) and Abul Ala Mawdudi (d. 1979), or even Ayatollah Khomeini. In the past decade, many African Muslims have also become familiar with the ideas of the Qatar-based Egyptian Yusuf al-Qaradawi (b. 1926), Tariq Ramadan (b. 1962), the Swiss grandson of Hasan al-Banna, and others, not least through the medium of satellite television. Many of the Africans who have looked to such Muslim reformists and/or modernists are "new Muslim intellectuals," though some have also been involved in Sufi orders (Otayek 1993a, cf. Roy 1994). These new Muslim intellectuals have frequently promoted modern forms of education, often in Arabic, in Africa (see Otayek 1993b, Brenner 2001). They and their followers have also frequently advocated individual personal or ethical reform and particular forms of piety. These are the social actors, whom Olivier Roy dubs "neo-fundamentalists" (1994). However, it is important to remember that many Muslims involved in Sufism and Sufi orders have been equally concerned with ethical reform and piety. Moreover, the search by African Muslims for ideas, models, and inspiration for their own societies, even from outside Africa, should not be understood as an attempt to simply remake African societies in the image of Iran or the Arab world, as found, for example, in Saudi Arabia or Egypt.

The Current Historical Conjuncture

Although Western countries have long been attentive to the internal and external policies and ambitions of such players on the African continent as Libya, with its expansionist and pan-African objectives, and Sudan, with its Islamist trajectory dating from the 1980s, their attitudes began to shift after the end of the cold war and the collapse of the Soviet Union. At that time some, seeking to identify a new "menace," predicted that Islam might easily become a main focus of the West's attention (Esposito 1994). In fact, a series of events and circumstances have led to heightened interest in Islam and Muslims in Africa. With the long civil war in Algeria and the increase in Islamist violence and government repression in Egypt in the 1990s, the possibility of Islamist insurgency elsewhere on the African continent was of immediate concern. After the 1998 attacks on U.S. embassies in Kenya and Tanzania, involving considerable loss of life, attention turned increasingly to the question of Islam and the possibility that individual Muslims and groups in Africa might have ties to outside radicals or to al-Qaeda. With the extension of sharia criminal law in twelve states in northern Nigeria beginning in 1999, Nigeria also became the focus of considerable attention. However, it was after the events of September 11, 2001, in the U.S. that previously unprecedented attention was paid to Islam and Muslims in

Africa. As Mahmood Mamdani has put it (2004), many people are now making a concerted effort to identify the good and bad Muslims in the world.

With the recent wars in Afghanistan and Iraq, scholars, the media, and policy-makers have focused even more closely on Islamism and political Islam in Africa. After September 11, there were demonstrations in support of Osama bin Laden in various places on the African continent; t-shirts and posters depicting him were sold, and babies were named after him. While these public displays may have primarily indexed dissatisfaction among many Africans with U.S. foreign policy (especially the wars in Afghanistan and Iraq) and with Westernization (see below) rather than actual support for bin Laden (cf. Masquelier and Seesemann, infra), they were nevertheless surprising to many observers of Africa, who, as we have suggested, assume African Muslims are necessarily politically quiescent and tolerant. In addition, many have warned that collapsed states such as Somalia (but also Sierra Leone and Liberia) might provide spaces for the spread of radical Islam or harbor radical Muslims, including those linked to al-Qaeda. The fact that so many of the September 11 hijackers were from Saudi Arabia meant that the U.S.'s close ally, its citizens, and their networks (including those in Africa) faced intense scrutiny. One of the first U.S. responses was to invest in various counterterrorism initiatives, such as the Pan Sahel Initiative, which ran from 2002 to 2004, and the more ambitious follow-up program, the Trans-Sahara Counterterrorism Initiative, which began in 2005.[8] Official U.S. policy of "outreach" to Muslims has also been intensified.

In our view, much of the commentary on Islam and Islamism in Africa produced since the late 1990s has been both superficial and alarmist, focusing almost exclusively on issues of international security. Many are now pointing to possible links between Islam/Islamism and terrorism in Africa, and commentators are looking everywhere in Africa for links to Muslim radicals, as well as for presumably nefarious Saudi and South Asian connections. Such security concerns are certainly legitimate, but a focus on them seriously risks misrepresenting Islam in sub-Saharan Africa (see Otayek 2003–2004, 52–53). As we have noted, Sufi orders are important in many countries in contemporary Africa, and Muslim reformists, modernists, and even Islamists have become more prominent. Polemical anti-Western, anti-American, anti-Christian, and anti-Jewish literature, videos, and CDs are readily available for sale in shops and outside mosques, and bin Laden t-shirts and posters are ubiquitous in many countries in sub-Saharan Africa. It would nevertheless be unwise to assume that such views or their spokespersons have widespread support. It would be equally unwise to ignore their presence. However, the view that the dichotomy between the "traditional" "African Islam" of Sufis, on the one hand, and "Islamists" or fundamentalists and neofundamentalists, on the other, is the key to understanding Islam and Muslim societies in Africa is seriously misleading (cf. Piga 2003, Rosander 1997).

Since 9/11, this conventional but deficient way of understanding Islam in Africa—advocated by many scholars—has been given new life, especially in U.S. policy circles. In a 2005 publication of the Center for Security Policy in Washington, DC, *An African vortex: Islamism in sub-Saharan Africa*, one can read that

Wahhabi ideology and massive infusions of Saudi cash are rapidly transforming the once syncretic and peaceful Sufi-inspired sub-Saharan Islam into militant Islamism.

The likely result . . . is "unmanageable inter-communal strife between Muslims and non-Muslims," and a "hospitable environment for terrorists with an international agenda."[9]

In a recent Rand Corporation report, "Civil democratic Islam," one of the policy prescriptions is to identify and promote presumably tractable Muslim "partners."[10] Its author suggests "encourag[ing] the popularity and acceptance of Sufism," presumably as a bulwark against radical Islam or Islamists. This policy prescription seems to be based on the premise that "Wahhabis" are generally anti-Sufi in orientation. If one accepts that the enemy of one's enemy is one's friend, it would seem to follow that policymakers should recommend the promotion of African Sufis (read "African Islam").

Such dichotomous ideas about Islam, which clearly draw on academic research, are now widely diffused in policy circles in Washington but are by no means limited to discussions of Africa. In fact, such ways of thinking about Islam, according to which "Wahhabis" are the principal danger, are nearly identical to those that many in Russia have used to make sense of post-Soviet Russia's southern border (see Knysh 2004). These new attempts to identify good and bad Muslims are strikingly similar to colonial efforts to determine whether Muslims in Africa were loyal or potentially seditious. But despite such recent scholarship and policy documents, we would like to emphasize that most Muslims in Africa today are neither members of Sufi orders nor reformists or Islamists. This is not to downplay the importance either of Sufi orders or of Muslim reformists and Islamists. But it is an incontrovertible fact that African Muslims cannot be reduced to a simple dichotomy between the two. Such a reduction makes it impossible to understand, for example, why the Islamist government in Sudan has appealed to many who have ties to Sufi orders (Ahmed, infra), or how so many Sufis and self-styled Islamists joined together to extend sharia to include criminal law in twelve states in northern Nigeria (Sanusi, infra).

If one can no longer assume that ordinary African Muslims are Sufis, reformist Muslims, or potential recruits to Islamist causes, then who exactly are the millions of ordinary African Muslims—and also Muslim elites—and how might we characterize them? The fact is that we still know very little about the history and sociology of Islam in contemporary Africa, Muslim identity formation, new forms of Muslim leadership, and Muslims' engagement with politics and the state. Some of the major social and political-economic transformations of the colonial and postcolonial periods have continued and deepened in the recent era of political and economic reforms and liberalization, disengagement of the state, and increased global interconnections. We need to understand how African Muslims and others are involved in, affected by, and making sense of these momentous changes of the past ten or fifteen years, and how the practice of Islam and Muslim politics in Africa have been changing. In the chapters that follow, the contributors suggest ways of coming to such understandings. In our view, it is through dynamics internal to African societies, such as the crisis of the state, the failures of economic development, the deterioration of educational and health care systems, massive urbanization, and demographic expansion, that the recourse to religion, and to Islam in particular, must be largely understood.

In the remainder of this Introduction, we focus on three sets of interrelated issues that help us to understand Islam and Muslim politics in contemporary sub-Saharan

Africa: first, Islam and transnationalism; second, changes associated with political liberalization and the expansion of the public sphere; and, finally, political Islam or Islamism and recent possible alternatives.

Islam and Transnationalism

Many have emphasized the increased transnational exchanges and global interconnections between Africa and the rest of the world. However, little sustained attention has been paid to the actual implications of transnational Islam in sub-Saharan Africa.[11] The globalization of Islam has, of course, a long history. The *umma*, the global community of Muslims, is, after all, supranational by definition. But in recent years the speed and intensity of the interconnections between Muslims in Africa and the rest of the world have increased rapidly. Despite current preoccupations with the "deterritorialization" of radical Islamism, the articulation of the local and the global in Islam and Muslim societies and transnational Islam (Coulon 2002, Soares 2005, Loimeier and Seesemann 2006) cannot be reduced to the shadowy activities of Islamist networks. We want to briefly consider some of the transnational connections linking Muslims in Africa and those elsewhere in the world.

We begin with the relations between African countries and Arab and other Muslim countries. We do so both because Islam is a major element structuring these relations and because many claim that the spread of Islam and Islamism in sub-Saharan Africa is the direct result of the activism of Arab states or Iran or both. However, it is important not to exaggerate the influence of Arab and Muslim countries' policies in sub-Saharan Africa. Indeed, only a few countries are (or have been) capable of executing a real "Africa policy." Under Muammar al-Qaddafi, Libya has long been eager to impose its leadership in Africa, and it is no less so since resolving its differences with the U.S. and Europe. Once a beacon of Third World anti-imperialism, Algeria has been preoccupied by its own internal problems. Since the death of Nasser in 1970, Egypt, which still capitalizes on the symbolic power of Cairo's prestigious Islamic university, al-Azhar, has lacked the resources to back up any policy pretensions in sub-Saharan Africa. After actively promoting Islamism, Sudan, where Osama bin Laden lived in the 1990s, has been partly rehabilitated by its cooperation with the U.S. in the so-called war on terror but also remains preoccupied with its own problems. Only oil-rich Saudi Arabia and Iran have been able to mobilize considerable economic resources in support of their (opposed) ideological orientations. Although Saudi influence has risen in such countries as Ethiopia and Nigeria (Abbink and Sanusi, infra), such influence, like Iran's, has often been less than straightforward.

Although such institutions as the Organization of the Islamic Conference (OIC) might be expected to advance the cause of pan-Islamic integration even more than individual Arab or Muslim countries, ongoing conflicts and rivalries among member states have limited the achievements of the OIC (see Eickelman and Piscatori 1996), and African states, more than twenty of which are OIC members, remain junior partners in it. Indeed, the divisions and rivalries among Arab and Muslim countries should not be underestimated. Although some countries occasionally cooperate to advance specific diplomatic objectives in sub-Saharan Africa, they usually remain opposed to each other in the long run. This was clearly the case with Egypt under Nasser and with Saudi Arabia, two countries with divergent conceptions of Islam. Since the Iranian revolution, such divisions and rivalries have been even more apparent, with Iran and Saudi Arabia openly competing for influence across the Muslim world. While the Iranians have sought to export their revolutionary model and to challenge the influence of the West and pro-Western Arab governments, the Saudis have aggressively tried to counter Iran's influence. Relying on their status as Guardians of the Two Holy Places (Mecca and Medina), the Saudis have long used their vast resources to fund and support the Muslim World League (Rabita al-'Alam al-Islami) and the World Assembly of Muslim Youth (WAMY), both of which seek to promote Saudi interests, the Saudi monarchy, and particularly conservative ideas about Islam.

The longstanding rivalry between the Saudis and the Iranians has had important effects in certain African countries. Beginning in the 1980s, the two countries used petrodollars to channel funds into foreign aid, education, and scholarships in Africa. In some African countries, young Muslims eagerly looked to the Iranian Revolution for inspiration for the transformation of their own societies at a time when the space for political debate was very restricted, and many Muslims looked to Saudi Arabia for educational opportunities and funding. In Nigeria, for example, Saudi Arabia provided support to the country's leading Muslim reformist intellectual, Chief Kadi Abubakar Gumi (d. 1991), and Iran sought to court some of his intellectual and political rivals, with effects that can still be felt today (Sanusi, infra). In addition, Israel's ability to reestablish full diplomatic relations with many African countries, though sometimes controversial (Ould Ahmed Salem, infra), is highly significant. It clearly demonstrates the limited ability of major players in the Arab and Muslim world to isolate Israel and promote pan-Islamic integration.

Although relations with Arab and Muslim states have undoubtedly been important in the spread of Islam and Islamism in Africa, various transnational networks involving Sufi orders, Muslim elites, and Islamic humanitarian assistance have also helped to integrate Muslims in sub-Saharan Africa into the global *umma*. Sufi orders have long been an important vehicle of transnational Islam in Africa. They accompanied the spread of Islam in Africa, readily crossing colonial and postcolonial borders and often bridging social, ethnic, and linguistic differences. In the postcolonial context, some Sufi orders have successfully gone global. For example, the Mourides, long considered an almost exclusively Senegalese Sufi order, have become progressively transnational.[12] They have developed their religious and commercial networks in the rest of Africa, as well as in Europe and North America, and they have skillfully appropriated new media and information technologies in their religious, social, and commercial practices.

Beginning in the first half of the twentieth century, many self-styled Muslim reformists and modernists intensified their contacts with other like-minded Muslims in Africa and beyond, helping to animate transnational Islam in Africa. Many of these Muslim reformists and modernists were educated in Arabic; they are the so-called *arabisants*, those who frequently express themselves in Arabic and promote its use. Some of them sought more advanced education in Egypt, Saudi Arabia, and other places in the Muslim world in the late colonial period and after independence.

These Muslim intellectuals eventually became part of a new, sometimes highly educated, postcolonial Muslim elite that one finds throughout sub-Saharan Africa. This Muslim elite sometimes sees itself in contradistinction to the Westernizing and secularizing postcolonial political elite in many African countries. Some of them joined the civil service and were instrumental in forging and strengthening ties with the Arab and Muslim worlds. They served as diplomats in Arab and Muslim countries, and endeavored to ensure that scholarships to universities in the Arab and Muslim world were offered to African students and that aid was channeled to Africa. They also organized and staffed the national Muslim organizations set up in many countries. Subsequent generations of reform- and modernist-minded Muslims followed, and their trajectories sometimes included advanced secular education in European languages.

An important area in which some of these Muslim elites have been involved is Islamic humanitarian aid and the development of Islamic nongovernmental organizations (NGOs) in Africa. The development of international Islamic humanitarian aid can be traced to the 1970s.[13] From the start, sub-Saharan Africa, along with Afghanistan under Soviet occupation, was a favored field of activity for international Islamic aid organizations. Such organizations extended their activities throughout Africa with the explicit aim of competing against Western NGOs, which they suspected (not always unreasonably) of similarly using humanitarian aid for religious ends. Like secular organizations, they are involved in relief, development work, and education (Adama, Brégand, Kaag, Ould Ahmed Salem, and Sadouni, infra), but they usually combine humanitarian aid with an "Islamic" agenda. For example, while providing assistance to widows and orphans, they may promote proselytizing and provide Islamic education. They often coordinate their activities with local Muslim organizations, granting them technical assistance and financial support for mosque and school construction or sponsoring preachers trained in the Arab world. The rapid growth of such organizations in Africa is due in part to the aforementioned rivalries among Arab and Muslim states. For example, under Saudi leadership the oil-rich Gulf states created a network of Islamic aid organizations to counter the influence of Libya and, subsequently, postrevolutionary Iran.

The development of Islamic humanitarian assistance must also be understood within the context of greater transnational interconnections for education, funding, and expertise where African Muslims (like most Africans) have faced cutbacks in state services and considerable economic uncertainty, given neoliberal reforms and structural adjustment programs. With the state's progressive disengagement from some of its functions, such private religious actors have been relatively free to move into those spaces public authorities have vacated. Such critical areas as health, education, and even security have sometimes been turned over to religious institutions. Although the recent cases of strife-ridden Chad and Somalia (Kaag and Renders, infra) illustrate this quite clearly, in many places entrepreneurial Muslims turned to humanitarian aid, benefiting from easier access to Islamic funding via transnational networks (Abbink and Sadouni, infra).

In any case, one should be careful not to overestimate the volume of such aid flows through Islamic humanitarian channels or their long-term effects, ideological or otherwise. As the case of Southern Africa suggests, certain South African Muslims, who sometimes looked to Shiism and Iran for ideas, have been able to accept Saudi funds for their organizations, all the while maintaining a measure of independence in their activities, as well as ideological distance from the Saudis' conservative ideas about Islam (Sadouni, infra). One must also not forget that the new Islamic NGOs and associations are sometimes the initiatives of development entrepreneurs more interested in capturing external financial resources than in *da'wa*, the call to Islam or the propagation of Islam. In the post-9/11 world, Islamic NGOs have become the object of study and sometimes repressive measures by various states. The U.S. has tried to shut down certain high-profile international Islamic NGOs, including some working in Africa (Kaag and Seesemann, infra), and one African country, Mauritania, has actually banned Islamic NGOs altogether (Ould Ahmed Salem, infra). However, this might only make the quest for transnational Islamic funding more clandestine.

The recent attention to Islamic humanitarian aid notwithstanding, the most important agents of transnational Islam in Africa are undoubtedly ordinary African Muslims. Today, more than forty years after most countries in Africa gained their independence, countless African Muslims have studied in Islamic educational institutions and secular schools throughout the continent, in addition to the many thousands who have studied in institutions in Cairo, Medina, Khartoum, Qom, and Kuala Lumpur, as well as in Europe and North America. Many of the young African Muslims who have conducted their studies in Arabic face considerable challenges entering sectors of the economy, including government service, in their home countries, where literacy in European official languages is required. Many African Muslims are migrants living and working in Africa, Europe, North America, the Middle East, and East and Southeast Asia, and many of these diaspora Muslims are affecting the religious and sociopolitical realms in their home communities through their remittances and the new ideas and practices they help to introduce (Abbink, Renders, and Ould Ahmed Salem, infra; see also Soares 2004a). The world's largest transnational Islamic missionary (*da'wa*) movement, Jama'at al-Tabligh, has been very active with Africans in diaspora and is increasingly important in sub-Saharan Africa (Brégand, Renders, Loimeier, and Ould Ahmed Salem, infra). Its members' pietism and visible asceticism stand in sharp contrast to the ostentatious wealth of many African elites and Arab philanthropists. Although this volume does not consider in any depth those African Muslims involved in clandestine networks who might advocate violent means for advancing particular goals, the authors do shed light on the more informal, increasingly complex and shifting networks of Muslims in Africa (and beyond) that often escape state control.

The Public Sphere and the Political Arena

Although some (e.g., Huntington 1996) have argued that Islam and democracy are incompatible and Muslim societies incapable of secularization, the political liberalization that began in the early 1990s in Africa is in sharp contrast to the situation in most places in the Arab Middle East.[14] Indeed, the political opening in Africa provides a significant opportunity for reflecting upon the questions of religion and politics. With the political liberalization and greater freedoms of expression and association that followed the end of one-party rule in Africa, religion came to play a more prominent public role. Islam, Christianity, and even African traditional religions have all to varying degrees "gone public" and entered into politics. One should not understand this as the "re-traditionalization" of society (Chabal and Daloz 1999) but rather as a result of the political void during three decades of authoritarian rule. However, African Muslims' engagement with politics must also be understood within the broader context of an expanded public sphere.

For more than two decades, Islam has had a more pronounced public presence, with the proliferation of mosques, the foundation of new Islamic educational institutions such as the *madrasa* ("school" in Arabic; a modernized form of the traditional school where both religious and secular subjects are taught), and more visible and audible expressions of public piety. While not limited to urban areas, this public presence of Islam (and other religions) has had an enormous impact on Africa's rapidly urbanizing spaces, in which massive migration has in some cases led to tensions and violence across religious boundaries and in others to new styles of religiosity. The vast popular assemblies for Friday communal prayers, Muslim holidays, visits with Muslim saints, and local pilgrimages throughout Africa attest to the greater public presence of Islam. In Senegal, the Mourides' Grand Magal annually draws several hundred thousand people from across the world to the city of Touba (Coulon 1999). In neighboring Mali, Chérif Ousmane Haïdara, the country's most famous Muslim preacher and head of Ançar Dine, the largest modern Islamic association, convenes his followers in a football stadium to accommodate them all (Soares 2005). As this example suggests, there are new and changing modes of Muslim religiosity and Muslim socialities in Africa, ones quite different from quaint notions of "African Islam."

With political liberalization and greater freedom of association, new forms of associational life began to flourish in Africa. Suddenly, national Muslim organizations were no longer the only officially recognized modern Islamic organizations, and new Islamic associations for women, youths, and students became vehicles for expressing Muslim religiosity and sociality. Until 9/11, Western observers ignored these organizations, since they seemed to contradict conventional ideas about civil society. That is, they are religious and sometimes Islamist in name or orientation. As cases from Cameroon, Kenya, Mali, Somaliland, South Africa, and Tanzania (see infra) suggest, such associations attempt to respond to a growing demand for Islam: they organize conferences on topics many Muslims find compelling (Islam and democracy, women's rights in Islam, social justice, etc.), as well as evening prayer sessions, and provide instruction in "proper" Islamic practice. In some cases, marginalized social groups such as women and youth have been able to express and affirm themselves through such associations, which allow them to participate in political debates from which they are usually excluded (Adama, infra; see also Samson 2005). Active in urban areas, the new Islamic associations rely on a rapidly expanding sector of deregulated mass media, including print media, television, private radio stations, and audio- and videocassettes to learn about the wider world, including the global *umma*, and to participate in public debate.

The effects of the newly liberalized mass media in Africa extend well beyond such institutional forms as Islamic associations or even an expanded Islamic educational sector. Learning about international politics and the plight of Muslims in Palestine, Iraq, Afghanistan, or Europe through the media affects how Muslims imagine themselves as part of the global *umma*. The liberalized media can also influence how Africans (Muslims or not) think about their relationship to or alienation from the state and/or "the West." In allowing many Muslims in Africa more access to a variety of information about Islam, politics, and other ways of being Muslim, the media sometimes prompts Africans to question, reassess, and even change their own practices.[15]

New generations of Muslim intellectuals, preachers, and activists (both men and women) have come of age in the era of liberalization. Since the liberalization of the media in the 1990s, media-savvy Muslim activists have employed new media technologies to promote religious, political, and social agendas that are sometimes at odds with those of Westernizing and secularizing postcolonial elites. These activists range from radical Islamist preachers in Mauritania and Kenya to radio commentators promoting reformist ideas about Islam, Sufism, or even women's rights. Such Muslim intellectuals have sometimes been able to call into question the religious authority of existing Muslim scholars, the ulama, leading to the fragmentation of religious authority that Eickelman and Piscatori (1996; cf. Zaman 2002) have identified in the Muslim world more generally.

Political Islam in one form or another has accompanied, if not preceded, the growing public presence of Islam in sub-Saharan Africa. In the 1990s, Muslim religious leaders in sub-Saharan Africa were largely absent from the initial debates about such issues as human rights, multiparty rule, and the rule of law in many countries. That would, however, soon change. With greater spaces for political expression, many African Muslims eagerly and actively engaged in political debate, often as concerned citizens who happened to be Muslim and sometimes as Muslim activists, even as Islamists. But only a minority of Africans seem to advocate political Islam or Islamism as an agenda.

In addition to Sudan, where Islamist projects have been actively pursued from the 1980s, individual activists and groups have sought to advance various Islamic political projects in many African countries. However, Islamists often find their ventures cut short when they do not end in anonymity, as with the stillborn candidacy of Moustapha Sy, leader of a dissident branch of the Tijaniyya Sufi order, in the 2000 presidential elections in Senegal, or the ephemeral revolutionary Iran-inspired Hizbullah or "Party of God," also created in Senegal by Ahmed Khalifa Niasse in the late 1970s, or the equally ephemeral Malian Hizbullah of the 1990s. In most places in sub-Saharan Africa, politicized Islam has not really been a function of the creation of Islamic parties, since parties with an ethnic, regional, or religious character are ordinarily not recognized, prohibited, or banned (like the Islamic Party of Kenya and the Mauritanian Hizb al-Umma or Party of the Umma). It is the rise of a Muslim counter-elite, often arabophone and increasingly active in the public sphere (with new Islamic associations, access to liberalized media, and complex transnational interconnections), that helps to explain some of the ways Islam has been politicized.

In many countries, the critique of the Muslim counter-elite focuses on the Westernized and secular elite in power and the principle of state secularism. Certain individuals and groups have attempted to put the West on trial, denouncing secularism as contrary to God's plan and calling for Islamization. In some cases, Islamists set moral and political renewal at the center of their hopes: hence the struggle against allegedly un-Islamic religious practices (associationism, magic or *maraboutage*, saint veneration, and "superstition"), the denunciation of moral decline and of mimicry of the West, the critique of family law codes as too "Western" (see Otayek 1996), and the controversies over inheritance law. In some cases, the critique is even more radical, with calls to implement sharia and to Islamize the state. However, other than in Sudan (Ahmed, infra) and in northern Nigeria, where sharia criminal law has been extended (Sanusi, infra), this critique, systematic as it may be, rarely presents a well-formulated counterproject for the Islamization of the state. Arguably, these efforts have not been strategies to take over the state but rather assertions of Muslim identities. Indeed, in Kenya and Tanzania (Seesemann and Loimeier, infra), many Muslims are struggling with their status as citizens in plural societies and think (rightly or wrongly) that they are marginalized and threatened as Muslims within the secular (read "Christian") state. Similar dynamics, where Muslims see themselves as marginalized vis-à-vis secular elites and the state apparatus, have appeared in other countries, including Ethiopia, Mali, Niger, and Nigeria. The extension of sharia law in northern Nigeria, the recent heated debates about Kadhis' Courts governing family law in Kenya, and the considerable Islamist activism in Mauritania provide evidence of the mobilizing potential of Islam, and political Islam in particular. The presence of large numbers of Christians, as in Sudan, Nigeria, and Kenya, makes sharia law or even the right of Muslims to apply Islamic legal principles in family matters highly contentious and inflammatory, not least because of the rise of intolerant Christian fundamentalist groups who demonize Islam and Muslims. If many Muslims in Sudan think a Christian could never be head of state, many African Christians find the notion of a Muslim head of state equally unthinkable.

There have been important cases of radicalization in sub-Saharan Africa with some notable examples in Sudan and Nigeria. Both of those countries have a long history of millenarian movements seeking to violently overturn the established order, as in the Mahdiyya in nineteenth-century Sudan and the long war the Islamist regime in Khartoum waged against the populations of the south under the banners of Islam and Arab civilization. In Nigeria, there was the Maitatsine uprising in the 1980s, the recurring clashes between Muslims and Christians, and the recent emergence of self-styled Taliban groups in the north.[16] But, however appropriate the focus on such radicalization in Africa might be, it would be hazardous to overestimate its strength. Outside Nigeria and Sudan, Islamism, as we have noted, remains a relatively marginal phenomenon. This marginality is due in part to the failure of Islamist groups to convincingly put forth a compelling political program. In many places, Islamists have been unable to effectively challenge those Muslim groups and elites who have privileged ties to the state and have been able to act as authoritative interpreters of Islam. Islamists also seem unable to transcend the ethnic and religious pluralism and important regional differences that characterize sub-Saharan Africa. However, the ability of the secular state—even when relatively weak—to coerce, repress, and exclude its critics, Islamist or otherwise, should not be forgotten. The active, even enthusiastic support for the U.S.'s "war on terror" might allow certain African governments to deflect internal or external criticism and could serve as a cover for abuse and repression.

Islamic activism has sometimes been accompanied by serious conflict and violence (see, e.g., De Waal 2004), and this violence has sometimes, as in the case of Maitatsine, been linked to massive migration and rapid urbanization, which have helped to reconfigure the social and religious landscape, further contributing to tensions. But such violence is still relatively exceptional (though for how long?). In fact, African societies have for the most part accommodated themselves fairly well to religious pluralism. Rather than extrapolating from extreme cases of violence in Nigeria, Sudan, or elsewhere and waving the specter of a "clash of civilizations," one should analyze each case individually and consider the relevant social, political, and economic factors in conflicts that may have or take on a religious dimension. In Sudan, Islamism has been very much a project of northern Sudanese political elites, and religious disputes in that country frequently relate to the struggle of those elites to obtain or retain political power (Ahmed, infra). In Nigeria, the recurrence of religious disputes is due at least in part to the foreclosure of all democratic debate by the military regimes that succeeded one another until 1998, the difficulties of managing plural identities in a federal state system, and the competition between political and religious factions to retain power, for which purpose both cynically use religion and ethnicity (Sanusi, infra; cf. Haynes 1996). The radicalization of religious identities, Muslim as well as Christian, threatens to bring the "Lebanonization" of Nigeria, the breakup of Sudan, and an end to the relatively peaceful coexistence of Muslims and Christians in Ethiopia (Abbink, infra) and elsewhere.

Africa is clearly not immune to the deleterious effects of the politicization of religion, not least because the aggressive proselytizing and demonizing rhetoric of certain Muslim groups matches that of equally intolerant Protestant fundamentalist movements (Hackett 1999, 2002). In Côte d'Ivoire, for example, Pentecostal and Evangelical churches have developed a discourse demonizing Islam that eerily echoes the policy of "*Ivoirité*," or "Ivorianness," as a mode of discrimination between "true" Ivorians (members of southern ethnic groups, mostly Christian and "animist") and "strangers" (northerners, lumped into the generic categories of Dyula and Muslims). It is a historical irony that this anti-Islamic discourse does not stigmatize a radical or sectarian Islam but rather that embodied by the Centre national islamique, the National Islamic Center, that is, a version of Islam that is both "reformist and relatively respectful of the local pluralism of Muslim traditions [and] which is, for obvious reasons, the only religious faction to fully support the principle of the secularism of the Ivoirian state" (Mary 2002, 86; see also Otayek 2002, Miran 2006).

One of the hallmarks, as well as the paradoxes, of democracy is that it allows criticism by its detractors. It is in the name of democracy and its foundational principle, majority rule, that some call for sharia in sub-Saharan Africa. Thus, in Nigeria, sharia, which was for decades only applied to matters of personal law, was extended to cover criminal law for Muslims in northern states only after the return to a constitutional regime in 1998, following a long interlude of military regimes. This was done in the most democratic way possible, by vote, and under pressure from the poorest members of society, who saw in sharia the only form of justice capable of remedying endemic corruption (Last 2000). As the cases of Kenya, Mali, Niger, Nigeria (Seesemann, Soares, Masquelier, and Sanusi, infra), and other countries show, the Islamic critique of political institutions has developed all the more surely as transitions to democracy in Africa have generated expectations that have too often been rapidly disappointed, while the ideologies of development on which single-party regimes had relied for their legitimacy have similarly proven themselves incoherent. In this context, African proponents of political Islam have a field day denouncing what they consider the obvious failures of Western-style modernity and its organized political expression, the secular Jacobin nation-state, incapable of performing even the most basic tasks. In their way of thinking, the crisis that African countries face can be resolved only by a return to Islam as the supreme moral, legal, and political code. This was, for example, the line of argumentation developed by radical Islamic movements in the 1980s and 1990s. Nonetheless, some self-styled Muslim reformists have been progressively integrated into the political arena in various countries. By incorporating such Islamic movements, for example, the regime of former Senegalese president Abdou Diouf partly succeeded in neutralizing direct challenges to the secular state while reducing its dependence on the Muslim establishment of Sufi leaders (Villalón 1999, Loimeier 2001). In Mauritania and Kenya, the government has instead chosen a path of confrontation with radical Islam and some Muslims, at the same time reinforcing ties with moderate Islamic organizations and persons (Ould Ahmed Salem, infra; cf. Seesemann, infra, and Oded 1996).

Advocates of political Islam in sub-Saharan Africa have clearly strained to formulate a project that has broad appeal. But it is also true that, given the recurring debates around social issues that galvanize many Muslims, the discourse of Islamists tends to lend credence to the idea that the religious and the political are indissociably linked and that political Islam provides an alternative to Westernization and the challenges of modernity. The discourse of Islamists is even more widely diffused because it pushes other Muslims and leaders of national Muslim associations in particular, generally legitimist and reluctant to engage in political action, to "Islamize" their own discourse by emphasizing the themes of a return to Islam and so-called Islamic values, in order to protect their dominant position in the religious field and privileged access to power. And of course many secular Muslims, including politicians, also seek to emphasize their own Islamic credentials.

While many warn of the dangers of Islamism's spread in Africa and that it might become an unstoppable juggernaut, some Islamists in Africa have recently called for democracy (Ahmed, Soares, and Ould Ahmed Salem, infra). At the same time, Islamists in some places have lost ground. In Sudan, Islamists, while still in control, have been forced to concede major parts of their political and social programs with the signing of peace accords with Southern rebels and the agreement to share power with non-Muslims. Such pragmatism might indeed herald the beginnings of a post-Islamist phase in Sudan. As Nigerians express their disillusionment with the erratic state-implemented sharia project, which does not seem to be producing the hoped-for results, it is even possible that this project might lead to a strengthening of the secular state (Ostien 2006). At the same time, though Muslim minorities in Benin and South Africa seem well integrated in their respective countries, there is a danger in countries such as Ethiopia, Kenya, and Tanzania that the marginalization and exclusion of Muslims could push some to seek radical solutions. Although some Muslims have turned to *da'wa* in times of repression, they might not always do so.

New Ways of Being Muslim

As we have suggested, the liberalization of the early 1990s has had some unexpected effects in sub-Saharan Africa. Today the Islamic landscape is much more diverse, partly reflecting both the sometimes-unconstrained multiparty competition in some countries and the competitive strategies of Arab and Muslim states that attempt to use various Islamic factions to further their own objectives, with various degrees of success. It is difficult under such conditions for a singular Islamic discourse to prevail and remain uncontested. As some have noted, the increased religious "supply" within Christianity in Africa has helped to facilitate processes of individualization. To use the market metaphor, there is a more plural religious market, with more options among which individuals can choose. This also applies to Muslims, with Islam increasingly an affair of individuals. In the words of Christian Coulon, "the iron law of the group, of the 'community' or 'ethnic group' in its relationship to religious affil-iation as in other domains, to the extent that it ever existed, is tending to give way to considerations, behaviors, and strategies stemming from a patent process of individ-ualization" (Coulon 2002, 21; see also Marie 1997). Of course, social actors and attendant processes of individualization face constraints that derive from various hierarchies and socioeconomic differences, which help to limit what is possible for individuals.

It is evident that many Muslims from all sectors of society in contemporary Africa are concerned with their identities as Muslims. In many places in the Muslim world, not just in Africa, Muslims are increasingly concerned with questions of religiosity, the correct practice of Islam, and ethical reform and improvement. Whereas some are radicals or even self-styled Islamists with transnational ties and aspirations, many are not necessarily Islamists or even advocates of any political project with Islam as its focus. Some scholars of Islam and Muslim societies have pointed to this apparent shift, and certain observers, such as Olivier Roy (2004) and Asef Bayat (2005; cf. Burgat 2005, White 2005), have referred to it as "post-Islamism." We, however, would urge caution in announcing the end of Islamism, in Africa or elsewhere. At the same time, our understanding of Islam and Muslim politics in Africa compels us to recognize new ways of being Muslim.

In this context, one might ask, as have Patrick Haenni and Tjitske Holtrop (2002, 45–46), whether it would not be "more heuristic to abandon approaches overly centered on politics for which 'Islamism' implicitly remains the model to which one relates all forms of religious revival." In other words, would it not be more appropri-ate, in order to understand current reformulations of Islam in Africa, to investigate the emergence of what we might call, paraphrasing these two scholars of Islam in the Arab world, *islam mondain* in French? One might translate this term as "Islam in the present world." Although *mondain* can be translated as "secular" in English, it is not quite secular. Rather, it points to ways of being Muslim that exist in secular societies and spheres, without necessarily being secular. Such a notion of new ways of being Muslim contrasts considerably with the recent work of Saba Mahmood (2005) and Charles Hirschkind (2006), who have both sought to apply a Foucauldian model of the cultivation of pious subjects among those involved in "piety movements" or the so-called Islamic revival in Cairo. Not unlike such Foucauldian readings of Muslim subject formation, *islam mondain* is also a moral and moralizing Islam. However, it does not necessarily replace that of political Islam and does not in any way call into question the scholarly attention devoted to the latter; but it raises new questions because it seems to capture more adequately many Muslims' ways of being in the contemporary world. Those Muslims inhabiting this *islam mondain* might focus on self-improvement, the correct practice of Islam, and not just politics or the political, though they might attend to the latter as well. *Islam mondain* points to a new kind of Muslim sociality that we can see in many places in the world where individual Muslims are often, though not exclusively, concerned with coping with economic decline and cutbacks in state services and considerably disenchanted with multiparty elections that often seem only to reelect the governing elites and perpetuate existing neopatrimonial systems (cf. Haenni 2005).

One can see this way of being Muslim especially among ordinary African Muslims, including certain groups usually excluded from public space, most notably youth and women. We are thinking of those young Nigerien Muslims who ask themselves, in media outside the control of religious authorities as well as of the state, about "what it means to be a Muslim, a citizen, or simply a youth with moral convictions" (Masquelier, infra), questions which underlie the fashionable preaching of Amr Khalid in Cairo, studied by Haenni and Holtrop. Granted, the Egyptian preacher's audience hails from Cairo's affluent elites, whereas the young Nigeriens are socially and economically marginal. But, in both cases, the cultural practices—hip hop style and music among young Nigeriens, unrestrained and ostentatious consumerism among trendy Cairenes—and ritual practices—nonobservance of ritual prayer times among the former, "the refusal of a religious practice where ritual punctiliousness is sufficient in itself" (Haenni and Holtrop 2002, 47) among the latter—signal nearly identical processes of individual self-fashioning and generational affirmation, which are perhaps more revealing about changes in the practice of Islam in Africa and elsewhere than repetitive mantras about Islamism or totalizing notions of the cultivation of virtue as in the work of Mahmood (2005). What does it mean to be Muslim? How can one live according to the religion and reconcile it with modernity, social success, and globalization? The re-Islamization of African societies, or, more accurately, the affirmation of Islam, should, we think, be interpreted in terms of these questions rather than the Islamist paradigm, the "symbolic confrontation" (Cruise O'Brien 2003) with the West notwithstanding.

Similarly, most Muslims in Benin are neither affiliated to a Sufi order nor reformists—nor Islamists, for that matter. There is, however, considerable emphasis in Benin on the importance of moralizing social and public life, as there is in many other places (Brégand, infra). In Mali, while many Malian Muslims worry that the "un-Islamic" is more readily available in the era of liberalization, some Muslim preachers and public intellectuals have developed a moralizing discourse targeting both individual Muslims and the government (Soares, infra). In Cameroon the media celebrity and Islamic radio personality Souleymane Bouba has written "Islamic" plays, which entertain while delivering moral messages to his aspirational and self-consciously modern audience. In one play, he satirizes upwardly mobile Muslims who abandon their religious practices and give in to the temptations of corruption and marital infidelity once they reach the top (Adama, infra). Among the Senegalese

Moustarchidine, which teaches Muslim youths appropriate behavior and dress and offers classes in family planning, cooking, and housekeeping (see Samson 2005), there is a similar morality emphasizing individualism, social success, and religious practice in step with modernity. In all these cases, *islam mondain* is a conception of religion that is socially and ethically compatible with the neoliberal economy (cf. Soares 2004b, Haenni 2005). It stems just as much from the process of modernizing religion (Haenni and Holtrop 2002), which productively helps to destabilize the image of Africa either as a prisoner of its traditions (including so-called African Islam) and its communitarian allegiances or as an inevitable fount of Islamist terrorism. Such analysis opens new and challenging research perspectives but does not delegitimize research on political Islam. Rather, it suggests that, even if Islamism has not completely failed as a political project (cf. Roy 1994, Burgat 2005), Islam also provides a social and cultural model for African Muslims. This is particularly true for ordinary African Muslims, the countless people who work, study, and socialize together, join organizations and political parties, organize study groups at mosques or in homes, listen to radio programs and audiocassettes, watch videos and satellite television, log on to the Internet, and discuss and debate Islam, being Muslim, politics, and so forth.

*   *   *

The chapters that follow are grouped into sections reflecting three loosely overlapping themes. The authors in Part I consider Islam at the intersection of the local and the global. Those in Part II focus on the question of the state for African Muslims. Finally, those in Part III highlight new ways of being Muslim that are not limited to Sufism or Islamism. The detailed case studies of ordinary Muslims, Muslim youths, Muslim students' associations, activists, preachers, transnational networks, Islamic NGOs, debates about Islamic law, secularism, and minority rights, and Muslims and the political process in both conflict and postconflict settings in Africa show limits to the conventional understandings of Islam and Muslim politics in Africa. They also demonstrate the need for new terms of analysis and styles of interpretation of Islam and Muslim politics in Africa and beyond.

Notes

We are grateful to Adeline Masquelier, Rüdiger Seesemann, and Leonardo Villalón for their comments on an earlier draft of this Introduction.

1. For estimates of Muslims in the world, see Delval 1984, and specifically for Africa, see Lyman and Morrison 2004 and Dickson 2005.
2. On Muslim-Christian encounters in Africa, see Soares 2006.
3. The classic statement about African Islam or *Islam noir* is by Monteil 1980.
4. For an overview of Sufi orders in African history, see Vikør 2000.
5. On such modes of apprehending Islam in Africa, see Harrison 1988, Triaud 1992, Launay and Soares 1999, Robinson 2000, Seesemann 2002, and Soares 2000, 2005, 2007.
6. In contrast, some scholars (e.g., Otayek 1993a, Kane and Triaud 1998) have shown the complexity of such categories as Islamic reform and Islamism and of the social and religious groups involved.

7. On Mali, see Kaba 1974, Brenner 1993, Hock 1999, and Soares 2005; on Senegal, Gomez-Perez 1997 and Loimeier 2001; on Nigeria, Umar 1993, Loimeier 1997, and Kane 2003; on Côte d'Ivoire, Launay 1992, LeBlanc 2006, and Miran 2006; on Kenya, Seesemann 2006; and from a comparative perspective, Coulon 1988, Otayek 1993b, Kane and Triaud 1998, Loimeier 2003, Piga 2003, and Gomez-Perez 2005.

8. On the Pan Sahel Initiative, see Ellis 2004. On recent U.S. policy toward Africa, cf. Schraeder 2005 and Lyman and Morrison 2004.

9. Alex Alexiev, preface to David McCormack, *An African vortex: Islamism in sub-Saharan Africa*, Center for Security Policy, Occasional Papers Series, no. 4, Washington, January 2005, available at http://www.centerforsecuritypolicy.org/Af_Vortex.pdf, 1. See also the U.S. National Intelligence Council's *Mapping sub-Saharan Africa's future*, Conference Report, March 2005, which mentions Saudi Arabia and the "export" of its "Wahhabi tradition" (14).

10. Cheryl Benard, "Civil democratic Islam: Partners, resources, and strategies," Rand Corporation, 2003, available at http://www.rand.org/pubs/monograph_reports/2005/MR1716.pdf.

11. In contrast, Christianity, particularly Pentecostalism, and transnationalism in Africa have been fairly well studied. See Meyer 2004.

12. Recent contributions to the ever-expanding literature on the Mourides include Babou 2002, Coulon 1999, Diouf 2000, Guèye 2003, Riccio 2004, and Roberts and Roberts 2003. For a critical perspective on some of that literature, see Soares 2007.

13. On international Islamic NGOs, see Benthall and Bellion-Jourdan 2003, and for Africa, Salih 2004.

14. With some notable exceptions (e.g., Constantin and Coulon 1997, Ellis and Ter Haar 2004, Gifford 1995, Otayek 2000, and Villalón 1995, 1999), most scholars have not considered religion in relation to the history of political liberalization in Africa. For a broader discussion of democratization in Africa, see Villalón and VonDoepp 2005.

15. On Islam, media, and the public sphere in Muslim societies, see Eickelman and Anderson 1999, Salvatore and LeVine 2005, and Soares 2005. For religion, media, and the public sphere more generally, see Meyer and Moors 2006.

16. On Maitatsine, see Nicolas 1981, Lubeck 1981, and Watts 1996. The Nigerian "Taliban" has been reported on in international and Nigerian media outlets since at least 2004.

References

Babou, Cheikh Anta. 2002. Brotherhood solidarity, education, and migration: The role of the Dahiras among the Murid Muslim community in New York. *African Affairs* 101:151–70.

Bayart, Jean-François, Achille Mbembe, and Comi Toulabor, eds. 1992. *Le politique par le bas en Afrique noire*. Paris: Karthala.

Bayat, Asef. 2005. Islamism and social movement theory. *Third World Quarterly* 26 (6): 891–908.

Benthall, Jonathan, and Jérôme Bellion-Jourdan. 2003. *The charitable crescent: Politics of aid in the Muslim world*. London: I. B. Tauris.

Brenner, Louis. 1993. Constructing Muslim identities in Mali. In *Muslim identity and social change in sub-Saharan Africa*, ed. Louis Brenner, 59–78. Bloomington: Indiana University Press.

———. 2001. *Controlling knowledge: Religion, power and schooling in a West African Muslim society*. Bloomington: Indiana University Press.

Burgat, François. 2005. *L'islamisme à l'heure d'al-Qaida: Réislamisations, modernisation, radicalisations*. Paris: Découverte.

Chabal, Patrick, and Jean-Pascal Daloz. 1999. *Africa works: Disorder as political instrument*. Oxford: James Currey.

Constantin, François, and Christian Coulon, eds. 1997. *Religion et transition démocratique en Afrique.* Paris: Karthala.

Coulon, Christian. 1988. *Les musulmans et le pouvoir en Afrique noire.* 2nd ed. Paris: Karthala.

———. 1999. The *Grand Magal* in Touba: A religious festival of the Mouride brotherhood of Senegal. *African Affairs* 98:195–210.

———. 2002. Les nouvelles voies de l'*umma* africaine. In *Islams d'Afrique: Entre le local et le global,* L'Afrique politique 2002. Paris: CEAN-Karthala, 19–29.

Cruise O'Brien, Donal B. 2003. *Symbolic confrontations: Muslims imagining the state in Africa.* London: Hurst.

Delval, Raymond, ed. 1984. *A map of the Muslims in the world.* Leiden: Brill.

De Waal, Alex, ed. 2004. *Islamism and its enemies in the Horn of Africa.* London: Hurst.

Dickson, David. 2005. Political Islam in sub-Saharan Africa: The need for a new research and diplomatic agenda. United States Institute of Peace Special Report no. 140. Washington, May.

Diouf, Mamadou. 2000. The Senegalese Murid trade diaspora and the making of a vernacular cosmopolitanism. *Public Culture* 12 (3): 679–702.

Eickelman, Dale F., and Jon W. Anderson, eds. 1999. *New media in the Muslim world: The emerging public sphere.* Bloomington: Indiana University Press.

Eickelman, Dale F., and James Piscatori. 1996. *Muslim politics.* Princeton: Princeton University Press.

Ellis, Stephen. 2004. Briefing: The pan-Sahel initiative. *African Affairs* 103:459–64.

Ellis, Stephen, and Gerrie Ter Haar. 2004. *Worlds of power: Religious thought and political practice in Africa.* New York: Oxford University Press.

Esposito, John. 1994. Political Islam: Beyond the green menace. *Current History* 93 (January): 19–24.

Gifford, Paul, ed. 1995. *The Christian churches and the democratisation of Africa.* Leiden: Brill.

Gomez-Perez, Muriel. 1997. Un mouvement culturel vers l'indépendance: Le réformisme musulman au Sénégal (1956–1960). In *Le temps des marabouts,* ed. David Robinson and Jean-Louis Triaud, 521–38. Paris: Karthala.

———, ed. 2005. *L'islam politique au sud du Sahara: Identités, discours et enjeux.* Paris: Karthala.

Guèye, Cheikh. 2003. New information and communication technology use by Muslim Mourides in Senegal. *Review of African Political Economy* 30 (98): 609–25.

Hackett, Rosalind I. J. 1999. Radical Christian revivalism in Nigeria and Ghana: Recent patterns of conflict and intolerance. In *Proselytization and communal self-determination in Africa,* ed. Abdullahi A. An-Na'im, 246–67. Maryknoll, N.Y.: Orbis Books.

———. 2002. Discours de diabolisation en Afrique et ailleurs. *Diogène* 199:71–91.

Haenni, Patrick. 2005. *L'islam de marché: L'autre revolution conservatrice.* Paris: Seuil.

Haenni, Patrick, and Tjitske Holtrop. 2002. Mondaines spiritualités: Amr Khâlid, "shaykh branché" de la jeunesse dorée du Caire. *Politique africaine* 87:45–68.

Harrison, Christopher. 1988. *France and Islam in West Africa, 1860–1960.* Cambridge: Cambridge University Press.

Haynes, Jeffrey. 1996. *Religion and politics in Africa.* London: Zed Books.

Hefner, Robert W. 2005. *Remaking Muslim politics: Pluralism, contestation, democratization.* Princeton: Princeton University Press.

Hirschkind, Charles. 2006. *The ethical soundscape: Cassette sermons and Islamic counterpublics.* New York: Columbia University Press.

Hock, Carsten. 1999. *Fliegen die Seelen der Heiligen? Muslimische Reform und staatliche Autorität in der Republik Mali seit 1960.* Berlin: Klaus Schwarz.

Huntington, Samuel P. 1996. *The clash of civilizations and the remaking of world order.* New York: Simon and Schuster.

Kaba, Lansiné. 1974. *The Wahhabiyya: Islamic reform and politics in French West Africa.* Evanston, Northwestern University Press.

Kane, Ousmane. 2003. *Muslim modernity in postcolonial Nigeria: A study of the Society for the Removal of Innovation and Reinstatement of Tradition.* Leiden: Brill.

Kane, Ousmane, and Jean-Louis Triaud, eds. 1998. *Islam et islamismes au sud du Sahara*. Paris: Karthala.

Knysh, Alexander. 2004. A clear and present danger: "Wahhabism" as a rhetorical foil. *Die Welt des Islams* 44 (1): 3–26.

Last, Murray. 2000. La charia dans le Nord-Nigeria. *Politique africaine* 79:141–52.

Launay, Robert. 1992. *Beyond the stream: Islam and society in a West African town*. Berkeley: University of California Press.

Launay, Robert, and Benjamin F. Soares. 1999. The formation of an "Islamic Sphere" in French colonial West Africa. *Economy and Society* 28 (4): 497–519.

LeBlanc, Marie Nathalie. 2006. De la tradition à l'Islam: L'orthodoxie à l'encontre des rites culturels.*Cahiers d'études africaines* 182: 417–36.

Levtzion, Nehemia, and Randall L. Pouwels, eds. 2000. *The history of Islam in Africa*. Athens: Ohio University Press; Oxford: James Currey.

Loimeier, Roman. 1997. *Islamic reform and political change in Northern Nigeria*. Evanston: Northwestern University Press.

———. 2001. *Säkularer Staat und islamische Gesellschaft: Die Beziehungen zwischen Staat, Sufi-Bruderschaften und islamischer Reformbewegung in Senegal im 20. Jahrhundert*. Hamburg: LIT Verlag.

———. 2003. Patterns and peculiarities of Islamic reform in Africa. *Journal of Religion in Africa* 33 (3): 237–62.

Loimeier, Roman, and Rüdiger Seesemann, eds. 2006. *The global worlds of the Swahili: Interfaces of Islam, identity and space in 19th- and 20th-century East Africa*. Berlin: LIT.

Lubeck, Paul. 1981. Conscience de classe et nationalisme islamique à Kano. *Politique africaine* 4:31–46.

Lyman, Princeton, and J. Stephen Morrison. 2004. The terrorist threat in Africa. *Foreign Affairs* 77:75–86.

Mahmood, Saba. 2005. *Politics of piety: The Islamic revival and the feminist subject*. Princeton: Princeton University Press.

Mamdani, Mahmood. 2004. *Good Muslim, bad Muslim: America, the cold war, and the roots of terror*. New York: Pantheon.

Marie, Alain, ed. 1997. *L'Afrique des individus: Itinéraires citadins dans l'Afrique contemporaine*. Paris: Karthala.

Mary, André. 2002. Prophètes pasteurs: La politique de la délivrance en Côte d'Ivoire. *Politique africaine* 87:69–94.

Meyer, Birgit. 2004. Christianity in Africa: From African Independent to Pentecostal-Charismatic churches. *Annual Review of Anthropology* 33:447–74.

Meyer, Birgit, and Annelies Moors, eds. 2006. *Religion, media, and the public sphere*. Bloomington: Indiana University Press.

Miles, William F. S. 2004. Islamism in West Africa: Conclusions. *African Studies Review* 47 (2): 109–17.

Miran, Marie. 2006. *Islam, histoire et modernité en Côte d'Ivoire*. Paris: Karthala.

Monteil, Vincent. 1980. *L'islam noir*. 3rd ed. Paris: Seuil.

Nicolas, Guy. 1981. "Guerre sainte" à Kano. *Politique africaine* 1:47–70.

Oded, Arye. 1996. Islamic extremism in Kenya: The rise and fall of Cheikh Khalid Balala. *Journal of Religion in Africa* 26 (4): 406–15.

Ostien, Phil. 2006. Sharia and national law in northern Nigeria. Paper presented to the Faculty of Law, Leiden University, June 15.

Otayek, René. 1993a. Introduction: Des nouveaux intellectuels musulmans d'Afrique noire. In *Le radicalisme islamique au sud du Sahara: Da'wa, arabisation et critique de l'Occident*, ed. René Otayek, 8–18. Paris: Karthala.

———, ed. 1993b. *Le radicalisme islamique au sud du Sahara: Da'wa, arabisation et critique de l'Occident*. Paris: Karthala.

————. 1996. L'islam et la révolution au Burkina Faso: Mobilisation politique et reconstruction identitaire. *Social Compass* 43 (2): 233–47.

————. 2000. *Identité et démocratie dans un monde global.* Paris: Presses de Sciences Po.

————. 2002. Ethnicisation du politique et transition démocratique: La Côte d'ivoire entre crispations identitaires et invention de la citoyenneté. In *L'imaginaire des conflits communautaires*, ed. Elise Féron and Michael Hastings, 113–39. Paris: L'Harmattan.

————. 2003–2004. Religion et globalisation: L'islam subsaharien à la conquête de nouveaux territories. *La revue internationale et stratégique* 52 (winter): 51–65.

Piga, Adriana, ed. 2003. *Islam et villes en Afrique au sud du Sahara: Entre soufisme et fondamentalisme.* Paris: Karthala.

Quinn, Charlotte A., and Frederick Quinn. 2003. *Pride, faith, and fear: Islam in sub-Saharan Africa.* New York: Oxford University Press.

Riccio, Bruno. 2004. Transnational Mouridism and the Afro-Muslim critique of Italy. *Journal of Ethnic and Migration Studies* 30 (5): 929–44.

Roberts, Allen F., and Mary Nooter Roberts. 2003. *A saint in the city: Sufi arts of urban Senegal.* Los Angeles: UCLA Fowler Museum of Cultural History.

Robinson, David. 2000. *Paths of accommodation: Muslim societies and French colonial authorities in Senegal and Mauritania, 1880–1920.* Athens: Ohio University Press.

Rosander, Eva Evers. 1997. The Islamization of "tradition" and "modernity." In *African Islam and Islam in Africa: Encounters between Sufis and Islamists*, ed. Eva Evers Rosander and David Westerlund, 1–27. Athens: Ohio University Press.

Roy, Olivier. 1994. *The failure of political Islam.* Trans. C. Volk. Cambridge, Mass.: Harvard University Press.

————. 2004. *Globalized Islam: The search for a new ummah.* New York: Columbia University Press.

Salih, M. A. Mohamed. 2004. Islamic NGOs in Africa: The promise and peril of Islamic volunteerism. In *Islamism and its enemies in the Horn of Africa*, ed. Alex De Waal, 146–81. London: Hurst.

Salvatore, Armando, and Mark LeVine, eds. 2005. *Religion, social practice, and contested hegemonies: Reconstructing the public sphere in Muslim majority societies.* New York: Palgrave.

Samson, Fabienne. 2005. *Les marabouts de l'islam politique: Le Dahiratoul moustarchidina wal moustarchidaty, un mouvement néo-confrérique sénégalais.* Paris: Karthala.

Schraeder, Peter J. 2005. La guerre contre le terrorisme et la politique américaine en Afrique. *Politique africaine* 98:42–62.

Seesemann, Rüdiger. 2002. "Ein Dialog der Taubstummen": Französische vs. britische Wahrnehmungen des Islam im spätkolonialen Westafrika. *Africa Spectrum* 37 (2): 109–39.

————. 2006. African Islam or Islam in Africa? Evidence from Kenya. In *The global worlds of the Swahili*, ed. Roman Loimeier and Rüdiger Seesemann, 229–50. Berlin: LIT.

Soares, Benjamin F. 2000. Notes on the anthropological study of Islam and Muslim societies in Africa. *Culture & Religion* 1 (2): 277–85.

————. 2004a. An African Muslim saint and his followers in France. *Journal of Ethnic and Migration Studies* 30 (5): 913–27.

————. 2004b. Muslim saints in the age of neoliberalism. In *Producing African futures: Ritual and reproduction in a neoliberal age*, ed. Brad Weiss, 79–105. Leiden: Brill.

————. 2005. *Islam and the prayer economy: History and authority in a Malian town.* Edinburgh: Edinburgh University Press; Ann Arbor: University of Michigan Press.

————, ed. 2006. *Muslim-Christian encounters in Africa.* Leiden: Brill.

————. 2007. Rethinking Islam and Muslim societies in Africa. *African Affairs* 106:319–26.

Triaud, Jean-Louis. 1992. L'Islam sous le régime colonial. In *L'Afrique occidentale au temps des Français (colonisateur et colonisés, c. 1860–1960)*, ed. Catherine Coquery-Vidrovitch, 141–55. Paris: Découverte.

Umar, Muhammad Sani. 1993. Changing Islamic identity in Nigeria from the 1960s to the 1980s: From Sufism to anti-Sufism. In *Muslim identity and social change in sub-Saharan Africa*, ed. Louis Brenner, 154–78. Bloomington: Indiana University Press.

Vikør, Knut S. 2000. Sufi brotherhoods in Africa. In *The history of Islam in Africa*, ed. Nehemia Levtzion and Randall L. Powells, 441–76. Athens: Ohio University Press.

Villalón, Leonardo A. 1995. *Islamic society and state power in Senegal: Disciples and citizens in Fatick*. Cambridge: Cambridge University Press.

———. 1999. Generational changes, political stagnation, and the evolving dynamics of religion and politics in Senegal. *Africa Today* 46 (3–4): 129–47.

Villalón, Leonardo, and Peter VonDoepp, eds. 2005. *The fate of Africa's democratic experiments: Elites and institutions*. Bloomington: Indiana University Press.

Watts, Michael J. 1996. Islamic modernities? Citizenship, civil society, and Islamism in a Nigerian city. *Public Culture* 8 (2): 251–90.

White, Jenny B. 2005. The end of Islamism? Turkey's Muslimhood model. In *Remaking Muslim politics: Pluralism, contestation, democratization*, ed. Robert W. Hefner, 87–111. Princeton: Princeton University Press.

Zaman, Muhammad Qasim. 2002. *The ulama in contemporary Islam: Custodians of change*. Princeton: Princeton University Press.

Part I
Between the Local and the Global

CHAPTER 1

ISLAM IN MAURITANIA BETWEEN POLITICAL EXPANSION AND GLOBALIZATION: ELITES, INSTITUTIONS, KNOWLEDGE, AND NETWORKS

Zekeria Ould Ahmed Salem

When M. Ould Taya, the president of Mauritania, was deposed in a coup d'état on August 3, 2005, the Military Council for Justice and Democracy (Conseil militaire pour la justice et la démocratie) which acceded to power promised to reestablish a true democracy and to allow open participation in politics. The members of the Council and of the transitional government were even legally excluded (by decree) from competing in the election, planned to restart the democratic process after the resolutely authoritarian rule of the previous regime, which had been in power since 1984. Consultative meetings allowed the signing of a national pact that was warmly welcomed by nearly all Mauritanian political forces. The new authorities rapidly implemented the measures they had promised: institutional reforms, recognition of new political parties, liberation of political prisoners, a new electoral calendar, creation of an independent electoral commission, and so on. But unlike all other elements, the Islamist movement (by which I mean the totality of projects and discourses which propose the political reform of Muslim states or societies according to an explicitly Islamic ideology) has not benefited from the new political climate. On one hand, the new regime did not consider certain "Islamist" prisoners to have been jailed only for expressing their opinions; on the other hand, it immediately and categorically refused to recognize any party based on religion. It is true that the research for this chapter was conducted before this notable political change; but it is unlikely that the state will recognize the Islamist movement in the near future. Even so, Islamist leaders are favorably disposed to the new authorities and seem to have suspended their political activities.

Initially, the goal of this study was to collect data documenting the globalization of Islam in Mauritania and the state's disengagement. The working hypothesis was that the relationship between the state and political Islam had a long and tumultuous history which had recently seen new developments. This relationship evolved in tandem with profound changes in the state as well as the growing globalization of Islam in Mauritania. Given the nature of this problematic and the broad scope of the study, only a multifaceted approach can allow us to grasp the complexities of the situation. There is a subtle articulation between the role of the state, Islam, and globalization, which we can illustrate only by exploring several different fields of activity; the recent history of the relationship between the state and Islam and the development of reformist discourses can be understood in terms of the relationship which Islam(ism) has enjoyed with the outside world, notably through diasporas, in the Persian Gulf and the United Arab Emirates. Moreover, the institutions which most symbolize localism, such as national nongovernmental organizations (NGOs) and mosques but also traditional Qur'anic schools, are inseparably linked at the same time to both the Mauritanian and the foreign Islamist movements, as can be seen in the financing of mosques or the international recruitment of students in the *mahadir* (Islamic schools for advanced studies; singular *mahadra*). The analysis of all these structures and their interrelationships allows us to better understand the important fact that a few Mauritanians are very prominently implicated in international terrorist networks (despite the relatively modest influence of the Mauritanian Islamist movement at home).

Islam in Mauritania: National Logics and Transnational Dynamics

On June 3, 2005, a Mauritanian military outpost at Lemgheity, 530 kilometers from Zouérate (the northernmost Mauritanian town) and near the Algerian and Malian borders, was attacked at dawn by a group of heavily armed commandos. The government attributed the attack to an Algerian terrorist group called the Groupement salafiste pour la prédication et le combat (GSPC, Salafist Group for Preaching and Combat), well known for operating in the uncontrollable areas bordering Algeria, Mali, and Mauritania and notably for kidnapping foreigners for ransom.[1] Leaving about thirty dead (including nine of the attackers) and dozens seriously wounded, this terrorist attack was the first ever perpetrated in Mauritania, let alone by a foreign terrorist group like the GSPC. In an Internet posting claiming responsibility for the attack, the Algerians cited as justification the "impious" Mauritanian government's hostility toward the Islamist movement and its harassment of religious activists.[2] Whatever the (still unclear) dimensions of this affair, the old regime found in it a justification for the pressure it had placed for the previous two years on Islamist milieus. In April 2005, the authorities had announced that they had arrested seven young Mauritanians who had allegedly received training from the GSPC in Algeria. The arrest was accompanied by the umpteenth imprisonment of the spiritual and political leaders of the Islamist movement in Mauritania, who had no known links with the terrorists. Although the new government immediately freed the principal Islamist leaders, the seven alleged terrorists were still held in detention. But all these arrests took place at a critical moment in Islam's relationship with the state.

The State against the Islamists

In the Islamic Republic of Mauritania, the importance of "Islamic activist" trends had always been perceived as normal. After having long been limited to religious affairs, this influence was extended to the political domain under the reign of Colonel Mohamed Khouna Ould Haidalla (1979–84), during which reformist Muslims were integrated into the management of public affairs. This situation was concretized by the adoption (never fundamentally challenged since) of sharia as the exclusive source of juridical norms. This period of partial Islamization of the state and of its law (Monteillet 2002) was also marked by the application of Islamic legal punishments (*hudud*) following trials in sharia courts.[3] It is from this period that a political movement inspired by the Muslim Brotherhood truly dates. However, with the exception of this short but decisive parenthesis, the state often kept its distance from religious circles, leaving them to manage religious practices, and did so until mid-2003. Keeping the custodians of a reformist religious discourse at a respectful and respectable distance was not difficult. On one hand, the "Islamic" nature of the country always protected it to some degree against the accusations that proponents of Islamic renewal often make (that the state is secular, communist, atheist, etc.); on the other hand, Mauritanian religious leaders were usually law abiding and commanded the respect of the authorities.

The Islamist movement was founded at the end of the 1970s, echoing the development of political Islam in the rest of the Arabo-Muslim world. It defends an Islam of protest spread through the medium of live and recorded sermons and nongovernmental associations. The Institute d'études et de recherches islamiques (ISERI, Institute of Islamic Research and Study), a state body intended to train graduates of the *mahadir*, was the crucible from which young Islamists emerged, some of whom would occupy leadership positions, such as Jamil Ould Mansour and Mohamed El Hacen Ould Dedew. At the same time, various figures became progressively active, reproducing the cleavages and affinities found elsewhere: *tablighis* (members of the Tablighi Jama'at), Muslim Brothers, pro-Wahhabis, "traditionalists," and others. These finally banded together in the mid-1980s under the aegis of Hasim (Harakat al-siyasiyya al-islamiyya fi Muritaniyya, the Islamic Political Movement in Mauritania). This small group is led by young teachers, imams, and cadres of diverse backgrounds. During the introduction of multipartyism in July 1991, the state refused to recognize the party promoted by this group, Hizb al-Umma (the Party of the Umma).[4] The party nevertheless survived for a short period, during which several incidents were attributed to an "Islamist fanatic";[5] in addition, inflammatory preaching in mosques increased, and the associational movement grew significantly. The government began strict surveillance of activists; in 1994 it launched a hunt for Islamists and a massive expulsion of foreign preachers (Pakistanis, Algerians, Tunisians, and others) whose presence supposedly contributed to the radicalization of Mauritanians, who, the government asserted, are "habitually peaceful." Many clubs, associations, and Islamic foundations, which had begun to flourish in the country, were banned, and their leaders were arrested and accused of "plotting" before being freed for lack of evidence. This pressure did not prevent militant religion from making progress—not only by criticizing those in power but also by opposing traditional representatives of Islam. Emblematic of the purveyors of radical discourse, Shaykh Mohamed Ould Sidi Yahya, the best-known preacher in the country (Ould Ahmed Salem 2001–2002), continued his critique of the regime and of society largely unhindered. He was, moreover, the only such person who was not severely repressed in early 1994, although he was placed under brief house arrest.

Following these events, which gave the movement a new political visibility, its leaders rapidly dispersed. Some of them emigrated to the Gulf, whereas others rallied to the regime or were incorporated into the bureaucracy managing "official" Islam, such as the Islamic High Council (Haut conseil islamique), the Association of Ulama of Mauritania, the Ministry for Islamic Orientation, and other organizations. Certain others, including Jamil Ould Mansour, Ould Saleck, and El Hacen Ould Moulaye Ely, joined the opposition. The progress of Islamist sentiments in Mauritania did not weaken, and the authorities' determination to check it grew correspondingly, culminating in the regime's final years in an international struggle against "Islamism and terrorism."

Establishment in Society

In the second half of the 1980s, preachers (du'at) intensified their efforts at the level of everyday society and the Tablighi Jama'at was again tolerated because of its conspicuously apolitical character. It was even able to establish two preaching centers in the poorer neighborhoods of Nouakchott, all the while being officially supported by the major theologians and imams of the country. In fact, although its political influence had virtually disappeared, Islamism in Mauritania apparently redeployed itself in da'wa or the call to Islam. This "retreat" from politics allowed it to gain ground and to win acceptance and understanding from its immediate rivals, the ulama.[6] In any case, it was through preaching in the mosques that the Islamist movement regained its vigor. It recruited in all the most vulnerable sectors of society, for example among haratines (former slaves or descendants of slaves), where it made spectacular inroads.[7] Successive periods of repression and calm paradoxically helped to publicize the formerly secretive Islamist movement, which was increasingly demonized, especially after the events that took place on the international scene in the early 2000s. Political debates about foreign relations allowed the Islamist discourse to become increasingly audible. For example, when Mauritania began establishing diplomatic ties with Israel, there was a deep split among religious leaders who had close ties to the state. Given the state's disengagement from the Palestinian cause and the internal decline of the pan-Arab movements—which had suffered considerably from purges within the Mauritanian regime that had long supported them—the Islamists were able to position themselves as defenders of the abandoned Palestinian and pan-Arab causes. This was the context within which new leaders emerged. In less than two years, one of them, the young Mohamed El Hacen Ould Dedew, would become the charismatic leader of Islamism in Mauritania.

The Emergence of a Leadership

Ould Dedew, the nephew of Shaykh Mohamed Salem Ould Addoud (a well-known official theologian who is a former minister of Islamic orientation and former president of the Islamic High Council), is a graduate of a Mauritanian *mahadra*, the former imam of a mosque in Riyadh, Saudi Arabia, and a professor at the Muhammad Ibn Sa'ud University in Mecca. He works to strengthen the radical Salafi tendency of Islamism in Mauritania. Although his widely circulated cassettes were for a long time limited to technical and theological matters, he was provided an entry into the political scene by the large opposition movement denouncing the establishment of diplomatic relations between Mauritania and the state of Israel in 1999. This is an example of the "boomerang effect," whereby global issues have local repercussions on the relationship between state, society, and Islam in Mauritania.

In 2002, Ould Dedew managed to "prove" through arguments drawing on Islamic sources that Muslim states cannot enter into relations with the state of Israel as it currently exists. The petition (fatwa) which he circulated was signed even by ulama who had always been close to the regime. This symbolic and political victory gained Ould Dedew exceptional notoriety. More and more people listened to his sermons, especially when the preacher who had been the best known and most popular in Mauritania, Mohamed Ould Sidi Yahya, retired from preaching for personal reasons. Ould Dedew emerged as a militant contesting relations with Israel and thus as a leader of the Palestinian cause, which enjoyed overwhelming support in the streets and in the mosques. Henceforth, proponents of the re-Islamization of Mauritania would see in him a leader who linked not only charisma, popularity, and youth (he was born in 1965) but also family connections and social legitimacy. The Dhikr mosque in Tinsweilim, a Nouakchott neighborhood, quickly became his base. Ould Dedew was as a matter of course joined by a long-time Islamist, Jamil Ould Mansour. Relatively young (about forty-five), Ould Mansour was known as an activist in the radical opposition. He was elected in 2001, from the electoral list of the Rassemblement des forces démocratiques (RFD, Union of Democratic Forces), as mayor of Arafat, the most populous neighborhood of Nouakchott. He is also founder and secretary general of Ribat, an association not recognized by the government, which struggles, as it declares in all its public statements, "against the normalization of relations with Israel and for the defense of al-Quds" (Jerusalem). The Dedew-Mansour duo was quickly joined by a former Mauritanian ambassador to Syria, Moctar Ould Mohamed Moussa; the three formed a trio which would spark the renewal of radical reformist discourse. Beginning in 2003, the renewal organized itself more effectively, orchestrating a variety of demonstrations from marches to pro-Palestinian strikes at the University of Nouakchott—where the Islamists won student elections in 2002—to days of solidarity with Iraq. But the decisive turning point in relations between the state and the Islamists only occurred in 2003.

The Islamists under Attack

In April 2003, the government decided to take back control of Islam in the country: NGOs, university institutes, clubs, associations, and other Islamist networks were suddenly banned. After the minister of culture and Islamic orientation threatened to destroy their mosques, the imams, who had heretofore been free of any state control, were warned and then arrested in droves, accused of spreading "subversive messages" and of tolerating "parasites who preach in the mosques." The prime minister alleged connections between Mauritanian mosques and "international terrorist movements."

The people arrested were alleged to have incited violence and were suspected of ties with foreign extremist and terrorist circles. The first thirty-five arrestees included a number of magistrates, *qadis* (judges), teachers, NGO employees, and, last but not least, the well-known leaders Ould Dedew, Ould Mohamed Moussa, and Jamil Ould Mansour; the latter was also divested of his mayorship, although he had begun to make noteworthy improvements in Arafat. The arrests of Islamists provoked lively popular protest for the first time. As long as the regime had attacked political leaders who had no real reputation in the milieus of traditional Islamic learning, it had not excited any mass reaction. But in this case, the arrested imams and ulama were far too visible for their arrests to leave their followers and sympathizers, and indeed the whole of society, indifferent. In the Nouakchott market, strike days were even organized, as merchants constituted a large contingent of the Islamist ranks.

The Islamists were hunted, harassed, and accused. They turned the prison where they were held into a place for preaching and religious activities. Visiting days became major popular events. When, on June 8, 2003, a bloody military coup was thwarted in Nouakchott (leaving fifteen dead and thirty-nine injured, according to official counts), President Ould Taya directly linked the Islamist activists to the attack, even if no formal ties could be established between them. In the course of that day, there was such disorder in the capital that the prisons were opened and all the prisoners escaped. But when order was reestablished, all but three of the Islamists, as good citizens, voluntarily returned to prison. The exceptions included Jamil Ould Mansour and Ahmed Ould Wedia (director of the Islamist weekly *Al-Raya*), who fled and sought political asylum in Belgium. Ould Mansour eventually returned to Mauritania in October and was imprisoned for a few days before being freed. His colleagues, including Ould Dedew and Ould Mohamed Moussa, had been freed before his return. They had nonetheless initially refused to leave prison and tried, unsuccessfully, to get a trial. Just several weeks after the failed coup, on June 30, a law was proclaimed regulating the status of mosques in a belated attempt to take back control of the places of worship, whose numbers in Nouakchott had increased twentyfold over the previous decade.

The leaders of the coup attempt who had fled were arrested, and a period of relative calm ensued between the Mauritanian regime and the Islamists. But, on August 8, 2004, the government arrested thirty-one army officers. The minister of national defense appeared on television on August 10 to declare that an attempted coup d'état had been foiled and that it had been planned by officers with ties to the same group that had attempted a coup the year before. The minister also added that this failed coup attempt was linked to threats against Mauritania, which had supposedly been made by the Jordanian Abu Musab al-Zarqawi! Together with the officers, the leaders of the Islamist movement were arrested and accused of ties with the soldiers who had planned the 2003 coup attempt. The arrested alleged conspirators were the same as before: Ould Dedew, Jamil Ould Mansour, and Ould Mohamed Moussa. During their detention, the Islamist leaders were put face to face with young "Islamists," who, according to the regime, had been trained abroad alongside the organizers of the coup in order to attempt another putsch. On leaving prison a month later, the Islamist leaders testified to the harshness of their detention and triggered a considerable outcry when they declared that prisoners, including the young Islamists, had been severely tortured by the police. The government reacted violently when the Internet site of a Mauritanian human rights monitor, Observatoire mauritanien des droits de l'homme, based outside the country and considered to be close to the Islamists, published photos of alleged prisoners who had suffered torture. The Islamist leaders were once again arrested and indicted for "spreading false information." It was expected that the "Islamists" would be tried along with the leaders of the coup, whose trial began in November 2004 in Ouad Naga, near Nouakchott. But this was not to be the case. They remained in prison until the end of the trial and were finally freed in February 2005 after having begun a hunger strike.

The Mauritanian Islamists benefited politically from their repression. Ould Dedew, in a credible enough attempt to position himself at the center of Mauritanian political debate, called for a dialogue between different political forces in a declaration on the Qatari television station Al Jazeera. Jamil Ould Mansour insisted that the movement, which was part of a worldwide Islamic revival, had taken root in Mauritania. But the details of their ideological options or of their political program were never really spelled out. Both leaders declared that they unconditionally supported the democratic selection of leaders by means of the ballot box. Ould Dedew even declared, in interviews with Mauritanian newspapers, that democracy was "the best formula for governing ever conceived by the human mind."

In April 2005, the regime claimed to have identified ten young Mauritanians (seven of whom were arrested) accused of planning terrorist attacks in Mauritania after having undergone extensive training in the Algerian camps of the GSPC. The Mauritanian Islamist leaders were once again arrested, except for Jamil Ould Mansour, who fled the country. The regime launched a campaign to enforce the 2003 law forbidding unauthorized preaching in mosques, and also condemned the doctrinal links between Mauritanian Islamists and youth involved in international terrorist movements. It was at this tense moment that the murderous attack against the military outpost at Lemgheity, on the northern border, took place.

Whatever the future effects of this bloody event, the GSPC's raid and the reasons the group gave for it were the self-fulfillment of a prophecy: the Mauritanian Islamists had been accused for two years of violent terrorist projects, but it was a foreign group which sought to avenge them. It thus becomes difficult to know whether it is the state or the religious activists who are truly responsible for the violent turn their relationship has taken. Admittedly, it is impossible to find the slightest organic or political link between this attack and the Mauritanian Islamists. Even so, in the eyes of the regime, the preachers, politicians, and imams are responsible for facilitating this grave transformation, which must significantly affect the complex relationship between Islamism(s) and the Mauritanian state. After the coup d'état of August 3, 2005, the Islamist leaders were freed, but twenty-one other Islamists did not benefit from the "general, full, and entire" amnesty granted by the new authorities to those who had been imprisoned or exiled for their opinions. It is clear that all of this is played out in the interstices between the interior and the exterior, and between the internal and the external. Even if Mauritanians have been identified in regional or international terrorist movements (such as, respectively, the GSPC or al-Qaeda), as we will see below, the nature of the religious diasporas is far more complex.

A "Religious" Diaspora: Mauritanian Islamic Networks in the United Arab Emirates

The field research that Yahya Ould al-Bara and I conducted in the United Arab Emirates (UAE) was concerned primarily with the number, personal characteristics, and itineraries of expatriate theologians and with their relations with Islamist trends in Mauritania itself. It is essential to bear in mind the celebrity of and the respect accorded to the present leader of Mauritanian Islamists, Mohamed El Hacen Ould Dedew, by Muslims of the Emirates as well as Mauritanian expatriates. Considered one of the finest specialists on hadith in the Muslim world, he is well respected throughout the Gulf. In the Emirates, where his cassettes are distributed and to which he has traveled many times, the name of Mauritania is beginning to be linked to his own. His prestige is even greater among Mauritanian immigrants. Certain young immigrants even collected funds to support Mohamed Khouna Ould Haidalla during the presidential elections of November 2003. As shown above, Haidalla, a former colonel who was head of state in Mauritania from 1979 to 1984, is known as the only Mauritanian leader amenable to Islamist ideas. During his ill-fated 2003 candidacy, he was backed by a wide spectrum of Mauritanian Islamists, and above all by the three emblematic local Islamist leaders. He was arrested after the election and tried on charges of receiving foreign funds.

The Mauritanian community in the UAE is concentrated in a highly circumscribed territory between the town of Abu Dhabi and Dubai, in a little place called as-Samha ash-Sha'abiyya. A collection of prefabricated housing first built to lodge policemen, shepherds, and jockeys from Nouakchott, this hamlet has progressively become a sort of Little Mauritania. According to an estimate from the Mauritanian embassy in the UAE, there are around four thousand Mauritanians in that country. These immigrants are largely shepherds and herders brought over in the 1970s and 1980s because of their skill in managing camel herds, but there are also a significant number of policemen and other security officers. Their jobs are provided under an agreement between Mauritania and the UAE, as are those of most of the imams, teachers, and *qadis*.

The Mauritanians participating in the religious domain in the Emirates can be divided into five principal categories, along with a number of individuals who do not fall into any of these. Sixty or seventy are imams in various mosques. Some of them were directly recruited in Mauritania, and a minority of them in the Emirates themselves. Others are former traders: a former grocer in Congo-Brazzaville who was impoverished during the civil war in the mid-1990s and another expelled from Senegal after the crisis with Mauritania in 1989 have found positions as imams. Professional imams come from various groups of Muslim religious specialists (*zwaya*) in southwest Mauritania and elsewhere. They are sympathetic to the Mauritanian Islamist movement, but it is uncertain whether most are truly interested in the political struggle, given that some of them owe their recruitment to official religious circles. The security of employment abroad, which also allows them to engage in commercial activities, seems preferable to militant action. Nonetheless, their solidarity with their colleagues who remain in Mauritania is evident.

About a dozen Mauritanians hold the prestigious position of *qadi*. Before 2000, the role was not subject to any agreement with the Mauritanian state, and a key member of the Mauritanian community in the UAE played a decisive role in recruiting the first *qadis*. This was Mohamed Abdellahi Ould Siddik, a scholar from the Tadjakanet tribe from the town of Guérou (in the Assaba region of eastern Mauritania). He is a Salafi theologian who taught for a long time in the official Islamic institute in Boutilimit (150 kilometers southeast of Nouakchott), a half-traditional, half-modern institute of religious learning, since closed. Settled in the UAE for more than twenty years, he has become an important religious counselor (with contracts from the Ministry of Justice, the Islamic Bank of Dubai, and the Islamic Bank of Abu Dhabi), permitting him to recruit seven members of his own tribe as magistrates. Known for his Salafism, he even wrote a follow-up to the classic polemical work written in the 1920s by Mohamed al-Khadir Ould Mayaba entitled *Mushtaha al-kharif*, in which he denounces Sufi orders, Sufism in general, and the Tijaniyya in particular. Ould Siddik has become an influential personality linked to financial and economic circles as well as to local and international theological ones. His prominence is locally recognized, and he is a dominant figure in the Mauritanian community. In the summer of 2004, a commission of the UAE Ministry of Justice came to Nouakchott to interview the candidates presented by Mauritania for the position of *qadi*. But the commission did not select a single one of the candidates interviewed.

The UAE recruits Mauritanian magistrates for both religious and political reasons. Mauritanians are Sunnis, and *fiqh* (jurisprudence) in the country follows the Maliki school of jurisprudence and the Ash'ari school of theology, essentially situated in the line of thought of Khalil Ibn Ishaq and his famous *Mukhtasar* (*Abridgment*), which is mastered in Mauritanian theological schools and *mahadir*. In the Emirates, only the families of the emirs are Maliki, while most of the population is Hanbali or Shafi'i. The UAE regime seems to want to make the administration of religion and justice more Maliki. Its efforts to recruit imams, judges, and scholars from this tradition are deliberate and manifestly political.

The third category of Mauritanians are *al-muwa'zin* (preachers). Although they are not *du'at* in the *tablighi* sense of the term (that is, they do not belong to a specific religious group with set practices, dress codes, methods, and discourse), they have made a profession of lecturing on the Islamic meaning of daily life, reminding the faithful of the end of the world. This millenarian theology is preached in private as well as in public spaces. These men generally come from the tribes of eastern Mauritania. They are often imams waiting for a job; some are small-scale brokers in the world of commerce who hope for a more profitable career in the religious domain or who aspire to a public position.

About seventeen Mauritanians are professors in the Emirates' universities and institutes of higher learning. Only three are proclaimed *du'at*, and they consider themselves apolitical even though they preach without payment, in the *tablighi* manner. Several founders of Mauritanian Islamism settled twenty years ago in the UAE. These ideologues were easily able to remake themselves as university professors. The two most significant are Boumiya Ould Boyah and Mohamed Lemine Ould Mezid, who became professors in local universities such as the University of Sharjah. The ruling family of the Sharjah Emirate wishes to see the town become a guardian of Islamic and cultural values within the confederacy. Anxious to attract intellectuals from the Arab and Muslim worlds, this emirate opens its doors to all Islamist intellectuals in trouble at home. The emirate's television station (Shariqa TV) is a multilingual (Arabic, French, English, Urdu) forum for popularizing the precepts of Islam. Its essentially religious programs are presented by anchors of a wide variety of nationalities, Western, African, and Middle Eastern, all with a decidedly Islamist look: beards, white robes, and so on.

The founding fathers of political Islam in Mauritania who took refuge in the UAE have been joined in the 1990s and 2000s by other Islamists who have modern and scientific training. This includes activists who claim to have been trained in science and technology in the West, for example, in the U.S. or in France. There are also Western-trained engineers in cutting-edge fields. Some of them claim to have contributed intellectually to the diffusion of Islamist ideas.

The last category is the *marabouts*, or Muslim religious specialists. In spite of the Emirates' official Salafi ideology, the market for Islamic esoteric services is flourishing there and throughout the Gulf. There is a strong and growing demand from people in all social classes throughout the Emirates, but especially from the well-off, for miraculous cures, religious interpretation of dreams, divination, and other Islamic esoteric ways of obtaining health, wealth, and success. This demand is clandestine, unofficial but real. It is satisfied by Muslims of diverse origins and of several categories: healers using religious formulas and operating in middle-class circles, and prestigious healers who come to live with their clients for several months of the year, or who travel back and forth among Dubai, Abu Dhabi, Paris, and Nouakchott. The case of Cheikh Youba is exemplary. He is a high-class *marabout*, with numerous followers, and has prospered for twenty years in the Gulf circuit. There are also persons better known in Saudi Arabia but also familiar in the Emirates, such as Mohamed El Hussein, an important financier of the former party in power in Mauritania, the Parti républicain démocratique et social (PRDS, Democratic and Social Republican Party). Still more numerous are those sometimes called fetish men, whose competence is unverifiable and who hope to have a lucky break, dreaming of finding an emir or, more likely, a "princess" to whom they can propose their services or those of a supposedly even more "powerful" *marabout*.

Actors and Institutions: NGOs, Associations, Networks

State Islam and its institutions have largely been abandoned by the central authorities over the past twenty years, to the benefit of religious and financial networks, some of them foreign. The neglect of certain sectors of society has left a considerable field open to the Islamist networks' charitable activities. The results of our study of Islamist NGOs, groups, and organizations which were or still are active in Mauritania can be divided into two parts: the first relates to international NGOs, and the second to Mauritanian organizations structured in institutional networks sometimes recognized by or attached to the Mauritanian state.

Islamic NGOs: A Long-Term Influence

Transnational Islamic NGOs have been active in Mauritania for more than twenty years and have had notable material achievements as well as sociopolitical and institutional effects. Most local NGOs were "structured" by the offer of international Islamic humanitarian assistance. Before they were banned in 2003, these NGOs were essentially under the aegis of four large international structures:

1. the International Islamic Relief Organization (Hayat al-Igatha al-Islamiyya), funded by the Muslim World League;
2. the Africa Muslim Agency, financed by Kuwait;
3. the International African Relief Agency (IARA) (Al-wakala al-islamiyya al-ifriqiyya li-l-igatha), financed by Sudan;
4. the Emirate Aid Agency (Hayat al-igatha al-imaratiyya), financed by the UAE.

The analysis of these organizations' structure, achievements, and organizational methods will allow us to appreciate their impact on Mauritania, an impact which has survived the closing of their national offices.

Although it was a humanitarian organization, the International Islamic Relief Organization was nevertheless headed by a bureau called Da'wa wa-l-irshad (Preaching and Orientation) that ensured its management reflected a sort of subtle blend of charity and ideology. It undertook important projects such as the construction of an orphanage in Nouakchott, with a boarding school for 120 students. In addition, five hundred orphans in Nouakchott received a daily allowance covering their subsistence needs and those of their families, sometimes as much as US$20 per day. In various Nouakchott neighborhoods, a committee was responsible for taking a census of orphans and paying for their school enrollment and clothing, as well as giving them a monthly cash allowance. The NGO also built and equipped a clinic in Arafat, staffed by Mauritanian doctors provided by the Ministry of Health. In principle, health care was free. Primary schools in Rosso and Boghé (both on the Senegal River) were constructed. During the Tuareg rebellion in neighboring Mali, refugee camps were established in eastern Mauritania and this organization furnished considerable material assistance to refugees. Each year, it brought over Pakistani doctors who performed numerous free surgical operations and distributed prescription eyeglasses. The NGO distributed sheep during the celebration of the 'Id or Feast of the Sacrifice. It also dug wells in areas which lacked water. One of this NGO's long-term directors was a Mauritanian of *halpulaaren* ethnicity with Islamist convictions who belonged to the Tijaniyya. After this NGO was banned, this man joined the official Association of Ulama of Mauritania as an "inspector." Another of the NGO's leaders was trained in the ISERI and was imam of a mosque which he himself had constructed, all the while acting as director of Iqra, a Mauritanian institute devoted to training graduates of traditional schools (*mahadir*) in manual work.

The Africa Muslim Agency, a humanitarian NGO, is affiliated with the Kuwaiti Muslim Brothers and has mostly enabled pilgrims, selected in many cases along clientship lines, to go to Mecca. But it has also offered aid to the poor, building mosques, digging wells, and supporting orphans. It was led by an Islamist activist trained in the ISERI who also founded a locally famous Islamist club, Nadi Musab, which was banned in 1994. This man is now in the construction business. The NGO was later managed by an Algerian, Habib Al Jazairi. His programs for assisting orphans survived the group's banning and are today managed by a well-known legal expert who is close to the regime.

A branch of a Sudanese Islamic aid agency, the International African Relief Agency, has sporadically intervened in Mauritania and has never been managed by a Mauritanian. Little is known about its activities other than that it conducts Islamist preaching and offers aid to orphans and the sick.

The activities of the Emirate Aid Agency, a pilot international NGO of the UAE, are similar to those of other international NGOs. Initially managed in Mauritania by a Sudanese affiliated with the Islamic Front, a certain Ata al-Menan, it was afterward managed by a member of the Islamist movement in Mauritania who is nevertheless an advisor to the current minister of Islamic orientation, and then by another locally known Islamist activist.

It should be recalled that the international Islamic NGOs were all banned, without exception, and their offices closed down in May 2003, in the course of the anti-Islamist campaign discussed earlier. Most of the important local Islamic NGOs were also suspended and their offices closed, and the Saudi centers for preaching, as well as the Islamic Institute of Nouakchott (a Saudi Islamic university providing scholarships to students throughout West Africa), were unceremoniously shut down. Indeed, the style and method of this clampdown are worth noting: on May 7, 2003, the police raided the premises of the Saudi Institute, ignoring diplomatic subtleties, and sixty people were immediately arrested, including all the teaching staff of Mauritanian nationality. At the same time, police also raided the headquarters of the UAE aid agency. In Abu Dhabi, the authorities immediately asked the Mauritanian embassy for an official explanation, while insisting on the apolitical and humanitarian nature of their organization. The official Mauritanian response was that the closure was aimed principally at the director of the office, a Mauritanian national. But the fact that all the agency's activities continued to be banned proves that it was the NGO itself that was targeted.

The banning of international NGOs, and of most of the local ones that acted as their intermediaries, did not put a stop to their activities but rather rendered them more uncontrollable and clandestine. It opened up opportunities for intermediaries to travel directly to the Gulf in search of funds. One of these says his targets are the *haratines* of the Senegal River valley. He digs wells while proselytizing, concentrating his efforts on the poorest sectors of society. He proclaims that he and others are attempting to replace government programs which refuse to recognize the specific problems of the community of *haratines*, from which he does not personally come. His objectives are not clear and his explanations of his choice of sites conform to a general pattern whereby Islamist agents on the ground target the most vulnerable sectors of the population. The activist in question is the representative of a Qatari NGO which has never had any official presence in Mauritania. The presence of several other NGOs similarly remains informal or linked to a specific individual, making it difficult to ban them or to intercept their local agents. Among these are the World Assembly of Muslim Youth or WAMY, which concentrates on building schools and digging wells, and the Saudi-funded al-Haramain Foundation, which finances mosque building, represented by the Islamist Salafi Ahmed Kowry. It should be mentioned that, as the directors or former directors of Islamic NGOs freely admit, there is absolutely no control over the allocation of funds. According to certain informants, this carelessness on the part of donors reached its peak between 1987 and 1994, a period which corresponds to the local Islamist movement's transition from secrecy and ideological action to activity in political and humanitarian arenas.

The current secrecy surrounding the activities of these Islamic aid organizations is reminiscent of the period before their formal arrival in Mauritania, when they risked reproof from the ministry[8] for the lack of transparency of their funding, their activities, and the management of their programs; their refusal to communicate with the government or to submit to audits; the lack of official contacts with the local authorities; and so on. In any case, all the embassies of the Gulf states continue to provide subsidies and gifts to these aid networks and Islamic figures.

Alongside these transnational NGOs, there exists a set of Mauritanian organizations structured in institutional networks, sometimes recognized by or linked to the state and sometimes linked to international Islamic bodies. It is through this network that traditional elites have had access to state political and administrative positions. The Islamic Cultural Association (ICA, Al-Jami'at al-thaqafiyya al-islamiyya) was founded under the aegis of and with the encouragement of the Haidalla regime in the early 1980s. It fostered the creation of a veritable Islamic scout movement in Mauritania and allowed the allocation of considerable funds, the first of their kind in Mauritania, to finance a network of clubs for boys (Club Musab Ibn Oumeir) and for girls (Club Aïcha), which exposed many young Mauritanians to the values and language of Islamism and Salafism. The founding members of this association were for the most part businessmen and executives who still wield influence. The ICA was both the precursor of the associational movement and the crucible in which Islamist elements simmered for a long time. The funds it was allocated enriched many of its founders and ultimately served to finance the first Islamic networks. Its moral authority remains uncontested today. As for the Iqra institute mentioned earlier, it is a branch of a Saudi network of similar institutes aimed at providing technical training, but in Mauritania it was founded and managed by El Hacen Ould Moulaye Ely, one of the very first leaders of the Islamist movement. We must also mention the Higher Institute for Islamic Thought (Al-mahad al-ali li-l-fikr al-islam), an affiliate of an international institute based in the U.S. The Association for Wisdom and the Preservation of the Patrimony sponsored by Ould Dedew himself provides supplementary classes for the benefit of students working toward a baccalaureate in letters, the degree awarded graduates of the *mahadir*. It also manages the sale of recorded sermons on cassette.

Mosques and *Mahadir* between the Local and the Global

The building and upkeep of a mosque are among the pious works for Muslims. To build a mosque here "down below" is to guarantee oneself a home "above," in God's paradise, *al-Janna*. It is thus hardly astonishing that some of the most important investments by Muslims are in this field. Ever since the 1980s, funds from oil-rich nations intended for mosque construction have flooded Mauritania, thanks in particular to the diaspora and the Islamic NGOs. The state graciously provided the land.

In the past fifteen years, most public establishments (hospitals, government offices, stadiums, universities, and institutes) have received their own mosques: forty-nine such mosques existed in Nouakchott in 2003. In general, the proliferation of these places of worship is entirely unplanned and disorganized. It is difficult for the Mauritanian state to refuse to permit a mosque's construction. A law[9] passed in 2003 was supposed to establish control over the process, but it has never been implemented, although meetings held in mosques controlled by Islamists are sometimes dispersed on its authority. Mosques are places of prayer but also of Qur'anic teaching and *da'wa*. Nowadays in Mauritania, as elsewhere in the Muslim world, they serve multiple functions on which we cannot dwell here.

In Nouakchott, the number of mosques increased from 46 in 1989 to 617 in 2002, and, in April 2005, the Ministry of Communication affirmed that it had reached 730. The rate of increase named by the minister in charge of Islamic orientation (10 per year) is thus incorrect: during Ramadan, at least 1 mosque is opened every day. According to the authorities of the League of Imams of Mauritania (founded July 4, 2000), in 2002, 162 mosques were built by the collective efforts of neighborhood residents; 37 were built by rich Mauritanians; and 248 were built with individual contributions from inhabitants of the Gulf nations. NGOs and charitable Islamic organizations built another 166. Foreign countries (Qatar, Saudi Arabia, Morocco) only financed the building of 3 mosques and the Mauritanian state has built only 1 in 1963. Government subsidies and salaries were awarded to about one hundred imams and mosques. Only 37 percent of these mosques are *jami'* mosques, that is to say, large enough to hold the Friday communal prayers.

Mosques are considerably more common in poorer, more populous neighborhoods than in richer neighborhoods. Still, Al Sabkha, the most populous arrondissement of Nouakchott, paradoxically has the fewest mosques (36): this is a neighborhood inhabited by immigrants from African countries and by Black African Mauritanians. It is also here where preaching has the fewest followers. Its population has less access to the resources of the Gulf nations, and charitable Islamic associations are less active there.

Nouadhibou, during the same period, saw a steady but equally spectacular growth. Of the ninety mosques now in existence, only ten existed in 1989. The proportions are the same as in Nouakchott, except that industrial sites include a considerable number of small mosques.

The *Mahadir*, Sites for Training Islamic Elites

Although the traditional Mauritanian Islamic schools for advanced studies (*mahadir*) have always attracted Muslims from throughout the world, Muslims who attended them in different periods have been attracted for different reasons. We studied foreign students in Mauritanian *mahadir* in 2004 with the hope of better understanding the people attracted by this mode of acquiring Islamic knowledge, determining their motives and the rewards they gain from this particular environment.

There exists in Mauritania an Islamic culture which is scholarly, prestigious, elaborate, and centered on traditional Qur'anic and theological study (Ould Cheikh 1985; Lydon 2004). Although Islam in Mauritania is characterized by powerful Sufi orders, its real distinction lies in the almost "industrial" production of religious elites trained in Maliki *fiqh* (jurisprudence) and enjoying a considerable reputation both in international Islamist circles and in other Muslim countries. The Mauritanian ulama have long traveled to the Maghreb and the Middle East in order to advertise and diffuse their knowledge. The image of the *mahadir* has certainly benefited; it is very favorable in the Maghreb, in the Gulf, and beyond.

We do not know exactly when this kind of teaching began. The term *mahadra* does not exist in Arabic dictionaries and appears quite typical of the dialect of Arabic spoken in Mauritania by the Moors (Bidan). The origin of the word is thus unknown, but it has the same root as *muhadara* (lecture, class), *mahdar* (report), and *hudur* (presence, assembly). We can thus say that it connotes a lecture and its listeners. At their origin, the *mahadir* were truly nomadic universities under the direction of a shaykh whose learning was nationally or regionally acknowledged, and some of them could be passed down from father to son. The success of the *mahadir* is a function of the number of religious leaders and renowned scholars who have been trained in them. Learning is simultaneously the acquisition of knowledge through memorization and a test of physical endurance. The conditions of a shaykh's life remain, even today, those of the desert, frugal and spartan. The *mahadra* is supported by pious gifts that cover only the community's basic needs. For the pupils, it is a test of endurance, of destitution, of exile. These schools are separate from the *zawiyas* of the Sufi orders, but this does not exclude shaykhs from having close ties to the orders (Ould Ahmed Salem 1996, 178–83). As a rule, the *mahadir*'s curriculum is strictly religious, but it does not include Islamic mysticism. The principal subjects taught are the Qur'an, hadith, *'aqida* (basic religious beliefs), *fiqh* (jurisprudence), and *sira* (the biography of the Prophet Muhammad), but Arabic language, literature, and grammar are also covered. Only large *mahadir* cover all these subjects exhaustively; the great majority are of modest size and simply teach the Qur'an and hadith.

Teaching in the *mahadir* has remained largely outside the state's orbit, and the considerable attempts by the state to include them have failed. After the drought of the 1970s, the *mahadir* often ceased to move about, becoming sedentary in order to more easily receive aid from the state or from international Islamic organizations and to better manage their resources. Some of the *mahadir* attempted to constitute themselves as independent villages, or, for that matter, as small religious towns (Boubrik 1999). Government figures are striking; they report that there were 3,054 *mahadir* in 2003.[10]

Although religious exchanges between the traditional Mauritanian schools and sub-Saharan Africa (e.g., Futa Jallon, Senegal, and Mali) have existed for so long that they need not be discussed in detail, the number of people arriving from other countries has grown. The appearance of Maghrebis and Europeans, as well as students from North America, dates back only to the 1980s. In particular, students often come from diasporic Muslim communities. Presumably, teaching carried out under a tent better corresponds to the image of early Islam, not yet altered by modernity: the fact that teaching is offered for free, its liberty and absence of rigidity, and the desert environment's similarity to that of the Prophet and his companions bolster this image, and the Moors thus acquired a reputation as learned scholars in Islamic sciences. Word of mouth effectively spreads this reputation.

Attending the *mahadra* is also a spiritual experience, and all foreign students invoke this as a reason for attendance. The foreign students who attend Mauritanian *mahadir* come from many places;[11] Asians (Pakistanis) are scarcer now, since their expulsion in 1994.

We chose four *mahadir* which we consider emblematic of this tradition of scholarship, and which are among the most popular with foreign students, and visited them in the summer of 2004. (The fact that it was summer may have affected the number of foreign students in the schools.) The following is a discussion of our findings.

Oum el Qura seems to embody the most striking contradictions of this system.[12] Its head is among the most famous ulama in the country, Shaykh Mohamed Salem Ould Addoud. A former minister of culture and Islamic orientation (1989–92), in 1992, he was named president of the newly created Islamic High Council. This recognition of a typical *mahadra* teacher, acknowledged as a worldwide specialist in Maliki *fiqh*, constitutes recognition of a representative of official, legalistic, moderate Islam, who happens also to be the uncle of Ould Dedew, himself trained at Oum el Qura. There are intensive exchanges between this austere Bedouin school and the universities of Saudi Arabia, and the school enjoys considerable symbolic and religious influence.

The village built around the *mahadra* is sixty-five kilometers from Nouakchott. Addoud's Salafi tendencies are well known and the principal subjects of instruction are hadith and Arabic. When we visited, there were 132 students, with fewer foreign students than in the past. At the time of our visit, there were students from Algeria, Tunisia, and various West African countries.

The village of Ma'âta Moulana, "The Gift of God," is situated 123 kilometers to the east of Nouakchott. It was founded by a Tijani religious leader, Shaykh Al Michri, and all its inhabitants are affiliated with the Tijaniyya. Nevertheless, the *mahadra* concentrates on teaching the Qur'an. Its current head is the founder's son, a member of the Idaw Ali tribe, one of the country's most powerful because of its intellectual, financial, and economic weight. This *mahadra* profits from the international ties constructed by its founder along the lines of Tijani networks. It receives considerable local and foreign assistance and is particularly renowned for educating the sons of Nouakchott's nomenklatura. In August 2004 the school had 161 students, including students from Senegal, Algeria, France, the U.S., Tunisia, Mali, Gambia, and Guinea.

According to authorities in the *mahadra*, the relationships established by the founder with his Tijani brethren throughout the world were responsible for its attracting foreign students. Western students come to it through a Senegalese Tijani channel, that of Cerno Mansour Baro, the Halpulaar leader of the Mbour *zawiya* of the Tijaniyya, who directs all those who come to him seeking Qur'anic instruction or mystical study, but especially Western converts to Islam, to Ma'âta Moulana. Cerno Mansour Baro (who died in early 2007) was himself one of the centers of Tijani influence in the Senegalese as well as the Mauritanian Tijani diaspora.[13]

Noubaghiya is a small town on the so-called Road of Hope (*Route d'espoir*) leading east from Nouakchott. It is primarily occupied by a group of kin from the Idaw Ali tribe, especially the families of Ahl Abderrahmane and Ahl Al Qadi. Its inhabitants are also members of the Tijaniyya, and two famous Tijani *zawiyas* are located there. But these *zawiyas* are the only ones in Mauritania which follow neither the path of Ibrahima Niasse nor that of Shaykh Hamahullah, which together encompass almost all Tijanis in Mauritania. The *mahadra* is one of the oldest and best organized in the country. Founded in the seventeenth century by Abdallah Al Qadi, it is the beneficiary of considerable resources from the Idaw Ali tribe, even more than the *mahadra* of Ma'âta Moulana. It is, moreover, a *mahadra jami'a*, where all the religious sciences and Arabic are taught. Since 1970, the principal teacher at the *mahadra* has been Mohamed Fall Ould Abdallahi Ould Bah, who is sixty years old. The village authorities willingly admit they receive funds from Gulf states without specifying the countries or naming the donors. At the time of our visit the school had 220 students, including some from Mali, Guinea, Algeria, Morocco, Chad, Senegal, France (from Paris), and the U.S. (from Texas). The *mahadra* receives no state subsidies.

Et'teysir is a village about fifty kilometers from Nouakchott. Its inhabitants belong to the Niassène branch of the Tijaniyya, and most of them are members of the Ideyghoub tribe. Led by Shaykh Mohamed Al Hassan Ould Ahmed Al Khadîm, the *mahadra* is joined to the Tijani *zawiya*. It was founded in 1968 as a continuation of an old school the shaykh's ancestors founded. It includes as many as 304 students, and it acknowledges that it is partly financed through charitable contributions from the Gulf along with subsidies from the Mauritanian government. It includes students from Guinea, Algeria, Morocco, France (of Moroccan origin), Austria, Tunisia, and the U.S. (sent by Shaykh Hamza of the Zaytuna Institute in California).

Mauritanians in International Terrorist Networks?

Since 1998, the arrests made from time to time by the authorities have targeted certain Mauritanian Islamist activists and accused them of being connected to international terrorist networks. There has rarely been concrete evidence of such connections. Granted, in 1999, the police declared that they had dismantled a network that arranged transportation through Sudan to al-Qaeda training camps in Afghanistan. An NGO called Noor—since then banned[14]—supposedly received funds from the bin Laden family. The famous Abu Hafs, alias Mahfoudh Ould Al Waled, who would play an important part in the al-Qaeda network (see later), had been taken in for questioning before he could flee the country.[15] In December 2004, the authorities also arrested several young men who allegedly threatened terrorist attacks on the Dakar rally in the name of al-Qaeda. In 2000, the Associated Press published a report from Afghanistan which mentioned "Mauritanians" considered very close to al-Qaeda's leader (Associated Press 2000a, 2000b). The Mauritanian Islamists who participate in these international networks are not numerically significant, but their presence is remarkable in light of the many nationalities involved and the modest number of high-ranking Mauritanian Islamists ready to take this kind of risk. Information implicating Mauritanians in terrorist networks comes from verified local and international public sources which leave little room for speculation: the presence of two Mauritanians in key positions in al-Qaeda's chain of command has been confirmed.

The first is Mahfoudh Ould Al Waled, alias Abu Hafs Ech-chingitti, who is wanted by the American authorities after the attacks of September 11. Close to Osama bin Laden, he was, as *mufti*, responsible for issuing fatwas and led his colleagues in prayer. After September 11, he appeared on several Arabic television stations and spoke in the name of al-Qaeda. According to Mauritanian newspapers, which cite Iranian sources, he is currently a prisoner of the Iranian authorities, who allegedly proposed to extradite him to Mauritania, which refused to accept him.

The second is Mohamedou Ould Slahi, whose role the National Commission on Terrorist Attacks upon the United States (the 9/11 Commission) has highlighted. He earned a diploma in telecommunications engineering in Germany, and, while there, spent time with and advised the men who went on to carry out the September 11 attacks. Later he led prayers at the Al Sunna mosque in Montreal, Canada. Canadian newspapers provide plentiful information about Ould Slahi's time and activities in Canada. According to the report of the National Commission, Ould Slahi played a key role in the orientation in Afghanistan of four young men, three of whom would go on to pilot planes on September 11. The commission drew its information on Ould Slahi's role from the fourth member of the group, who was their coordinator and who would not be aboard a plane, namely the Yemeni Ramzi Binalshibh: "The four were Mohamed Atta, Marwan al Shehhi, Ziad Jarrah, and Ramzi Binalshibh. Atta, Shehhi, and Jarrah would become pilots for the 9/11 attacks, while Binalshibh would act as a key coordinator for the plot." According to statements given to the commission, the so-called Hamburg group was constituted in Germany at the end of the 1980s and took definitive form in 1999.

> According to Binalshibh, by sometime in 1999, the four had decided to act on their beliefs and to pursue jihad against the Russians in Chechnya. . . . Binalshibh claims that during 1999, he and Shehhi had a chance meeting with an individual to whom they expressed an interest in joining the fighting in Chechnya. They were referred to another individual named Mohamedou Ould Slahi—an al Qaeda member living in Germany. He advised them that it was difficult to get to Chechnya and that they should go to Afghanistan first. Following Slahi's advice, between November and December of 1999, Atta, Jarrah, Shehhi, and Binalshibh went to Afghanistan, traveling separately. (National Commission on Terrorist Attacks 2004)

The commission thus allotted Ould Slahi a decisive role as a recruiter. Fleeing Montreal in 2000, he was detained and questioned in Senegal, then released before being arrested in Nouakchott, and eventually extradited to the U.S. at the end of 2002. His family claims to have received a letter from him, and Canadian newspapers allege that his health has deteriorated seriously.[16]

Even though it is a state religion, the public authorities in Mauritania have not managed to hold Islam to the preestablished norms they would prefer. The activists who want to use dogma to become political actors paradoxically benefit from the state's attempts to interfere in an Islamic field, which is no longer dominated by small groups and is no longer only a national issue. Even without elaborating a political proj-ect, the Islamist movement can now count on new recruits, on the intensive long-term work of associations, on the presence of innumerable mosques, and on global net-works and diasporas which can be useful in many ways, including financially. It remains to be seen to what extent these advantages can be put to use by local Islamist actors who have national credibility and who are not compromised by the involvement of a very few of their colleagues in international terrorism. The state, in any case, still has available to it those repressive measures which it has used both justly and unjustly, to the great advantage of those Islamist activists who have been repeatedly accused of serious crimes only to be subsequently cleared. The bloody attack on a military outpost on Mauritania's Saharan frontier may signal the targeting of Mauritania by regional terrorist movements such as the GSPC, which is both well established in the uncontrollable desert border regions and linked to the smuggling that flourishes there. But this attack may also dampen public support for the Islamist cause. In any case, the dilemma facing the Mauritanian state is enormous: it seeks to limit the religious activities of local and generally peaceful Islamists without attracting the wrath of their local and international terrorist sympathizers. The military regime which seized power in 2005 might be able to deal with this dilemma because it has no direct quarrel with Mauritanian Islamists, although it has refused to officially recognize their movement and still detains twenty-one people associated with them. However, the transition toward democracy it has inaugurated has been well received by the so-called Islamist leaders, as part of a nationwide sentiment in favor of the Military Council for Justice and Democracy and its program of democratization. The Islamist masses and their leaders will hold the regime which emerges from the elections scheduled for 2007 accountable for the place granted Islamist trends in the Mauritanian political and institutional landscape. In the meantime, we are witnessing a period of relative calm.

Notes

With the assistance of Yahya Ould al-Bara in field research.

1. In 2003, the GSPC had freed thirty-one Western tourists after ransom money had been paid.
2. *Liberation*, June 8, 2005.
3. Ordinance 80-085 of May 10, 1980, instituted a special criminal court charged with applying Maliki *fiqh* (jurisprudence). On September 19, 1980, a prisoner condemned to death was executed and three thieves had their hands amputated.
4. Article 4 of the Ordinance on the Freedom of the Press and of Political Parties stipulates, "Islam cannot be the platform of a political party" (Mauritania 1991, 2). This article is retained in the constitution proposed in the June 2006 referendum.
5. In October 1993 this same person attacked a priest in the church in Nouakchott and in November a group of ministers who had gathered for an official ceremony. The victims were not seriously injured, and nothing indicates that "Islamism" was the only motive behind the attacks. The man has never been identified; some claim he is a "madman."
6. On the Mauritanian ulama and their relationship to politics, see Ould al-Bara 2000.
7. Political aspects of Islam are sometimes lived and perceived differently by the different categories and ethnic groups that make up Mauritanian society. On this point, see Ould al-Bara 2000.
8. Interview with Mohamed Lemine Ould Chawaf, director of Islamic orientation, Department of the Struggle against Illiteracy, of Primary Schooling, and of Islamic Orientation, Nouakchott, July 2004.
9. Law no. 031.03 of July 24, 2004, *Journal Officiel de la RIM*, no. 1052, August 15, 2003.
10. The modest subsidies accorded annually to these schools allow the Ministry for Islamic Orientation to furnish these statistics, which may thus be slightly biased.
11. Attempts to conduct extended interviews with foreign students were fruitful but not in the way we had envisaged. The students refused to talk about political subjects, which they claimed did not interest them. They said that they had come for religious studies and mystical discovery, and for nothing else. They had generally been given the address of a

mahadra by a friend, a family member, or an expatriate Mauritanian, whom they met in circumstances which were not always clear, and on average they spend no more than three years at the school.

12. At the time of our study, the daily *Nouakchott-Info* had repeated a story from an electronic Nigerian newspaper *(Thisdaynews)* on Nigerians arrested in Nigeria and accused of having been trained in a terrorist camp in Mauritania called Oum el Qura. We thus arrived there during a climate of suspicion of questions in general and of researchers in particular. The *mahadra* sued the Mauritanian newspaper, and the matter was eventually settled out of court (*Nouakchott-Info*, July 12, 2004).

13. On Cerno Mansour Baro and his followers in West Africa and Europe, see Soares 2004.

14. *La Tribune*, March 17, 1999.

15. *Le Calame*, October 2, 2001.

16. Numerous articles appeared in the *Globe and Mail* in January and February 2000 and June 2004, and in *La Presse* in March 2001, among other places. See, in particular, Colin Freeze, "Ex-Montrealer 'suffering' in Guantanamo, site says," *Globe and Mail*, June 2, 2004, A9.

References

Associated Press 2000a. Osama: America's latest punching bag. Story by Kathy Gannon. March 5. http://www.ap.org.

———. 2000b. Afghan camps: Training ground for terrorists. Report from Jalalabad, Afghanistan. http://www.ap.org.

Boubrik, R. 1999. *Saints et société en Islam: La confrérie ouest saharienne Fadiliyya*. Paris: CNRS.

Lydon, G. 2004. Inkwells of the Sahara: Reflections on the production of Islamic knowledge in Bilad Shinqit. In *The transmission of learning in Islamic Africa*, ed. S. Reese, 39–71. Leiden: Brill.

Mauritania. 1991. *Textes élementaires relatifs aux partis politiques et à la liberté de la presse*. July 25. Nouakchott: Imprimerie nationale.

Monteillet, Vincent. 2002. L'islam, le droit et l'État dans la constitution mauritanienne. *L'Afrique politique 2002*, 69–100. Paris: Karthala.

National Commission on Terrorist Attacks upon the United States. 2004. Outline of the 9/11 plot. Twelfth public hearing, staff statement 16. http://www.9-11commission.gov/staff_statements/index.htm, accessed March 22, 2006.

Ould Ahmed Salem, Z. 1996. Retour sur le politique par le bas: De quelques modes populaires d'énonciation du politique en Mauritanie. PhD. diss., Institut d'Études Politiques de Lyon.

———. 2001–2002. Prêcher dans le désert: L'univers du Cheikh Sidi Yahya et l'évolution de l'islamisme mauritanien. *Islam et sociétés au sud du Sahara* 14–15: 5–40.

Ould al-Bara, Yahya. 2000. Société et pouvoir: Étude des soucis et préoccupations sociopolitiques des théologiens-légistes mauritaniens (*fuqaha*) à partir de leurs consultations juridiques (*fatawa*) du XVIIe au XXe siècle. PhD. diss., École des hautes études en sciences sociales, Paris.

Ould Cheikh, A. W. 1985. Nomadisme, islam et pouvoir politique dans la société maure précoloniale (XIe–XIXe siècles): Essai sur quelques aspects du tribalisme. Ph.D. diss., Université René Descartes–Paris V.

Soares, B. F. 2004. An African Muslim saint and his followers in France. *Journal of Ethnic and Migration Studies* 30 (5): 913–27.

Chapter 2

Global Concerns, Local Realities: Islam and Islamism in a Somali State under Construction

Marleen Renders

Introduction

Somalia is the quintessential "collapsed state." Since 1991 it has not seen even a minimally functional central government. An international military intervention set up in 1993 under the aegis of the United Nations, intended to get the state back on its feet, bogged down in Mogadishu soon after its inception. As the capital sank into a quagmire of competing clan militia, the UN troops were pulled out again. Somalia was largely forgotten as the eyes of the world and the attention of policymakers turned to the civil war in Yugoslavia, which had broken out in the same year. After the events of September 11, 2001, however, policymakers suddenly remembered Somalia. As the ultimate stage of state "disengagement," Somalia's disarray offered cause for worry, particularly because its population is nearly 100 percent Muslim.

Somalia figured high on the list of potential hideouts of the world's most wanted, including Osama bin Laden. One Somali organization in particular attracted attention in the so-called war on terror: the Islamist group al-Ittihad al-Islami, or Islamic Union. The global dimension of Islam has been more and more emphasized since September 11. Political Islam, or Islamism, is increasingly analyzed as a global or even a globalized movement. At first sight, the latter assessment seems to make some sense: Islamic or Islamist movements increasingly use similar discourses and refer to injustices against Muslims in Palestine, Kashmir, Bosnia, and elsewhere. The reality on the ground, however, is much more complex. International events and conflicts are far less of a concern to local Islamists than may be inferred from their discourse.

Amid real or imagined concerns about what is called global Islamic terrorism, political analysis seems to forget about the local space in which Islam and Islamism "happen." In the case of Somalia, factors such as clan and state (or the absence thereof) cannot be disregarded. Two issues stand out. First, Somalia saw the development of a number of localized polities—some more sustainable than others, but all of them clan-based. One of these, called Somaliland and situated in the northwestern region of the collapsed state, developed into a multiclan arrangement that looks, smells, and tastes like a state.[1] It has a government, a claim on a territory, and a bicameral parliament that passes laws; it raises taxes, issues license plates for cars, and even holds elections. Second, in Somaliland and elsewhere in Somalia, clan remains an important political factor which significantly affects Islam and Islamist movements.

This chapter emphasizes the interconnectedness of Islam and Islamism with Somaliland's local society and politics. The appearance, ideology, or sociopolitical role of Islam and Islamism depend on the context. Like other philosophical frames of reference (religious or otherwise), Islam and Islamism in a given polity are the product of politics.[2] To be sure, Islam and Islamism do shape society and politics, affecting, for example, the decisions and actions of individuals. But at the same time Islam and Islamism themselves are shaped by society, by the actions of political actors making use of these frames of reference. Although Islamic or Islamist groups may use a "globalized" discourse or ideology, their actions are very much shaped and driven by their local context.

Islam, State, and Clan in Somalia

The Somali clan system and Islam are inseparable. When Islam was imported into Somalia from the Arabian Peninsula, as early as the seventh century, it immediately blended with the emerging clan system. In the stateless society of the Somalis before the British and Italian colonizations, the clan system was the paramount mode of social organization. In the absence of a central, overarching (state) structure, it was the network of clan relations that provided people with physical protection and social security. In the Somali clan system, every person identifies him- or herself as a member of a particular clan-family, a clan, a subclan, and even of a sub-subclan, down to the level of immediate kin. Clansmen are obliged to assist and protect each other, financially and otherwise.

Customary law (*heer*) governs relations between the clans. When customary law is broken, blood compensation (*diya*) has to be paid to the victim's clan, and the wrong-doer's clan is collectively responsible for doing so. It is the clan elders of the respective groups who agree on how a breach of the law is to be settled and what the compensation for different infractions in particular cases should be. Clan elders can also decide on armed revenge for wrongs committed against the clan. Clans and some subclans are headed by so-called titled elders, although they have no coercive authority. The titles vary: the head of a clan may be called, for example, a sultan (*suldaan*), *garaad*, or *bokor*.

As Lewis (1955) points out, the Somali initially adopted not the rational, legalistic Islam that is better known in the West but a more mystical Islamic theosophy. According to Lewis, the Sufi understanding of Islam was more suited to the Somali clan system, as it did not emphasize Muslim law (which to a degree conflicted with *heer*) as much as religious experience and the relation between the believer and God. This relation is experienced under the moral guidance of a spiritual master in the context of a Sufi order, that is, a *tariqa*. The Qadiriyya, introduced in the fifteenth century, is the oldest Sufi *tariqa* among the Somali. In the first half of the nineteenth century the Qadiri shaykhs founded *tariqa* settlements (called *jama'a* by the Somali) in the interior, religious communities where Somalis of different clan backgrounds lived together as brothers (*ikhwan*), engaging in agriculture, animal husbandry, religious study, and worship (Kapteijns 2000, 235). The *jama'a* of Shaykh Maddar in northwestern Somalia would form the nucleus of what is now Somaliland's capital, Hargeysa.

In the twentieth century, the concept of the state was introduced to the Somali territories. Under British and Italian tutelage in their respective territories,[3] the Somali polity saw the emergence of nationalism. Somali nationalists wanted to do away with the clan system, which they saw as hampering modernization and progress. This opinion was adapted and extended by the military regime of Siyyad Barre, which came to power after a brief period of civilian rule between 1960 and 1969.[4] The military regime believed that building a state and a corresponding national identity entailed doing away with all forms of subnational allegiance, especially solidarity or legal ties based on lineage. Clan allegiance was outlawed. Islam, on the other hand, was deemed a useful national ideology, the declared socialist orientation of the regime notwithstanding. Islam, albeit a peculiar "Siyyadized" version, was used in political manipulation and propaganda. Despite the regime's discourse, it did the same with clan allegiance; it followed a divide-and-rule strategy, singling out particular clans for favors and others for punishment. By manipulating clan and religion, the dictatorship bred opposition in exactly these spheres.

Islamist Opposition

Small groups, inspired by movements in Saudi Arabia (the Wahhabiyya) and in Egypt (the Ikhwan al-Muslimin or Muslim Brotherhood) started to emerge in the early 1970s. These Islamist movements promoted a more legalist and moralist understanding or interpretation of Islam and the grounding of both society and state on the sharia. Both secularism and Sufism were denounced as deviations from the straight path. The Somali Ikhwan criticized government corruption. They were most notably implicated in the protests against the 1975 Family Law, which accorded equal inheritance rights to women. Siyyad Barre promptly had a number of Muslim leaders arrested (and executed within a week), making clear that it was the prerogative of the state—or rather, the head of state—to interpret the message of the Prophet Muhammad. Although several underground Islamist organizations were formed during the 1970s, notably al-Nahda and al-Ahli (Abdurahman 2001), they were far too weak to challenge the regime (Marchal 2001, 4).

Siyyad Barre played the religious card himself. During the 1980s, the religious settlements set up by the Sufi orders were engaged in social and economic experiments. Some of them were forced to label themselves cooperatives to help boost the record of Barre's cooperative movement (Helander 1999, 46). In some cases, their leaders were given certain powers and privileges in return for their allegiance to the Barre regime. One example is the *jama'a* of Shaykh Raabi, nicknamed "Timo Weyn" ("Big Hair"), near Yagoori. Raabi seems to have started out as an offshoot of the Qadiriyya order. Yet, over time, his focus shifted from spirituality to the economic and political power that can be associated with it. The Barre regime took an interest in Raabi's *jama'a* because the shaykh had significant influence in a strategic area bordering on

Somalia's archenemy Ethiopia, which Barre wanted to keep under control.[5] Members of the Timo Weyn community were reportedly given money, cars, and weapons by the government. The *jama'a* developed into a sophisticated organization, with its own income-generating activities, which survived the downfall of the military regime and the ensuing collapse of the Somali state.

Interestingly, the Islamist movements denounced the clan system just as Barre did. The clan system, so profoundly connected with Sufi understandings of Islam, would stand in the way of uniting Muslims under an Islamic banner. It was a backward institution, harmful to any future Islamic state. As the Barre regime visibly weakened toward the end of the 1980s, the small Islamic study and activist groups were confronted with the question of how to push their ideas forward. Islamist students at Mogadishu National University debated whether it would be useful and legitimate to take up arms and seize control of the state,[6] but events soon made the question irrelevant. Siyyad Barre fell from power in January 1991. He was deposed not by the Islamists but by clan militia organized by demoted and antagonized politicians who no longer shared the spoils of power.

As armed clan militia took control of strategic infrastructure and assets, some of the Islamists also organized militias and tried to take direct control of a portion of Somali territory. They were, however, rarely in a position to stand up against clan militia: when the Hawiye clan militia (under the name of the United Somali Congress, USC) took over Mogadishu, all Islamists who were not Hawiye were forced to flee the capital and either take refuge with their own clans or go to Kismayo, where some of them took up arms against the Hawiye warlord Mohamed Farah Aideed.[7] On September 22, 1991, an armed Islamist movement called al-Ittihad al-Islami was proclaimed.[8] Its founding document, the "Manifesto of an Islamic Party," declared its primary objective to be the establishment of an Islamic state. In addition, it sought the installation of Islamic justice, economic reform, the propagation of Islam, and the countering of deviant beliefs. Finally, al-Ittihad declared its intention to create a strong army after it had established an Islamic state. Until that was done, it refused to make alliances with non-Islamist forces (Abdurahman 2001, 236). However, the manifesto did not clearly present the group's ideology.

Al-Ittihad became another military faction in the Somali civil war and, like the clans, tried to gain and hold territory and strategic assets. It had only limited success, however. In January 1991, al-Ittihad took control of the seaport of Kismayo but was soon driven out by the Hawiye (USC) militia. The same thing happened in Bossaso; once more the al-Ittihad militia was defeated by clan militia—this time the Majerteen Somali Salvation Democratic Front under the leadership of Abdillahi Yusuf (Le Sage 2001). Wherever the Islamist militia did not succeed in forging a military alliance with a strong clan-based political faction, it was unable to hold its position. After suffering a number of military defeats, al-Ittihad withdrew from direct military activity in Somalia. The militiamen and their leaders returned to their clans, rejoining the day-to-day life of their communities.

Clan-Based Opposition

Like the United Somali Congress, the Somali National Movement (SNM), which ended up founding Somaliland in 1991, was a result of the oppressive policies and the divide-and-rule strategy of the Barre regime. It was begun in 1977 by émigré intellectuals belonging to the Isaaq clan family in Saudi Arabia and the UK, who intended it to be a Somalia-wide opposition movement against the military dictatorship.[9] It was initially known as the Somali Democratic Islamic Movement, but the word "Islamic" was soon dropped. Although some of its founders explicitly took issue with the regime for appropriating and misusing Islam in its pursuit of total political control, this was not their only grievance. People with an "Islamist" inclination were joined in the group by people with other grievances, such as politicians who had been sidelined and military officers who had defected. The SNM became an amalgam of opposition forces with different aims and backgrounds, which led to ideological cleavages within the movement (Lewis 1994; Compagnon 1992).

In 1982 the SNM took up arms against the Barre regime. The military campaign transformed the SNM from an elite undertaking which—at least in theory—superseded clan allegiance to a true popular movement, deeply rooted in the clans of the Isaaq clan family. It was the Isaaq clans who provided the SNM's fighting power and logistical support. Therefore, it was the Isaaq clan structures and clan leaders who took over power in the movement. Ideological differences among the original cadre became less relevant, whereas clan allegiance became increasingly important. As the Isaaq clan leaders became crucial actors in the war, they were given a more prominent role in the administrative structures of the SNM movement, which was institutionalized in the Council of Elders (the Guurti). Founded as an advisory body to the Central Committee of the SNM, the Guurti gained considerable political weight under the aegis of a few of its members, including its speaker, Shaykh Ibrahim Shaykh Yussuf Shaykh Maddar, a direct descendant of Shaykh Maddar, the founder of the Hargeysa *jama'a*. Although Shaykh Ibrahim's religious prestige undoubtedly added to his political respectability, it was his position within his clan and his political skill that determined his political weight.[10] The SNM guerrillas called themselves *mujahideen*, but the name was misleading, as it gave the impression that they were a unified Islamic or even Islamist fighting force, which they decidedly were not. Islam was a rallying cry and a moral support, but as an ideology it was fairly unimportant in the movement.[11]

Although the SNM had not been directly involved in the removal of Siyyad Barre in 1991 (Mogadishu was overrun by the Hawiye USC clan militia), the organization now found itself with military control over the northwest. The SNM and the clan leaders of the Isaaq decided to focus on the northwest first, rather than waiting until the situation in the south subsided and political opportunities arose there. The non-Isaaq clans inhabiting the northwest, who had previously sided with the military regime against the Isaaq, were invited to participate in a local northern peace process. At the Grand Conference of Northern Peoples in May 1991, delegates from the Isaaq, Gadabuursi, Warsangeli, and Dulbahante decided to proclaim the independence of the northwest under the name of the former British protectorate, Somaliland.

The Grand Conference mandated the SNM to govern Somaliland for a transitional period of two years. After these two years, a new clan conference adopted a transitional charter. This preconstitutional document established a presidency and a bicameral parliament, consisting of a House of Representatives and a House of Clan Elders or Guurti. Members of both houses were appointed according to clan allegiance and with the estimated (and agreed-upon) demographical weight of the clans taken into account. Gradually a fragile peace took root and state structures began to be institutionalized in those regions which were under formal government control. A constitution was drafted in 1997 and approved by popular vote in 2001. Peaceful local, presidential, and parliamentary elections, considered "free and fair" by international observers, took place in 2002, 2003, and 2005, respectively.

The Somaliland government claims authority over the territory of the former British Protectorate. Its power was initially consolidated in the Hargeysa-Berbera-Boorama triangle and was later extended to Bur'o. Further east, the situation is less straightforward, and government control beyond Bur'o is very weak. Somaliland's authority over the eastern regions of Sool and Sanaag is disputed by the Puntland State of Somalia, founded by Abdillahi Yusuf in 1997. But large portions of Somaliland have seen no major violent conflict over the past decade. Although Somaliland is not recognized by the international community, it certainly has at least some of the characteristics usually attributed to a state. Ironically, perhaps, it was not the Islamists who were able to build this polity. The Somaliland "state" declares itself to have been built on the foundations of clan allegiance, which had been considered the impediment par excellence to state building.

Despite its origins as a clan-based political arrangement, Somaliland has from the beginning presented itself as an Islamic state. Its constitution stipulates that Islam is the national religion. Any law that contradicts the sharia is void, and an official eleven-member ulama council watches to make sure such laws are not passed. Promotion of other religions is forbidden, and men standing for election to parliament or the presidency must be Muslims. Religious freedom is interpreted by the constitution essentially as the right and the duty of Muslims to remain Muslims (the sharia forbids renouncing Islam) and the right of non-Muslims (should there be any) to become Muslims (Somaliland Constitution).

Islam and Islamism within the Realm of Somaliland Governance

Islam is manifested and practiced in various ways in Somaliland. It is not always clear what makes an "Islamist." There are many religiously inclined people—devout, hardworking, and religiously motivated in their social and political actions. There is keen interest in religion among the Somaliland educated elite. Amran Ali, a local businesswoman and the wife of Ahmed Haashi, a former mayor of Hargeysa, has set up a women's Islamic study group. Calling herself a "born-again Muslim," she has dedicated herself to the cause of teaching people "proper Islam," cleansed of historical and local deviations. Her teachings do not attack the theology of Sufism but rather its sociopolitical effects and implications. Amran criticizes the use of Sufism as an excuse for bad behavior. For instance, Sufi religious exercises may well involve consuming herbal stimulants to enhance concentration and religious experience, but—contrary to what some men like to think—Sufism is not about sitting down to chew khat all day with friends. Men who chew all day do not take care of their families. This is most certainly un-Islamic, she maintains, and it is also contrary to Sufism. Amran insists that more people should learn about Islam so they can no longer be misled by bad teachers or by their own misinterpretations or limited knowledge. This is especially true for women, who in the past have been denied formal education in religion. Her study group meets every Thursday night; women come together to listen to a lecture by a shaykh, watch a film, or read a book and discuss their findings and questions.[12]

"Lady Amran" is respected in Hargeysa as a virtuous and knowledgeable Muslim. So is Ahmed Haashi himself. One of the Saudi founders of the SNM, Haashi became mayor of Hargeysa in 1995. He quickly built a reputation as an efficient and honest administrator: he made city officials work in the afternoons (which they had usually spent chewing khat) and improved Hargeysa's waste management and water sanitation. In the spring of 2003, Lady Amran was appointed secretary of state for family affairs. The women-only reception organized at the Hotel Maan-Soor in Hargeysa to mark the occasion was attended by many prominent women from the capital—from rather secular-minded businesswomen to a young woman trained as an engineer who had renounced her professional career because she had come to think that it is un-Islamic for women to work with men.[13] A few months later, Ahmed Haashi was called to high office as well and appointed minister of trade and commerce.

The discourse and morals of both Ahmed Haashi and Amran Ali are reminiscent of the "reformist" or "Islamist" moralist discourse. However, they do not regard themselves as Islamists, and neither do their elite peers. They are simply seen as exemplary Muslims. Indeed, Somaliland's social climate seems decidedly more conservative now than it must have been during the SNM struggle or before. Modesty in dress is insisted upon, especially since the late 1980s. Although Somali women, like the Senegalese and other West African Muslim women, did not traditionally wear the *hijab*, they do now. East of Berbera, in Bur'o or Las Aanood, it is fairly common to see women fully covered: face, hands, and feet. The sale and consumption of alcohol is prohibited, and some shaykhs disapprove of music being played before a mixed crowd.

Although Haashi and Amran do not identify themselves as "Islamists," other individuals and groups do publicly claim that label. This seems acceptable to the Somaliland government as well as to the community leaders (notably the clan elders), as long as these individuals and groups do not resort to violence. Islamist groups do exist in Hargeysa, although not much is known about them, their origins, manifestos, activities, or membership. Whereas under the Barre government any religious or political activity was suppressed, today this is no longer the case. Members of Islamist groups whom I interviewed in Hargeysa declared that they are free to organize meetings and can freely disseminate their views and teachings. No significant government restrictions on their activities seem to exist.[14] Indeed, in September 2002, the Tablighi mosque in eastern Hargeysa hosted a major conference (with seven thousand Somali and three hundred foreign participants), featuring keynote speakers who were former members of al-Ittihad (International Crisis Group 2005b, 18). However, when in 2003–4, in a series of related incidents, a small cell of jihadi terrorists directed from Mogadishu killed a number of foreign aid workers in Somaliland, the attackers were eventually apprehended by villagers and handed over to the Somaliland authorities to be questioned and tried (International Crisis Group 2005a, 5).

The first Islamist group in what is now Somaliland is believed to have been al-Wahda (Islamic Youth Unity), founded in Hargeysa in 1969 by Mahamed Hadj

Du'aale Shaykh. Its members were primarily students. Although al-Wahda opposed the socialist regime, its attitude toward the clan-based opposition movements was somewhat ambiguous. Whereas the armed struggle of the SNM guerrillas was clearly aimed at liberating the northwest with an Isaaq army, al-Wahda seemed torn between Isaaq and Islamist solidarity. Its members did not participate in the armed insurrection. According to some of them, Islamist groups in Somaliland had good relations with their counterparts in the south and elsewhere. The Isaaq bias of the SNM clashed with their ideology of Muslim unity. Despite the insistence of the SNM leadership, al-Wahda did not actually take up arms against the Somali regime.[15] On the other hand, they claim to have offered moral and perhaps some material support in the Isaaq refugee camps in Ethiopia, preaching to the soldiers, setting up schools, and collecting money for refugee children.[16]

Social services, especially schooling, still constitute a very important part of the activities of Islamist activists associated with al-Wahda. Reportedly, local groups have set up a number of schools, teaching Islamic sciences and Arabic but also other subjects, such as math. The teachers are Somali graduates from universities in Egypt, Sudan, or Saudi Arabia, and classes are conducted in Arabic. There are said to be sixty-five such schools, including three or four secondary schools, in Hargeysa alone, with an estimated enrollment of ten thousand. Another school is located in Boorama (a western town near the border with Ethiopia) and is said to have a student population of a thousand, including fifty girls.[17] It is not known where these schools get the necessary financial resources. According to the Islamist activists involved in promoting, organizing, and running them, the money is raised locally, but I could not confirm this. It is at least possible: amid almost general unemployment, Hargeysa has seen the rise of a generation of religiously observant young professionals who are primarily working (and making money) in the big telecom and money-transfer companies. Proudly sporting beards and ankle-length trousers, they make no secret of their religious and political preference. This has not, however, led to the emergence of a political movement in the narrow sense of the word. One man I interviewed stated that he had tried to set up his own political party, inspired by the views of North African Islamists such as the Tunisian Rachid Ghannouchi,[18] but the project never really took off.[19]

In the end, clan loyalty seems to be stronger than Islamist ideas of Muslim unity. The Islamist groups are said to be largely mixed, counting among their members people from the different clans of the city. But interviewees repeatedly pointed out that lineage is still very relevant. If two clans with members in the same Islamist group should come into conflict, even in a context unrelated to the group, the group might split along clan lines. Islamist organizations or networks function as a social security net for their members, much as a clan would, but they can never actually replace the clan. Members of Islamist groups who own businesses could, for example, give preferential treatment to fellow members when hiring employees. However, kinsmen and the obligations to the clan come first.[20] Generally, Islamist groups are not believed to have a very important impact on political life in Hargeysa, as is confirmed by the work of Roland Marchal (2001) and Marc-Antoine Pérouse de Montclos (2003).

Not only Islamists, but also Sufi Muslims have organized themselves in ways adapted to Somaliland's current sociopolitical context. The personal trajectory of one of my interviewees is peculiar in this respect. Originally from Boorama in western Somaliland, born into a shaykhly family, he attended secondary school and became a banker in the national bank in Mogadishu, where he led a secular life. Then on a government scholarship he went abroad to Italy, where he studied banking and earned a degree in sociology at Greenwich University and a Ph.D. in social anthropology from London University. While doing his doctoral work he joined the BBC Somali Service. Here his interest in Sufism was reawakened: on his return to Somaliland, more than a decade later, he took up religious teaching. He now has a small group of pupils whom he invites to Qadiriyya prayer sessions in his home, where they recite the *dhikr* (religious exercises) passed on to him by his father, the Boorama shaykh.

Professionally, he wants to remain active in journalism; like many Somali intellectuals and professionals, he has set up his own NGO to attract foreign funds for his projects. Sometime in the future, he would like to open a literary café in Hargeysa, with foreign newspapers and computers offering Internet access. He is fascinated by French writers such as Sartre, Lacan, Derrida, and Foucault, he told me. He considers this interest not at all incompatible with Islam, for Sufism, he said, is only about love and knowledge, not about politics. The Islamists, on the other hand, do have political goals, he claimed: they are concerned with power and money. In this way, they threaten the Sufis, who were the original Muslims in Somalia. Islamism has been imported from Saudi Arabia, and this imported ideology now clashes with the original Islam, which is organizing itself against this imposition. According to him, numerous Qadiriyya groups are being set up in Somaliland by "moderate people whose fathers were shaykhs"—that is, not by opportunistic newcomers. He intends to support that process, he said. In this respect it was important that he "disciplined his own people" when they gave Sufism a bad image of "useless undisciplined khat chewers."[21]

This is indeed how Islamists like to portray Sufism. One of their favorite examples is the Qadiriyya Shaykh Raabi or "Timo Weyn," the Sufi master discussed above.[22] My interviewee admires him greatly, avidly telling stories about his visit to Yagoori. But according to the Islamists, Shaykh Raabi was a wild-haired, pot-smoking heretic. The competition between Sufis and Islamists takes place on a religious level, but the real stakes are probably political and economic. Where Sufism is organized, as it is in Shaykh Raabi's community, competition can grow especially fierce. It occurs on the village level; whoever controls the mosque and the madrasa controls the community, because he has sole control of propaganda. It takes a lot of political maneuvering to get the clan elders on one's side,[23] but they are the ones who ultimately decide who the local religious leaders will be (and from which denomination they will be drawn).

According to one Islamist source in Hargeysa, the Islamists have displaced the Sufis in urban areas, whereas the Sufis retain most of their power base in the countryside. The Timo Weyn community, for example, is said to function much like a sect and to control significant resources. It is a hierarchical chain of communities within the Qadiriyya order. Its economic assets include trucks, Toyota Land Cruisers, and at least a thousand camels in the Taleeh area, east of Las Aanood. In former times it was financially supported by the Barre government, but now it earns income through its own activities: Raabi created a tomb for Shaykh Darood, which generates some income, and the shaykh is also given money by his followers all over Somaliland and even abroad. The Islamists, however, disapprove of begging and saint veneration, and they say so. In their opinion even religious people should work for their living instead of taking money and resources from their followers. They also have their own economic activities, notably in trade and commerce, which presumably compete with Timo Weyn activities. Insulted and feeling their interests threatened, the Timo Weyn allegedly attached themselves to Abdillahi Yusuf in the east and the Somaliland government in the west to use them against the Islamists. Other sources indeed confirm that the Timo Weyn have relations with people within the Somaliland government, but it is not at all clear with whom or to what extent.[24]

Where There Is No Government

Armed militia groups (Islamist or clan militia) are disapproved of by the general population.[25] They are outlawed and suppressed where the government has the political and military power to do so. Although virtually all adult male Somalilanders have their own AK-47s or other small arms at home, west of Bur'o real militia groups are a thing of the past. The bands of armed young men that used to roam the countryside or set up checkpoints to "tax" passers-by have been mostly dealt with by local clan elders. In most cases, the elders and the militia came to an agreement, and the militiamen demobilized, returned to their families and clans, and submitted to the authority of their elders. In other cases they just left, after being told by the elders that they were unwelcome. For instance, according to local reports, in 1993 the land of what is now Boorama University was occupied by al-Ittihad militiamen. The Boorama clan elders, who were setting up a local administration and wanted to do away with freelance militia, asked them to leave, and they complied (Menkhaus 1997, 13).

In some cases, militia members were disowned by their clans: if these men killed or injured anyone, their clans would not pay compensation but would kill the perpetrator instead. This was true not only of clan militia but apparently also of militia that called themselves Islamist. As governmental institutions were consolidated in Hargeysa after the Somaliland civil wars, local administration was taken over by the Somaliland government. According to official accounts, Islamist militia have not been treated differently from any other kind of irregular militia; consequently, like clan militia they have disappeared from government-controlled areas.[26]

In any case, clan seems to be the paramount political asset where conflicts of interest arise. Once the worst disarray of the civil war was over, independent militia were driven out of areas where "traditional" (clan) authority was strong. This was even the case in areas where the elders did not look particularly kindly on being governed from Hargeysa. When the al-Ittihad militia was chased out of Bossaso by Abdillahi Yusuf in 1992, it sought refuge further west and moved to take over the smaller port of Las Qoray in Sanaag, in disputed territory between Somaliland and Abdillahi Yusuf's neighboring Puntland. For a year, the port and the city were controlled by the al-Ittihad militia. Allegedly, the militia sought the support of local Warsangeli subclans, much to the displeasure of their sultan. I was told that, with the help of a clan-based NGO (the Somali Development and Relief Agency) operating from Djibouti with the assistance of the diaspora of the region, an operation was set up to purge the al-Ittihad militia from the area.[27]

In Somaliland, the presence of a strong traditional authority apparently allowed fairly rapid removal or dissolution of (Islamist) militia. Where traditional leadership was not so strong, freelance (Islamist) militia bands persisted. This seems to have been true of both the Sool and Sanaag regions, especially since the death of the widely respected old Warsangeli sultan. Traditional leadership in Sool and eastern Sanaag is very much divided, especially over whether to ally with Somaliland or Puntland. Both Somaliland and Puntland claim to have government structures in place in the region. When I visited the area in the spring of 2002, there were Puntland and Somaliland police stations and local governors present in the area, but they could do nothing except try to be visible. Any action on their part would have provoked an immediate reaction from the other side, triggering conflict.[28]

The Sool traditional leaders are said to have been bought by either Somaliland or Puntland, or even both. They are accused of only looking out for themselves. Unlike their Isaaq and Gadabuursi counterparts, the traditional leaders in Sool and Sanaag seem not to feel themselves accountable to their communities. In western Somaliland the war has promoted the integration of traditional leadership, modern politicians, and clansmen or civilians, first in the context of the SNM and later in the gradual state-building process. The inverse has happened in the east, where the war and its aftermath profoundly disrupted society: the clans of the easterners (who were the closest allies of Siyyad Barre) lost the civil war, and subsequently they felt more or less excluded from the state-building process (and the spoils attached to it) going on in the Boorama-Berbera-Hargeysa triangle. Divided and opportunistic, the traditional leaders in the east are weak and unable to exercise authority or control. Islamist militia are said to still be operating in the area, although very little is known about them. In any case, in Somaliland at least, strong traditional leadership seems to have led to recognized government and the elimination of Islamist (and indeed all) militia.

In Hargeysa the existence of al-Ittihad is simply denied. It is said to have disappeared after its defeat by Abdillahi Yusuf. In Las Aanood, interviewees tended to call all people with a religious inclination "al-Ittihad." Yet it is altogether unclear what al-Ittihad actually stands for. Is it a loose coalition of individuals, a formal organization, a coalition of organizations, or just the local generic word for "Islamist"? Interviewees were often reluctant to clarify this issue, or did not know themselves. Some of the garaads (titled elders) in the Sool region would downplay the Islamist presence, claiming that "Islamists" are merely learned people teaching the Qur'an to the children and that people in fact do not like new forms of Islam, because they are not in keeping with Somali culture. Other garaads, by contrast, accused their peers of working with al-Ittihad because they did not have the support of their legitimate constituency, their kinsmen.[29] Such accusations may be correct but are hard to assess, especially since it has become common practice among rivals for political power to accuse their competitors of being "fundamentalists," in the hope of obtaining foreign support against them.

Some interviewees said that they do not even know who is an Islamist and who is not. One claimed that "al-Ittihad people are not different from other religious people; they are just very knowledgeable and people ask them questions." According to one former politician, it had never mattered who was a member of al-Ittihad until after the September 11 attacks. On the other hand, a member of a women's group described al-Ittihad as much more readily recognizable and told me, "Every Friday, they have a sermon in the street. Five or six men would take a microphone and many men and women would come and listen." Yet she emphasized that "nobody is really against them; they are respected people in the community. Their respect depends on their religious knowledge and their ability to explain."

Since its disbandment as a militia, al-Ittihad has been elusive. Opinions differ as to whether it still exists at all. The name "al-Ittihad" seems to be given to various groups or organizations that are only very loosely (if at all) connected to one another. Menkhaus (2002, 8) confirms that al-Ittihad movements appear to vary significantly by region, with some appearing more moderate and others more radical. According to Menkhaus, their agenda in Somalia and Somaliland is primarily domestic, not global. Evidence I collected in Las Aanood indeed points to the importance of the local situation. Al-Ittihad is said to control sizable economic assets, including most shops and businesses in Las Aanood. Men associated with al-Ittihad enjoy a good reputation as business partners and contractors and thus are frequently hired (including by international aid agencies). They work hard, respect deadlines, and do not chew khat—which saves them time and money that they can reinvest. None of them are seen to be unemployed or sitting about; most of them are well-to-do and respected.[30] The Islamists in Las Aanood also play an important role in the delivery of social services. They run a number of orphanages funded with money from the Gulf, which, I was told, are so well built and managed that people would bring their children there even if they were not orphaned. In medical emergencies such as traffic accidents, al-Ittihad provides the injured and their families with food and transportation, something the hospital would not be able to do.[31]

Although to a certain extent al-Ittihad seems to supersede or at least bypass the divisiveness of the clan system, this capacity is limited. According to a women's group member in Las Aanood, they seem to be trustworthy negotiators and peacemakers in a context fragmented by clan politics, because they do not use clan as a divisive strategy.[32] Yet al-Ittihad and other Islamic or Islamist groups do not operate outside the clan system. Al-Ittihad does not attack or denounce the clan system or the clan leaders, as it did before 1992. On the contrary, it uses the clan system to its own advantage and works to gain influence in the clan structures. One way of doing this is by influencing the selection of a new traditional leader, such as a clan sultan. It may even play each side against the other. In 2001, al-Ittihad reportedly played a major role in the clan conferences following a leadership conflict in Puntland.[33] But, at the same time, it attempted once more to take over the harbor of Bossaso: in exchange for a considerable part of the port revenue, it offered to manage the port for Abdillahi Yusuf's opponent, Jama Ali Jama. Al-Ittihad was supported by traders from minority Majerteen clans who were not strong enough to stand up against Yusuf.

Marchal aptly points out that the Islamists, willingly or unwillingly, became part of the clan politics in the region. Political actors supported them, not to promote Islamic reform but to counter other clans (Marchal 2001). Clan cannot be ignored without risking one's political position or power base. I was told that one of al-Ittihad's most prominent associates, Shaykh Ali Warsame (based in Bur'o), was once summoned by his clan leaders and instructed to withdraw his men from rebel military actions in Ethiopia, because relatives of clansmen killed in the fighting were coming to Bur'o to ask Ali Warsame's clan elders for compensation. The shaykh was told to either choose the side of the clan and bear its interests in mind or leave for Mogadishu.[34]

We do not have reliable information on al-Ittihad's current nature, strength, or influence. But it is clear, in any case, that the Islamists have had to abandon their strategy of operating independently of the clan structures. When clans do make peace, al-Ittihad tries to become involved as a mediator or peacemaker to influence the terms of the peace and the leadership of the clan. On the other hand, it may work to prolong leadership conflicts within a clan. Some interviewees in the Sool region suggested that al-Ittihad keeps local conflicts alive to prevent administrative structures from being established in the area, because any form of regional or national government or authority would be harmful to al-Ittihad businesses.[35] Government control or taxation would diminish profits and al-Ittihad's power in the region. To prevent this from happening, al-Ittihad reportedly supports freely roaming militia in Sool, arming and paying them to cause insecurity.

Conclusion

Islam and Islamism have many different appearances and roles in Somaliland. In fact, it is not always clear which individuals or groups can be called Islamist. Somalilanders do not always use the label; sometimes they make no distinctions among "religious people." At other times, they do use it. Labeling is part of the political game: calling someone an Islamist can be a political move. In other cases, the label "Islamist" is self-chosen. But even then, it does not necessarily indicate where a person or a group stands politically. Much depends on the specifics of the local situation.

The "Islamic state," as envisioned in the 1980s by the Islamist movements at the University of Mogadishu, remains a distant ideal. As the Somali Republic collapsed, the Islamists were confronted with the divisiveness of clan politics, which affected even their own ranks: Islamism proved utterly unsuccessful as a unifying ideology. Somalia disintegrated along clan lines, taking with it all national structures and organizations. Clan allegiance is a political fact that the Islamists (and all other Somali politicians, for that matter) cannot disregard. A few new political entities emerged after the collapse. Some were very fragile and withered away quickly. Others, such as Somaliland, proved more solid. But invariably they were clan-based. Islamists had to adapt themselves to the situation at hand.

Islamists in the Somaliland capital, Hargeysa, seem reconciled to the existence of the Somaliland republic. They conduct their social, business, and charity activities with the passive consent of the Somaliland government. The Islamists are integrated into the clan-based power structure and engage in conventional urban power brokering. In Hargeysa, Islamic solidarity networks coexist with clan-based ones. In the east of Somaliland, on the other hand, where there is no effective government, Islamist groups—notably al-Ittihad—may be actively trying to prevent any state or other administrative structures from taking root. In areas where the state is absent and traditional leadership is weak, Islamists have aimed to co-opt the latter.

This does not come as a surprise when we take into account the processes at work in western and eastern Somaliland. Whereas in the west the war has promoted the integration of traditional leadership, modern politicians, and ordinary clansmen or civilians, first in the context of the SNM and later in the gradual state-building process, the inverse has happened in the east, resulting in a very different context. Where a state exists, as the result of a clan-based consensus, the Islamists—who are to an important degree also subject to clan politics—accept and participate in the existing order. Where clan consensus and a clan-based governance arrangement did not take root, conflict persists (on clan and other levels) and the Islamists are involved in it.

The local level has the greatest effect on the nature and the impact of Islamist movements in Somaliland. Very few Islamist activists are interested in anything beyond the immediate locality. Most observers agree that Islamists (whether in a state or not) can affect the local power balance only in conjunction with clan structures.

While Islamist movements are adapted to the clan context, the presence (or absence) of a secular state structure, and the changing sociopolitical environment in Somaliland, Sufi organizations such as the Timo Weyn adapted themselves as well. Islamist organizations have not displaced all Sufi organizations or networks, nor are all Sufi adherents and ideology "traditional," backward, indigenous, and incapable of religious or organizational innovation and political activity. Both modern Islamist and Sufi organizations and ideology are the result of the historical evolution of the Somaliland polity. So are the concepts of clan, traditional leader, and state.

It would be a mistake to suppose that the clan system has not evolved. It is not a static institution; it has been influenced by colonization, the introduction of the modern state system, urbanization, globalization, and the civil war. The nature of traditional leadership is changing as well. The number of sultans is increasing rapidly and the position has become more urban-based. Former soldiers, civil servants, and even businessmen now become "traditional" leaders or "religious men." It is widely felt that both these roles have become increasingly politicized (in the east as well as in the west) under the influence of Somali states and governments.

Islamism, clanism, and the state can combine, as in eastern Somaliland, to make a very complex picture, difficult for the observer—or even the participant—to disentangle. A "traditional clan leader" in Sool—who is, perhaps, a former militia leader—might be paid by the Somaliland treasury to pledge alliance to Somaliland, and at the same time he might seek cooperation with people associated with al-Ittihad to enhance his position within his subclan. An "Islamist" can seek a "traditional" office by brokering peace deals in clan wars or try to rise within his clan in order to enter government service.

Although the population of the Somali Republic was almost entirely Sunni Muslim, the country's collapse did not simply result in a takeover by Islamist terrorist groups. Although there is evidence that Islamist groups inclined to violence exist (as they do in Belgium, France, Spain, the UK, the Netherlands, and Germany), the same evidence indicates that they are a tiny minority (International Crisis Group 2005b). Failing to appreciate the complexity of Islam and Islamism, in Somalia and elsewhere, may lead to uninformed and misguided actions on the part of international policymakers, and these marginal groups may become stronger and more popular.

Notes

The data and interviews for this chapter were collected in fieldwork in Somaliland, Nairobi, and London between 2002 and 2004. In particular, I interviewed traditional leaders, staff of local and international NGOs, members of women's and youth groups, local health professionals, local politicians, and intellectuals in Las Aanood in June 2002. The writing of this chapter was completed in early 2006.

1. I borrow this phrase from Matt Bryden.
2. I do not intend to denounce Islam as a religion or a spiritual belief held by individual Muslims or communities. I am speaking of it here as an ideology, a mode of social organization, rather than as a theology.
3. Great Britain had a protectorate in the northwest of what later became independent Somalia, while Italy governed the south-central regions, first as a colony, then, after the Second World War, as a trust territory.
4. Siyyad Barre took power in the so-called bloodless coup of October 1969. The preceding civilian regime was accused of being corrupt and too vulnerable to clan politics.
5. Somali journalist and Sufi master, interview.
6. Islamist intellectual, interview.
7. Islamist intellectual, interview.
8. This name means something like "Islamic unity," possibly referring to the Islamic concept of the oneness of God (*tawhid*).
9. Mohamed Haashi, interview; Saad Noor, interview.
10. Osman Axmed Xassan, interview, June 27, 2004.
11. Islamist intellectual, interview, confirmed by Prunier 1990.
12. Amran Ali, interview.
13. I was told this story by one of the other women present at the reception.
14. Businessman and religious scholar, interview.
15. Businessman and religious scholar, interview; Islamist intellectual, interview.
16. Businessman and religious scholar, interview.
17. Muslim activist, interview. Other, non-Islamist interviewees confirmed the schools' existence, but I could not verify their enrollments. Figures such as these are the subject of much speculation. The Somaliland administration has been unable to keep proper records or statistics on private education, and the organizers of private schools might tend to overstate their importance.
18. Rachid Ghannouchi founded the Tunisian Islamist organization Mouvement de la tendance islamique, later renamed al-Nahda.
19. Muslim activist, interview.
20. Islamist intellectual, interview.
21. Somali journalist and Sufi master, interview.
22. Raabi died in autumn 2005.
23. Islamist intellectual, interview.
24. Somali businessman, interview.
25. Osman Axmed Xassan, interview, June 27.
26. Osman Axmed Xassan, interview, June 27.
27. Former chairman of the Somali Development and Relief Agency, interview.
28. Somaliland pulled its personnel out of the area after an incident occurred during a visit by the Somaliland president to Las Aanood in December 2002. The description, however, is still accurate.
29. Garaad Gani, Garaad Abshir, Garaad Suleiman, interviews.
30. Employee of an NGO operating in Sool, interview. This was confirmed by some local Somali interviewees in Las Aanood.
31. Health professional employed at Las Aanood Regional Hospital, interview.
32. Women's group member, interview.

33. The Sool region was also concerned here because traditional leaders from Sool, who at that time sided with Puntland, also participated in the clan conferences as representatives of the Dulbahante.
34. Osman Axmed Xassan, interview, June 27.
35. Youth group member, interview.

References

Published works

Abdurahman, M. A. "Baadiyow." 2001. Tribalism and Islam—Variations on the basics of Somaliness. In *Variations on the theme of Somaliness: Proceedings of the EASS/SSIA International Congress of Somali Studies, August 6–9, 1998*, ed. Muddle Suzanne Lilius, 227–40. Turku, Finland: Centre for Continuing Education, Åbo Akademi University.

Compagnon, D. 1992. Dynamiques de mobilisation, dissidence armée et rébellion populaire: Le cas du Mouvement national somali (1981–1990). *Africa* (Rome) 47 (4): 503–30.

Helander, Bernhard. 1999. Somalia. In *Islam outside the Arab world*, ed. David Westerlund and Ingvar Svanberg, 39–55. Richmond, Surrey: Curzon.

International Crisis Group. 2005a. Counter-terrorism in Somalia: Losing hearts and minds? Africa Report no. 95. Brussels and Nairobi, July 11.

———. 2005b. Somalia's Islamists. Africa Report no. 100. Brussels and Nairobi, December 12.

Kapteijns, Lidwien. 2000. Ethiopia and the Horn of Africa. In *The history of Islam in Africa*, ed. Nehemia Levtzion and Randall L. Pouwels, 227–50. Athens: Ohio University Press.

Le Sage, Andre. 2001. Prospects for Al Itihad and Islamist radicalism in Somalia. *Review of African Political Economy* 28 (89): 472–77.

Lewis, Ioan M. 1955. Sufism in Somaliland: A study in tribal Islam. Parts 1 and 2. *Bulletin of the School of Oriental and African Studies* 17: 581–602, 18:145–60.

———. 1994. *Blood and bone: The call of kinship in Somali society*. Lawrenceville, N.J.: Red Sea Press.

Marchal, R. 2001. Islamic political dynamics in the Somali civil war. Paper presented at "Islam in Africa: A Global Cultural and Historical Perspective," a conference of the Institute of Global Cultural Studies, Binghamton University, New York, April 19–22.

Menkhaus, Kenneth. 1997. *Awdal region*. United Nations Development Office for Somalia, Studies on Governance 2. Nairobi: United Nations Development Office for Somalia.

———. 2002. The threats of radical Islam in Somalia: A typology and assessment. Paper presented at the Giornata di reflessione nella Somalia, Roma, February 15.

Pérouse de Montclos, Marc-Antoine. 2003. *Diaspora et terrorisme*. Paris: Presses de Sciences Po.

Prunier G. 1990. A candid view of the Somali National Movement. *Horn of Africa* 13 (3–4): 107–20.

Somaliland constitution. Unofficial English translation by Ibrahim Hashi Jama. http://www.somalilandforum.com/somaliland/constitution/revised_constitution.htm.

Interviews

Amran Ali, Somali businesswoman, June 3, 2002, Hargeysa.

Businessman and religious scholar, former member of al-Wahda, June 9, 2002, Hargeysa.

Employee of an NGO operating in Sool, June 17, 2002, Las Aanood.

Former chairman of the Somali Development and Relief Agency, a local Sanaag NGO, June 8, 2002, Hargeysa.

Former politician, June 18, 2002, Las Aanood.

Garaad Abshir, titled clan elder, June 16, 2002, Las Aanood.

Garaad Gani, titled clan elder, June 15, 2002, Las Aanood.

Garaad Suleiman, titled clan elder, June 20, 2002.

Health professional employed at Las Aanood Regional Hospital, June 22, 2002, Las Aanood.

Islamist intellectual, April 3, 2003, Hargeysa.

Mohamed Haashi, former mayor of Hargeysa and SNM veteran, April 19, 2003, Hargeysa.

Muslim activist, June 9, 2002, Hargeysa.

Osman Axmed Xassan, official Somaliland representative in the United Kingdom, June 27 and 29, 2004, London.

Saad Noor, official Somaliland representative in the U.S. and SNM veteran, April 14, 2003, Hargeysa.

Somali businessman, June 29, 2004, London.

Somali journalist and Sufi master, March 23, 2003, Hargeysa.

Women's group member, June 22, 2002, Las Aanood.

Youth group member, June 20, 2002, Las Aanood.

CHAPTER 3

TRANSFORMATIONS OF ISLAM AND COMMUNAL RELATIONS IN WALLO, ETHIOPIA

Jan Abbink

Introduction

Ethiopia holds a special place in the history of Muslim–Christian relations in Africa. Islam has a very long history in the country, going back to the time of the Prophet Muhammad (Cuoq 1981, 28). Despite a history of tension and occasional violence over the past five to six hundred years, the relationship between religious communities in Ethiopia, especially since the era of Emperor Menelik II (r. 1889–1913), has predominantly been one of accommodation and compromise, not of antagonism and strife. Muslims in Ethiopia are of diverse ethnolinguistic backgrounds, and Islam has acquired a strong indigenous character.

This chapter looks at possible transformations of Muslim life in Wallo, Ethiopia, a region with one of the oldest and largest Muslim populations in the country, and assesses how these might affect both local communal relations and national politics. The background is one of increasing globalization and political liberalization, which in Ethiopia has meant a devolution or decentralization of state power to the regional level and a measure of local autonomy. A closer study of the Wallo region is both interesting (because of the mixed and tolerant nature of Christian–Muslim relations) and relevant (because recent developments may upset the balance and could have political repercussions).

Ethiopia, and the Horn of Africa in general, has received renewed attention in the current context of the global hegemony of international powers,[1] transnational religious linkages, tension between Christian and Muslim communities in Africa and the Middle East, and so-called Islamist terrorism, which some see as a real security threat in Northeast and East Africa (Marchesin 2003; McCormack 2005; Shinn 2004a, 2004b; West 2005; Pan 2003). This latter concern, however, tends to cloud views of Muslim culture and society in Northeast Africa, and can lead to erroneous conceptions of the politics of identity and the political implications of Islam in the region.

To properly assess Islam and its relations with Christianity and the state in the Horn of Africa, it is essential to understand it as a long-established way of life and a system of meaning for large groups of people rather than only as a potential source of a radical, politicized worldview. I will demonstrate this in an exploratory account of the Wallo region in northern Ethiopia, a remarkable instance of religious intermingling (Abbink 1999; Berhanu 1998, forthcoming; Ficquet, forthcoming). I do not intend to emphasize the exceptional nature of this region but only to demonstrate the variety and richness possible in intercommunal relations in an African setting. The Wallo region, with a population of some four million, exemplifies sociocultural hybridity, pragmatic tolerance, and the accommodation of diversity. Also relevant here are social-science discussions of identity politics and of cultural hybridity (Kapchan and Strong 1999; Anthias 2001), that is, the combination of elements from differing cultural traditions into new wholes.

In the following, I describe the historical roots of Wallo religious culture, the sociocultural context of local society, and give a sketch of crucial changes in the past decade or so. It has to be noted that there is considerable diversity within the Muslim communities of Ethiopia, as well as debate as to the future of their religious practices and identity, their place in the wider society, and their relations to the Muslim world outside Ethiopia. There are also notable regional divergences: the situation and experiences of Muslims outside of Wallo—e.g., in Harär, Arsi, Jimma, 'Afar, or the Somali region—can be quite different. But all Ethiopian Muslims must confront reformist–revivalist (often referred to as "Wahhabist") currents (i.e., purist and strictly scripture-based forms of Islam), originating mostly in Saudi Arabia and inimical to much of the Muslim ethos in Northeast Africa. During interviews in late 2004 with Wallo informants, both Muslim and Christian, this subject always came up.[2]

I also address the question of religious accommodation or tolerance in Wallo— whether it is durable or whether it has always been a temporary and vulnerable outcome of contingent historical processes, with tensions under the surface. In other words, was the "compromise" or cooperation between Christian and Muslim populations only a precarious balance, or was it based on a shared way of life and recognized—for example, by community leaders—as a solution to the challenges of religious diversity? The question is relevant in view of both the current revivalist movement and the fact that a major jihad devastated this region in the sixteenth century and is still a tacit reference point in current perceptions and attitudes. I will argue that the particular combination of politics, state power, and religious identity in Wallo enabled a constellation of hybrid and negotiated communal relations to emerge, but that this balance is vulnerable, first, to changes in the political system and the state's attitude toward religion in the public sphere, and, second, to a decline in Wallo's social infrastructure of religious coexistence and civility. Such shifts might set the stage for antagonistic religious politics and exclusionism in both Muslim and Christian communities that will have major political repercussions on the national level (cf. Abbink 1998).

Wallo's pattern of communal accommodation is quite unusual in Ethiopia, although the extent of religious intermingling and coexistence should not be idealized. Despite the popular Ethiopian image of the "Walloye" (people of Wallo) as relaxed or "superficial" in their religious practices, there has been a constant, though muted, undercurrent of tension and rivalry between religious communities in Wallo since the sixteenth century.

An underlying socioeconomic constraint in Wallo society is the grinding poverty and insecurity (see Little et al. 2004). Wallo became notorious during the dramatic Ethiopian famines of 1973–74 and 1984–85. This poverty and insecurity drives people to make choices, look for new survival options, and try to secure other sources of income. Issues of access to land, to cash, to healers or spiritual guides, or to anything else that may improve their lives have an effect on religious adherence, because under certain circumstances they can create new social bonds and networks of mutual support. Both Christians and Muslims in Wallo—and in Ethiopia in general—are to a large extent nonliterate and depend on oral and ritual transmission of the faith. Paradoxically, their shared poverty and desperation may have contributed to local coexistence and mutual sociability.

Islam in Wallo: A Historical View

Islam in Ethiopia dates from the seventh century, when the Prophet Muhammad, faced with Quraysh persecution, sent a number of his followers to Orthodox Christian Ethiopia to seek refuge. The Christian king in Aksum received them and treated them well. The asylum seekers later returned to Arabia, though some remained and converted to Christianity. Muslim tradition (the hadith recorded by al-Tabari) claims that some years later (in AD 628), the Ethiopian king (or *negus*) converted to Islam, but corroboration of this claim cannot be found.[3] In Muslim tradition, Ethiopia was neutral, *dar al-hiyad*, and exempt from jihad (also see Erlich 2003).

Islam began to gain adherents in the coastal areas of Ethiopia in the ninth century, and expanded gradually through Sufi orders and itinerant teachers, saints, and traders. The main Sufi orders were the Khatmiyya, Sammaniyya, Tijaniyya, Shadhiliyya, and Qadiriyya. The latter arrived in the sixteenth century, the others in the course of the eighteenth and nineteenth centuries; but the Qadiriyya order remained dominant and was especially widespread in Harär and Wallo (Hussein 2001, 69–70).

Muslims in Ethiopia are Sunnis, mostly of the Shafi'i rite (some are Hanafi). Knowledge of Arabic is limited. In Ethiopia, Muslims constitute an estimated 35 to 40 percent of the population (extrapolating from the 1994 national census) and live dispersed across the country, but predominantly in the east, in parts of the center, and in the southeast. The Christian heartlands of Ethiopia—Gondar, Tigray, western Shewa, and Gojjam—have always had Muslim minorities, illustrating the fact that Islam is virtually indigenous in Ethiopia.

The religion has long been established in South Wallo, probably since the tenth century.[4] The region was located on important trade routes to the coast, along which Muslim traders and travelers entered the country. The area of western Wallo was then known as the "Bete Amhara" (domain of the Amhara) and was historically a core region of the Christian empire. Ulama from the sultanate of Ifat in eastern Ethiopia came to missionize the area in the fourteenth century, but Islamization commenced in full force in the jihad (in the years 1529–43) of Ahmed ibn Ibrahim "Gragn," a militant Muslim imam from Harär.[5] Scores of Amharic-speaking Christians were forcibly converted. This episode of devastating war almost led to the demise of the Christian Ethiopian kingdom and created a "trauma" in Ethiopia, instilling enmity and fear of violent Muslim expansion in highlanders. An influx of Oromo people from the south late in the century temporarily halted the expansion of Islam. In the seventeenth century, however, the Oromo in Wallo largely converted to Islam and in the process also adopted the local Amharic language. Present-day Wallo is an ethnic amalgam of Amhara, Argobba, Agaw, Oromo, and 'Afar peoples. A strong local Muslim dynasty emerged in the early eighteenth century (Hussein 2001, 27). These "Mammadoch" later became affiliated with the imperial government. Imperial authority in Ethiopia from the late seventeenth to the late nineteenth century was in large part dependent on control of Wallo.

Islam in Wallo is marked by a preponderance of, and great respect for, "saints" (*walis*), shrines (tombs), mystics, and panegyrists.[6] All contemporary Muslim shrines (*ziyyara*) in Wallo were founded by saints from the Qadiriyya Sufi order, with the exception of Geta, which is Tijaniyya-founded. In the early centuries of Muslim expansion in eastern Ethiopia, groups of Yemeni and Arab teachers and traders settled in the country, intermingling with local people. The number of Arabs was not large, however, and Arabic did not become a common language. The local Argobba people became an important intermediary for spreading Islam. The Muslim founding fathers started religious institutions and centers of learning and gave rise to dynasties of local rulers, and after their deaths their graves became shrines. For instance, the shrine of Abbaye Shonké,[7] a noted Wallo Muslim leader or saint, is still located in Boqoqé village in the Argobba area. Saints are appealed to for help in illness, infertility, business ventures, disputes, and so on; and the advice and prayers of their living descendants, the incumbent *wali* line, are sought as well. The Sufi saints of Wallo are linked by filiation and teacher–student bonds, and ranked in a hierarchy of prestige. The main shrine in South Wallo is in Annâ (in the Rayya area); then others follow, like Dägär, Dâna, Gaddo, Jamma-Negus, Geta, Worewayyu, and Châli. They are places of Muslim learning, and religious students will visit a number of them to learn the branches of religious knowledge in which they specialize, such as *tawhid* or *fiqh*. Such centers were often established in a neutral area, on the border between various ethnic or local groups. The shrine of Châli, for instance, lies in a no man's land between the 'Afar and Amhara areas in eastern Wallo.

Local chiefs in Wallo were economically powerful, and some were contenders for the throne. In general, Wallo was a very fractious territory with many internal rivalries. In the late nineteenth century the incumbent Mammadoch leader Mohammed 'Ali allied himself with two Christian Ethiopian emperors, first Yohannes and later Menelik II, and converted to Christianity, an act that often indicated a change in political allegiance. Mohammed 'Ali was baptized Mikael and given the title Ras, and his allies supported him against his rivals in Wallo. He became a sponsor of Christianity, founding several churches. In 1909 his son Iyasu was designated heir to the throne by Emperor Menelik II himself, although he reigned only three years (1913–16) before being deposed by force.

In the twentieth century Wallo lost its former political and economic importance, as the political center of Ethiopia shifted south. However, Emperor Haile Sellassie I (r. 1930–74) aligned himself with the Wallo nobility by marrying the granddaughter of Ras Mikael. He also conducted a number of campaigns to quell unrest in Wallo. During the Italian occupation (1936–41) the Muslim community in Ethiopia was supported by the Italians, who wanted to break the power and institutional role of Ethiopian Orthodox Christianity, which they identified with Ethiopian nationalism and which they thought was not strong among Muslims. The Italians promoted the building of mosques (Trimingham 1952, 137; Borusso 2001) and in general fur-thered the interests of Muslims in public life to "balance" the two faiths. This led to the resurfacing of old rivalries in some areas of Wallo, notably in the west (such as the isolated and staunchly Christian region of Amara Sayint), but not to actual clashes. After Emperor Haile Sellassie was restored to the throne in 1941, Wallo tended to be relatively neglected in national development policy, perhaps because locals had been less than enthusiastic in supporting resistance to Italian rule. In modern times the Walloye have prided themselves on their tolerance and flexibility in religious matters, which may be partly explained by their ethnically mixed nature. They often use the Amharic phrase *mečačal abro mänor*, "living together so that we accommodate, reach consensus."

Islam, Society, and Politics in Ethiopia, 1878–1991

The dominant religion of the Ethiopian empire had been Orthodox Christianity since the fourth century, but, in the centuries after the jihad of Ahmed Gragn, reli-gious relations stabilized. The imperial order was largely able to prevent violent confrontations between the religious communities. Socioeconomic processes and cultural similarities worked toward the accommodation of differences. But tensions remained under the surface. The last dramatic, violent confrontation between Muslims and Christians in Wallo was in 1878–82, after Emperor Yohannes pro-claimed an edict demanding religious unity in the empire and conversion of the Muslims. This coercive policy was a return to the conflict of medieval times, but it was ultimately unsuccessful because of the protests it generated among local Muslims and even among Christians, who resented the disturbances it caused. Local Muslim leaders (such as Shaykh Talha b. Ja'far, Mohammed Qanqe, Amädé Tsadiq, and Hussein Jibril) organized armed resistance, demonstrating that a strong undercurrent of Muslim identity and revivalism was native to the country, not merely "imported" from elsewhere.[8] This resonated with attitudes elsewhere whereby Muslims need not be second-class citizens. At that time, many Sufi leaders had already received religious education in Arab countries, such as Yemen, Sudan, or Egypt (cf. Hussein 2001). Their revolts were defeated, and scores of Muslims did convert, but in the time of Emperor Menelik II (r. 1889–1913) many reverted again to Islam. The emperor stated that he respected the wish of people to "adhere to the religion of their fathers."

During the imperial conquest of southern territories at the end of the nineteenth century, Christianity was usually seen as part of the politics of the conquering emperor, and the banner of Islam was used in various regions to resist the conquest and forge a kind of ideology of resistance (see Abbas 1999; Hassen 1994); among the conquered peoples, many adherents of traditional religions converted to Islam.[9] After the establishment of Menelik's empire in the 1890s, however, which resulted in the subjugation and economic exploitation of the southerners, in practice a "live and let live" policy developed here as well, with neither Christians nor Muslims allowed to mount conversion campaigns. Ethiopian Christians showed no fervent urge to conversion, being satisfied with establishing the presence of the church in the new areas, especially the towns.[10]

Emperor Haile Sellassie maintained the predominance of the Ethiopian Orthodox Church (EOC) in Ethiopia and discouraged or banned the participation of Muslims in high government functions. Muslims' demands for land and for recognition of their religious holidays were not honored. On the other hand, the 1944 Muhammadan Courts Act legally recognized Muslim jurisprudence and sharia for personal, family, and inheritance law. The emperor also had the Qur'an translated into Amharic (published in 1958). The emperor's religious policy was inspired by a famous dictum ascribed to him: "The country is a public, religion a private matter" (in Amharic, *Hagär yägara näw, haimanot yegil näw*). Although Islam in Ethiopia maintained relations with Muslim centers outside the country—sending community leaders and teachers to Egypt, Lebanon, or Iraq for religious education, for example—it largely turned inward.

The Ethiopian revolution of 1974 led to changes. On April 20, a few months after the revolution had broken out, almost a hundred thousand Muslims demonstrated in Addis Ababa for equality and recognition under the law. Many Christians joined the event. The committee of revolutionary officers or Derg that led the revolution soon declared the equality of religions, recognized Islamic holidays, permitted more mosques and educational establishments to be built, and increased the number of people allowed to go on the hajj. It also recruited people of Muslim background into the political apparatus and tried giving them their due recognition in the country. This also had the effect of balancing if not weakening the powerful Ethiopian Orthodox Church. However, when the revolutionary regime adopted a stronger Marxist ideology after 1977, an antireligious—and also anti-Muslim—policy emerged that forced Ethiopian Muslims to be more circumspect about expressing their religious identity and that led to a slackening of their international connections. The inward turn was thus reinforced.

Army leaders and regional administrators under the Derg often violently repressed both religious people and political opponents. They made no distinction between people of Muslim and Christian background. 'Ali Musa, the militia commander in Wallo's capital, Dessé, was known for his brutal policies.[11] The political violence of the Derg thus affected Wallo inhabitants of both religions equally, furthering solidarity and joint tactics of subversion. The unsuccessful economic policies of the Derg, which resulted in impoverishment and social decline, contributed to this cooperation.

In 1991 the Derg regime of Mengistu Haile-Mariam was ousted by the Ethiopian People's Revolutionary Democratic Front (EPRDF), an alliance of four groups including the northern Tigrayan People's Liberation Front (TPLF), which is still in power in 2007. The EPRDF committed itself to a democratic, ethnofederal Ethiopia and opened up space for ethnicity-based politics and cultural and religious revival. The past fifteen years have seen a remarkable broadening of horizons, new opportunities for travel and exchange for religious leaders, and an influx of NGOs and missionary organizations in the country that is transforming Ethiopian Muslim communities as well.[12] The process of globalization has tended to decenter localized forms of belief and allowed pressure from well-funded transnational forms of religion to increase, such as Evangelical-Pentecostal Christianity and revivalist Islam, notably Wahhabism from nearby Saudi Arabia. Wahhabism is a significant phenomenon—a massive, well-financed movement to remold what is usually called popular or "folk" Islam in Africa into new, "stricter," or what the Wahhabis consider "proper" shape. It is, however, difficult to investigate, because its workings are informal and unregistered. The movement and its aims are contested and controversial, but it considers itself the center of the Islamic faith.[13]

Muslim and Christian Culture in Wallo

These new forms of religion are at variance with local Christianity and Islam and pose a serious social, ideological, and political challenge to the pattern of coexistence and accommodation. In this section, I briefly describe this traditional pattern as it exists today, with a focus on Islam.

Islam in Wallo has a "popular," local aspect; the Walloye maintain a rich variety of practices and beliefs which are not derived from the scriptural tradition but reflect a variety of older cultural beliefs, though adapted to the Muslim worldview.[14] Islam in Wallo is distinguished from Islamic practice in Egypt or Saudi Arabia or Indonesia not only by veneration of saints, who are mediators between God and humans, and by reverence of and pilgrimages to their tombs (*ziyyara*), but also by other customs, like elaborate celebrations of *mawlid* (the birthday of the Prophet), communal ritual prayer gatherings called *wadajja* (see Berhanu, forthcoming), and devotion to Sufi mystics and panegyrists, who for didactical purposes perform and lead religious songs of praise (*dhikr*) and rituals for ordinary believers (Berhanu 1998). Wallo Muslims also honor the dead in postburial remembrance rituals called *sedaqa* (equivalent to the Christian *täzkar*) and join in ceremonies praying for rain. Muslim shaykhs also treat people touched by spirit possession. An important function is served by the *abagar* ("father of the land"), a Muslim mediator in the countryside who reconciles people in the name of divine authority (God) but not on the basis of sharia. Both Christians and Muslims may appeal to an *abagar*.

Most Muslims, especially in rural Ethiopia, are committed to this "popular" and spiritually versatile form of Islam, cherishing it as their way of life and religious identity. It has to be noted that illiteracy was always common among ordinary people, and ignorance of Arabic still more so, necessitating oral and ritual transmission of the faith. Indeed, oral Muslim culture (in Amharic) has undergone a remarkable development in Wallo. Moreover, in conditions of poverty, frequent disease, and general insecurity, religious rituals and beliefs are tested on their pragmatic merits and maintained according to the satisfaction they provide in the daily struggle for survival. Reformists' claims that most of these practices are "un-Islamic" miss the fact that ordinary people have invested so-called non-Islamic ritual practices with Islamic meaning. The emerging tension between Sufi understandings of Islam and reformist–revivalist Islam has often been seen in Africa, but in Wallo the situation is different because of the age-old pattern of reciprocal conversions, the underlying cultural and linguistic similarities across religions, and the intertwining of religion (Islam and Christianity) and politics in Ethiopia, in which Wallo has featured prominently.

When faced with such examples of "un-Islamic" religious expression, non-Wolloye outsiders often suggest that Muslims in Wallo are "lax and weak" in their adherence to the faith, and that they "do not perform the rituals properly," are "ignorant," and too easily convert to Christianity and back to Islam. These charges deny ordinary Muslims religious agency and spiritual commitment, but there is no doubt a grain of truth in them. Some of the characteristics of the Walloye, however, are seen as positive. In this mixed setting of Christians and Muslims, both indigenous to the area and sharing many customs, a pattern of open borders and accommodative social practices developed. Muslims and Christians frequently intermarry, socialize, attend each other's festivities, and undertake joint activities. Sometimes Muslims accept the mediation efforts of Christian priests and the healing power of Christian priests and saints, to whom there are also some shrines in the area. On the other hand, many Christians visit the tombs of Muslim shaykhs (for instance, at *mawlid*) and consult the shaykhs' living descendants in cases of personal problems, illness, and other affliction. Most remarkably, there are also many cases of people converting to the other faith and then returning to the first. Such successive conversions result in mixed personal names, such as "Indris Mekonnen" or "Teferra Yimam."

This is a pattern of what I earlier called "religious oscillation" (Abbink 1998). This pattern characterizes not only the lives of individuals but also the course of community relations, in which Christians sometimes help Muslims in their religious duties and vice versa. Kalklachew (1997, 83–85) has provided quite remarkable examples of this, including Christian neighbors helping Muslims to build a mosque and Muslims campaigning for the preservation of a Christian village church in danger of being closed down. Muslims and Christians are also joint members in burial societies (*qire*) and savings clubs. One might see all this as evidence of a pragmatic ethics of tolerance in conditions of poverty and insecurity, as well as an expression of commitment to mutual support and social cohesion among the adherents of the two religions. It has not kept Muslim and Christian communities and their leaders from being self-conscious, and some have been known for strong, and at times fanatic, adherence to the faith. Examples include the nineteenth-century Muslims Shaykh Hussein Jibril,[15] Liben Amedé, Shaykh Mohammed Qanqé, Haji Bushra Mohammed, and Shaykh Talha bin Ja'far, the latter an orthodox Muslim who opposed the conversion campaigns of Emperor Yohannes IV. Wallo has also produced a notable number of Islamic scholars (see Hussein, O'Fahey, and Wagner 2003).

There was not any doubt of the differences between the two faiths: in religious law and rituals, in conceptions of God/Allah and the mortal or divine nature of Jesus Christ, in burial customs, in prayer formulas, and in dietary rules. In particular, the taboo on eating the meat of an animal slaughtered by someone of the other faith was strictly observed; indeed, it became the unambiguous dividing line.[16] The bans on the stimulant leaf khat (*Catha edulis* Forsk., chewed by Muslims, banned by Christians) and on alcohol (drunk by Christians, banned by Muslims) were less strictly observed. Overall, the combination of historical factors and the religious demography of Wallo—which has approximately equal numbers of Muslims and Christians[17] living together intermingled—made social interaction and mutual help inevitable. Joking and playful references to religious difference were common, given a situation that might be described as institutionalized ambiguity.

The core values of Islam, as expressed by its adherents in Wallo, are a pious and just life in the eyes of God; nonviolence; a striving for ethical conduct and justice; knowledge of the Qur'an and Islamic law; religious education and awareness; respect for knowledgeable and charismatic religious leaders (saints, mystics, panegyrists), healers, and mediators; material progress; and the accommodation of differences with others. In Wallo the situation of Muslims was also relatively good because of their dominance in trade and their social integration—they were never banned from owning land, like Muslims elsewhere in the country. In short, Wallo provides us with a model of Islam that was not antagonistic nor nationally divisive, the effectiveness of which depended on its indigenous character and its historical interactions with Christianity, on economic integration, on tolerance or at least creative integration of preexisting ethnocultural characteristics into a Muslim way of life, and on a structural rejection of exclusivist identities.

Religion and Community in the Political Space of Post-1991 Ethiopia

The new political space created since 1991 by the EPRDF regime, which issued from an ethnoregional insurgent movement, has allowed the resurgence of organized religion, long suppressed by the Derg. Although it had abolished the privileged status of the Ethiopian Orthodox Church, nationalized all church property, and eliminated all state subventions and had formally recognized the equality of Islam and allowed the public celebration of its holidays, the Marxist-oriented Derg government was hostile to religion in general, and both the Christian and Muslim faiths were seen as undesirable historical heritages.

The current regime has welcomed investments of all kinds, including those by religious organizations. Ties with Muslim countries have been reinforced, and Islamic NGOs have mushroomed. Salih (2004, 156) claims that in 2000 there were 13 Islamic NGOs in Ethiopia (of a total of 150), compared with none in 1980. Little is known about their activities, but they seem to be almost exclusively focused on religious affairs and on assisting Muslims. Islam has thus become more prominent on the national level. Its prominence is also seen in the media, with new Amharic-language Muslim weeklies such as *Salafiyya, Hijira,* and *Quddis.*[18] Many Muslim books and didactic publications, as well as cassettes and videotapes of prayers and sermons, are on sale, especially in the area around the Anwar or Grand Mosque of Addis Ababa. New bookshops were opened in urban centers, with notably more Arabic-language Islamic publications on sale than in the past.

Globalization has intensified notably in the religious domain during the last fifteen years. After 1991, the Muslim community of Ethiopia reconnected with developments in Islam worldwide through travel, study abroad, the activities of Islamic NGOs in Ethiopia, and international trade and business.[19] As a result, reports of Islamic resurgence in Ethiopia are frequent. Some observers see the shift as "Socialism out [after the fall of the Derg] and Islamism in" (Jabłońska 2004). Massive financial support from mostly informal, private circles in Saudi Arabia and the Gulf states is funding Islamic revivalism and expansion in Ethiopia (Erlich 2003, 3; Ficquet, forthcoming). I saw new mosques in about twenty towns and villages in Wallo, and local people always told me the same story: an NGO member or a local Muslim (usually a migrant worker or a religious student or teacher) had gone to Saudi Arabia or another Arab country, established contact with a private religious financier or organization, and brought back the funds to start a mosque or a madrasa.

On the national level, it seems that the Ethiopian government, which guarantees religious freedom, has not paid much attention to the creeping impact of reformist–Wahhabist Islam in the past fifteen years, or to internal strife among the Muslim population, except for trying to keep public activism under control. There is, however, heavy competition in the Muslim councils (local representative groups recognized by the state) between mainstream adherents and reformists, and the latter are reputed to use all means available, including bribing voters. For example, in December 2004 two competing candidates reported in the press that Saudi Arabian sources had allocated 4 million riyals (ca. €750,000) to get their candidates voted onto the Muslim councils and thus become the dominant voice of organized Islam in Ethiopia.[20]

But certain social processes in Ethiopia contribute to the growth of the reformist current. The young generation in urban centers—facing high unemployment, poverty, a health crisis, and often desperate prospects—are taking up the message of Islamic revivalism, and in some instances Islamism, for political reasons. Thwarted in the socioeconomic and political spheres—which are still undemocratic, with a lack of respect for rights and for local autonomy—urban youth turn to Islam to develop a counterdiscourse and to belong to a community.[21] Conflicts between members of the Christian and Muslim faiths, and between adherents of Sufi understandings of Islam and revivalist Islam, are more frequent than in the pre-1991 period.[22] Government action and legal measures are usually not sufficient to either prevent or handle such incidents.

The Changing Balance? Local Muslims, Reformists, and Christians and the Shift of Identities in Wallo

Transformations of Islam and local communal relations in Ethiopia are clearly set in a globalized discourse concerning a transnational Islam as well as Christianity. As in many other African countries, there is a public debate among Ethiopians, sometimes quite polemical, about both religions, and especially Wahhabism (Alem 2003; Johannes 2004; Hibret 2004). This is the general term under which diverse forms of revivalist, "fundamentalist," and reformist Islam are grouped, though there are also movements, teachers, and NGOs that have connections with Iran, the Gulf states, or Pakistani Muslim circles.[23] The Saudi factor in Islamic revivalism, however, is most prominent. Wahhabism rejects so-called popular Islam as practiced in Ethiopia, and aims at Muslim disengagement from allegedly "non-Islamic" institutions and peoples. It considers the locally inflected forms of Islamic belief and practice to be "contaminated" with bid'a—so-called unlawful innovations or accretions by "igno-rant" people that have to be excised. Such neoorthodox versions of the faith aim to "deculturalize" and recast Islam. The paradox is that the popular Sufi understandings of Islam are characterized by great devotion, calls for moral behavior, and spiritual wealth, which elsewhere were the main reasons for Islam's appeal and success in winning adherents over the past centuries.

Are Wallo Muslims moving to adopt the Islamic reformist message, based on strict scriptural interpretation (Desplat 2002), and redefine their Muslim identity? We can answer the question only by analyzing the processes of social interaction between Christians and Muslims and the reproduction of local society: community relations; patterns of conversion; mutual help; intermarriage; respect for Sufi mystics, mediators, shaykhs, and shrines; and the practice of popular Islamic rituals. I can only give a modest answer to it here.

From field research it appears that the Wallo rural population is so far not greatly attracted to this reformist message. Elites in towns and villages may plead for a stricter, "better" practice of Islam, but even they do not approve of social disengagement from the secular state and from Christians. But the steady increase of reformist–Wahhabist influence and other stricter versions of Islam in Wallo lead to changes. On the basis of surveys and interviews I carried out in Dessé and in rural South Wallo, the following tendencies can be confirmed:

- Mosques were (re)built in virtually every town and rural center in Wallo in the past fourteen years (many Christian churches were also built or renovated).
- Interfaith marriages are slowly declining, but mainly in the towns.
- Reformist Islamic teachers and religious leaders are established in many towns, in madrasas and in local NGO operations.
- The shaykhs at the rural shrines are aware of the reformist Muslims' challenge to their practices on the grounds of strict scriptural interpretation and respond by emphasizing literacy in Amharic and Arabic and the study of the Qur'an, the hadith, and didactic books on Islam. But they reject what they call fanatics and "Wahhabis."
- Mixed-faith burial societies (*qire*) in the towns are declining (especially in Dessé, the capital of Wallo): Muslims leave them and set up their own (although Christians do not).
- Many Muslim youth in the towns are attracted to reformist Islam and are less inclined to develop friendships with Christians or to intermarry. They ignore and shun non-Muslims, including former friends.
- Both the number of Muslim madrasas and regular schools and the number of students attending them have increased, and more people are studying Arabic.
- In Wallo, and in Ethiopia in general, people evidence greater interest in Muslim history and in the future role of Muslims and Islam. This occasionally leads to an interpretive "rewriting" of history, which can be seen in stories of Wallo history, especially those told by community or religious leaders.
- Expatriate Wallo Muslims (and to a lesser extent Christians) have an increasing impact; they send home remittances and donations for religious causes and may come to see Wallo through the filter of their new, more monolithic, diaspora religious identity.

These changes signify a rethinking of communal relations and an openness to revivalism. Wallo Muslim elites reemphasize or reinvent their Muslim identity in the new political and religious context of federal Ethiopia, taking advantage of the opportunities offered by the post-1991 era of liberalization. They do not openly politicize

Muslim identity; they only work toward its social consolidation and dominance in local conditions. But this reflects the different constituencies and populations: young, urban, and newly trained religious teachers, leaders, and activists have a political agenda to be realized in due course, whereas ordinary people, living in conditions of mutual dependence and socioeconomic interaction, continue to support the hybrid culture and communal contacts characteristic of Wallo society. Indeed, core elements of Islam in Wallo, while contested in the emerging debates with reformists in the urban centers and the Islamic NGOs, remain in place and inspire continuing commitment: reverence for saints and shrines, admiration of popular Muslim panegyrists and poets, Muslim folk healers and dispute mediators (*abagars*), the practice of *wadajja*, and life cycle rituals like *sedaqa*. Most ordinary people continue to cultivate accommodative relationships with Christians as a matter of principle. However, the representatives of "popular" Islam may not have good (doctrinal) answers to the religious–scriptural challenges issued by the newly emerging elite of the often orthodox or even radical revivalists.

A core point of difference between Wahhabist understandings of Islam and the local Sufi understandings is that the former emphasize the sole authority of the basic Muslim scriptures (the Qur'an and hadith), sober ritual form, and doctrinal "purity" (in an almost physical sense). The latter stress spiritual experience and adherence to the basic organizing ideas and ethics of the Muslim faith, flexibly interpreted. People acknowledge the formal Islamic knowledge and aims of Wahhabist-inspired teachers, educators, and imams. But they do not see why they should abandon Muslim practices that gave spiritual meaning to their identity, or why they should turn their backs on Christian neighbors and friends. Some informants in Dessé and villages in the Wallo countryside asked why they should stop going to the saints' shrines, or stop *mawlid* celebrations, or hate the Christians with whom they have lived for so long and who have helped them many times. As one farmer in the Tänta area said, "Knowing the Qur'an and sharia is good, but is the new teaching meant to refuse our friends and to repudiate our shaykhs? Who said we are not Muslims?"[24] People like him tend to reject what they call "fanatics" (Amharic, *akrariwoch*, sing. *akrari*). Wallo informants generally also spoke with shock and incomprehension about the situation in the Jimma area in southern Ethiopia, where in the past couple of years more than one hundred Sufi mosques had been burned down, allegedly by Wahhabist-inspired religious zealots. They also reject the destruction of Muslim tombstones, which are banned by Wahhabis. Wahhabism also draws great skepticism in Ethiopia because it rejects female political and legal equality and public roles for women. In rural Ethiopia, women are considered perhaps not equal to men but certainly as strong and independent-minded, and, in many regions, they have strong customary rights to property and are vital in economic and family life. The veiling of women is also unpopular. One Muslim informant in Kemise town said, "Why the veil? It says nowhere in the Qur'an that women have to go veiled. We don't like it."[25] This statement was widely echoed in Wallo.

Wahhabism is not the only reformist–revivalist trend in Muslim Ethiopia, but it is certainly one of the more wealthy and powerful ones, because of its foreign connections and resources, which attract potential converts.[26] Evangelical churches also offer access to resources, such as scholarships and community aid. The challenge from

Wahhabist-leaning movements in Ethiopia is quite important and is seen as having a direct impact on social peace and the public order. Wahhabis' underlying attitude that Muslims who are not like them are "unbelievers" (i.e., their practice of *takfir*) is rejected by other Muslims, in rural Wallo in particular. As David Shinn, a regional expert and former U.S. ambassador to Ethiopia, has noted in one of his analyses of the politics of Islam in Northeast Africa, "it is an inescapable fact that Wahhabi proselytism has contributed to religious tension in Ethiopia" (2004b, 2).

After the sudden opening up of political space in the early 1990s, religious activists from both Muslim and Christian reformist movements eagerly increased their activities. But they made many mistakes in their fierce campaigning and met with skepticism and rejection. Now they work more patiently and less publicly and have adapted their message. More recently, Ethiopian state security has kept a closer lid on Muslim activities, arresting "troublemakers," forbidding certain public events, and bringing Muslim schools under stricter control by the national Education Ministry, which supervises curricula and teaching.

A full study of the changing religious balance must also include an analysis of the response of the established Ethiopian Orthodox Church. Here I can only note that increased mosque building and the expansion of Muslim schools and NGOs have evoked a somewhat similar response from the EOC: churches have been built, youth organizations reinvigorated, and public processions held. The locations of some new mosques have been contested. Obviously, the third factor in the equation is the Pentecostal-Evangelical movement, which is growing fast and recruits youths mainly from among the Orthodox constituency, where it evokes a negative response. As one EOC member in Dessé said, "The Pentecostals [or 'Pent'es' in local parlance] are 'our Wahhabis': they are fanatical, unjust, cheating and they work under false pretenses. We oppose their separatism and anti-EOC behavior."

This religious competition in both the Muslim and the Christian communities extends into other domains, such as the struggle for converts, community aid projects for the poor and for HIV-AIDS victims and orphans, and efforts to pressure and lobby the authorities.

Conclusion: A New Politics under the Surface?

In a perceptive paper of 1980, Haggai Erlich noted the tendency toward the politicization of Islam and the depoliticization of Christianity in Ethiopia. Globalization processes of the past two decades have reinforced this trend. Islam in Ethiopia benefits strongly from transnational contacts with more wealthy and powerful Muslim countries, but the EOC has no comparable transnational links, because foreign Christian groups prefer to work with the fast-growing Pentecostal and Evangelical churches (whose adherents now constitute about 10 percent of the population). As I have said, the current government does not interfere much in religious life, conversion campaigns, or foreign missionary activity, except to neutralize any overt political expression and keep the religious elites pro-government. It has "co-opted" local religious leadership, such as the EOC Patriarchate (dominated by regime supporters) and the Supreme Islamic Affairs Council in Addis Ababa (seen by many Muslims as virtually a government body). Both institutions have therefore drawn skepticism and even disdain from believers. Since 1991, Muslim institutions and councils have become an arena of competition between elites bent on establishing their version of Islam. An essentialization of faith and doctrine is the result, which works against pluriformity. On the national level, religious identity is becoming more important to the Muslim community than nationality (Østebø 1998, 445–50). This is occurring especially among Muslims because they are much more strongly oriented toward international Muslim centers of learning and of funds than are Ethiopian Orthodox Christians to church organizations elsewhere in the world.[27]

In Wallo, interreligious relations are still nonconflictual and accommodative. In fact, relations between Christians and Muslims over the past century have been almost an exemplary model, because of the explicit recognition of differences and their enactment in a setting of cultural relatedness. Wallo inhabitants are inclined to present their history this way, and they are proud of it. Wallo's current position as a secondary, and comparatively marginalized, political unit within Ethiopia has perhaps increased local solidarity.

Wallo society is not static, isolated, or immune to change, and revivalism has been an undercurrent at least since the late nineteenth century. However, the current challenge to local Islam comes primarily not from within Wallo society but from outside. Islamic organizations and individuals from well-endowed countries like Saudi Arabia have an increasing impact, providing both resources and an insistent but controversial version of Islam, thus sowing the seed of revivalism and reformism. In addition, members of the top body of Ethiopian Muslims, the Supreme Islamic Affairs Council in Addis Ababa, although not sharing a Wahhabist version of Islam, have stated that "Wallo Muslims, because of their mixture of all kinds of cultural and non-Islamic elements, are basically not real Muslims. They are mostly illiterate and lack proper religious knowledge."[28] Such views suggest that the Muslim establishment as well as the reformist movements will not let Wallo retain its own form of Islam and will work for change. It is therefore by no means sure that the patterns of tolerance and accommodation, and the ambivalence of religious identification in Wallo, can be maintained. This society, which local people see as a historical achievement in toleration of difference, is in danger of decline. If this occurs, we can expect an increase in religiously fueled tensions, if not conflict (both within Muslim communities and between Muslims and Christians), and the undermining of a rather unique way of life marked by historically evolved compromises that recognize religious diversity and symbiosis. "Reformed" Muslims deemphasize elements of folk Islam, defining Muslim identity exclusively on the basis of faithfulness to the holy scriptures, and promote transnational, "deculturalized" ideals of Muslim identity. This will certainly have political repercussions: on the regional level, on Ethiopia's secular political system, and on the activities of Islamist groups who seem to actively recruit in the Horn of Africa (United States Institute of Peace 2004). If the hardening of communal relations continues, it will affect Ethiopia's relations with the international donor community and the Muslim world.

Both the Ethiopian state and the international community can further the evolution of Wallo society—and interreligious relations in Ethiopia in general—by their commitment to a nonsectarian development agenda. Wallo, like most rural areas in Ethiopia, suffers from entrenched poverty and insecurity, problems that are foremost in the minds of people of any religious persuasion. Policies that improve the local economy and living conditions will garner goodwill. Conversely, approaching people primarily as Muslims or as Christians, instead of in their social and economic roles (as farmers, traders, workers, mothers, wives, or heads of families, etc.), thus forcing them to put their religious identity first even when it is only a situational or partial identity, is not helpful.

The Ethiopian state will probably continue its commitment to secularism in the legal and public sphere, while recognizing religious law and institutions in personal status matters where they do not infringe on the public sphere. Indeed, because of its entrenched diversity, the public sphere can only be secular or "neutral." The international community, and the donor countries and their projects, would be well advised not to let themselves be identified with religious or sectarian aid or development agendas but to concentrate on issue-directed, pan-religious projects geared to initiatives arising from local society.

Notes

This chapter is based on fieldwork in Ethiopia in October–November 2004. I am grateful to many people in Addis Ababa, Dessé, and the South Wallo countryside for their willingness to talk about religious relations in Ethiopia and share their stories and reflections. Particular thanks are owed to Shaykh Indris Mohammed, Shaykh Sayyid Mohammed, Ato Mohammed 'Ali, Qes Tayye Tsägga, Shaykh Adem Hussein, and Ato Siraj Mohammed. I am also deeply grateful to my main field assistant, Ato Hassän Mohammed, and to Ato Berhanu Gebeyehu of Addis Ababa University. I thank the Institute of Ethiopian Studies of Addis Ababa University, especially its director, Ms. Elisabet Wolde-Giorgis, for facilitating my research.

1. These powers include not only the U.S. and the EU but also Saudi Arabia, China, and some other countries.
2. Saudi Arabians are not popular in Ethiopia and do not have a good reputation. Many Ethiopians of various faiths spoke of their "arrogance," their "womanizing," and their often degrading treatment of the many thousands of Ethiopian migrant workers and female domestic servants in Saudi Arabia.
3. The Ethiopian king at the time (Armah) had coins minted bearing the symbol of the cross (Sergew 1972, 190), so the story is quite unlikely. No Ethiopian or other source mentions a conversion. See also Cuoq 1981, 33–34.
4. An essential study of the history of Islam in Wallo is found in Hussein 2001. See also Trimingham 1952.
5. See the eyewitness account of the first phase of this war, written by a pro-Ahmed contemporary ('Arabfaqīh 2003). With its contentious views on the religious value of destruction (of non-Muslim holy places) and making war on "infidels," it almost reads like a modern-day Islamist tract.
6. Panegyrists (*madih*) are local oral performers who recite epics, didactic poems, and religious texts in the vernacular (and sometimes in Arabic) relating to saints, scholars, and other important Muslim figures in local history.
7. Abbaye Shonké is the popular name of Shaykh Jawhar b. Haydar b. 'Ali (c. 1837–1937). See Hussein 2005 for a sketch of his life.
8. It is most likely, however, that Shaykh Talha b. Ja'far allied himself politically to the Sudanese Mahdists, who invaded Ethiopia in the 1880s and sacked the city of Gondar (Hussein 1989, 21).
9. I will not attempt to define "conversion," as distinguished from "adhesion" or "affiliation" to a new faith. There is a continuum of religious commitment and practice.

10. As A. B. Wylde, a British vice consul, noted in 1901, "The Abyssinian does not push his religion like the European. . . . My experience of the Abyssinian clergy has been that they want to be left alone and to pray in peace" (142).

11. He later became a governor of the Gamu-Gofa and Bale regions. Incidentally, 'Ali Musa was also a scion of the formerly ruling Muslim dynasty in Wärä Himano. He committed suicide in 1991 when the Derg fell.

12. An excellent survey of Islamic NGO activities in Ethiopia and the Horn is found in Salih 2004.

13. According to Alex Alexiev's testimony in June 2003 before the U.S. Senate Subcommittee on Terrorism, Technology, and Homeland Security, citing the Saudi government newspaper *Ain al-Yaqin*, Saudi Arabia alone has invested tens of billions of dollars in Africa in the past twenty years in "overseas aid": building mosques and religious schools, distributing copies of the Qur'an, and training Islamic teachers and missionaries (http://judiciary. senate.gov/testimony.cfm?id=827&wit_id=2355). This happened largely under the aegis of the Muslim World League (Rabita al-'Alam al-Islami), founded in 1962.

14. In using the term "popular Islam," I do not mean to suggest that there is an "African Islam" that is in essence different from other forms of Islam but only that the faith is differently articulated. Local culture and society have to some extent shaped the Muslim experience in Africa, gearing it more toward conditions of diversity. See also *Encyclopaedia Britannica*, 15th edition, vol. 9, pp. 922–23 (section on "folk Islam"). Recent contributions on this issue include Lewis 1998, De Munck 2005, Vahed 2003, and De Waal 2004, 2–3.

15. See Bogalä 2001, a book of Hussein Jibril's prophecies, recorded from oral traditions in Wallo.

16. At mixed holiday celebrations and weddings, Christians and Muslims eat only meat slaughtered according to their own religious tradition. The host provides for both groups, and the system still works perfectly well.

17. However, according to the 1994 Ethiopian census, the population of the South Wallo zone is about 70 percent Muslim and 30 percent Christian. The eastern parts of South Wallo, like Riqqe, Qallu, Worebabo, and Tehulädere, are 90–95 percent Muslim.

18. Some earlier ones, like *Bilal*, which was published partly in Amharic and partly in Arabic, no longer exist. *Salafiyya* ceased publication in 2005.

19. Mohammed Al-Amoudi, the richest man in Ethiopia, is often seen as one example of "Muslim revival," though not in a spiritual or religious sense. No doubt this successful Saudi-Ethiopian mega-entrepreneur—he is the owner of, among other things, the Addis Ababa Sheraton, one of the most lavish Sheratons in the world—has stimulated Muslim resurgence through, for instance, funding the building of Muslim schools and mosques in many places. But he also supports Christian and general Ethiopian causes through his charity foundations. He has a pan-Ethiopian vision that recognizes the multiplicity of religious identities. It may come as no surprise that he is a native of Wallo.

20. *The Reporter* [Amharic], December 29, 2003.

21. An additional factor in the "religious turn" may be the constant disappointment or disillusion people feel with politics, as seen recently after the highly controversial parliamentary elections of May 2005, which were followed by repressive violence and a massive clampdown on the emerging democratic culture.

22. In 2004 and 2005, for example, local Muslims agitated against the remaining Christians in the town of Alaba: see http://www.persecution.net/news/ethiopia6.html and http:// www.persecution.net/news/ethiopia7.html. These are missionary websites perhaps prone to some exaggeration, but much of the information is confirmed locally.

23. For critical responses to Wahhabism, see Pasha 2004 and Kabha and Erlich 2004.

24. Interview, October 28, 2004.

25. Interview with Siraj Mohammed, October 16, 2004.

26. Several informants alleged that Muslim NGOs offer money to people who convert (up to €300–400 per person).
27. The online mobilization of identities also strongly contributes to this. Websites of ethnic, political, and religious communities create self-contained spaces of discourse that glorify their own tradition. The self-presentation of these sites and the way they promote identity formation deserve study. In 2006–7 there were at least twelve websites about and for Ethiopian Muslims that give clear evidence of a transnational orientation, deemphasizing Ethiopian history, collegiality, and culture in favor of a wider and often stricter Islamic identity. See the website of the Network of Ethiopian Muslims in Europe at http://www.ethiopianmuslims.net (and the other websites to which it links, many of them quite polemic, anti-Christian, anti-Jewish, and dogmatically religious).
28. Interview with the secretary of the council, October 13, 2004, Addis Ababa.

References

Abbas Haji Gnamo. 1999. La conquête impériale éthiopienne des Oromo-Arsi (1882–1892). *Africa* (Rome) 54 (1): 85–115.

Abbink, J. 1998. An historical-anthropological approach to Islam in Ethiopia: Issues of identity and politics. *Journal of African Cultural Studies* 11 (2): 109–24.

———. 1999. Ethiopian Islam and the challenge of diversity. *ISIM Newsletter* 4:24.

Alem Zele-alem. 2003. Saudi Arabia's Wahhabism and the threat to Ethiopia's national security. http://www.dekialula.com (accessed February 15, 2005).

Anthias, F. 2001. New hybridities, old concepts: The limits of "culture." *Ethnic and Racial Studies* 24 (4): 619–41.

'Arabfaqīh (Šihāb ad-Dīn Ahmad bin 'Abd al-Qāder bin Sālem bin 'Utmān) 2003. *The conquest of Abyssinia, 16th century: Futūḥ al-Ḥabaša*. Translated by Paul Lestern Sternhouse, with annotations by Richard Pankhurst. Hollywood, Calif.: Tsehai Publishers.

Berhanu Gebeyehu. 1998. Islamic oral poetry in Wallo: A preliminary descriptive analysis, M.A. thesis, Addis Ababa University.

———. Forthcoming. Intercultural relations in Wallo: A folkloristics perspective. In *The cross and the crescent: Inter-religious dialogues in Ethiopia*, eds. Shiferaw Bekele and Hussein Ahmed. Addis Ababa: German Cultural Institute.

Bogalä Täfärra Bäzu. 2001. *Tänbite Shéh Hussén Jibril*. 2nd ed. Addis Ababa: Branna Printing.

Borusso, P. 2001. L'impero Etiopico e la crisi dell'identita cristiano-amarica durante l'occupazione italiana (1935–41). *Africa* (Rome) 54 (1): 1–45.

Cuoq, J. 1981. *L'Islam en Éthiopie des origines au XVIe siècle*, Paris: Nouvelles Éditions Latines.

Desplat, P. 2002. Muslime in Äthiopien—Die Heiligenverehrung in Harar in Auseinandersetzung mit islamischen Reformströmungen. *Afrika Spektrum* 37 (2): 141–57.

De Munck, V. 2005. Islamic orthodoxy and Sufism in Sri Lanka. *Anthropos* 100 (2): 401–14.

De Waal, A., ed. 2004. *Islamism and its enemies in the Horn of Africa*. London: Hurst.

Erlich, H. 1980. The Horn of Africa and the Middle East: Politicization of Islam in the Horn and depoliticization of Ethiopian Christianity. In *Modern Ethiopia: From the accession of Menilek II to the present*, ed. Joseph Tubiana, 399–408. Rotterdam: A. A. Balkema.

———. 2003. The Saudis and Ethiopia: Which Islam? In *Proceedings of the XVIth International Conference of Ethiopian Studies, Hamburg 2003*, ed. Siegbert Uhlig, 233–241. Wiesbaden: Harrassowitz.

Ficquet, E. Forthcoming. Interfaces of diversity: Islam and Christianity in Wello, central Ethiopia. In *The cross and the crescent: Inter-religious dialogues in Ethiopia*, ed. Shiferaw Bekele and Hussein Ahmed. Addis Ababa: German Cultural Institute.

Hassen, Mohammed. 1994. Islam as a resistance ideology among the Oromo of Ethiopia: The Wallo case, 1700–1900. In *In the shadow of conquest: Islam in colonial northeast Africa*, ed. Said S. Samatar, 75–101. Trenton, N.J.: Red Sea Press.

Hibret Selamu. 2004. Proof of Wahabi activities in Ethiopia. http://www.ethiomedia.com/newpress/proof_of_wahabism_in_ethiopia.html (accessed April 10, 2005).

Hussein Ahmed. 1989. The life and career of Shaykh Talha B. Ja'far (c. 1853–1934). *Journal of Ethiopian Studies* 22: 13–30.

———. 2001. *Islam in nineteenth-century Wallo, Ethiopia: Revival, reform, reaction.* Leiden: E. J. Brill.

———. 2005. Shaykh Jawhar b. Haydar b. 'Ali (d. 1937): A mystic and scholar of Shonke, Southeast Wallo, Ethiopia. *Annales d'Éthiopie* 20: 47–56.

Hussein Ahmed, R.S. O'Fahey, and E. Wagner. 2003. The Islamic and related writings of Ethiopia. In *Arabic Literature of Africa, volume 3: The writings of the Muslim peoples of Northeastern Africa,* ed. R.S. O'Fahey, 16–68. Leiden: Brill.

Jabłońska, A. 2004. Mosques instead of committees: Radical imams appeared in Africa when emissaries of Red Moscow left. *Wprost* (Warsaw), July 11.

Johannes Sebhatu. 2004. The emergence of radical Islam in Ethiopia (1991–2004). http://ethiomedia.com/commentary/radical_islam_in_ethiopia.html (accessed December 15, 2004).

Kabha, M., and H. Erlich. 2004. "Al-Ahbash" and Wahhabiyya—Interpretations of Islam. Unpublished paper.

Kalklachew Ali. 1997. Religion, ritual, and mutual tolerance in Wallo: The case of Kabe, s.-w. Wallo. M.A. thesis, Addis Ababa University.

Kapchan, A. D., and P. T. Strong. 1999. Theorizing the hybrid. *Journal of American Folklore* 112 (445): 239–53.

Lewis, Ioan M. 1998. *Saints and Somalis: Popular Islam in a clan-based society.* London: HAAN.

Little, P. D., M.P. Stone, Tewodaj Mogues, A.P. Castro and Workneh Negatu. 2004. "Moving in place": Drought and poverty dynamics in South Wollo, Ethiopia. Paper presented at "Combating Persistent Poverty in Africa," BASIS CRSP Policy Conference, Washington, D.C., December.

Marchesin, Philippe. 2003. The rise of Islamic fundamentalism in East Africa. *African Geopolitics* 12 (fall). http://www.african-geopolitics.org/show.aspx?ArticleId=3497 (accessed April 11, 2006).

McCormack, David. 2005. *An African vortex: Islamism in sub-Saharan Africa.* Occasional Papers Series, no. 4. Washington, D.C.: The Center for Security Policy,

Østebø, T. 1998. Creating a new identity: The position of Ethiopian Muslims in contemporary perspective. *Swedish Missiological Themes* 86 (3): 423–54.

Pan, Esther. 2003. Africa: Terror havens. Washington, D.C.: Council on Foreign Relations. http://www.cfr.org/publication/7716/africa.html (accessed January 20, 2006).

Pasha, Ayyub Sabri. 2004. Wahhabism and its refutation by the Ahl as-Sunnat. Extract from *The Sunni path.* http://www.ummah.net/Al_adaab/suwahhab.html (accessed April 13, 2005).

Salih, M. A. Mohamed. 2004. Islamic NGOs in Africa: The promise and peril of Islamic volunteerism. In *Islamism and its enemies in the Horn of Africa,* ed. Alex De Waal, 146–81. London: Hurst.

Sergew Hable-Sellassie. 1972. *Ancient and medieval Ethiopian history to 1270.* Addis Ababa: United Printers.

Shinn, D. 2004a. Fighting terrorism in East Africa and the Horn. *Foreign Services Journal* 81 (12): 34–42.

———. 2004b. Islam and conflict in the Horn of Africa. Lecture delivered at the American University of Beirut, December 20.

Trimingham, J. S. 1952. *Islam in Ethiopia.* London: Oxford University Press.

United States Institute of Peace. 2004. *Terrorism in the Horn of Africa.* Special report no. 113. http://www.usip.org/pubs/specialreports/sr113.html (accessed April 11, 2006).

Vahed, G. H. 2003. Contesting "orthodoxy": The Tablighi-Sunni conflict among South African Muslims in the 1970s and 1980s. *Journal of Muslim Minority Affairs* 23 (2): 313–34.

West, Deborah L. 2005. Combating terrorism in the Horn of Africa and Yemen. Program on Intrastate Conflict and Conflict Resolution, Belfer Center for Science and International Affairs, John F. Kennedy School of Government, Harvard University.

Wylde, A. B. 1901. *Modern Abyssinia*. London: Methuen.

CHAPTER 4

AID, *UMMA*, AND POLITICS: TRANSNATIONAL ISLAMIC NGOs IN CHAD

Mayke Kaag

Introduction

Transnational Islamic nongovernmental organizations (NGOs) have been active in many parts of Africa since the 1980s, and, particularly since the 1990s, have expanded their activities and outreach across the continent. As transnational organizations, they act across national borders; and as Islamic organizations, they represent one of the significant power blocs in today's world. In addition, they are of local importance in that they try to enhance people's material and moral livelihoods by humanitarian aid and proselytizing activities. For instance, in addition to offering medical help, food, and educational facilities, they also offer rules of behavior and a sense of belonging to the *umma*, the global community of the faithful. Because of these characteristics, global backing and local action, they often also acquire a charged political meaning in the national context.

In view of this, it is rather surprising that up till now the interventions of Islamic transnational NGOs have received only scant scholarly attention. Studies on intervention and transnationalism in Africa have mainly focused on Western forms of intervention and have neglected the Islamic transnational influence in sub-Saharan Africa (see, for instance, Callaghy, Kassimir, and Latham 2001). Scholars of Islam in Africa have for the most part also turned a blind eye on the phenomenon. Is this because their studies tend to focus on local variety and local traditions of Islam, as opposed to the so-called great tradition of Islam, and thus tend to neglect transnational influences coming from the Arab countries? Or is it because NGOs are considered too Western and too economic a concept, that is, not relevant to the study of Islam? There are signs, however, that things are changing for the better: two interesting studies on Islamic NGOs have recently been published, *Jihad humanitaire* by Abdel-Rahman Ghandour (2002) and *The Charitable Crescent* by Jonathan Benthall and Jérôme Bellion-Jourdan (2003).

Although the two works differ in style and approach, the drift of their arguments is very similar. Both studies emphasize that the Islamic NGOs, from their creation at the end of the 1970s and the beginning of the 1980s, based themselves on an understanding of Islamic solidarity that is composed of three elements: *ighatha* or humanitarian relief, *da'wa* or Islamic call, and *jihad* in the sense of armed support of the Islamic cause. They show that in different contexts, such as in Afghanistan and Bosnia, these three elements have all been present in Islamic NGOs' activities. They also show that over the years, the NGOs evolved toward professionalization (Benthall and Bellion-Jourdan 2003); some developed a more humanitarian outlook, others became more politically active (Ghandour 2002; see also Salih 2004). Although these two books give a good insight into the development, ideas, and working strategies of Islamic NGOs in general, their focus remains predominantly on the Middle East and on the well-known hot spots where wars are fought between Muslims and non-Muslims, such as Afghanistan, Bosnia, and Somalia in Africa.

Unfortunately, the rest of Africa is only marginally treated. This is all the more regrettable because as early as 1984 Africa was identified as a "Land of Islam" by the Muslim World League during its annual meeting (Institut pontifical d'études arabes 1984).[1] Islamic NGOs have been working in Africa to implement this identification, and *ighatha* and *da'wa* have been important parts of that effort. Armed support has been less important; the political aspects and consequences of their work appear in more subtle ways.

In this chapter, I will focus on international Islamic NGOs in Chad. I will show how they give material and moral support and in doing so also affect political dynamics. Chad makes a challenging case study for several reasons. First, the needs on the ground are manifold, Chad being very poor and facing continuous political and ecological instability. Second, in social and political tensions at both the local and the national level, religion is an important element of rivalry and identification. Third, Chad has long been at the crossroads of Western and Arab spheres of influence, and for this reason has been a strategic area of intervention for Arab and Christian NGOs.

My analysis is based on interviews I did with the directors of transnational Islamic NGOS during fieldwork in Chad in spring 2004 and the following September. In addition, I conducted interviews with other informants, such as staffers of Christian NGOs and Muslim authorities. To grasp what happens on the ground, in the interaction between the NGOs and the population, I conducted interviews in different quarters of N'Djamena and in several villages in the south of Chad.

After an introduction to Chad, I will give an overview of the different international Islamic NGOs operating in the country. It will become clear that in their work, aid and *umma* are tightly entangled. This entanglement means that they become political actors, because others suspect them of using aid to enlarge the *umma*, while they themselves indeed feel that they are there to defend the Islamic cause. I will discuss two examples of their involvement in political dynamics. The first is the rivalry between Christian and Muslim NGOs in Chad, which is a struggle both for followers and for moral high ground. Both Christians and Muslims, however, accuse each other of being a tool in the hands of territorial powers as well. The second example concerns the international arena, where transnational Islamic NGOs currently are a target in the U.S.'s so-called war on terror for their alleged role in supporting terrorism.

It is in this latter context that transnational Islamic NGOs have been discussed in the press and public debate. In terminology inspired by the "war on terror," they are often portrayed as the materialization of evil, as representatives of the fundamentalist "Other," and, where attention is paid to their work as relief NGOs, they are accused of merely copying Western NGOs—and doing even this with malevolent intentions. The data presented in this chapter counter these clichés. I will show that it is simplistic to consider transnational Islamic NGOs as the primary instigators of a fundamentalist Islam in Chad and elsewhere in Africa. Further, their image as stubborn and unapproachable fundamentalists cannot be upheld when looking at how they work in practice. Finally, I will argue that taking Muslim ideas of charity seriously implies that the activities of these NGOs cannot be reduced to a mere mimicking of Western NGOs.

Chad: A Poor Country at the Crossroads of Arab and Western Spheres of Influence

With a life expectancy at birth of forty-five years, an adult literacy rate of 45.8 percent, and an adjusted GDP per capita of US$1,002, Chad is ranked no. 11 on the list of least livable countries in the world (United Nations Development Programme 2004). The long and severe civil war that affected the country in the 1970s and 1980s coincided with prolonged droughts. Today, clanic management of state resources continues to contribute to political instability, while the ecological fragility of the area remains a constant threat to many people's existence. Streams of refugees from the Central African Republic and Sudan pose an additional burden. The oil fields near Doba, in the south of Chad, have recently been brought into production by an American/ Malaysian consortium under the supervision of the World Bank; this has raised expectations among the Chadian population but also gave rise to significant unrest over control of the profits (Bennafla 2000; Guyer 2002; Ellis 2003). Recently, the Pan Sahel Initiative has made Chad an important element in the U.S.'s "war on terror." This program of the U.S. military's European Command to train and equip Sahel countries in the fight against groups linked to al-Qaeda started in 2003. Chad is one of four countries that are the focus of the program, along with Mali, Niger, and Mauritania (Ellis 2004).

The country has long been a transition area between Islamic zones and "animist" and Christian zones. The north has been progressively Islamized over the past seven centuries, through the influence of, among other things, trans-Saharan trade and Arab migration from the east from the fourteenth century onward. Christian missions arrived in Chad from the Central African Republic and Cameroon in the 1930s.

In recent history, religion has frequently been instrumental in struggles for state power by both northern and southern clans. At Independence in 1960, a southerner became the first president and most positions in the administration were occupied by southerners. They had been educated in French schools, which had been boycotted by the majority of Muslims. Another factor contributing to this southern dominance was that France had particularly focused on developing the south (*le Tchad utile*). This situation and the openly negative attitude of the president and his fellows led to growing tensions between the Muslims and those in power. After a long period of guerrilla and civil war (in which the northerners did not form one cohesive front), the northerners were able to seize power in the 1980s. Under Hissene Habré, the first Muslim president, the southerners felt that the northerners progressively occupied their area: not only were northern administrators installed, but also massive numbers of Muslim traders and cattle holders arrived, fleeing the droughts in the north. The tensions between these Muslim cattle holders and southern Sara-speaking farmers are among the most explosive problems in the south (Arditi 2003), and religion is instrumental in reinforcing them. The categories are not static, how-ever: in southern towns like Sarh, for instance, successful Muslim traders are role models for Sara youths, and provide a reason for them to convert. Despite the absence of hard data, most authors agree that Islam is on the rise in southern Chad (Magnant 1992; Magrin 2001).

In 1990, Habré fell from power, partly because France (which has had significant economic, political, and military influence in Chad until today) decided to withdraw its support of him. Idriss Deby, one of his former collaborators, took the presidency. Although democratization has been set in motion, it is still the case that the group in power uses state resources for its own sake, and consequently the conflicts and ten-sions between the Muslim north and the Christian south continue to exist. The dual-istic opposition between Islam/north and Christianity/south has become dominant in all thinking about religious, social, and political dynamics, which makes it difficult (and often politically also undesirable) to perceive variation and differentiation within the two "camps." The exploitation of the oil fields in the south that began in 2004 has nourished secessionist sentiments among southerners but has also increased the desire of those in power to control these sentiments, and hence surveillance and threats of violence have mounted.

Although the oil reserves have recently brought the country to the Western world's attention, Chad had been intensifying its ties with Arab countries since the 1980s. This heightened orientation toward the Arab world is both economic and religious/cultural in character. Thus, Chadian imports from the Gulf states have increased, while Arab investments in real estate, public works, and industries have also grown (Bennafla 2000). Sudan can be considered an old player in Chad, but its influence in the country is facilitated by its alliance with President Deby (he came into power with Sudanese support). Libyan investments in Chad have also become significant since the settlement of the twenty-year conflict over the Aouzou Strip halfway through the 1990s. In addition to investments, Arab bilateral and multilateral aid have become increasingly important. King Faisal University and the central market in N'Djamena, for instance, have been financed by Saudi Arabia. Multilateral support has mainly been provided through the Islamic Development Bank and the Arab Bank for Economic Development in Africa. Ties with the Arab world are also increased by the growing number of Chadians who have studied in Sudan, Egypt, or Saudi Arabia; the increasing number of immigrants to Saudi Arabia, who often keep in touch with their families back home; the growing number of people from Chad who go on the hajj (enabled by improved transportation, among other things); and so on. This intensification of contacts with the Arab countries is accompanied by processes of changing perceptions of Islam and a process of Arabization. The latter is defined here as an increased cultural orientation toward the Arab world, expressed in the adoption of elements of transnational Arab elite culture, such as language, style of clothing, and social and cultural values.

The Islamic NGOs studied in this essay form part of this growing influence of the Arab world. In the following I will explore how they intervene in the Chadian context, characterized as it is by poverty, internal political and religious tensions, and a growing geopolitical importance, both because of its oil and as a concomitant of the increased tensions between the West and the Muslim world.

The Entanglement of Aid and *Umma*

The following table gives an overview of the transnational Islamic NGOs operating in Chad in spring 2004. There are eleven, out of approximately forty-two transnational NGOs currently working in Chad.[2] Among them are one Libyan, three Sudanese, one Kuwaiti, and six Saudi organizations.

The table also shows that the Islamic NGOs arrived in Chad in two waves. The first arrived in the mid-1980s, at the time of the great droughts in the region and Hissene Habré's ascent to power. The late 1970s and early 1980s had seen the birth of the first transnational Islamic NGOs, triggered by the war in Afghanistan and made financially possible by the oil boom in the Arab countries (Ghandour 2002). In the following years, these NGOs started to work in other parts of Asia and in Africa. The International Islamic Relief Organization (IIRO), one of the first Saudi transnational NGOs (created in 1978 by the Saudi government), began working in Africa in the early 1980s. The arrival in Chad of the Sudanese organizations al-Dawa al-Islamiya and the International African Relief Agency (IARA) is due in part to Sudan's foreign policy, which was oriented toward the spread of Arabo-Islamic culture in Africa (Grandin 1993). Al-Dawa al-Islamiya at that time was, however, not only a Sudanese tool, as it was also largely funded by Muammar al-Qaddafi and received increasing amounts from the Saudis. The latter were particularly afraid that al-Qaddafi would use the organization to increase Libya's influence in Chad and tried to outbid Libya financially (Benthall and Bellion-Jourdan 2003, 115).

The second wave began at the end of the 1990s. In 1993 a national conference in Chad had set into motion a process of formal democratization and pacification, leading to a constitutional referendum and elections in 1996–97.[3] In this context of new beginnings, some highly placed individuals started a lobby in the Gulf states to attract Islamic NGOs. They organized meetings and conferences at which it was explained that Chad was a poor country in need of material, social, and cultural support. "The Christian organizations do not wait until they are invited, so why should you?"[4] Saudi Arabia in the mid- and late 1990s had seen an upsurge of new NGOs that were more independent from the Saudi state (but often still administered by members of the Saudi elite). These sought an outlet for their funds and were willing to respond to this Chadian call. The Libyan World Islamic Call Society only arrived in Chad after the settling of the Aouzou conflict and al-Qaddafi's historic reconciliatory visit to N'Djamena in 1998 (Haddad 2000).

NGO	Country of Origin	Arrival in Chad	Main Domains of Intervention
Al-Dawa al-Islamiya	Sudan	1985	Infrastructure, aid to orphans, humanitarian aid
International African Relief Agency (IARA)	Sudan	1985	Emergency aid, construction of wells, aid to orphans
Agence des Musulmans d'Afrique (AMA)	Kuwait	1985	Education, construction of mosques, aid to orphans
International Islamic Relief Organization (IIRO)	Saudi Arabia	1986	Construction of mosques, education, aid to orphans
World Association of Muslim Youth (WAMY)	Saudi Arabia	1996	Education, emergency aid
Al-Muntada al-Islami	Great Britain/ Saudi Arabia	1997	Construction of mosques and wells, education, emergency aid
World Islamic Call Society	Libya	1998	Education, construction of mosques, construction and operation of hospitals
Commission spéciale du Prince Sultan Ben Abdoul-Aziz pour le secours	Saudi Arabia	2000	Emergency aid, medical caravans
Al-Makka al-Mukarrama Foundation	Saudi Arabia	2002	Education, aid to orphans, construction of mosques
Al-Haramain	Saudi Arabia	2002	Emergency aid, construction of mosques and wells, education
Al-Biir/International Benevolence Foundation	Sudan	2002	Health, social services, education, emergency aid

Material Aid

The NGOs concern themselves primarily with concrete aid: constructing mosques and wells, supporting orphans, providing health care and education. The construction of wells and mosques often go together, as the faithful need water to purify themselves before praying. The care of orphans is a core activity for most NGOs, whether they finance orphanages (like the IIRO) or sponsor orphans who stay with relatives (like al-Dawa al-Islamiya). The care of orphans is rooted in Islam: the Prophet Muhammad himself was an orphan, and many hadiths refer to the value of taking care of them.

As for health care, several NGOs run small clinics in towns such as N'Djamena, Abeche, and Sarh. Many (including the Commission spéciale du Prince Sultan, the

AMA, and al-Muntada al-Islami) organize medical caravans, in which a team of doctors and nurses travel through the country to offer care. These caravans generally create very good publicity for their sponsors.

In the field of education, Islamic NGOs have constructed schools (both schools that follow the official state curriculum and Qur'anic schools) and assured their functioning. They also pay the salaries of teachers in existing schools. The AMA, for instance, has financed eleven schools following the state curriculum, with a total of 2,764 pupils, and pays the salary of 128 teachers. In addition, it has constructed seven Qur'anic schools, with a total of 450 pupils (Agence des Musulmans d'Afrique 2002). Al-Dawa al-Islamiya finances schools in Sarh and Abeche with a total of 600 pupils, and a school in N'Djamena with 1,000 pupils. The World Islamic Call Society, based in Libya, finances a secondary school and a library in N'Djamena, as well as other educational projects. All these organizations consider the teaching of, and in, Arabic very important. For them, the Arabic language stands for a way of living and perceiving that is inspired by Islam and Arab culture, values that in their view are marginalized in the Chadian state's lay educational system.

Organizations such as the AMA and the World Islamic Call Society predominantly focus on education, whereas IARA and al-Haramain have a more diversified portfolio. Al-Biir is the most specialized of the NGOs: in Chad, it focuses explicitly on health care. Its other activities derive from this primary focus, and include social services, health education, and emergency aid. Some organizations (such as al-Makka al-Mukarrama, the AMA, and al-Muntada) invest predominantly in the construction of large centers in which a mosque, a school, an orphanage, a center for professional education, a women's center, etc., are all integrated, whereas others, such as the IARA, have more dispersed and smaller projects.

Taken together, the international Islamic NGOs cover all of the country except the extreme north, which is not open to foreigners because of the presence of rebels. There seems to be some division of labor: in the south, for instance, the AMA operates in the zone of Moundou, while al-Muntada operates in the zone of Sarh. The al-Haramain Foundation predominantly operated in Central Chad (the Guera).

Missionary Activities

As Islamic NGOs—and not merely NGOs run by Muslims—the organizations studied also have a missionary function: they are ultimately concerned with advancing Islam, be it by converting non-Muslims (Islamization) or by deepening current Muslims' understanding of Islamic principles and improving their religious practices (re-Islamization). This missionary urge comes most explicitly to the fore in their activities in the field of religious education and the promotion of Islam (sponsoring Qur'anic teachers, distributing educational materials, etc.), but in fact it underlies all their other activities as well. Al-Haramain's website, for instance, listed among the organization's most important goals "Being quick to provide aid to the Muslims who suffer from catastrophes, disasters and calamities and to benefit them with material assistance to enliven the *eemaan* [Arabic *al-iman* or faith] in the hearts and implant knowledge in their breasts if Allah Most High so wills."[5]

Missionary activities are directed at Muslims who, in the eyes of these organizations, have only a very limited knowledge of Islam. In the south of Chad, which is predominantly Christian and animist, missionary activities are first and foremost directed at the non-Muslim population. In this area, organizations such as al-Makka al-Mukarrama, the AMA, and al-Muntada have centers for recent converts. Often preachers are sent to the villages and bring men who show an interest in becoming Muslim back to the center, where they are enrolled in a one- to nine-month course of study, during which they are fed and given a place to sleep. After their course, they go back to their villages and start spreading the message themselves. Another strategy is to approach local power holders such as the *chefs de canton*, on the principle that when they convert, their family and partisans will follow their example. Sometimes such leaders are offered presents or money, a ticket to Mecca, or a community project. The *chef de canton* of Dunia, for example, was given a trip to Mecca by the AMA and from there went on to Kuwait, where he even met the ruler, through whom he obtained a center with a mosque, a school, and a small clinic for his canton. The AMA's yearly report for 2001 includes the cost of seven people's pilgrimage to Mecca (Agence des Musulmans d'Afrique 2002).

It must be stressed, however, that Islamization is a complex process that cannot simply be attributed to the efforts of one organization. Let us take the example of a village in the south of Chad, where, I was told, the village chief had recently been Islamized, together with a large group of villagers. When I visited the village, it appeared that this had been not an instant event but a composite process involving Muslim merchants from the north who had settled in the village some years before, the chief of an adjacent village who had spent some time in Nigeria and had converted to Islam there before returning home, the efforts of preachers affiliated with the Grand Mosque in Moundou, and, finally, missionary efforts by the AMA which had prompted progressively more people to Islamize over the past few years. It is also important that people associate Islam with power, as most higher-ranking local administration officials and military officers are Muslims.

When I asked religious specialists and NGO staff whether there are differences between the messages of the different organizations, they all said that these NGOs' *da'wa* is basically the same. This unanimity is also illustrated by the fact that the Saudi, Kuwaiti, and Sudanese organizations use one another's promotional and educational material: thus, a booklet produced by WAMY was found in an AMA center, and booklets from the AMA were used by a center for recent converts run by the al-Makka al-Mukarrama Foundation. The Libyan organization seems to operate more independently in this respect, which stands to reason because al-Qaddafi claims that his socialist-inspired form of Islam is different from the reformist or Wahhabist messages of the other Islamic NGOs (Mattes 1993). One could argue that the understanding of Islam propagated by the Sudanese state, inspired as it is by the Muslim Brothers (Bennafla 2000, Ghandour 2002), is different from that prevalent in Saudi Arabia, but as al-Dawa al-Islamiya is also financed by donors from the Gulf countries, its message does not differ much from that of the Saudi organizations, and other Arab organizations seem to consider it part of their NGO community; its director regularly visits the others, for instance.

In theory, the Wahhabist stand of the Arab NGOs opposes the Tijaniyya Sufi order that is prevalent in Chad. The Superior Council of Islamic Affairs, which is the highest Muslim authority in Chad, is dominated by the Tijaniyya; on the one hand, it is somewhat wary of these new players in the field, but, on the other, it also collaborates with the Islamic NGOs, such as in the construction and supply of mosques.[6] The directors of the Islamic NGOs for their part are also generally willing to collaborate with the council. In practice, both the council and the NGOs are more pragmatic than might be predicted from their ideological stances.[7]

How strongly humanitarian and missionary activities are stressed depends not only on the organization but also on the public and the context. To a Western researcher like me, NGOs may tend to stress their humanitarian work,[8] whereas to their donors in Saudi Arabia they may stress their Muslim character and missionary function. This most probably also holds true for the different forums in which they participate: several organizations, such as the IIRO, WAMY, and the AMA, participate both in humanitarian forums (such as the NGO forum of the UN and UNICEF) and in Islamic forums (such as the Muslim World League).

The Sudanese organizations constitute a particular way of handling this double identity: al-Dawa al-Islamiya, founded in 1980, remained committed to *da'wa* activities but created the IARA as its humanitarian branch. Later on, the IARA became an independent organization for different reasons (see Bellion-Jourdan 1997). The division of labor is still visible today, however: al-Dawa al-Islamiya still has a more "Islamic" outlook, whereas the IARA presents itself explicitly as a humanitarian organization and also tries to attract funds from non-Muslim sources (and has no reference to Islam in its name).

How Are These Activities Financed?

Although not all NGOs were willing to share details of their budgets with me, on the basis of the data that are available we can conclude that the budgets of the NGOs studied range from €30,000 to €1,125,000 per year. They receive funds from a variety of sources. At one extreme, the IARA has to find donors for every new project it wants to undertake, which evidently does not make its work easy. At the other extreme, the Commission spéciale du Prince Sultan Ben Abdoul-Aziz pour le secours is wholly funded by the Prince Sultan himself, and it is thus assured a flow of funds. Most of the organizations, however, have multiple sources of funding. WAMY, for example, receives half of its funds from the Saudi government and half from private and institutional donations. The AMA depends on individual and organizational (both private and public) donations and on investments. Al-Biir's fundraising is the most diversified: it finances its activities through personal and governmental donations, contributions by its members, and investments in health care, private schools, and businesses, and it has fundraising offices in Switzerland, the Netherlands, and Great Britain. Interestingly, it has founded specialized private medical centers for the rich in Yemen and Sudan, and with the profit it finances small community health centers in poor regions, such as Chad.[9]

At the basis of the NGOs' financing is the Islamic concept of solidarity, already mentioned in the introduction. The financial aspect of this solidarity is formed by *zakat* and *sadaqa*: *zakat* is an obligatory almsgiving and thus a religious duty,[10] while *sadaqa* is a voluntary contribution. *Zakat* is a kind of "financial worship," and constitutes both an act of social solidarity and an affirmation of faith (Benthall and Bellion-Jourdan 2003, 26).

The Qur'an states who has a right to *zakat*. First are the poor and needy, then those who have responsibility for them, "those whose hearts are to be won," debtors, travelers, and those on jihad (see also Benthall and Bellion-Jourdan 2003, 10). Traditionally, *zakat* was paid to help the needy in one's own community (local or national), but more and more it is understood that "the community" can encompass the whole of the *umma*. This idea took root when Muslims in rich countries, such as Saudi Arabia and Great Britain, began to feel that real poverty did not exist there, or existed only sporadically, at the same time that the mass media was exposing poverty and calamities in the rest of the world. It is sometimes debated whether *zakat* is for needy Muslims only or also for non-Muslims. Generally, it is considered to be for Muslims only. But if the concept is widened to include not only Muslims but also those who can become Muslims ("those whose hearts are to be won"), aid to non-Muslims becomes appropriate. This means, however, that *da'wa* remains an important component of an Islamic NGO's strategy.

Aid, *Umma*, and Politics

Aid and *umma*, the humanitarian aspect and the religious aspect, are intimately inter-woven and make up an essential part of the identity of the transnational Islamic relief organizations. The concept of aid is rooted in an idea of Muslim solidarity, but also serves to bring (more) people (closer) to God—both in giving and in receiving aid. The *umma* is a moral concept in the first place, indicating the community of those who obey the commandments of God. In addition, it has a territorial connotation, as a distinction is usually made between *dar al-Islam* (literally, "the house" or "the abode of Islam"), referring to Muslim countries, and *dar al-harb* ("abode of war"), indicating all countries where Islam does not reign. In between there is a zone called *dar al-sulh* ("abode of reconciliation"), referring to non-Muslim countries that are not hostile to Islam and where, consequently, the *umma* can grow; traditionally the *dar al-sulh* is situated on the African continent (Ghandour 2002). It is generally considered a Muslim's duty to help expand the *umma*, and it follows from the foregoing that this expansion can be interpreted in both a moral and a territorial way. As is normal in situations of expansion, there are political repercussions; this is a rivalry for people and territory.

It appears that in Chad, the Islamic organizations consider the Christian NGOs their primary rivals. It is they, Muslim opinion holds, who try to keep people away from Islam and who use aggressive methods of conversion to gain adherents. When taking an international perspective, the directors of Islamic NGOs see Americans, or more precisely the Bush administration, as their most important enemy. It is American ideas and policies that stigmatize Islam in general and Islamic organiza-tions in particular, and seriously hinder their work. In the background are the Israeli–Palestinian conflict, in which the U.S. is considered a significant actor, and the invasion of Iraq. Remarkably, directors of the NGOs did not mention as a prob-lem the fact that Americans are in Chad to exploit the oil fields (as I had expected before starting my research)—competition over oil was seen more as a rivalry between the Americans and the French than as an attempt to enhance American hegemony to the detriment of Arab and Muslim influence.

In the following, I will elaborate on these two fields of animosity and contestation. At the national level, I will focus on the rivalry between Muslim and Christian NGOs (and we will see that the Christian NGOs, for their part, have much the same ideas and prejudices concerning the Muslim NGOs as the Muslim NGOs have concerning their Christian counterparts). At the international level, I will focus on the American accusations that the Islamic organizations support terrorism.

Politics: Islamic versus Christian NGOs

More than the rest of the country, the south of Chad is an arena of Christian–Muslim competition. The area was originally predominantly "animist" and Christian, but Muslim influence has become stronger from the 1980s onward, thanks to the immigration of traders and cattle holders from the northern parts of Chad, mainly triggered by drought and war and by the fact that the administration and the military were progressively taken over by Muslims after the northerners seized power. Géraud Magrin, in his elaborate study of changes in the south of Chad these past decades, states that the opposition between Christians and Muslims does not take on the violent antagonistic form it has in Sudan but that it is nevertheless strongly fed by both the increase in the number of Muslims in the south and the influence of movements promoting more rigorous Islamic practices (2001, 344). I would like to stress that the politicization of religion by both northern and southern parties has also contributed to the tensions.

The Islamic and Christian NGOs are actors in this arena, and they do generally feel that they are there to defend a cause. Both sides suspect the other of using aid as a means to gain converts (Benthall and Bellion-Jourdan 2003). What is more, each often suspects the other of having hidden political objectives or of being a political instrument in the hands of states or global power blocs. The director of an Islamic NGO, for instance, suspected the Christian NGO World Vision of being politically active in a town where both organizations were operating. A staff member of an American Protestant NGO described the transnational Islamic NGOs as puppets in a master plan by the Saudi state, especially, he said, because Chad is a strategic country. More often, however, Christian organizations (and Christians in Chad, more generally) see the "Islamic threat" as coming from Sudan. They fear that the Islamic influence of this neighboring country will cause Chad to become an Islamist state too, with the concomitant consequences for the Christian population that have been seen in Sudan. Christian organizations often also suspect the Islamic organizations of being given preferential treatment by the Chadian administration. Of staffers I spoke with from both Christian and Islamic NGOs, only a nun-fieldworker from a Catholic mission near Bongor was able to critically reflect on her own position, saying that "every party tries to win the population by gifts; we also impose, for instance through health care."

It must be kept in mind that Christian organizations may intend to proselytize, just as Muslim organizations do. The Entente of the Evangelical Churches and Missions in Chad (Entente des églises et missions évangeliques au Tchad; EEMET), for instance, the Chadian national association of Protestant churches, explicitly mentions evangelization as one of its objectives, next to the improvement of religious practices and the fighting of "wrong doctrines" within its own community, the defense of the interests of the evangelical community vis-à-vis the state, etc. In its vision statement, proselytization appears still more strongly: the organization's aim is "to make the whole Chadian nation the followers of Jesus Christ" (EEMET 2003). These three objectives—education of one's own community, conversion of others, and defense of the group's interests—are basically the same as those of many Muslim organizations.

There is little direct confrontation between the Christian and Islamic organizations, but the people who are the target groups of the NGOs' activities feel the tension all the same, as is shown by the following case.

In a small village in the south of Chad, I met a former priest who had recently converted to Islam. He had collected money for the church every Sunday, but he had never felt that the church did anything for him and his community. He told me passionately that he had found the light when he read a small booklet entitled *The Way to Islam*, given to him by people who had come to the village to preach. He went to the mosque in another village, near to the main road, and said that he wanted to convert, but they said that he had to think it over first and they sent him away. After five days he returned to say that he was decided, and then they warmly welcomed him. And a few days later, ten other men with their families followed his example. But a nun from the diocese came to the village and told them that it was the devil who had brought them to Islam and that they should not listen to him. They answered her that they had not converted for money, or anything like that, and when she saw that she could not convince them, she left. But, the former priest said bitterly, everywhere in the diocese it is taught that he is the embodiment of the devil. I saw that this was very painful for him. What I found very painful was that he had sent a letter to the Islamic NGO operating in the area, which was directly or indirectly involved in his conversion, to ask for a mosque, and he never got an answer. It seemed to me that he was treated in much the same way by both institutions.

Christian intellectuals in Chad share a common discourse on transnational Islamic NGOs. The political views elaborated at the beginning of this section are important elements in this. They also accuse Islamic NGOs of mimicry: "When we build a school, they also build a school; when we build an orphanage, they also build an orphanage." The idea that Islamic NGOs predominantly react to Christian/Western NGOs is also discernable in the literature (Coudray 1992). Benthall and Bellion-Jourdan (2003) sometimes fall into this trap as well, such as when they say that the founding of Islamic NGOs is a reaction to the presence of Western NGOs, or that their later professionalization is a mimicry of what is going on within Christian/Western NGOs. But many of these developments can be understood as being based on ideas and developments within Islam or the internal development of Islamic NGOs. The IIRO's building of an orphanage in N'Djamena might look from the outside like a mere copying of the Christian orphanage that was already there, but, as we have seen already, the care of orphans is very important in Islam, and the construction of this orphanage could be inspired as much by this imperative as by the wish to rival the Christian initiative. Also, the increasing "humanitarianism" of Islamic NGOs discussed by Benthall and Bellion-Jourdan cannot be explained merely as the result of a wish to become more like the Western

NGOs. Professionalization is apparent in the NGO world in general from the 1990s onward; perhaps the Christian and Islamic NGOs are moving down this path in parallel. In this process, NGOs influence one another, but developments within Islamic NGOs cannot be reduced to mere imitation.

Catholic organizations are generally more open to collaboration with Islamic organizations than are Protestant ones. In general, the staff of any given organization may be more pragmatic and more open in practice than might be expected from their group's theoretical orientation or from the strained relationship between different religious groups in Chad.[11] The Commission spéciale du Prince Sultan Ben Abdoul-Aziz, for instance, may collaborate with priests in distributing its goods. The director of WAMY is a member of an international group for Islamic–Christian dialogue. A Catholic organization helped a Muslim NGO in a refugee camp to distribute meat during the feast at the end of Ramadan.[12]

It appears to be easier for Muslims than for Christians to maintain an openness toward the other. The Christians' sense of being in the minority contributes to a defensive attitude. This is nicely illustrated by the fact that a director of an Islamic NGO expressed his open attitude toward his Christian colleagues while stressing that he saw the rivalry between them as nothing bad; a Christian director, by contrast, experienced this rivalry not as amusing or natural but as truly threatening. A Protestant group organized a seminar with the title "How to Respond to the Objections of Muslims to the Christian Faith," to enable its members to defend themselves. The booklet accompanying the seminar provides information on Islam, as well as the correct answers to six Muslim objections to Christianity (to the idea of the Trinity, Jesus being the Son of God, etc.). The booklet ends with the question: Who will win the battle? The answer is that Christianity will only win when all Christians are mobilized. Otherwise, it will be the contrary: Christians will become Muslims (al-Haq 2004).

Although Muslims are obviously the dominant party in Chad, because of the national political situation and the fact that Islam is the majority religion (Coudray 1992), in the international arena the situation is reversed. After September 11, 2001, Muslims clearly find themselves in the dock. In the following section, we will see how this affects the Muslim NGOs that are the subject of this study.

Politics: Accusations of Terrorism

The position of transnational Islamic NGOs, both internationally and in Chad, can only be understood by also taking into account the current global context of increasing antagonism and animosity between the Muslim world and the West, which has been strongly reinforced by the "war on terror." Islamic NGOs are sometimes directly accused of supporting terrorist groups and activities. Other effects of this tension are more indirect, affecting the atmosphere in which the NGOs have to work.

Islamic NGOs have been accused of promoting and supporting terrorism since the early 1990s in Afghanistan, Palestine, Pakistan, Bosnia, and elsewhere (Benthall and Bellion-Jourdan 2003). After September 11, however, the accusations became more severe and gained political clout, as they have become an integral part of the Bush administration's "war on terror." In this framework, transnational Islamic

NGOs are accused of providing financial, material, and logistical support to the al-Qaeda network and organizations such as Hamas. A director of a transnational Islamic NGO working in Chad, however, stated that members of his organization are treated as enemies by the U.S. because they take care of orphaned children of Hamas members and rebuild houses in the Palestinian areas that were destroyed by the Israeli army. (In saying this, he also indicated that their support is strictly humanitarian and that they are not involved in armed struggle.) All staff of the Islamic NGOs stressed that terrorists are not good Muslims and that Islam is a peaceful religion.

One of the reasons why it is difficult to judge these NGOs is the fact that they are transnational organizations: they often deploy different strategies in different countries, have different priorities, face different local environments, and employ different staff. Accusations of one branch may not be relevant to another branch in another country or on another continent. Until 2002, U.S. policy generally took these differences into account; al-Haramain, for instance, had been closed in only a few countries, such as Somalia and Bosnia. Recently, however, U.S. policy has become less discriminating and more repressive. Entire Muslim organizations have become the target of antiterrorism measures.

Thus, while I was in Chad in spring 2004, the Chadian branch of al-Haramain was forced to close its office as a result of the organization's elimination by the Saudi Ministry of Islamic Affairs, under pressure from the U.S. Other groups did not face such drastic measures, but many were also affected. WAMY, for instance, had its budget cut by the Saudi government as a result of U.S. pressure—the organization is still subsidized by the Saudi state, but private donors are no longer allowed to donate to it. When I returned to Chad in September 2004, all Saudi organizations were under scrutiny, their funds frozen until the investigations were complete. As a result of these measures and the pressure exerted by the Americans, the Commission spéciale du Prince Sultan Ben Abdoul-Aziz had ceased its activities and was preparing to leave the country. Its director told me that all delegations in Africa had been called back to Saudi Arabia. He said that all Saudi relief organizations would probably be dissolved and their activities brought together in an international organization, controlled and closely monitored by the Saudi state (see also *Middle East Online* 2004). The other Saudi organizations I spoke to were not convinced that this would happen and were awaiting the results of the investigations. Both the American and the Saudi administration want to end the flow of funds from private individuals to organizations over which they have no control. The fact that the Prince Sultan is also the minister of defense and aviation may explain why his organization was one of the first to react to this new policy. The director of the AMA said that his organization was already closely monitored by the Kuwaiti state administration and that hence U.S. pressure had no consequences for the AMA's functioning.

It is not possible for a researcher like me to judge the truth of the accusations of supporting terrorism, but it is certain that for Chad, the dissolution of the Islamic NGOs will have direct consequences: schools will have to be closed, orphans will no longer be supported. Even if this scenario does not materialize, the "war on terror" will have an effect. Most NGO directors complained that they meet with distrust and suspicion in the international humanitarian arena, which obviously hampers their work.

At the national level, the "war on terror" has other repercussions which also affect the working conditions of the Islamic organizations. On the one hand, there is the Pan Sahel Initiative, by which the U.S. provides weapons and training to the Chadian army to help it fight terrorist activities. This initiative is likely to lead to a more pronounced U.S. influence in Chad, and some directors of Islamic NGOs said that it makes working in Chad more difficult. Although the Chadian state in general has a positive attitude toward the Arab organizations, the influence of the Americans makes the relationship more complicated. This is especially true because both the Pan Sahel Initiative and the interventions of the Islamic NGOs offer profits to the Chadian leaders.[13] In addition, the design of this antiterrorism program has probably been influenced by the presence of important oil reserves in Chad (*De Volkskrant* 2004), in which both the U.S. and the Chadian administration are interested. On the other hand, observers state that the current international situation has nurtured an anti-Western and anti-Christian sentiment among the Muslim population that was not apparent before (al-Mouna 2004). All these elements will influence the work of the transnational Islamic NGOs in Chad in the near future, and it is probable that their material and moral interventions will become (still) more politically loaded.

Conclusion

This chapter has explored the character, working methods, and effects of transnational Islamic NGOs in Chad. Their transnational character comes to the fore in their funding, the geographical scope of their interventions, the composition of their staff, and their objectives, which are most often formulated in terms of the *umma*. They are Islamic organizations, and not merely organizations run by Muslims, in that their objectives, their activities, and their funding are guided by Islamic principles. This means that it is far too simplistic to consider their activities merely as mimicry of Western NGOs; I mentioned the founding of an orphanage in N'Djamena that could be seen as an attempt to rival a Christian initiative but can also be explained as arising from the Islamic principle that care of orphans is important. The Arab organizations differ primarily in their practical approach (some having large, integrated centers whereas others establish smaller, dispersed projects), the relative weight of *da'wa* and *ighatha*, and the source and extent of their funding (government or private).

Aid and *umma*, the humanitarian and the religious, are intimately interwoven in the work of these NGOs. This means, however, that they are also seen as political actors, using aid to enlarge the *umma* both in a moral or religious sense and in a geopolitical sense. Although at the national level it is the religious rivalry between Islamic and Christian NGOs that was most apparent, each side suspects the other of playing politics as well. This rivalry does not prevent NGO staff from being pragmatic and open to collaboration in practice, however; incidental collaboration may occur, for instance, between Islamic and Catholic organizations.

At the international level, geopolitical tensions are most pronounced as Islamic NGOs, accused of supporting terrorism by the U.S. (and, in its wake, by many other states), have become a target in the "war on terror." This global war has repercussions for the work of the Islamic NGOs in Chad. The data suggest that the "war on terror" will most probably change the charitable and political landscape in Chad as it will in other African countries, so the analysis of its impact should not be restricted to either the international diplomatic arena or the local situation in Afghanistan and Iraq.

It is difficult to say what the effects are of the transnational Islamic NGOs in Chad on the basis of this preliminary study. The first thing that can be said is that these organizations are very visible: they construct large educational centers and numerous mosques, and they often raise a sign or banner bearing their name in front of their projects, large and small. This visibility, however, may not mean as much as it seems to. In the capital, N'Djamena, smoothly running centers exist, but in the countryside many mosques are never opened and integrated centers often lack staff and financing. Also, the effects of their proselytization are difficult to measure. My impression is that the conversions effected by these NGOs are in many cases rather superficial, and reinforcements are needed to make them last, such as an existing, welcoming Muslim community, political or social advantages to be gained by being a Muslim, or the continued supervision and teaching of an imam or other Muslim authority. By themselves, these NGOs have a limited impact. Their real importance has to be sought in the fact that they are part of broader processes of Islamization and Arabization. The Arab Islamic NGOs at once embody and contribute to these processes, through their visibility and other means, and also profit from them, as they "ride the wave." In this also lies their ultimate political importance: they represent and are part of a larger phenomenon that is experienced by some as dangerous and by others as desirable.

More research should be done on the dynamics of intervention of transnational Islamic NGOs in Africa. I hope to have shown, first, that an approach combining a view of material, moral, and political aspects and analyzing the interrelation of global, national, and local dynamics is a promising one. Second, that the meeting of different strands of Islam and of Islam and Christianity should be studied in the field by looking at the interaction of people, not by looking at theories and ideologies only, as reality is more dynamic and people are more pragmatic than their ideologies would suggest. Finally, I propose that these organizations can best be studied as part of broader processes of Islamization and Arabization—in Chad and elsewhere in Africa.

Notes

I am grateful for the financial support given by WOTRO, the Van Coeverden Adriani Stichting, the "Islam in Africa" program (ASC/CEAN), and the African Studies Centre. In addition, I would like to thank Benjamin Soares and Mirjam de Bruijn for their comments on an earlier draft of this chapter.

1. The intensity of Christian–Muslim rivalry in Africa is illustrated by the fact that only a year later the recommendations of this meeting were published in a Vatican review.
2. In 2005, there were sixty-nine foreign NGOs registered with the Ministry of Planning, but only forty-two were operational; that is, they sent reports to the ministry (interview at the Ministry of Planning, NGO Direction, N'Djamena, April 2005).
3. See Buijtenhuijs 1993 for a thorough account of this conference and related dynamics, and Buijtenhuijs 1998 for the subsequent democratization process.
4. Interview with one of the lobbyists in N'Djamena, May 2004.
5. Al-Haramain's website is at http://www.alharamain.org. However, it is no longer accessible.
6. However, the council is not very pleased about the fact that these NGOs are supervised by the Ministry of Planning, and therefore the council has no control over them. It sees this as

unjustified, because its task is to supervise all Islamic activity in the country (see also al-Mouna 2004).

7. Probably contributing to this rather open attitude is the fact that many of the directors of these organizations are expatriates with wide international experience. The director of al-Makka al-Mukarrama, for example, is a Saudi who served in Bosnia before coming to Chad, and the director of the AMA is a Moroccan who previously worked in Burkina Faso.

8. They did not discuss their *da'wa* activities with me; I gained information on them only in the field.

9. Ghandour (2002, 144) states that this strategy is common among Islamic NGOs.

10. *Zakat* is fixed at one-fortieth of one's assets per year; what assets have to be counted is subject to discussion and Islamic jurisprudence. Muslims with assets below a certain threshold (*nisab*) do not to have pay *zakat*.

11. As I have shown, this is also true of the relationship between the Superior Council of Islamic Affairs and the Saudi NGOs.

12. These initiatives are, however, rather incidental. In organized forums, Muslim and Christian NGOs hardly meet each other, let alone collaborate. The NGO forum in Moundou, for instance, consists of Christian and lay organizations only. No Islamic organizations were invited to a conference on street children organized by the United Nations Development Programme in N'Djamena.

13. In an interview, Chad's former ambassador to the U.S. pointed to the danger that the Chadian president will use the equipment and better trained armed forces for his own ends (www.aljazeera.com). See also *Africa Confidential* 2004, stating that U.S. military cooperation will draw President Deby further into Washington's sphere of influence. A recent report by the International Crisis Group, however, stresses that although the initiative's goals are certainly ambitious, for the moment "the day-to-day activities are often rather mundane" (2005, 30).

References

Africa Confidential. 2004. Chad: Rebels all around. April 16 (vol. 45, no. 8), p. 7.

Agence des Musulmans d'Afrique. 2002. Rapport annuel d'activité année 2001. N'Djamena: AMA Bureau du Tchad.

Arditi, C. 2003. Les violences ordinaires ont une histoire: Le cas du Tchad. *Politique africaine* 91: 51–67.

Bellion-Jourdan, J. 1997. L'humanitaire et l'islamisme soudanais: Les organisations Da'wa Islamiya et Islamic African Relief Agency. *Politique africaine* 66: 61–73.

Bennafla, K. 2000. Tchad: L'appel des sirènes arabo-islamiques. *Autrepart* 16: 67–86.

Benthall, Jonathan, and Jérôme Bellion-Jourdan. 2003. *The charitable crescent: Politics of aid in the Muslim world*. London: I. B. Tauris.

Buijtenhuijs, R. 1993. *La conférence nationale souveraine du Tchad: Un essai d'histoire immédiate*. Paris: Karthala.

———. 1998. *Transition et élections au Tchad, 1993–1997: Restauration autoritaire et recomposition politique*. Paris: Karthala.

Callaghy, Thomas M., Ronald Kassimir, and Robert Latham. 2001. *Intervention and transnationalism in Africa: Global-local networks of Power*. Cambridge: Cambridge University Press.

Coudray, H. 1992. Chrétiens et Musulmans au Tchad. Unpublished paper.

De Volkskrant (Amsterdam). 2004. Terreur wekt interesse VS voor Afrika: Pan-Sahel initiatief moet strijd tegen terrorisme opvoeren tussen Rode Zee en Atlantische Oceaan. July 15.

EEMET (Entente des églises et missions évangeliques au Tchad). 2003. EEMET, sa vision, ses priorités, ses perspectives. N'Djamena: Entente des églises et missions évangeliques au Tchad.

Ellis, S. 2003. Briefing: West Africa and its oil. *African Affairs* 102: 135–38.

———. 2004. Briefing: The Pan-Sahel Initiative. *African Affairs* 103: 459–64.

Ghandour, Abdel-Rahman. 2002. *Jihad humanitaire: Enquête sur les ONG islamiques*. Paris: Flammarion.

Grandin, N. 1993. Al Merkaz al-islami al-afriqi bi'l-Khartoum: La République du Soudan et la propagation de l'Islam en Afrique noire (1977–1991). In *Le radicalisme islamique au sud du Sahara: Da'wa, arabisation et critique de l'Occident*, ed. René Otayek, 97–120. Paris: Karthala.

Guyer, J. 2002. Briefing: The Chad-Cameroon Petroleum and Pipeline Development Project. *African Affairs* 101: 109–15.

Haddad, S. 2000. La politique africaine de la Libye: De la tentation impériale à la stratégie unitaire. *Monde Arabe: Maghreb-Machrek*, no. 170 (October–December).

al-Haq, Abd al-Nour. 2004. Comment répondre aux objections des musulmans contre la foi chrétienne. N'Djamena: Entente des églises et missions évangeliques au Tchad.

Institut pontifical d'études arabes. 1984. Recommandations du 11ème séminaire Islamique Mondial sur l'Islam en Afrique. *Études arabes: Feuilles de travail* 66 (1): 46–55.

International Crisis Group. 2005. Islamist terrorism in the Sahel: Fact or fiction? Africa Report no. 92. Dakar and Brussels: International Crisis Group.

Magnant, Jean-Pierre, ed. 1992. *L'Islam au Tchad*. Talence: Institut d'études politiques de Bordeaux, Université de Bordeaux 1.

Magrin, Géraud. 2001. *Le sud du Tchad en mutation: Des champs de coton aux sirènes de l'or noir*. Saint-Maur-des-Fossés: Sépia.

Mattes, H. 1993. La da'wa libyenne entre le Coran et le Livre Vert. In *Le radicalisme islamique au sud du Sahara: Da'wa, arabisation et critique de l'Occident*, ed. René Otayek, 37–73. Paris: Karthala.

Middle East Online. 2004. "Al-Haramain Islamic Foundation dissolved." http://www.middle-east-online.com/english/?id=11474.

al-Mouna. 2004. Dossier: Les religions telles qu'elles sont vécues par les Tchadiens. *Carrefour*, no. 28 (July–August).

Salih, M. A. Mohamed. 2004. Islamic NGOs in Africa: The promise and peril of Islamic voluntarism. In *Islamism and its enemies in the Horn of Africa*, ed. Alex De Waal, 141–81. London: Hurst.

United Nations Development Programme. 2004. *Human development index, 2004*. New York: United Nations Development Programme.

CHAPTER 5

NEW RELIGIOUS ACTORS IN
SOUTH AFRICA: THE EXAMPLE
OF ISLAMIC HUMANITARIANISM

Samadia Sadouni

Islamic humanitarianism in South Africa represents new political, social, and economic horizons for the South African Muslim minority.[1] Its development in the 1970s was strongly linked to reformist and transnational Islamic trends. This essay will attempt to analyze current forms of Islamic aid from a sociohistorical perspective which takes into account the influence of religious globalization in the emergence of new Muslim actors as well as their relationship to the state. I will show that South African Muslims, especially those of Indian origin, initially entered into the humanitarian sphere with the goal of fostering Islamization and re-Islamization under the influence of international Islamic institutions. Then, in the 1990s, new practices of Islamic solidarity came to prevail in a context of economic liberalization, notably with the growing professionalism of South African Islamic NGOs. These latter would progressively link their Muslim identity to their identity as citizens, thus promoting the nationalization of Islamic associations and religious change.

The Globalization of Religion and
the Politicization of Islamic Solidarity

In South Africa, the charitable and social mission of Muslim associations was strongly characterized by the predominance of community ties. In the former province of Natal,[2] institutions of Indian origin, essentially under the leadership of Gujarati Muslims, were the first associational movements for the organization of Islamic solidarity. This pattern continues to mobilize associational energies and to awaken the awareness of Muslim citizens. In the 1970s, a variety of charitable organizations were created under the leadership of militant Indian Muslims, such as the Islamic Dawah Movement, the Islamic Medical Association, the South African National Zakáh Fund (SANZAF), and, in the 1980s, the Africa Muslim Agency (AMA).

These latter organizations were the products of a national Islamic movement, the Muslim Youth Movement (MYM),[3] whose roots date back to the 1930s. These early associations, placing social and educational work at the heart of their mission, were the initiatives of merchants and businessmen animated by the Aligarh movement and other forms of Indian Islamic reformism. Social activities were financed in the name of Islam and some of its institutions, notably *zakat* (obligatory alms), *sadaqa* (voluntary charitable contributions), and above all *waqf* (pious endowments). In later periods, Islamic associations were based on other kinds of ideologies: the Islamism of the Muslim Brothers and of Mawdudi's Jama'at-i Islami, the pan-Islamism of the World Assembly of Muslim Youth (WAMY).

These global Islamist ideas were circulated by the MYM within different ethnic communities in the country (Malay, Indian, Black African) and adapted to the specific context of Islam as a minority religion in the particularly discriminatory political context of apartheid. In addition, the integration of the MYM into transnational Islamic networks, dominated by the Islamist tendencies of the Muslim Brothers and the Jama'at-i Islami and financed by international institutions such as the WAMY, permitted South African Muslims to project themselves onto the global scene and to be an integral part of the *umma*.

However, this entrance into the global Islamic scene did not signal allegiance to an Islamism defined by its will to seize power. Even if these organizations for re-Islamization stressed the Islamization of the nation and the adoption of sharia in their literature and discourse, we can hardly consider them Islamist actors. Gaining power and confronting the government were not part of their political program, especially because the majority of Islamic associations in the country maintained relatively peaceful relationships with the state. The MYM certainly opposed racial segregation but hardly adopted a policy like that of the Call of Islam, which made its mark on the antiapartheid movement in Cape Province.[4] The Islamic organizations' tendency to remain neutral on the subject of the racial system made it easier for them to act in the social and charitable fields. Islam in South Africa thus furnishes an example of one modality of Islamic activism, defined in the present case as community-focused action. This political culture, combined with Islamic transnationalism, would strongly influence the relationship both between the state and established Islam in South Africa and between the Black African population and Indian Muslims.

Muslim Activism in Southern Africa

The construction of an Islamic humanitarian field in South Africa was initially marked by the creation of a regional organization, the Southern Africa Islamic Youth Conference (SAIYC). This organization, financed by the international Islamic institutions of the oil monarchies and especially Saudi Arabia, helped to integrate the Southern African region into global Islam. The Indian Muslim minority, in its role as the ideological conduit of these international institutions, would nonetheless keep control over this new policy of re-Islamization in Southern Africa from its South African base. These two sorts of actors, Saudi "financiers" and South African Islamic "managers," would strategically negotiate their joint leadership of the project of Islamization and re-Islamization in Southern Africa, but without establishing a relationship of dependency and clientship under Saudi leadership.

The SAIYC, created in response to resolutions taken by the Muslim World League[5] in Mauritania in 1976, became the instrument of the South African Islamic movement within the Southern African region. Its first conference, organized in Botswana in June 1977 and titled "Responsibility of Muslims to Humanity (with Specific Reference to Southern Africa)," was the product of the Islamic resurgence of the 1970s, which swept first through South Africa and then across the entire Southern African region. The policy of regionalization was intended to create a new approach to Islamic identity. South African Muslims were called upon to stop turning toward their countries of origin (such as India), their own ethnic communities, or the Arab world, whose holy cities were at the Islamic center. This was an important break with patterns of thought which invited Muslims living on the periphery of the Islamic world to integrate themselves into the Arabian (or in some instances South Asian) center.

The SAIYC has an office in Durban which coordinates the program of Islamization and re-Islamization in nine countries within Southern Africa: Botswana, Lesotho, Malawi, Swaziland, Mozambique, South Africa, Zambia, Zimbabwe, and Namibia. There are 11.5 million Muslims in these countries, constituting 3 percent of the total population of the African continent (Mumisa 2002, 285).[6] International conferences were organized every other year at which Southern African Muslims could meet one another, share their experiences of re-Islamization, and commit themselves to making Islam, in Mawdudi's words, "a way of life" in the region. Re-Islamization, much more than the conversion of Africans, was at the heart of the SAIYC's concerns, and it sought to energize ties of Islamic solidarity between different countries in the region[7] by inviting Islamist personalities such as Kurshid Ahmed, a leader of the Pakistani Jama'at-i Islami.

However, Sunni Islamism was not the SAIYC's only ideological source. After 1979, in the wake of the Islamic revolution in Iran, Shiism was also an important source of inspiration. It is thus important to understand the nuances of the role the SAIYC may play as an ideological intermediary for Saudi Wahhabism. Its South African leaders have cultivated their autonomy and their independence with respect to various Islamic currents in the world. They have explored different sources of reformism to find tools with which to conduct political and religious mobilization on their own terrain. This is why we find within the SAIYC the same Islamic activities that were initiated by the MYM. The exportation of a model of re-Islamization throughout Southern Africa essentially depended on activities put in place by the MYM in South Africa: the creation of libraries and Islamic centers, the distribution of Islamic literature, the organization of youth camps, the enumeration of the Muslim population, and the collection and distribution of *zakat*.[8]

Financing and Independence

It was a secretary-general of the WAMY whose idea it was to create the SAIYC. He had suggested to members of the MYM with whom he maintained close relationships that they extend their activities into neighboring countries of Southern Africa. The individuals at the heart of this process of regionalization constituted the bridge between Muslim groups in Southern Africa and the various international Islamic organizations of the oil monarchies.[9] Through groups such as the WAMY and the Muslim World League, the states of the Arabian Peninsula (with Saudi Arabia in first place) distribute funds for Muslim causes, encourage the SAIYC and study circles to organize regular conferences, and attempt to defend Muslim interests as well as to determine the program of the Muslim world at the national as well as the international level. These public international organizations propagate, for the most part, a Wahhabist ideology that serves the interests of the Saudi monarchy and helps to reproduce its pretension to hegemony over the Sunni world. It is nonetheless necessary to understand that this projection of a Wahhabist ideology on the international scene is not so straightforward. Unlike the Iranians, the Saudis buy their supremacy and their tranquility without worrying about maintaining close control, thus helping to allow the SAIYC to independently orient its Islamic activities and the mode of re-Islamization it exports throughout Southern Africa from its South African base.[10]

The presence and financial participation of international Islamic organizations (such as the Muslim World League, the Islamic Development Bank [IDB],[11] the International Islamic Federation of Student Organizations [IIFSO], and the WAMY) at the SAIYC's conferences were indispensable to its success and to the integration of the Southern African region into the Muslim world. The investment of these nongovernmental organizations in Africa can be explained by, among other factors, the vision which they project onto the African continent: to the IIFSO, for example, "Africa is . . . the continent of Muslims."[12]

Different actions were supposed to correspond to this internationalist ambition projected onto the African continent. First came the construction of Swaziland's first mosque, substantially financed by the WAMY in 1981, which became the agent of the MYM in the country. The WAMY, in conjunction with the IDB, has contributed millions of dollars to finance madrasas in South Africa, Zimbabwe, Zambia, and Namibia. The Muslim World League contributed US$80,000 toward an Islamic seminary in Harare.[13] Nonetheless, the lack of communication and collaboration between the principal institutions, such as the IIFSO and the WAMY, in the distribution of literature and the organization of centers for Islamic training has made the work of the regional SAIYC leaders more difficult. The duplication of activities within Africa by the IIFSO, the WAMY, the Muslim World League, and the Dar al-Ifta (the Saudi Department of Religious Affairs)[14] reflects a lack of organization within this network of Sunni financing, and perhaps even differences in their determination to implant Wahhabi ideology.

In spite of its institutional financing and its organization of international meetings, the SAIYC has not managed to democratize Black African access. The Africanization of Islam and the Islamization of the African population remain marginal phenomena. African Muslims' lack of access to the economic resources and Islamic network available to Muslims of Indian origin has hindered representation of the ethnic and cultural diversity which characterizes the Islamic landscape in Southern Africa. During the fourth conference of the SAIYC, in Harare in 1983, the delegation from South Africa included forty people whereas other countries in the region sent only four delegates each. The leadership of the SAIYC was strongly influenced by the Indian Muslim diaspora of Southern Africa, which privileged intra-ethnic solidarities and relationships. Thus, ethnonational cleavages have prevailed over Muslim universalism and ideological allegiance.

In general, the principal accomplishments of the SAIYC have been to give all the Muslim communities in the region the chance to get acquainted, to resolve difficulties encountered by agents of Islamic revivalism, and to integrate Southern Africa into the Muslim world through transnational networks capable of furnishing funds and support. But this financial assistance did not match the hopes and ambitions expressed at different conferences.[15] In 1990, the SAIYC interrupted its activities when the WAMY ceased to contribute financially toward its regional re-Islamization project. Since the Gulf War, public, official Saudi aid has diminished and the leaders of the SAIYC have failed to find other private financial backers, such as businessmen from oil monarchies.[16] However, the WAMY is still present in the region and finances other Islamic organizations promoting Islamic solidarity.

To summarize, the vitality of the transnational exchanges initiated by the SAIYC results from their instrumentality, the institutional character of the networks, and the disengagement of the apartheid state. The globalization of Islam and the particular political context of South Africa thus favored the transnational action of the SAIYC in the Southern African region, where opportunities for politico-religious action were available to African Muslims. Since the end of apartheid, South African Islamic associations have turned more toward their own country and progressively built cooperative relationships with the democratic state. Before embarking on the analysis of the postapartheid period, I will undertake the second part of the sociohistorical analysis of the SAIYC, which will reveal the principal stages which molded political relationships between Islamic organizations and public authorities.

The SAIYC's Political Activity in Mozambique

The fifth conference of the SAIYC was organized in January 1987 in Mozambique with the close collaboration of the WAMY. The presence of the WAMY and other international Islamic organizations in Mozambique can be explained by the development of Islamic activism in the country, which had begun in 1984. However, the status of Islam in Mozambique had not always been favorable to the spread of Islamic reformism.

Since the first conference of the SAIYC, in Botswana in 1977, the situation of Muslims in Malawi and Mozambique had been the subject of discussion. In that year, two years after Independence, Frelimo (the Mozambican Liberation Front), which had long struggled against Portuguese colonial rule, adopted a Marxist politics hostile to the cultural and religious traditions of the population. Muslims, who had already been the targets of repression under Portuguese colonialism, suffered strong restrictions on religious freedom after Independence, as did all Christians. Islam was marginalized by the transformation of madrasas and mosques into secular schools, by the banning of imported Qur'ans and the censorship of Islamic literature, and by restrictions on freedom of speech and on the movement of Muslims who wished, for instance, to pursue religious studies abroad (Bradlow 1987a, 6–7). Moreover, the exacerbation of ethnic tensions and conflicts, poverty, the low level of education, and mosques' lack of financial resources and competent imams also impeded Islamic activism. Faced with all these difficulties, Muslim organizations in Mozambique requested that Muslim countries intervene through diplomatic channels to pressure Frelimo and the government to guarantee religious freedom (Bradlow 1987b). Representatives of the SAIYC were requested to send Islamic literature and audio and video cassettes, as well as to allocate scholarships to train future Islamic leaders, through the intermediary of foreign embassies (Nigerian, Sudanese, Pakistani, and Egyptian) in Maputo (Muslim Youth Association of Mocambique n.d.).[17]

It was only in the 1980s that Frelimo decided to change its religious policy, creating a Department of Religious Affairs to oversee all religious organizations. This reversal made it easier for international institutions to intervene in the organization of Islam in Mozambique. It was in this favorable political context that the SAIYC decided to hold its fifth African conference in Mozambique, organized by the Islamic Council of Mozambique, in order to mark the rupture with its past hostility toward Islam (SAIYC 1987).

The title of this conference, "Islam, Religion for All Times and Places," suggested that it would be a highly politicized event. Portuguese colonization, with its support of Catholic missionary expansion, prohibition of Islamic religious practice, and closure of madrasas, was described as the principal cause of Islam's erasure from the country's public space. The colonial state's hostility toward Islam had effectively continued through the early 1960s. The SAIYC wanted to herald its different projects in Mozambique as an "Islamic comeback" in light of Islam's encounter with Western Christianity during the colonial period. The multifunctional vocation of the SAIYC also permitted it to act as an intermediary between international Islamic institutions—including the Islamic Development Bank—and the Mozambican government, offering the possibility of economic investment in a country which had reformed its policies concerning its Muslim population. In the context of this political mobilization, it would be imprudent to consider the SAIYC as no more than a political tool of the Saudi institutions which funded it. It would be more correct to see here a militant determination on the part of South African Muslims to employ the support of international Islamic organizations to assist Muslims who were in a minority situation and facing political, economic, and social difficulties. This network, of which the SAIYC is a part, can offer solutions to certain national crises that affect Muslims. The organization thus becomes a new agent for diplomacy by serving as a mediator in international relations.

Nevertheless, the politicization of the SAIYC's religious actions depends on the public space that the states of Southern Africa are willing to grant it. In the Mozambican case, the policy of legitimation and pragmatism on which the state embarked in the national and international arenas in the middle of the 1980s served the SAIYC's interests (Schutz 1995; Mwangi 2002). Mozambique, which had been marked in the past by its support for liberation struggles in Rhodesia/Zimbabwe and South Africa, was now constrained to negotiate with its South African neighbor in order to emerge from its political and economic crisis. Still, the changes in foreign policy that followed the signing of the Nkomati Agreements in 1984 (which required, among other measures, the restriction of the activities of the African National Congress [ANC] on Mozambican soil) did not signal the abandonment of the policy of denouncing the South African state and its policies of destabilization within the region. The participation of members of the Mozambican government in the SAIYC conferences can thus be explained by both their rallying to a policy of cooperation with different international actors and their determination to control the transnational activities of Muslims on their territory. But it is also appropriate to note the attention they accorded international Islamic institutions capable of disbursing funds.[18] In becoming a member of the Organization of the Islamic Conference (OIC) in 1994 and of the IDB in the following year, the Mozambican state redoubled its efforts to gain legitimacy in the eyes of its Muslim population, all the while pursuing its foreign policy of cooperation, accompanied from 1990 on with political and economic liberalization (Mwangi 2002).

In this context, favorable to transnational agents, the SAIYC offered a platform denouncing the foreign policy and racism of South Africa. During the Maputo Conference, the minister of justice referred to the "action of destabilization" and claimed that "the aggression which the racist South African regime promotes against the peoples of the Southern African states has intensified." He underscored the need to "consolidate the unity of the Southern African region," of which "the Muslim community is a part."[19] In these words, he referred specifically to the anticommunist rebellion led by Renamo that began in 1979. But it was only in August 1988, during its sixth conference (in Lusaka, Zambia), that the SAIYC explicitly challenged the South African state by inviting the ANC to participate. The ANC and President Kenneth Kaunda addressed the forty-two Muslim delegations, the vast majority of which were from Southern Africa. They encouraged Muslims in the region to foster a democratic government in South Africa (Rohan 1988). With this conference in Lusaka, the process of globalization was unquestionably an important factor in politicizing the activities of the SAIYC. However, the denunciation of authoritarian regimes on the international scene remained a marginal aspect of the SAIYC's transnational activities. Rather, the SAIYC sponsored a debate of an entirely different nature over the humanitarian and development assistance which would, in the years to come, represent a new modality of Islamic solidarity and political action.[20] This construction of a religious and political discourse centered on humanitarian intervention not only continues the actions of the earliest South African Muslim associations but also constitutes the principal contribution of the SAIYC.

In the course of the Maputo Conference of 1987, cooperation on development was officially considered inseparable from the *da'wa* (call to Islam), and resolutions were offered to aid Muslim communities that were victims of poverty, famine, war, or natural catastrophes. However, the SAIYC did not expand its domain of activity in the fields of humanitarian and development assistance; it remained an Islamic organization occupied on one hand with reinforcing ties between Muslims in the region, and on the other with constructing a network of Islamic educational institutions. Other organizations would follow up the SAIYC's efforts at re-Islamization by entering the field of emergency aid in Southern Africa. In effect, with the increasing ties between South African Muslims and the transnational network (largely of Saudi origin), new Muslim agents would begin to participate in the Africanization of Islam by creating Islamic NGOs seeking to assist the neediest Muslim populations.

The Proliferation of South African Islamic NGOs:
A New Category of Islamic Actors

Since the end of the 1980s, and especially since the advent of a democratic South Africa, *da'wa* in the local community has led Indian Muslims to pay attention to the political stakes in the economic and social development of the Black African community. Islamic organizations in South Africa no longer benefit from the relative freedom the SAIYC had enjoyed to set its own goals. The Indian Muslim community is now encouraged by international Islamic institutions to adopt a universal approach to *da'wa* and to no longer neglect African townships.[21] However, attitudes of indifference and sometimes contempt, strongly anchored in individual minds, weigh heavily on relations between Indians and Black Africans. To overcome the various conflicts between Indians and Black Africans, organizations have utilized means offered by transnationalism to fit themselves into this new paradigm of Islamic humanitarianism.

The Africa Muslim Agency

The domain of emergency assistance and humanitarian aid represents a new phase of *da'wa*, and in the 1980s it became a burgeoning field of Islamic action with the creation of Islamic NGOs such as the Africa Muslim Agency (AMA), which has branches in a number of African countries. Its first activities were concentrated in the domain of *da'wa*, particularly in Malawi. The third conference of the SAIYC, organized in that country in 1981, painted an alarming portrait of Malawian Muslims undergoing an identity crisis and associating Islam with illiteracy, slavery, and archaic traditions, and it called for emergency measures. A Kuwaiti doctor, Abdul Rahman Al-Sumait, answered the call and, with a representative of the Kuwaiti-based Islamic Africa Committee, created the Africa Muslim Committee, which would later become the AMA, with its headquarters in Kuwait.

The absence of Islamic organizations in the field of emergency relief impelled the AMA to make Malawi its principal target for re-Islamization. Five years after the SAIYC conference organized in the country, the AMA prided itself on having recovered the religious allegiance of Muslims, who, according to the group, once again constituted the majority of the population: more than 60 percent.[22] The AMA has also developed activities in Mozambique, where, as in Malawi, Muslims encounter problems of a religious and political nature in conducting a movement for re-Islamization. It has developed a sector of activity exclusively devoted to emergency aid, central to the ideology of Islamic NGOs, which is aimed at retarding the progress of Christian missionary organizations in sub-Saharan Africa. Neither the date of the AMA's founding nor its initial project of re-Islamization of the Muslim populations of Malawi and Mozambique is innocuous. Moreover, we can see that, wherever reformist movements have appeared, Islamic humanitarian NGOs have emerged. In the context of globalization, these organizations represent new enterprises of re-Islamization by virtue of their entry into public space and their transnational activities.

The AMA has gained the resources and the capacity to carry on multiple activities in different domains, such as *da'wa*, education, health care, and development aid (which consists of, among other projects, the construction of schools and medical centers and the organization of professional training courses). Its work is not limited to Southern Africa; the NGO is present in thirty-four sub-Saharan African countries. Its transnational network is the product of its strategy for managing charitable activity. According to its papers and reports, a variety of operations were undertaken in Africa in 1998, where 3,288 local people were hired: the AMA constructed 140 orphanages, 162 schools, 1,200 mosques, 840 madrasas, 100 medical dispensaries, 34 hospitals, and 100 centers for training women in handicraft production; and, in addition to that, it dug 2,000 wells, distributed 5.5 million copies of the Qur'an, furnished food aid and clothing, and more. Since the 1980s, Islamic humanitarian NGOs have become the worldwide collectors of funds and the managers of global Muslim solidarity.[23] The panoply of activities under the AMA's aegis illustrates its vision of a reformism which does not neglect any social or economic sector in its strategy of Islamizing and re-Islamizing underprivileged Black African populations.

By virtue of its proximity to international Arab institutions and its strategic role in the conduct of re-Islamization campaigns, the AMA of South Africa centralized activities throughout the Southern African region until the mid-1990s, making official visits to different countries, notably Mozambique. In a comparative perspective, we can ask questions about the relationship between the AMA of Mozambique and the group's headquarters in Kuwait. Unlike those of the South African organization, the leaders of the Kuwaiti branch are not drawn from the local population; most of them are Sudanese immigrants. In addition, the AMA of South Africa does not depend financially on the mother organization in Kuwait, unlike those of other African countries such as Mozambique, where most of the Muslim population is poor.[24] However, don't the Islamic NGOs frequently transform themselves into diplomatic tools to further the foreign policy of certain Arab countries?[25] Dr. Abdul Rahman Al-Sumait, founder of the AMA, insists that the NGO is not underwritten by the Kuwaiti state and that it does not represent Kuwait's political and religious interests in sub-Saharan Africa. The organization's resources primarily derive, he claims, from donations from individual Muslims.[26]

On the strength of its financial resources, the South African AMA was able to dominate the field of Islamic humanitarianism by modernizing its use of the media and its collection of donations. The marketing of charity in South Africa relies notably on the distribution of brochures, that is, pamphlets which exhort Muslims to support humanitarian actions that benefit "their brothers and sisters in Islam." The AMA deploys an Islamic argumentation in its mailing campaign, using quotations from the Qur'an and from hadiths on the occasion of Ramadan, followed by the holiday of *al-Fitr*, which concludes the month of fasting, and that of *al-Adha*, the feast of sacrifice, which lasts three to four days, during the period of pilgrimage to Mecca. Funds are collected during these holidays, during which Islamic organizations and NGOs energetically urge Muslims to participate in Muslim solidarity. The AMA uses appeals similar to those of a large number of Islamic NGOs. During Ramadan, it asks Muslims to contribute to the financing of the *iftar* (the meal which breaks the fast), on the basis of a hadith that affirms that those who contribute to the *iftar* will receive the same divine reward as those who fast. A mailing reinforces the message, asking, "Would you like to double your fast during Ramadan?" The mailings sent out by the AMA of South Africa include a bank address for contributing *zakat* and *sadaqa* funds, with the option of paying in installments. The alarmist tone used in appeals for contributions exercises a moral pressure on Muslims, who are, according to the AMA, under a religious obligation to come to the aid of needy Muslim populations, especially those at risk of becoming the victims of Christian proselytization. In a brochure, the AMA describes the situation of Black Africa as critical: "We treat each contribution and donation on the part of our donors as urgent." The NGOs and Islamic associations emphasize that *zakat*, one of the pillars of Islam, has a central place in community organization, and most of them forcefully remind Muslims of this religious obligation.

Finally, they more and more often make use of modern marketing techniques, such as text-messaging campaigns, telethons, websites that can receive online contributions, and advertisements in the Muslim press and the mass media, and they do not hesitate to employ sacred texts or promises of paradise. The South African AMA (unlike the Mozambican) is self-financed, having developed its own system to collect the donations that fund its activities.[27]

Transnational NGOs, Local NGOs: The Stakes of Development Aid in Postapartheid South Africa

For the past few years, transnational NGOs such as the AMA have had difficulties with the image of their activities presented in the media, as they are at the center of ethnic conflicts dividing the South African Muslim community. Despite their important role in the emergence of the Islamic humanitarian field, transnational NGOs have not managed to adapt to the challenges of democratization in South Africa. The public image of the AMA suffers as a result of numerous accusations from Black African Muslims and Somali immigrants who accuse the humanitarian organization of unfairly distributing aid because its ethnic Indian leadership is racist (Vahed and Jeppie 2004). These conflicts between Black Africans and Indian Muslims are an important obstacle to the nationalization of the Islamic aid associations, whose disenchanted leaders most often prefer to divert their efforts toward international aid organizations.[28]

On the other hand, locally based Islamic NGOs are more able to integrate pluralism and openness toward the social environment. In addition, organizations strongly anchored in the local social fabric seem to better manage the transition to professionalism. Study of Islamic NGOs in the Cape, such as the Mustadafin Foundation and the Tuan Yusuf Center, shows that their humanitarian activities express new forms of Muslim citizenship in a context of political and economic liberalization. Development has become a new terrain for action, and this new generation of Islamic NGOs considers the universality of aid a norm. In effect, as one of the leaders of the Mustadafin Foundation says, "Our various projects like pre-school, adult education, feeding scheme, disaster programmes, madressas and training of business initiatives has grown beyond our own expectation. . . . feeding was done to the overall community irrespective of the religion or culture" (Johnstone-Adams n.d.). The process of democratization certainly influenced the emergence of these religious actors concerned with linking their Islamic identity to their identity as citizens. The people I interviewed considered the "repertoires" of Muslim citizenship, including aid to the needy and to underprivileged social groups, the primary motives for joining these humanitarian organizations.

The Mustadafin Foundation and the Tuan Yusuf Center are particularly interesting and distinctive because they were created by women concerned with projecting a modern image of Islamic activism.[29] The reconfiguration of Islamic charity involves important changes, notably the activism of Muslim women belonging to both the Indian and Malay communities. Created in 1986, the Mustadafin Foundation strongly insists on bettering the condition of women who, according to its leader, are the first to suffer from poverty in the province of the Western Cape; at the same time, she challenges the religious monopoly of men in Islamic institutions.[30] The universality with which this NGO distributes aid to underprivileged populations has buttressed its popularity not only with the Muslim community but also throughout Cape Town. The Mustadafin Foundation has received donations from large companies such as Woolworths and BP (British Petroleum), and the Canadian government has subsidized its construction of a primary school. It is also part of a national network of women's associations, which enabled its director to testify before a parliamentary commission investigating the condition of women and domestic violence in South Africa. We can see that the Mustadafin Foundation operates simultaneously at three levels: identity, economy, and politics.

As mentioned earlier, the Tuan Yusuf Center has the distinction of having been created by a women's organization (the Muslim Women's Federation of Southern Africa Trust), in 2002. Financing from the IDB to the extent of US$200,000 has allowed it to become an NGO with a transnational capacity. Indeed, one of the members of the administrative council has managed to build ties of solidarity with a number of international Islamic organizations (Libyan, Saudi, etc.). The recent recruitment of professional volunteers, including businesspeople, has fostered the Center's modernization, and it has reorganized its activities and the presentation of its Islamic "ethic." The new members of the NGO would like, among other things, to give a new professional dimension to Islamic charity by freeing it from reliance on foreign aid. The production and sale of consumer goods—from a bakery, for example—are aimed at generating funds needed for the proper functioning of a development organization. Subsidies from the Ministry of Labor have allowed the Center, which already possessed a kitchen, to hire a restaurant professional to train adults. This innovative enterprise has permitted poor Black African women to receive the training they need to find work.

Even if it is difficult to measure the efficacy of these development activities, it seems to be easier for small organizations, such as the Tuan Yusuf Center, to professionalize. In contrast, observers both in South Africa and in Mozambique stressed the AMA's low level of professionalism and its lack of goals for development aid. Emergency aid seems to be its main activity, but many believe that the future of Islamic NGOs needs to be built on the accomplishment of economic and social projects. This requires technical competence, which the agents of Islamic humanitarianism need in order to clarify their financial objectives, but also greater cooperation with different social and economic partners.[31] In its concern to expand its partnerships in civil society, the Tuan Yusuf Center, for example, hosts the People's Empowerment Network (PEN), which includes psychologists and other social workers who commit to spending Saturdays helping people with family, marital, and psychological problems.

In Mozambique, Islamic organizations have not been able to mount many concerted actions. In the fields of AIDS prevention and the protection of children, the AMA has not had sufficient resources to care for orphans in its custody, some of whom carry HIV. A report commissioned by the World Conference for Religion and Peace (WCRP) in conjunction with UNICEF stresses its effort to establish orphanages but deplores the absence of prevention and health education programs, which is due to its principal members' lack of training (WCRP 2003). Because of their financial and material resources, transnational Islamic NGOs in both South Africa and Mozambique are encouraged to play an essential role in development aid and in the domain of health. In order to accomplish this, they need to successfully modernize their infrastructure and professionalize (Siméant 2001).

The professional activities and the universality of aid distribution exemplified by the Tuan Yusuf Center and the Mustadafin Foundation remain anchored in Islam, but the organizations do not legitimize their activities in the humanitarian and development sectors exclusively through religious rhetoric. The government's policy of affirmative action has certainly oriented the citizenship activities of Muslim organizations.[32] The members of the Tuan Yusuf Center, for the most part of Indian origin, have often acknowledged that they belong to a privileged community and that their national identity, reinforced by their religious values, points the way to a universal humanitarianism. This field of solidarity represents for many of them the expression of South African citizenship and the proof of their commitment to developing the country through the aid which they bring to the most underprivileged populations, irrespective of their ethnic or religious identities. This openness to pluralism is also expressed by religious tolerance, a new ideal to which the members of the Tuan Yusuf Center are much attached. For example, Muslim women who do not wear the veil are free to work within the organization.

Even if local and transnational Islamic NGOs define and treat poverty differently, they share a commitment to close cooperation with the government. The Mustadafin Foundation and the Tuan Yusuf Center have, for example, privileged the growing nationalization of their citizenship movement. In an ideal position to establish a working relationship with the state, associations—notably NGOs—are encouraged to increasingly commit themselves to a policy of "Black empowerment" and in the process to accept the norms of universal humanitarianism. On the other hand, Islamic transnationalism represents a considerable political resource for the postapartheid government, which is anxious to intervene throughout the continent to alleviate political conflicts or the effects of natural catastrophes. In August 2004, for example, the Ministry of Foreign Affairs financed the transportation of forty tons of food and medicine collected by the AMA for the region of Darfur in Sudan. A Ministry official justified the humanitarian action of the South African government in Sudan:

> The South African government is concerned about the plight of the people in Darfur and is trying to do all it can to alleviate their suffering. This trip is part of the support that the government is giving civil society organisations, like the AMA, to enable them to support the people of Darfur. This is part of an African attempt to assist and resolve issues in Africa. That's the essential message. (Voice of the Cape 2004)

In its practice of humanitarian *da'wa*, the AMA has learned to come to terms with the state, which remains a central actor in international relations. The state, in turn, is strengthened by this humanitarian cooperation, which permits it not only to play a powerful role in the region and to control the transnational Islamic flows initiated by South African Muslims[33] but also to confer legitimacy to the citizenship practices of these Islamic NGOs in the public sphere. The state thus plays an essential but ambivalent role in the actual configuration of Islamic humanitarianism in South Africa.[34]

The study of the multiple forms of Islamic humanitarianism represented by both types of NGOs, local and transnational, has allowed me to trace the evolution of contemporary aid. The development of the SAIYC, and later of the AMA, show that *da'wa* becomes progressively multifunctional, because the political integration of Islam, aid to the most needy, and development projects require a diversification of activities on the African continent. Ever since the period of democratic transition, the question of humanitarianism and development has been central to the religious activities of South African Muslims.[35] In particular, it requires Islamic organizations to be professionally managed, and most of them—like the Mustadafin Foundation and the Tuan Yusuf Center—become NGOs in order to appear as credible actors in the national and international arenas. This professionalization of NGOs induces religious changes, notably the growing activism of Muslim women, but also political changes, such as the close collaboration with the state on national development projects as well as the distribution of emergency aid abroad. The influence of the postapartheid government thus remains inescapable, imposing constraints on groups and individuals engaged in a field as specific as that of Islamic humanitarianism.

Notes

1. South African Muslims constitute less than 2 percent of the total population. Islam in South Africa includes four major groups: the Cape colored community and Muslims from the Indian subcontinent constitute the overwhelming majority of South African Muslims, but there are also Black Africans, and, finally, Muslims of European origin.

2. In postapartheid South Africa, Natal has become Kwazulu-Natal, and the majority of Indian immigration is concentrated there.

3. The MYM, founded in Durban in 1970, was at the avant-garde of the movement for the re-Islamization of all South Africa. The ideology of this Islamic movement essentially stressed the maintenance of Islamic ties within the Muslim community in order to preserve the social reproduction of Islamic identity. On the Muslim Youth Movement, see Tayob 1995.

4. The Call of Islam and the MYM split ranks because of the Call's alliance with the new antiapartheid front in 1983, represented by the United Democratic Front (UDF).

5. "Report on Afro Islamic Conference," Mauritania, May 3–5, 1976, unattributed typescript in the SAIYC archives, Durban. I thank E. Jadwat, coordinator of the SAIYC, for access to the archives.

6. This Muslim population is concentrated in Malawi, Mozambique, South Africa, Zimbabwe, and Zambia.

7. One of the coordinators of the SAIYC considered the situation of Muslims in the region critical: "We had very little knowledge about the condition of Muslims in the region and, whilst we researched the possibility of setting up a coordinating body, we were shocked to observe how serious the predicament was. Two major problems confronted us. Firstly, that

Muslims, while clinging tenaciously to their Islam, did so more out of instinct than intellect. The successive years of neglect of basic Islamic teaching meant that much of their Islam was rooted in superstition and myth. Added to this was the second problem of isolation. Not only were Muslims isolated from the mainstream of the ummah but also from other Muslims in the region. In many parts of the sub-continent it was as if Muslims were unaware of the existence of a world community of Muslims" (Bradlow 1987c, 59).

8. Report of the First Southern Africa Islamic Conference, Gaborone, Botswana, June 3–5, 1977, unattributed copy in the SAIYC archives, Durban; see also "Minutes of the First Southern Africa Islamic Conference Held at the Conference Hall, Holiday Inn, Gaborone, Botswana, Jumada Al-Akhirah 15–17, 1397/June 3–5, 1977."

9. As A. Colonomos stresses, the individuals at the center of these organizations "are the hub of the network which gives meaning to its functionality and its future" (Colonomos 1995, 169).

10. In the same vein, O. Roy notes that "the supranational institutions are networks of finance and diffusion rather than of command and organization" (Roy 1992, 144).

11. The IDB, based in Jeddah, was founded in 1974 by the Organization of the Islamic Conference, in the wake of the quadrupling of the price of oil.

12. Report of the secretary general of the IIFSO, presented at the fourth conference, Zimbabwe, May 5–9, 1983, unattributed copy in the SAIYC archives, Durban.

13. Fourth Southern Africa Islamic Youth Conference, Al-Birr (Harare), Muslim Youth League of Zimbabwe, September 1983; a brochure reproducing the conference program and containing extracts of presentations is in the SAIYC archives, Durban.

14. The Dar al-Ifta concentrates its financial efforts particularly on the spreading of Wahhabism.

15. The leaders express a certain optimism concerning projects accomplished in spite of the SAIYC's limited budget, which amounts to US$25,000 per year. Report presented at the fifth conference of the SAIYC, probably by E. Jadwat, Maputo, 1987, SAIYC archives, Durban.

16. One may wonder about the reasons for the WAMY's withdrawal. Perhaps it was a result of the changes of the 1990s, when connections between different Islamic organizations, along with Saudi financial support, became increasingly scarce (Kepel 2000).

17. See also "Memorandum on Mozambique, Durban, March 29, 1984," unattributed typescript in the SAIYC archives, Durban.

18. Beginning in 1974, Saudi Arabia developed its cooperation with sub-Saharan Africa. African countries which had severed relations with Israel hoped to benefit from financial aid from the oil monarchies and to forge closer ties with the Arab world. But African countries were not at the level they had hoped for. Rather, religious and cultural exchanges multiplied through the medium of different transnational networks put in place by Saudi Islamic organizations (Otayek 2000).

19. "Speech by His Excellency the Minister of Justice of the People's Republic of Mozambique," Maputo, January 8, 1987, in the SAIYC archives, Durban.

20. The action of charitable associations is political in that it is relative to the community, to the public at large. As Badie and Smouts underscore (1995, 61), such associations also have the capacity "to occupy empty social spaces."

21. This emphasis on the equality of opportunities for Muslims, regardless of their ethnic affiliation, masked another concern of Islamic NGOs. International actors from the Gulf states perceived the situation of Indian Muslims as precarious because of tensions with Black Africans, inherited from the past. Since 1991, Indians have not been considered powerful partners. They must, as a result, become the new agents of the Islamization and re-Islamization of Black African populations at both the national and regional levels.

22. Cheick Sa'ad, a member of the AMA, commented on this reversal of Islam's situation in Malawi: "Malawi exemplifies what a little money can do to change a nation's destiny" (Bradlow 1987a, 7). However, the estimate of Malawi's Muslim population proposed by the AMA does not correspond to reality. According to other counts, Muslims constituted between 10 and 20 percent of the population in the years 1980–90 (Mumisa 2002).

23. Since the events of September 11, 2001, the study of Islamic NGOs has involved questions about their financing. Islamic NGOs seem to have four sources of income: states and large, pan-Islamic organizations (such as the Organization of the Islamic Conference and the Muslim World League); Islamic banks; their own marketing of their charitable activities to the larger Muslim public; and, more shadowy, networks within an alleged "Islamist international."

24. In South Africa, the principal Muslim donors to Islamic organizations are members of the important merchant community.

25. A.-R. Ghandour retorts that this remark could also apply to certain Western NGOs, "political instruments of the institutions that finance them" (Ghandour 2002, 20).

26. The international prominence the Kuwaiti NGO achieved by expanding its activities on the African continent in less than twenty years earned Al-Sumait the King Faisal Prize.

27. For the Mozambican AMA, institutions are the most important source of funds. Interviews with the leader of the AMA of South Africa, Johannesburg, August 14, 1999, and with the national director of the AMA of Mozambique, Maputo, September 27, 2004.

28. Hirschman emphasizes the importance of such disenchantment in his analysis of militancy: "disappointment implies a prior erroneous choice or decision, and my analysis, in a sense, follows the traces of a succession of grave errors, without any certainty about the possibility of achieving freedom from disappointment" (Hirschman 1982, 228).

29. Women's participation in the domain of charitable assistance is increasing throughout the tertiary sector of the country. More and more women hold positions of responsibility, even if religious NGOs continue to be headed by men (Swilling and Russell 2002).

30. According to the leader of the Mustadafin Foundation, its project for the next five years is to reinforce the Islamic identity of women by encouraging them to enroll in madrasas to improve their education and knowledge of Islam. Interview, September 2, 2004, Cape Town.

31. Interview with a former member of the Mozambican AMA, now a leader in the World Conference for Religion and Peace (WCRP), Maputo, October 1, 2005.

32. The state, through the voice of its minister of social development, has defined action in the tertiary sector: "The government's second expectation is that NGOs will assist in expanding access to social and economic services that create jobs and eradicate poverty among the poorest of the poor. This requires cost effective and sustainable service delivery" (Swilling and Russell 2002, 4–5). Muslim politicians also influence the humanitarian activities of South African Muslims. Ebrahim Rasool, prime minister of the Province of the Western Cape, has encouraged charitable organizations to assist in development.

33. Globalization has favored the growing intervention of nonstate actors such as churches, NGOs, and multinationals in the foreign policy of African countries (Adar and Ajulu 2002).

34. M. Barthélemy stresses the ambivalent nature of the state. According to her, "One cannot limit oneself to noting that it instrumentalizes and controls associations. Its role as guarantor of equal treatment of its citizens and its institutions needs to be reaffirmed and its universal functions defended" (Barthélemy 2000, 266).

35. We see the same phenomenon in Mozambique, where Islamic NGOs establish programs of emergency aid and economic development.

References

Adar, K. G., and R. Ajulu, eds. 2002. *Globalization and emerging trends in African states' foreign policy-making process: A comparative perspective of Southern Africa*. Aldershot: Ashgate.

Badie, B., and M.-C. Smouts. 1995. *Le retournement du monde: Sociologie de la scène internationale*. 2nd ed. Paris: Presses de la FNSP-Dalloz.

Barthélemy, M. 2000. *Associations: Un nouvel âge de la participation?* Paris: Presses de Sciences Po.

Bradlow, A. 1987a. Islam in Mocambique: A struggle for survival. *Al-Qalam* (Durban), January 6–7, pp. 6–7.

———. 1987b. Islam under Frelimo. *Muslim Views* (Cape Town), March.

———. 1987c. Young Muslims of southern Africa reassert themselves. *Islamic World Review*, April, pp. 58–60.

Colonomos, A. 1995. Sociologie et science politique: Les réseaux, théories et objets d'études. *Revue française de science politique* 45 (1): 165–78.

Ghandour, A.-R. 2002. *Jihad humanitaire: Enquête sur les ONG islamiques.* Paris: Flammarion.

Hirschman, A. 1982. *Bonheur privé, action publique.* Paris: Fayard.

Johnstone-Adams, G. n.d. Directors report. In *Mustadafin Foundation*, a brochure published by the Foundation. Also available at http://www.mustadafin.com/html/director.html (accessed June 8, 2006).

Kepel, G. 2000. *Jihad, expansion et déclin de l'islamisme.* Paris: Gallimard.

Mumisa, M. 2002. Islam and proselytism in South Africa and Malawi. *Journal of Muslim Minority Affairs* 22 (2): 275–98.

Muslim Youth Association of Mocambique, Muslims Association of Mocambique (MYM). n.d. *Situation of the Muslims in Northern Mocambique.* Nacala.

Mwangi, O. G. 2002. Mozambique's foreign policy: From ideological conflict to pragmatic cooperation. In *Globalization and emerging trends in African states' foreign policy-making process: A comparative perspective of Southern Africa*, ed. K. G. Adar and R. Ajulu, 117–34. Aldershot: Ashgate:.

Otayek, R. 2000. *Identité et démocratie dans un monde global.* Paris: Presses de Sciences Po.

Rohan, R. 1988. Kaunda, ANC urge Muslims to help shape new SA. *Post* (Durban), August 24.

Roy, O. 1992. *L'échec de l'Islam politique.* Paris: Seuil.

SAIYC (Southern Africa Islamic Youth Conference). 1987. *The Proceedings of the Fifth WAMY-Southern Africa Islamic Youth Conference*, Maputo, January 8–12.

Schutz, B. 1995. The heritage of revolution and the struggle for governmental legitimacy in Mozambique. In *Collapsed states: The disintegration and restoration of legitimate authority*, ed. I. W. Zartman, 109–24. Boulder: L. Rienner.

Siméant, J. 2001. Urgence et développement, professionnalisation et militantisme dans l'humanitaire. *Mots: Les langages du politique* 65: 28–49.

Swilling, M., and B. Russell. 2002. *The size and scope of the non-profit sector in South Africa.* Durban: Centre for Civil Society, University of Natal.

Tayob, A. 1995. *Islamic resurgence in South Africa: The Muslim youth movement.* Cape Town: University of Cape Town Press.

Vahed, G., and S. Jeppie. 2004. Multiple communities: Muslims in post-apartheid South Africa. In *State of the nation 2: 2004–2005*, ed. J. Daniel, R. Southall, and J. Lutchman, 252–86. Pretoria: HSRC.

Voice of the Cape. 2004. Food not the problem in Darfur. Article posted on the radio station's website, http://www.vocfm.com, on August 10.

WCRP (World Conference for Religion and Peace). 2003. *Documentation Study on the Responses of Faith Based Organisations to Orphans and Other Vulnerable Children in Mozambique.* Maputo: WCRP-UNICEF.

Part II
The Question of the State

CHAPTER 6

MUSLIM REFORMISTS AND THE STATE IN BENIN

Denise Brégand

With the promulgation of its constitution in December 1990, Benin became a secular republic guaranteeing religious freedom and freedom of association and recognizing religious values while stipulating that no religious party may field candidates in elections.

The establishment of a new political regime, the outcome of a national conference held in February 1990 under the presidency of Monseigneur de Souza, then archbishop of Cotonou, was followed by a proliferation of religious movements, most of them Christian, and by a greater visibility of religion even in the political sphere: Nicéphore Soglo, elected president in 1991, turned toward vodou and established a holiday celebrating traditional cults, and, in the presidential elections of 1996, Mathieu Kérékou ran as a new man; he converted to Pentecostalism and never appeared in public without his Bible (Strandsberg 2000; Mayrargue 2004). Religious and political discourses were intermingled: "God loves Benin," as demonstrated by the fact that he gave it democracy and foreign aid (Mayrargue 2002).

If we compare the religious situation in Benin to that in other West African countries, in particular to the one in neighboring Nigeria, it appears to be a model of good religious coexistence, and Christians, Muslims, and adherents of traditional religions are often found in the same family. However, in the context of religious revival following the end of the revolutionary regime, certain leaders who perceived the risks of religious radicalization established, as early as the 1990 conference, an interreligious dialogue[1] which continued throughout the early years of the decade in lectures and publications.[2] Few Muslims participated in the national conference; they had until then emphasized trade and were not very interested in politics. But this situation is changing. Younger people are more involved in political parties and present themselves as candidates in elections.

Islam is gaining ground throughout the country. In the 1992 census, it was the declared religion of 20.6 percent of the population; that figure had increased to 24.4 percent in 2002.[3] Muslims are the majority in the north of Benin, constituting as much as 94.3 percent of the population of Malanville; they remain a minority in the south, where they are 14.2 percent of the population of Cotonou and 25.1 percent of that of Porto Novo, the two principal towns.

Introduced largely by traders, most of them affiliated with Sufi orders (the Tijaniyya and, more recently, its Niassène branch, associated with the Senegalese shaykh Ibrahima Niasse, have supplanted the Qadiriyya, which is nevertheless still active), Islam has been reinterpreted and reappropriated. It has experienced considerable growth in the second half of the twentieth century and into the twenty-first century because of numerous conversions. This "traditionalist" Islam, so labeled because it is anchored in local social practices, is a way of life. It structures time, organizing sociality around the mosque and around ceremonies marking major points in the life cycle: *aqiqa*, the naming ceremony for newborns on the seventh day after birth; marriage; ceremonies held one week, forty days, and three months after a death. It is inseparable from divination and "magic," and the *alfas* (Qur'anic scholars trained in this system), with their talismans and prayers, relieve earthly afflictions.[4] Alongside this "popular" Islam, the Sufi orders developed in intellectual circles and were largely oriented toward mystical quests. Sufism has been renewed by the establishment of two new orders in Benin: the Nimatullahi order, introduced in 1991 by Yacoubou Fassassi, grand master of the order for West Africa; and the Alawiyya order, introduced into Porto Novo in 1990 by al-Hajj Saliou Latoundji, a pharmacist and disciple of Shaykh Bentounès, who lives in France. The members of these two new orders, still few in number, are part of the country's intellectual and social elite.

In Benin, as in other West African countries, this understanding of Islam has been contested since the 1970s by graduates of Arab Islamic universities who, deriving authority exclusively from both the Qur'an and the Sunna, that is, the authoritative practice of the Prophet Muhammad, want to eradicate everything which does not stem from these texts. These *arabisant* graduates are joined by others who have studied in sub-Saharan Africa, in universities in northern Nigeria, Niamey, or Côte d'Ivoire. They receive support from international Islamic nongovernmental organizations (NGOs) which, at the same time as furnishing humanitarian aid, pursue their primary goal, *da'wa*: the call to Islam or propagation of the faith. The principal Islamic NGOs in Benin have their headquarters in Cotonou. These are the Kuwaiti-based Africa Muslim Agency (AMA); the World Organization for Islamic Aid, founded by the Muslim World League (under Saudi influence); the Libyan-based Association mondiale de l'appel à l'Islam (AMAI, World Islamic Call Society); and Al-Muntada al-Islami, a British NGO founded by Muslims of Arab and Asian origin.[5] Islamic NGOs of lesser importance, mostly Saudi and Kuwaiti, operate in the rest of the country. All the NGOs provide humanitarian aid, but their principal goal remains *da'wa*, and their "*da'wa* offices" hire graduates of Arab universities as preachers (on the average forty each in total for the bigger NGOs). They are also intended to spearhead the African policies of the states which finance them (Schulze 1993; Mattes 1993). This is particularly clear in the case of the AMAI (as evidenced in its brochures), in the corridors of its Franco-Arabic school,[6] and in the clinic of the Islamic complex of Cotonou, all of which prominently feature quotations from Muammar al-Qaddafi. In a very difficult social environment, these NGOs offer jobs in the religious field to graduates of Arab universities.

However, although the local Islamic arena is often characterized by tensions between old and new trends, a large number of Muslims are neither members of an order, nor reformists, nor fundamentalists; they are not militant and do not involve themselves in these internal Islamic conflicts.

After presenting the different trends and forms of action of the multifarious reformist and fundamentalist tendencies, I will examine the relationship between these trends and the state.

Islamic Renewal: A Fragmented Reformism

Islam and Modernity

The will to reform Islam, apparent throughout the Muslim world, has some of its roots in the Arabian peninsula with Abd al-Wahhab (1703–92), himself inspired by Ibn Taymiyya (1263–1328) and an advocate of a rigorist model. The term *reformism* designates more precisely the movement which, from the middle of the nineteenth century up to the years 1935–40, confronted Islam with the problematic of modernity, and whose best-known leaders were Jamal al-Din al-Afghani, Muhammad 'Abduh, and Rashid Rida. By *modernity*, they meant the mastery of science and of technological progress, which they deemed necessary to adopt without reservation, accompanied by a return to the religion of the pious ancestors (*al-salaf*). Since then, other thinkers have influenced the evolution of Islamic thinking in a more political direction, among them Mawdudi (1903–79), who founded the Jama'at-i-Islami in the Indian subcontinent in 1941, and Hasan al-Banna (1906–49), who founded the Muslim Brotherhood in Egypt in 1929, as well as Sayyid Qutb (1906–66) in the same movement. All these men continue to influence contemporary Muslims. In Benin, however, no one refers to these predecessors, nor to the "contemporary thinkers in Islam" (Benzine 2004), and the term *reformism* (rejected by the movement's proponents, who prefer *renewal* or *awakening*) is here pragmatic, aiming to purge Islam of its local adaptations (ceremonies, magical practices) and to return to the founding texts, the Qur'an and hadith. Different interpretations and meanings are given to the concept of modernity; here we find a dispersed reformism, ranging from a reading which situates texts in their historical contexts to a fundamentalist version which, following a literal interpretation, calls for a return to fundamental principles and wants to impose its own norms.

In any case, the relationship between Islam and modernity is at the heart of the question. Everything depends on what one classifies as modernity, and this classification changes from period to period. Reflecting on modernity within reformism, Olivier Roy states, "One can define modernity in terms of values (those of democracy). Or else one can define modernity in the sense of the individual's separation from inherited identities and affiliations and in terms of the affirmation of the subject" (Roy 2004). As Roy emphasizes, this definition encompasses values within the sociopolitical domain as well as those pertaining to the individual. By individualizing their religious engagement, everyone is freed from their primordial membership in family and village (Marie 1997); however, not everyone accepts the values of Western democracy, whose model has been transplanted to Benin, and the fundamentalists are distinguished by their radical critique of the West, of its values and its politics.

Although it is easy to delineate the extremes within this broad "renewal" movement, the situation is complex, and reformism encompasses a spectrum ranging from a liberal reformism which is open to the world's changes to the most normative fundamentalism. Moreover, there exists an indigenous reformism, advocated by men and women who are often educated and who have occupied important positions in government or private enterprise, and who categorically refuse the notion of reformism. Thus the anthropologist going to interview a supposedly "traditionalist" Muslim may find herself face to face with an interlocutor who has not studied in an Islamic university but who seeks answers to today's questions in the Qur'an; a pragmatist, he or she is involved in associations to develop Qur'anic instruction among Muslims and to promote a return to a more orthodox practice, all the while maintaining ties with the imams. These are the individuals who make "bridges" (Otayek 1993, 8) possible between reformism and Sufi orders, though such bridges still remain exceptional.

For the purposes of this chapter, I will call "reformists" those who work to reform Islam, while continuing to envisage it within its present context, and who see no contradiction between their religion and the political and social changes occurring in Benin. They are to be distinguished from "fundamentalists." Fundamentalism consists in wanting to adhere more closely to religious texts understood literally and, with a mythic understanding of the early period of Islam, wanting to reestablish its practices, such as by imitating the clothing of the Prophet Muhammad and going bearded as he did. The fundamentalists do not reject modernity but consider that it is already contained in the Qur'an. They accept scientific and technical progress but oppose the idea that this progress should change society or lifestyles. As one of them explains,

> is it seen in the Western manner, encouraging liberty and libertinism? According to me, modernity is what allows man to stay up to par, to accept scientific discoveries and adapt them to his Islam. If this is modernity, it is already within Islam. The first sura is an incitement to research. The Qur'an speaks of biology, of physics, of medicine. You cannot be a Muslim and avoid modernity, except that a Muslim places limits on himself.[7]

One example illustrates the difference in ways of understanding contemporary problems: one of the few people I interviewed who declared himself a "reformist," a graduate of al-Azhar who taught in a Franco-Arabic school in Porto Novo, participated in awareness days organized by UNAIDS and discussed AIDS prevention in his sermons, considering that attacking this problem is a part of reform. On the other hand, a fundamentalist affirmed that prevention can "only encourage debauchery" and that, in countries where sharia is applied, there is no AIDS problem.

A Heterogeneous Fundamentalist Tendency

Alongside two highly structured and easily identifiable groups, the Tablighi Jama'at and the Ahmadiyya, there is also a diffuse, unorganized movement which defines itself as Sunni and presents every degree of dogmatism and rigor.

The Tablighi Jama'at, a missionary organization founded near Delhi in 1927 by the scholar Mawlana Muhammad Ilyas, has as its goal the propagation of the faith and the improvement of Muslim belief and practice (Gaborieau 1998). It has spread throughout the world since 1947, reaching Benin in 1986 from Nigeria and developing primarily in the south. Its grand assembly in Glodjigbe, on the outskirts of Cotonou, attracted seven hundred people over three days in February 2005. There are perhaps a thousand *tablighis* in Benin. In accordance with their methods of outreach, they travel in groups, preach, and sleep in the mosques. Although they belong to a transnational movement, they receive no money; they live in poverty, travel mostly on foot, and must earn a living while remaining entirely at the movement's disposition, since belonging to the Tablighi Jama'at requires total commitment. Very mobile, they do not hesitate to leave Benin to preach in neighboring countries, and in turn they host Pakistani, Nigerian, and Ghanaian missionaries. They attempt to re-create the model of the early Muslim community, the golden age, the age of the Prophet, and they follow a very strict code of daily behavior. They live deeply concerned with purity, in fear of hell, and the women among them are always entirely veiled in black.

Another transnational proselytizing movement, the Ahmadiyya, was founded in India at Qadian, where Mirza Ghulam Ahmad (1838–1908), "the promised Messiah and Mahdi," was born; in 1882, he declared himself a reformer chosen by God (Friedman 1989). He called on Muslims to renounce holy war and to devote themselves to peaceful proselytism. He encouraged missionary activity throughout the British Empire and beyond, a program which would be realized by his followers. Jihad in the sense of holy war was replaced by *da'wa* or the call to Islam (Gaborieau 2000).

The Ahmadiyya movement arrived in East and West Africa in the first quarter of the twentieth century (Ajayi and Crowder 1988). It was introduced into Benin in the 1960s, and, after having been evicted under the revolutionary regime, was allowed to reopen its missions in the context of democratic revival. The movement's spiritual and temporal leader, the amir, lives at its headquarters in Porto Novo and sends missionaries into other provinces. Many other Muslims do not recognize the Ahmadis as fellow Muslims, and even prohibit them from making the pilgrimage to Mecca. An ambivalent movement, the Ahmadiyya can be described as fundamentalist in that its members refer strictly to the Qur'an and to the teachings of Mirza Ghulam Ahmad; on the other hand they call for adaptation to the world, social success, and interfaith dialogue, and they accord women an important role. In a sermon for the Feast of the Sacrifice ('Id al-Adha or Tabaski) in February 2002, the amir condemned the attacks of September 11 and all violence in the name of Islam, insisting on an understanding of "greater *jihad*," a struggle within oneself. The Ahmadiyya has an excellent rapport with the current regime, and its November 2004 publication *Le message* told followers, "Every Ahmadi citizen is free in his political allegiance, but after the electoral contest, he should support the state and the government in power."

Fundamentalists with Wahhabist leanings do not distinguish themselves from other Muslims by setting up their own associations, but rather they exercise a diffuse influence from where they happen to be situated, their ambition being to promote the "awakening" of all Muslims. Those with religious diplomas try to obtain positions as imams in order to lead the Muslim community. "Traditionalist" Muslims and non-Muslims call them "Wahhabis," but they do not define themselves in terms of the founders of that ideology, such as Ibn Taymiyya and Abd al-Wahhab; rather, they strictly observe rules which they have brought back from universities in Medina or

Kuwait and insist on holding as closely as possible to the texts—that is to say, to their own reading of them. Their most influential ideologue is certainly Abubakar Gumi (1922–92; Loimeier 1997, 2003), who in Nigeria in 1978 supported the founding of the radical movement 'Yan Izala (Jama'at Izalat al-Bid'a wa Iqamat al-Sunna, Society for the Removal of Innovation and Reinstatement of Tradition [i.e., the Sunna]), whose ideology and activities contributed to the application of sharia criminal law in the states of northern Nigeria. The 'Yan Izala movement of Malanville, a frontier town and international marketplace, is directly overseen by the Nigerian organization. It was only able to obtain control of one mosque after bitter local conflicts (Abdullaye 2003). Other than 'Yan Izala, very small groups calling themselves Ahl al-Sunna or "people of the Sunna," mostly in Porto Novo and Cotonou, represent the most radical wing of this Wahhabist tendency. Finally, there is a broad range of fundamentalisms circulating within the networks of local mosques, Qur'anic and Franco-Arabic schools, and international Islamic NGOs.

Islam's Greatest Visibility in the Public Sphere

Fundamentalism is highly visible in the public sphere, giving non-Muslims an exaggerated impression of its importance. Very attached to form, fundamentalists wear a *jellaba*, a long white tunic, over calf-length pants; some wear turbans; and all sport beards trimmed to a "regulation length." They seem to enforce this dress code; anyone seeking entry into the circles that control religious employment needs to observe it. Women must veil themselves from head to toe in black. Wearing the *hijab*, the headscarf of women student members of the Association culturelle des étudiants et élèves musulmans du Bénin (ACEEMUB, Cultural Association of Muslim Students of Benin), is more a sign of protest.

Islam has achieved greater visibility both in towns and in rural areas. Financed by NGOs, "Kuwait mosques" have proliferated throughout Benin; the urban religious landscape has changed with the construction of Islamic complexes that include a mosque, a clinic, a Qur'anic school, and sometimes an orphanage. The fundamentalists have opened libraries to attract further public attention. Over the past decade, they have conquered public space in the city of Djougou in a particularly spectacular manner (Brégand 1999). The concern for madrasa or Franco-Arabic education was part of the twentieth-century reform movement. All reformists and fundamentalists insist on the necessity of educating children in religion and developing teaching in French. School has become a major instrument of *da'wa*.

In the early 1990s, Arabic-language instruction accompanied Islamization and was heralded as an "instrument of identity formation and a language of politics" (Otayek 1993, 11). In Benin nowadays, although learning Arabic to understand the Qur'an is still considered a necessity, campaigns of proselytism are conducted in French, the language into which the Qur'ans distributed by NGOs are translated. This is certainly one of the reasons for the spectacular success of *da'wa*. The NGOs, and also small individual entrepreneurs, open schools, encouraged by the strong demand for education. Since the liberalization of the economy, the public schools' insufficient capacity and poor reputation have encouraged the multiplication of private schools which welcome students from all social backgrounds; even parents with modest incomes (for example, domestic servants and drivers of motorcycle taxis) send their children to private schools, because in Benin, at least in towns, education is highly valued. The educational sector has experienced the same development as the health sector: the withdrawal of the state has left room for private initiatives, and Muslim establishments, new to this market, make up for the state's inadequacies. There is thus a place for new Franco-Arabic schools, which in addition provide jobs for graduates of Islamic universities. The growing success of Franco-Arabic schooling reflects the belief that it guarantees Muslim morality, whereas public or Christian schools presumably lead students away from their faith.

In this context, fundamentalists attempt to control specific spaces, a mosque or a school, thus creating the nuclei of a network within which they circulate to teach or to preach. If there exists an international flow of capital (NGO financing through petrodollars) and of preachers, it is through daily local work that they slowly gain an audience. The local trumps the global; certain graduates, who on their return harshly contested the imams in place, have now set themselves up as religious entrepreneurs, reinserting themselves into their society as soon as they accept the position of imam in an important mosque.[8]

One must be careful not to lump all reformists together. Reformism is a plural phenomenon in the making whose diversity is expressed by different attitudes and political positions held by a variety of actors. If, as Muslims, all consider themselves part of the *umma* and share the will to return to a more orthodox Islam, their discourse about the world, their assessment of political changes in Benin over the past fifteen years, and their projections for the future do not allow any generalizations. All have their discourses on politics, but the content of these discourses and the concrete forms of action they promote vary considerably.

Reformists, Politics, and the State: "The Situation Is under Control"

The Fundamentalists: "Regenerating Society to Regenerate Public Life"

With the exception of the members of 'Yan Izala, the fundamentalists are not Islamists, those who use Islam for political ends: conscious of being a Muslim minority, especially in the cities along the coast, they do not aim at acquiring power in the name of Islam. They belong to the category which Olivier Roy calls "neofundamentalist," defined by a very strict and literal vision of the Qur'anic message and by an anti-Western stance (Roy 2002).

Throughout the world, anyone who owns a satellite dish can receive foreign television broadcasts. In Benin, all the people I spoke with were well informed: they regularly follow news broadcasts on francophone networks and receive Arabic stations. As Internet users, they find arguments to support their positions on Islamic and Islamist websites. Although one need not be a fundamentalist to criticize the global order, the fundamentalists distinguish themselves from other Muslims by the virulence of their anti-Western discourse. Like other Beninois, they criticize the World Bank and its structural adjustment programs, but it is in the domain of international relations that they affirm their radicalism. Their critiques are also aimed at the deviant use of scientific progress, the decline of family values, and moral depravity.

In interviews I conducted from January to March 2005, my informants displayed a lively interest in the issues in French news having to do with Islam, denouncing Islamophobia and the law of March 2004 that banned religious insignia in public schools, and vehemently defending Tariq Ramadan, who they felt had been unjustly treated by the media. It is consequently logical that they are not satisfied with a political system patterned after a Western model whose conceptions of democracy and of public liberties they do not share. Like many of their fellow countrymen, they condemn corruption, but they distinguish themselves from their fellows by the solutions they propose for the country's problems.

They consider that the moralization or regeneration of society will lead to the regeneration of public life. They concentrate on proper conduct and morality, and they advocate a flawless social morality. In answer to the question "How do you participate in your country's development?" a member of the Ahl al-Sunna group answered,

> we participate in development in our own way, by regenerating social life, because we think that if we fail to improve society's morals, public life will be immoral. When someone sees that he is already fleeced of his money at the mosque or in church, he will then fleece money from the public coffers. Through *da'wa*, we can purify, we don't have to seize political power. Acquiring power is not contrary to Islam. If you feel you can do something to improve the situation, you have to go for it, because if you think you can do something and don't try, you are sinning. The Prophet was not only a spiritual leader, he was a statesman; he organized society.[9]

In matters of religion, they denounce all forms of corruption and embezzlement, which are far from having been eradicated in Benin (Blondo and Olivier de Sardan 2002). Younger men engage in politics through the religious domain. Even conflicts for control over mosques express the struggle of "juniors" against elders who hold up the transfer of power from one generation to another. Their proposals for change are based on moral rules. They think that the application of sharia will solve all problems and uncritically idealize the states that apply it:

> For us, that is where there is divine law. Here, it is not possible, unless everybody were Muslim. We are in a secular state, but we are inwardly persuaded that with sharia, you can regulate society, because with sharia all children have to go to school, the rights of man must be respected, he who has stolen has infringed on the rights of someone else, and God tells you, "Cut off his hand," and wherever they cut off people's hands, in those countries there is less theft. Wherever they stone and beat the adulterer, there is less of an AIDS problem. The stricter the law, the fewer problems with security. We have information from northern Nigeria that the [Christian] Igbo are returning because they feel safer there, their women are not raped. It is God who brought us sharia and it was applied in the time of the Prophet.[10]

For the reformists, sharia remains an ideal, but it is inaccessible because it is circumscribed within a historical context that contemporary society makes it impossible to reproduce.[11] Reformists and fundamentalists are sharply divided by their different relationships to history. The latter, lending credence to the myth of the ideal *umma*,[12] dream of a political and social system which takes as its model the era of the Prophet, but they do not situate it outside this world: that is, unlike the members of the Tablighi Jama'at, who proclaim that the goal of life is to "prepare for the next world," they think that Islamic law can change life on earth. In this, they are similar to the Islamists.

How to Reconcile the Desire for Sharia and the Secular State

Benin can be called "secular" (*laïque*) in the legal sense, even though it is a non-secularized society (Roy 2005) where religion and religiosity remain ever-present. Secularism does not present any problems for Muslims, and the fundamentalists who take the precaution to state that they respect it negotiate an arrangement between their desires for sharia on one hand and secularism on the other.

This contradiction, lived out in everyday life, concerns in the first instance marriage, the family, divorce, and inheritance. The first issue of the newspaper *Al-Oumma Al-Islamia*, published by the Zongo neighborhood mosque in Cotonou, appeared on July 27, 2001, at the same time as the Code of Family and Personal Law was being voted on. An article in it was entitled "Why not a legislative option for Muslims?" The author reaffirmed his recognition of the state's secularism, and in the name of freedom of conscience and of religion asked whether Muslims could be exempted from those measures of the law which, according to him, were contrary to Islam, concluding,

> it is now time to envisage the possibility that certain categories of citizens might choose a legislative option. Muslims could then have the chance to apply Qur'anic legislation in situations of demonstrated incompatibility with the Code of Personal and Family Law.

This proposal was not followed up in later issues, perhaps as a measure of prudence, as the authorities had called the Zongo mosque to order several times. Polygamy and the seclusion of women are at the heart of this contradiction between the law and sharia. In the north of the country, Muslim Hausa women often lived in seclusion, in particular in the families of *alfas* and imams. In Parakou during the Revolution, the army entered compounds and forced the women out (Brégand 1998, 223). In the south, on the other hand, where Islam was introduced by Yoruba traders, there was no tradition of secluding women, who enjoyed an important role in society. Like the *alhadji* of Parakou (those who have completed the pilgrimage to Mecca), the women *alhadja* traders in the Dantokpa market of Cotonou financed the construction of mosques, acquiring in this way a social prestige unthinkable in the north of the country.[13] The Muslims advocating polygamy and female seclusion get around the law by avoiding civil marriages, enabling them to believe that they are living according to sharia, at least in private life.

If, as a previously cited interviewee suggested, Islam is not opposed to political activity, in the absence of any hope of installing an Islamic regime, is it not contradictory to participate in a system modeled after the much-devalued West? At present, well-known fundamentalists do not seem to be involved in institutional politics, preferring to devote themselves to "Islamization from below," whereas reformists do not hesitate to engage in political activities.

Separating Religion from Politics,
and Engaging in Politics

The reformists affirm the principle that one cannot mix religion and politics,[14] but this does not signal discretion or withdrawal on their part; they expend considerable energy in associations, and the separation of religious and political spheres allows them to engage individually in politics, as citizens. The state intervenes directly in the affairs of Muslims only in exceptional circumstances, leaving other intermediate institutions the role of managing problems internal to Islam.

The number of Islamic associations registered by the Department of Worship and Customs of the Ministry of the Interior, Security, and Territorial Management, admittedly far fewer than that of Christian associations, expresses the will of these Muslims to constitute themselves as actors in civil society.[15] The registry of associations shows that leaders have emerged in the Islamic arena who are responsible for several associations. In 1992, thirty-two Muslim associations met in the Amitié stadium in Cotonou on the initiative of Yacoubou Fassassi, a politician and Sufi and the promoter of the National Conference of Islamic Associations of Benin (Conférence nationale des associations islamiques du Bénin, CONAIB-Shura), in order to coordinate their activities, but this initiative failed because of rivalries over power and was never pursued further. More recently, in 2000, the imam of the Zongo neighborhood mosque, a center of reformism in Cotonou, founded the Network of Islamic Associations and NGOs of Benin (Réseau des associations et ONG islamiques du Bénin) with the aim of federating the associations; about fifteen joined. In general, the associations pursue their activities independently, some of them devoting themselves to promoting Islamic education.

One example is the Organisation pour la culture islamique du Bénin (OCIB, Organization for Islamic Culture in Benin), which is a part of the Network. Its principal goal is Islamic education according to the Qur'an and the Sunna, and it holds two meetings a month at the mosque of the Association mondiale de l'appel à l'Islam, both where people educated in Arabic offer classes and where an imam gives a lecture followed by discussion. The OCIB declares itself apolitical as an association, but its members participate as individuals in institutional politics, joining parties which sometimes are in opposition to one another. They adopt a secularist posture and, as Muslims who since Independence have occupied seats as representatives or positions as ministers, participate in politics not as Muslims but rather as citizens.[16] As politicians, they have become secular Muslims.

Another example is the Union of Muslim Women of Benin, led by educated women either active in the workplace or retired.[17] Their program concentrates on health, education, and knowledge of Islam; they concern themselves with literacy and AIDS education and struggle for the schooling of girls and against their decreasing educational levels. They give lectures and, preoccupied by the condition of women, want to "let women know about their rights and their duties according to the Qur'an." Although they refuse the notion of reformism because "there is only one Islam," they adopt a reformist approach in that it is on the basis of their interpretation of the Qur'an that they work to better the condition of women, though their reading of the Qur'an is diametrically opposed to that of Ahl al-Sunna. The ACEEMUB also organizes lectures; by maintaining among their goals the "training of executives with integrity," the students in this association intend to influence the country's future. They want Muslims, whom they consider to be underrepresented in politics and in high-level administrative positions, to catch up to the rest of the country.[18]

Although the fundamentalists are made highly visible by their dress code, Muslim reformists, fundamentalists included, remain very discreet compared to members of Evangelical and Pentecostal churches in the south of Benin. The Christian religions have their own fundamentalisms; could radicalization threaten interfaith peace? The state, while guaranteeing religious freedom in a country where religion plays a prominent role, also needs to guarantee social peace.

The State and Muslim Communities: "The Situation Is under Control"

Whereas freedoms of religion and association are respected in Benin, the NGOs and associations must request recognition from the Ministry of the Interior, Security, and Territorial Management (Pirotte 2005, 35). The state thus has a means of control in its administrative services, but it is rare that it intervenes directly in Muslim affairs, leaving the Union islamique du Bénin (UIB, Islamic Union of Benin) to manage problems internal to the Muslim community. Because of the development of Islamism in the world and the proximity of Nigeria, fundamentalists, whom some believe to be under heightened surveillance, are objects of particular attention, and the monitoring of them has been discreetly increased. Islamic NGOs, like other NGOs, additionally depend on the ministry responsible for their particular domain of activity; for example, the construction of a clinic requires the authorization of the Ministry of Health. All the directors of NGOs declare that they cooperate with the state, which does not oppose their projects, because the construction of schools and clinics fills the void which the state has left. These government departments apply the law. Thus, in the name of secularism, the ACEEMUB was denied authorization to build a mosque on the campus of Abomey-Calavi University (in a suburb of Cotonou). This mosque, the base for *da'wa* in the university, was eventually built off-campus with Saudi financing.

The Ministry of National Education is careful in granting permission for the founding of Franco-Arabic schools. The imam of the Zongo mosque, a prominent personality in Islamic reformist (or, according to some opinions in Cotonou, funda-mentalist) circles and founder of the Franco-Arabic school across from the mosque, deplores the fact that it was a Muslim minister who raised the most obstacles to his opening the school. The election of the Pentecostal Mathieu Kérékou to the presi-dency finally resolved this situation, because this neighborhood in Cotonou, with a Muslim majority, voted for him in 1996.[19] Powerful Islamic NGOs easily obtain authorization because the education they offer is often superior to that in public schools. The situation is often more delicate for schools opened with meager funds by graduates who are attempting to create jobs for themselves; the buildings rarely meet the required standards, sometimes amounting to little more than a shed, and the teaching staff do not always have the necessary qualifications.

When internal problems arise within the Muslim community, the state only inter-venes in cases of public disorder. The UIB plays an intermediary role by ensuring that individual and collective Muslim actors cooperate with the central political authorities.[20] Founded in 1984, the UIB replicates in its structure that of the administrative divisions of Benin, with national and departmental offices. Its leaders have intervened on numbers of occasions in conflicts between "traditionalists" on one hand, and *arabisant* Muslims and Islamic NGOs on the other. These conflicts break out when, for example, an NGO that has built a mosque wants to impose its choice of imam, as was the case in Parakou, where the AMA built several mosques, including that of the Zongo Islamic complex. The situation was so tense that, when the imam was nominated, the minister of the interior traveled there in person. There was another serious conflict when the Africa Muslim Agency (AMA) wanted to inaugurate a mosque outside Parakou and declare it a Friday mosque despite the categorical opposition of the local imams. Similar problems have occurred in other localities, and, in each case, the president of the Islamic union of the department of Borgou had to mediate.

The question of the calendar is a recurrent problem. The beginning and the end of the month of Ramadan are fixed by the Conseil supérieur de l'Islam au Bénin (Higher Islamic Council of Benin, part of the UIB), but reformist imams who orient themselves by the moon's appearance in Saudi Arabia, which is a day off, do not observe this schedule. Religious holidays are consequently celebrated on two consecutive days, which complicates public life, especially as religious holidays are officially recognized in Benin.

Conscious of the fact that they have been weakened by their divisions and anxious to revitalize the organization's activities, members of the UIB elected a new slate at the December 2003 congress and decided to work harder to promote Islamic education. In the new leadership, where "traditionalists" work alongside those who are Western-trained, policies are not static and reformist ideas have penetrated the UIB; the priority given to Islamic education is one index of this change. In interviews, some members of the UIB appeared to be hovering between traditionalism and reformism; some were more modernist than others, in that they advocated abandoning certain practices and rethinking Islam in a contemporary context, but all shared the will to oppose the development of fundamentalism and invoked the example of Nigeria. Most declared that they were not worried, saying, "The situation is under control." The following statements from my fieldwork give an idea of their preoccupations and their determination:

> We were in the process of making an effort so that those who would like to dictate Islam calm down, and that we can create Islamic unity in the country. In Kano, they cross arms [in prayer]; if you don't cross them, they can kill you. We don't want these kinds of quarrels in our country; we are struggling for this, for an Islam in peace.
> There are young men just back from Arab countries and they want to change things, but they encountered resistance, and I think they have calmed down; they were obliged to. When they tried to impose their will, they were quickly overcome.

Control is exercised by Muslims themselves, which does not stop the state from having recourse to the usual means of exercising surveillance over individuals and groups.

Islam in Benin is experiencing an expansion which encourages different actors to engage in *da'wa*, and more and more are doing so. The dynamism of Islam is stimulated not only by the activism of these new trends but also by the rivalry of Pentecostal and Evangelical churches. Reformism and fundamentalism remain urban phenomena because urban life is open to outside influences, favors individualization, and allows change. Moreover, it is to the cities that graduates of Islamic universities flock to find employment in an Islamic NGO or a school. From there, preachers set out for villages where NGOs build mosques and, in fewer numbers, schools. Reformism, plural and pragmatic, is winning over new strata of Muslims, some of whom come from "traditionalist" Islam; among them, certain personalities have emerged as true agents of democratization, activists for social peace and for a peaceful Islam coexisting with other religions, heirs of the quietist Islamic tradition associated with al-Hajj Salim Suware (Wilks 1968). They are conscious of the changes taking place, and an imam indulgently remarks, "We can speak of an Islamic awakening provided that we avoid the euphoria of callow youth; they need to understand the environment."

Reformism and fundamentalism have affected Muslim communities the world over, but reformists in Benin, including their extremist fundamentalist branch, have finally shown themselves as devoted to their society and to peace, the local here trumping the global. There is only one society, composed of Muslims, Christians, and followers of traditional religions, and political rivalries in Benin do not translate into religious divisions. Confronted with this renewal, which is difficult to characterize, the state seems content to keep its distance and leave the UIB to manage issues concerning Islam; and the UIB is very confident, one of its members declaring that "in Benin, everything is under control, there is no problem, and when there is one, we are well situated to intervene." Under control, no doubt, but for how long? "Traditionalist" Islam lacks young leaders, and so the face of Islam will necessarily change as one generation is replaced by another. The Sufi orders are renewing themselves as well, with the arrival of new mystical orders which remain very elitist. Change may be dominated by an indigenous revival which, while it moves closer to the orthodoxy of the Qur'anic text, situates itself in continuity with the tolerance and openness which characterized and still characterize Islam in Benin. These forces exist, but they may be overwhelmed by strict and militant fundamentalism which acknowledges only the Qur'an and the Sunna and rejects any ideas of local culture.

Moreover, without resorting to determinism, we can wonder about the future relationship between political radicalization and growing inequality. A Muslim intellectual from Benin, a member of the Qadiriyya and very active in the local Islamic arena, who traveled to Islamabad in June 2004 for a seminar organized by Pakistan entitled "Enlightened Moderation against Islamism and Terrorism," concluded thus: "What creates radical fundamentalism? Social injustice and poverty pave the way for fundamentalism."

Notes

1. "With other religious leaders, we said to each other: we have to check the fanaticism of traditional religions, the Aino (in Fon, masters of the earth), the extremism of certain Christians in light of the multiplicity of churches, and the extremism of young *arabisants* who return from [Saudi] Arabia." Interview with Imam Ligali, Cotonou, March 11, 2005.

2. Two tendencies emerged in this effort to promote interreligious dialogue in the 1990s. One was the movement begun by Yacoubou Fassassi, leader of the Nimatullahi Sufi order, who in 1995 founded the African Group for Islamic Revival, which publishes the quarterly review *Iqraa Afrique*; the other was the intellectual movement centered on El Hajj Bachir Soumanou (the Niassène Tijaniyya), founder of the magazine *La lumière de l'Islam* (*The Light of Islam*) and of the Centre d'étude et de recherche Islam et développement (CERID, Islam and Development Center for Study and Research).

3. At the same time, Christian groups, largely Evangelicals and Pentecostals, increased from 6 percent to 12.5 percent.

4. On "traditionalist" Islam, see Piga 2003 and Coulon 1993.

5. "Similarly, the activities of International Islamic organizations like Al-Muntada al-Islami Foundation . . . their publications and enlightenment campaigns[,] provide additional impetus to Muslims' aspiration for Islamic system in Nigeria" (Bunza 2004, 54).

6. Madrasas, called "Franco-Arabic schools" in Benin, combine education in modern disciplines, according to a national curriculum, with religious and Arabic education. Some classes are conducted in French. In Qur'anic schools, by contrast, only religion and sometimes Arabic are taught.

7. B. M., interview at a Qur'anic school in the Dodgi neighborhood of Porto Novo, January 26, 2005.

8. This is very clearly true in the case of the mosque of the Zongo neighborhood complex in Parakou. I suspect that the case of the great mosque of the Zongo neighborhood in Cotonou is similar.

9. Collective interview in a mosque in the Tchébié neighborhood of Porto Novo, January 26, 2005.

10. Ibid. Murray Last recorded the same arguments and the same hopes in northern Nigeria when sharia was applied (Last 2000).

11. "For 'enlightened Muslims,' whom official Islamic institutions hardly take into account, the sharia, even in the domain of marital law, is an inspiration, a path that was expressed in a precise and long-past historical context" (Carré 1993, 34).

12. Appadurai (2001) insists on the imaginary dimension of life linked to transnational networks in a globalized world.

13. *Alhadji* (feminine *alhadja*) has become a common term for rich Muslims. Toukourou, a rich woman trader of Dantokpa very respected for her generosity, is currently financing an Islamic complex in her neighborhood of Akapakpa in Cotonou.

14. For Olivier Carré, a well-known scholar of Islam, the "few true reformists and reformers" show "that politics and religion are separate once and for all and that Islamic theory itself, and not only practice, has carefully separated the spiritual from the temporal, ever since the Prophet's time" (Carré 1993, 34).

15. On this concept, see Pirotte 2005.

16. Interview with Yaaya Salouf Alihou, president of the OCIB, Cotonou, March 3, 2005.

17. Interview with Madame Bio Tchané, president of the Union of Muslim Women of Benin; al Hadja Afsa Igué, the vice president; and al Hadja Lawani, responsible for school affairs; at Madame Tchané's home, Cotonou, March 10, 2005.

18. Interview with the leaders of the ACEEMUB, March 4, 2005. The amir Moudachirou Dramani, who participated in this collective interview, was killed in an accident in late 2005.

19. Most Muslims in northern Benin, and also those of the Zongo neighborhood in Cotonou, support Kérékou.

20. Marie Miran (2005) paints a negative portrait of the UIB, agreeing with its critics; she correctly points out that the Muslim community remains very divided. My discussion of the organization is based both on my field observation during several consecutive years in the north and from January to March 2005 in the south and on interviews with people who participated in the events in question.

References

Abdullaye, G. 2003. Les diplômés béninois des universités arabo-islamiques: Une élite moderne "déclassée" en quête de légitimité socio-religieuse et politique. Working Papers 18. Mainz: Institut für Ethnologie und Afrikastudien. http://www.ifeas.univ-mainz.de.

Ajayi, J. F., and M. Crowder. 1988. *Atlas historique de l'Afrique*. Éditions du Jaguar.

Appadurai, A. 2001. *Après le colonialisme: Les conséquences culturelles de la globalisation*. Paris: Payot.

Benzine, R. 2004. *Les nouveaux penseurs de l'islam*. Paris: Albin Michel.

Blondo, G., and J. P. Olivier de Sardan. 2002. La corruption au quotidien en Afrique de l'Ouest: Approche socio-anthropologique comparative: Bénin, Niger et Sénégal. Working Papers 18. Mainz: Institut für Ethnologie und Afrikastudien. http://www.ifeas.univ-mainz.de.

Brégand, D. 1998. *Commerce caravanier et relations sociales au Bénin: Les Wangara du Borgou*. Paris: L'Harmattan.

———. 1999. Les Wangara du Nord-Bénin face à l'avancée du fondamentalisme: Étude comparative à Parakou et Djougou. *Islam et sociétés au sud du Sahara* 13: 91–102.

Bunza, M. U. 2004. Muslims and the modern state in Nigeria: A study of the impact of foreign religious literature. *Islam et sociétés au sud du Sahara* 17–18: 49–63.

Carré, O. 1993. *L'islam laïque ou le retour à la Grande Tradition*. Paris: Armand Colin.

Coulon, C. 1993. Les itinéraires politiques de l'islam au Nord-Nigeria. In *Religion et modernité politique en Afrique noire*, ed. J. F. Bayart, 19–62. Paris: Karthala.

Coulon, C., and D. C. Martin. 1991. *Les Afriques politiques*. Paris: La Découverte.

Friedman, Y. 1989. *Prophecy continuous: Aspects of Ahmadi religious thought and its medieval background*. Berkeley: University of California Press.

Gaborieau, M. 1998. *Tablighi Jama'at*. In *Encyclopédie de l'Islam*, new edition, 39–40. Leiden: Brill.

———. 2000. De la guerre sainte au prosélytisme (*da'wa*): Les organisations musulmanes transnationales d'origine indienne. Paper presented at *L'internationalisation du religieux: Mutations, enjeux, limites*, conference of the Association française de sciences sociales des religions, IRESCO. Paris, February 7–8.

Last, M. 2000. La charia dans le Nord-Nigeria. *Politique africaine* 79: 141–52.

Loimeier, R. 1997. Islamic reform and political change: The example of Abubakar Gumi and the 'Yan Izala movement in northern Nigeria. In *African Islam and Islam in Africa: Encounters between Sufis and Islamists*, ed. E. E. Rosander and D. Westerlund, 286–307. London: Hurst.

———. 2003. Patterns and peculiarities of Islamic reforms in Africa. *Journal of religion in Africa* 33 (3): 237–62.

Marie, A. 1997. *L'Afrique des individus: Itinéraires citadins dans l'Afrique contemporaine*. Paris: Karthala.

Mattes, H. 1993. La da'wa libyenne entre le Coran et le Livre Vert. In *Le radicalisme islamique au sud du Sahara: Da'wa, arabisation et critique de l'Occident*, ed. R. Otayek, 37–53. Paris: Karthala.

Mayrargue, C. 2002. Dynamiques religieuses et démocratisation au Bénin: Pentecôtisme et formation d'un espace public. Ph.D. diss., Université Montesquieu–Bordeaux IV.

———. 2004. Les langages politiques en campagne électorale. In *Voter en Afrique: Comparaisons et différenciations*, ed. P. Quantin, 285–312. Paris: L'Harmattan.

Miran, M. 2005. D'Abidjan à Porto Novo: Associations islamiques et culture religieuse réformiste sur la côte de Guinée. In *Entreprises religieuses transnationales en Afrique de l'Ouest*, ed. L. Fourchard, A. Mary, and R. Otayek, 43–72. Paris: Karthala.

Otayek, R., ed., 1993. *Le radicalisme islamique au sud du Sahara: Da'wa, arabisation et critique de l'Occident*. Paris: Karthala.

Piga, A., ed. 2003. *Islam et villes en Afrique au sud du Sahara: Entre soufisme et fondamentalisme*. Paris: Karthala.

Pirotte, G. 2005. Société civile importée et nouvelle gouvernance: Le nouveau secteur ONG au Bénin. In *Gouverner les sociétés africaines: Acteurs et institutions*, ed. P. Quantin, 27–43. Paris: Karthala.

Roy, O. 2002. *L'Islam mondialisé*. Paris: Le Seuil.

———. 2004. Modernisation, réformisme et réislamisation. *Mouvements* 36: 22–31.

———. 2005. *La laïcité face à l'Islam*. Paris: Stock.

Schulze, R. 1993. La *da'wa* saoudienne en Afrique de l'Ouest. In *Le radicalisme islamique au sud du Sahara: Entre soufisme et fondamentalisme*, ed. R. Otayek, 20–35. Paris: Karthala.

Strandsberg, C. 2000. Kerekou, God and the ancestors: Religion and the conception of political power in Benin. *African Affairs* 99: 395–414.

Wilks, I. 1968. The transmission of Islamic learning. In *Literacy in traditional societies*, ed. J. Goody, 162–95. Cambridge: Cambridge University Press.

CHAPTER 7

PERCEPTIONS OF MARGINALIZATION: MUSLIMS IN CONTEMPORARY TANZANIA

Roman Loimeier

Introduction

African countries with Muslim populations can be divided into three categories. In countries of the first kind, such as Senegal, Muslims form a clear and undisputed majority of the population. Religion (Islam) is an accepted part of daily life, and there are no major conflicts between Muslims and non-Muslims. National conflicts are mostly related to political, economic, social, ethnic, or communal issues and do not necessarily acquire religious connotations. Religious disputes among Muslims are largely over matters of ritual and the interpretive authority of religious scholars or competing Islamic religious movements.

In countries of the second kind, such as South Africa, Muslims form a clear and undisputed minority of the population. Islam is not a significant part of most people's daily lives and there are no major conflicts between Muslims and non-Muslims, although countries differ in the degree to which Muslim minorities are integrated into national politics. National conflicts again mostly relate to political, economic, social, ethnic, or communal issues and do not necessarily acquire religious connotations, whereas religious disputes among Muslims again largely concern matters of ritual and the relative authority of religious scholars.

In countries of the third kind, such as Nigeria, Muslims form a sizable part of the population, perhaps even the majority, but not a decisive majority; or, if a minority, they are a large minority that can exert considerable influence on national development. National conflicts in these countries have multiple political, economic, social, ethnic, or communal dimensions; at the same time, these conflicts easily acquire religious connotations. In other words, in these countries religion constitutes a platform of political mobilization, for both Muslims and non-Muslims, to a larger extent than in the others. Religion (Islam) is consequently more often instrumentalized as a marker of identity in interreligious conflicts in those countries, where historical legacies and postcolonial policies have led to the emergence of disputes over development, national political leadership, or access to resources.

Tanzania risks becoming one of the countries of the third category, where religion may either contribute to national stability or become a destabilizing force. We see this especially when looking at interfaith relations and how they are negotiated in national politics. At the conference "Global Worlds of the Swahili," held in Zanzibar in February 2003, one of the participants from mainland Tanzania indeed described Muslims in contemporary Tanzania as feeling marginalized and pointed out a major feature of Muslim political strategy: "They are attacking the state by attacking the Christians" (Muhammad Said, personal communication, February 2, 2003). This sense of marginalization among Muslims may be surprising, as the number of Muslims in Tanzania has grown considerably since the late nineteenth century. Yet this growth has not been translated into a corresponding increase in the number of Muslims holding positions in the political, educational, or economic arenas. In the eyes of many Muslims, Tanzania has become a Christian country, and Muslims have been pushed to the wall. By attacking Christians, Muslims want to force the state to redress this imbalance.

The Historical Context

Although Islam had been established on the East African coast since at least the ninth century, Muslims started to expand into the East African interior fairly late, during the eighteenth and nineteenth centuries. Islam became familiar in the hinterland even before the colonial period, through the mediation of Swahili traders. Its expansion continued under colonial rule in both German East Africa and British Tanganyika. Nimtz explains conversion to Islam in these territories as resulting from the desire to bring "order into a chaotic situation" after the disruptions of the Maji Maji rebellion, 1904–7, and the First World War, 1914–18 (Nimtz 1980, 15; see also Iliffe 1979, 211–16 and Koponen 1994, 580–83). In addition, the German colonial administration largely relied on local cadres, the so-called *akidas* and *liwalis*, who were mostly Kiswahili-speaking Muslims. Swahili culture as well as Islam thus acquired and retained the nimbus of dominance and superiority. As a consequence, the interior was not only increasingly Islamized but also adopted Kiswahili as a lingua franca (Iliffe 1969, 1979).

Still, the colonial period was a time of hardship and crisis for Muslims, especially after 1919, when the bulk of German East Africa had become Tanganyika, a British mandate territory. The interference of the colonial administration in Muslim affairs, Islamic jurisdiction, and the administration of the religious foundations (*awqaf*) disrupted coastal Muslim societies considerably (Iliffe 1969, 1979). In the British colonial period, Muslims also became increasingly disadvantaged in terms of education; modern education remained largely confined to mission schools. Under Governor Cameron (1925–31), for instance, the British decided to "promote education by working in partnership with Christian missions" (Njozi 2003, 15).[1] Thus a Christian elite was groomed to replace the Muslim functionaries of the German administration (Ludwig 1999, 27–28). Muslims shunned the mission schools, seeing them as vehicles to promote conversion to Christianity. As a result, a new African elite emerged in the 1920s that was almost exclusively Christian, often Catholic. In 1955, even colonial statistics showed that Muslims had become disadvantaged in virtually every sphere of education: they had fewer schools of every kind, from primary schools to medical and technical schools and teacher training centers (Mbogoni 2004, 107–8):

School Type	Government Schools	Mission Schools	Muslim Schools
Primary schools	656	1692	28
Secondary schools	10	16	–
Rural middle schools	28	223	–
Teacher training centers	11	23	–
Medical and technical schools	7	5	–
Total	712	1959	28

About two-thirds of all schools (as well as half of all hospitals) were thus in missions' hands at Independence,[2] and the "Christian" and even "Catholic domination" of Tanganyika has remained a central topic of discourse in Tanganyika and Tanzania.[3] In 1987, Muslim groups in Zanzibar, for instance, claimed that Tanzania was dominated by Catholics (Forster 1997, 172).[4] Facing these challenges, Muslims reacted in different ways: although some leaders of the Qadiriyya and Shadhiliyya Sufi orders increased their *da'wa* (mission) efforts, hoping to increase the numerical weight of the Muslims, other Muslims started to advance ideas of reform and to participate actively in the struggle for independence.

Muslims in Tanganyika indeed featured prominently among the founders of Tanganyika's independence movement, the Tanganyika Africa Association (TAA),[5] which became, in 1954, the Tanganyika African Nation Union (TANU), led by Julius Nyerere. From the 1930s to the 1950s, Muslims made up the vanguard of Tanganyika's struggle for independence (see Said 1998, 167–88) and acquired considerable weight in pre-Independence politics. The first Muslim Tanganyikan political associations, the Muslim Association of Tanganyika (MAT; or in Arabic, Jam'iyat al-Islamiyya fi-Tanganyika, JIT)[6] and the East African Muslim Welfare Society (EAMWS, see later), also actively supported the struggle for independence. Concurrently, Muslim politicians such as Bibi Titi Muhammad, a famous *ngoma* singer and first president of TANU's women's organization (the Umoja wa Wanawake wa Tanzania, UWT, or Tanzanian Women's Union),[7] and Tewa Said Tewa, one of the seventeen founders of TANU in 1954, featured prominently in TANU as well as the EAMWS (Said 1998; Chande 1998). The membership of the JIT, the first Muslim association in Tanganyika to be controlled by Africans rather than by Indians, was identical to that of the TAA (and later TANU), and prominent JIT leaders such as Shaykh Hassan b. Ameir[8] and Shaykh Abdallah Chaurembo[9] in Dar es Salaam, Shaykh Abd al-Muhsin Kitumba in Ujiji, Shaykh Mze b. Fereji in Tabora, and Shaykh Muhammad b. Yahya in Bagomoyo were strong supporters of TANU and Nyerere. They saw their support for TANU and independence as a way to redress the imbalance in education created by the British colonial administration (Nimtz 1980, 88).

The Political Development
of Post-Independence Tanzania

Tanganyikan and Tanzanian post-Independence history may be divided into distinctive periods, according to the development of relations between the state and religion. The first is the time between Independence in 1961 and the Arusha Declaration in 1967, when Nyerere tried to consolidate control and to remove established elites, both Muslim and non-Muslim, from positions of power. As Muslims had been represented prominently in the struggle for independence, they were affected most. The second period, from the Arusha Declaration in 1967 to the end of Nyerere's administration in 1985, may be described as the *ujamaa* ("community") period of Tanzanian politics. A new Muslim bureaucratic elite developed that supported *ujamaa* politics, while the churches, especially the Catholic Church, grew disenchanted with them. A third period started in 1985 and still continues; it is characterized by the development of a multiparty democratic system and a liberal economy, as well as increasing disaffection among activist Muslims, who have started to criticize loyalist Muslim functionaries and their seeming inability to fight for Muslim interests.

Although Muslims had a prominent role in the struggle for independence, the relationship between Muslims and the state changed completely after 1961, when Nyerere gradually accepted "Christian" positions on national development, and possibly even accepted demands from the Catholic Church for the dissolution of the EAMWS (Njozi 2000, 68; Said 1998, 84; Sivalon 1992). The first national government included eleven Christian and only four Muslim ministers (Ludwig 1999, 40), which contributed to Muslim dissatisfaction and led to protests within TANU. Many Muslim party members in fact came to support Abdallah Fundikira, the leader of the EAMWS, who opposed Nyerere in the run-up to the 1962 presidential elections. According to TANU-party sources, "the Muslims backed Fundikira very strongly and it was not clear for several days that Nyerere would be in" (Ludwig 1999, 53). Reacting to the increasing influence of representatives of the church, Shaykh Hassan b. Ameir (as well as his followers) urged Muslims to become more active, particularly with respect to education, "so that they could share power with the Christians in governing the country" (Said 1998, 295). But before the Muslims could develop a new strategy, the government began a "de-Islamization" of the administration. This political maneuver became public on March 1, 1963, when Nyerere dissolved TANU's "elders' council," which had been dominated by Muslims (Said 1998, 268). In January 1964, Nyerere also used a mutiny of the Tanganyika Rifles to arrest some prominent Muslims such as Bilali Rehani Waikela, who had started to publicly criticize his government (Said 1998, 273).

Muslims thus encountered increasing problems in the sphere of politics. In a first reaction, a pan-territorial congress of all Muslim organizations in Tanganyika was convened in 1962, bringing together the EAMWS, the JIT, the Muslim Education Union, and other groups. All were supposed to unite, "from Kigoma to Dar es-Salaam, from Lindi to Arusha," in a new national Islamic organization, the Jumuiya ya Da'awah ya Uislamu (Arabic, Jam'iyat al-Da'wa al-Islamiyya), that was registered on August 26, 1963 (DUMT 2004, x). The congress elected Tewa Said Tewa as its president and decided to support the establishment of an Islamic university. In April 1964, in the context of a state visit to Egypt, Tewa Said Tewa signed an agreement which provided the funds for the university. Later that month, however, he was removed from the government in a cabinet reshuffle, in the context of Tanganyika's union with Zanzibar,[10] and became ambassador to China. The plan for an Islamic university was shelved.[11] At the same time, Bibi Titi Muhammad, the leader of the Umoja wa Wanawake wa Tanzania, was sidelined as well: in 1965, she lost her seat in Parliament, and when in February 1967 she protested against the Arusha Declaration, she was quickly accused of collaborating with Nyerere's enemies, especially Oscar Kambona.[12] In 1969, she was accused of having been involved in a plot to remove Nyerere from power. After a trial in 1970–71, she was condemned to life imprisonment, although she was released from prison in 1972 (Geiger 1997, 174–75).[13]

The next victim of Nyerere's policy of marginalizing old elites was the East Africa Muslim Welfare Society (EAMWS), which had been founded by the Aga Khan in 1937 but was formally established as the EAMWS only in 1945. In 1961, under the leadership of Abdallah Fundikira,[14] its headquarters were moved from Mombasa to Dar es Salaam. As a consequence of Tanganyika's turn to "African socialism" after the Arusha Declaration of 1967, the EAMWS, which had promoted unity among East Africa's Muslim populations, became increasingly obsolete; there was less place for a supranational organization in the context of emerging nationalisms in East Africa and the different development paths being followed by Tanzania, Uganda, and Kenya. The dissolution of the EAMWS was triggered, however, by internal rivalries which had started as a local dispute in Bukoba in 1965 over appropriate ritual in the Friday prayers.[15] This dispute led, in 1967–68, to the disintegration of the organization, when a dissident group led by Adam Nasibu organized an internal coup and pledged support for TANU politics of nationalization, as well as the 1967 Arusha Declaration ("Azimio la Arusha"), by proclaiming that "socialism was compatible with Islam" (Said 1998, 285). In this strategy, Nasibu was supported by local opponents of the EAMWS in Dar es Salaam, in particular by Shaykh Abdallah Chaurembo, who claimed that the EAMWS was too "Indian" and that it was anti-Arusha and thus "anti-Tanzanian."[16] At the same time, members of the old EAMWS elite, such as Tewa Said Tewa and Bibi Titi Muhammad, had lost their influence within TANU. There was, thus, nobody within TANU who could defend the EAMWS against Nasibu's dissident group. At a meeting of the EAMWS in Bukoba in June 1968, the Nasibu branch broke away, a decision rapidly accepted by nine other regional branches. The final break came at a conference in Iringa in December 1968, when Abeid Amani Karume, Tanzania's Zanzibari vice president, opened the meeting with wild attacks against the EAMWS and accused the organization of "colluding with foreigners" (Chande 1998, 138).

As a consequence of the dissolution of the EAMWS at the end of the Iringa meeting, a new organization, the Baraza Kuu la Waislamu Tanzania (BAKWATA, Supreme Council for Muslims in Tanzania) was established. BAKWATA essentially came to function as a Muslim wing of TANU, and in 1977 TANU was renamed the Chama Cha Mapinduzi (CCM, the Party of the Revolution). Muslims became increasingly dissatisfied with it (see also Chande 1998, 158–61), not only because BAKWATA was responsible for issuing legal documents such as permits and marriage certificates to Muslims, and was thus difficult to ignore, but also because the "supreme leader," the "Shaykh Mkuu" of BAKWATA (Shaykh Ali b. Hemedi al-Buhri, who was appointed *mufti* of BAKWATA in 1975), repeatedly defended government policies

(Chande 1998, 143). BAKWATA was consequently seen as a government institution which failed to promote Muslim positions and to unite Tanzania's Muslims.[17] On the other hand, in the 1970s BAKWATA was one of the few religious groups which supported Nyerere's *ujamaa* policies (Mbogoni 2004, 137). The churches had in fact, to Nyerere's chagrin, started to criticize some expressions of *ujamaa*, particularly the forced resettlement of villages (Ludwig 1999, 96). Because Nyerere needed the support of the churches for his policies and this support was not forthcoming as quickly as he wished, church–state relations turned rather volatile in the 1970s. Nyerere, in particular, "complained that the Catholic church in general failed to give him the support he needed." According to Nyerere, in the colonial period "the churches had seen the existing social, political and economic system as being fixed and unchangeable and had thus helped to preach resignation." Nyerere repeatedly criticized the "silence of the churches" in the postcolonial situation and accused them of being "shaped by hierarchical thinking and structures." Times had changed, and churches should have adapted to the new situation (Ludwig 1999, 111, 104–105). Also, Nyerere recognized the problem of Muslim–Christian inequality in education and appealed to the churches, in the 1960s, to open their schools to Muslims. As the churches were not willing to do so, Nyerere came to see nationalization of the mission schools as a major step in the implementation of *ujamaa* politics (Ludwig 1999, 55, 63), and carried it out through a law of March 15, 1970, a move that was interpreted as intended "to neutralize the religious influence of the schools" (Ludwig 1999, 134). The nationalization of mission schools was put into effect, however, without properly consulting the churches, and the "churches expressed their astonishment," although they did not ultimately oppose nationalization, especially after Nyerere declared that church and mission grounds (not school buildings) would remain church property (Ludwig 1999, 135). By 1974, Nyerere seems to have been thoroughly frustrated with the churches, particularly the Catholic Church, on account of their critique of *ujamaa* politics (Mbogoni 2004, 139–44). We may then ask why Muslims perceive themselves as disadvantaged in the post-Independence period, and why they were not able to better use their privileged position in the 1970s to translate political influence into power in other spheres of life, such as education, especially since, by nationalizing the mission schools, the Nyerere government had deprived the churches of a major source of socioreligious influence (Njozi 2003, 16). An answer to this question might be that organizations such as BAKWATA were unable to use Muslims' privileged political position to develop long-term strategies for the development of Muslim education and relied on privileged access to power and political representation within the regime. BAKWATA acted in essentially political terms, and saw its role as representing the government instead of representing Muslim aspirations for political development: BAKWATA continued, in fact, to act as a government institution and to enjoy the resulting political privileges, without taking the opportunity to redress the structural imbalance between Muslims and Christians.

New Muslim Organizations

The establishment of new Muslim organizations in Tanzania since the 1980s has to be seen in the context of the crisis of the *ujamaa* system and the subsequent "opening" of Tanzania to International Monetary Fund and World Bank demands for economic liberalization, which eventually led, in the 1990s, to the introduction of a multiparty system—which was still dominated, however, by the CCM. Economic superstructures should thus be considered a major defining factor for the development of state–religion dialectics in Tanzania's post-Independence history: economic structures indeed appear to be of paramount importance for the 1967–85 period, when *ujamaa* politics (and economics) dominated Tanzania's development and defined religious dynamics. The same is true for the period of economic liberalization since 1985, which seems to favor Christians who are disproportionately better educated and trained. The politics of economic and political liberalization in fact led to a considerable multiplication of choices in the arenas of religion and politics. As a result, Muslim activist groups were able, with the backing of Muslim international donor organizations based in the Near East, to build new schools and to improve their chances to gain public acceptance (Farouk Topan, personal communication, February 23, 2001). As a consequence, new and independent Muslim organizations developed, defined by their efforts to develop modern Islamic education and to oppose state-informed concepts of "true Islam" as presented by BAKWATA. The proliferation of new Muslim organizations gained momentum when Muslims realized that their far-reaching aspirations of an official "rectification" of existing conditions would not be realized under Ali Hassan Mwinyi, a Muslim politician from Zanzibar who became president of Tanzania in 1985. In 1987, Mwinyi declared, in a public speech in Dar es Salaam, "The government of our nation has no official creed and the same is true for our party: it has no religion" (quoted in Lacunza Balda 1989, 288). [Na chama chetu vivyo hivyo hakina dini.]

Many of the new Muslim organizations were critical of BAKWATA. In addition to influential Muslim dissidents, such as Shaykh Saidi Musa,[18] who have not built organizations of their own, there are some important Sufi order–linked associations, such as the Baraza Kuu a Jumuiya na Taasisi za Kiislamu, the Supreme Council of Islamic Organizations and Institutions in Tanzania (established in 1992–93), and a Shadhili nongovernmental organization (NGO) in Kariakoo, Dar es Salaam, led by Shaykh Nur al-Din Husayn, who has acquired a considerable national reputation on account of his independent views,[19] and numerous activist Muslim groups and Islamic NGOs that are not linked to a *tariqa* or Sufi order, often subsumed under the umbrella term *ansar al-sunna*, that is, followers of the Sunna, the authoritative practice of the Prophet Muhammad. Today, Tanzania is teeming with Islamic organizations, associations, and NGOs, a few with branches nationwide, some represented in only a few regions, and others confined to a single school. The most important of these associations are listed here:

1. The Baraza la Uendelezaji Kuran Tanzania (BALUKTA, National Association for the Promotion of the Qur'an in Tanzania) was founded in 1987 by Shaykh Yahya Hussein (Ludwig 1996, 227; see also Lodhi and Westerlund 1999, 106).[20]

2. The Warsha ya Waandishi wa Kiislam (Workshop of the Commission of Islamic Authors) actually started out, in 1975, as a BAKWATA workshop (Kiswahili *warsha*) at the Kinondoni Secondary School in Dar es Salaam for the development of

an Islamic curriculum (Chande 1998, 144; see also Lodhi and Westerlund 1999, 106; Ludwig 1996, 226). A number of Muslim youths, mostly affiliated with UVIKITA (see later), joined BAKWATA to support the independent scholars in the workshop against the government scholars. Although Nyerere asked the local leaders of BAKWATA, in particular Shaykh Muhammad Ali (the secretary-general of BAKWATA at that time), to stop these antigovernment activities, the participants of the workshop resisted. As a consequence, the dissident *warsha* members were expelled from BAKWATA in 1982 and became at independent organization of Muslim intellectuals, scholars, and teachers based at Masjid Qubah (Chande 1998, 147). Today, Warsha maintains a number of schools, such as the Masjid Qubah and Islamic Center in Dar es Salaam, and is trying to develop reformed forms of Islamic education (see also Lodhi and Westerlund 1999, 106).

3. The Muslim Students' Association at the University of Dar es Salaam (MSAUD, Jumuiya ya Wanafunzi wa Kiislamu) became influential in the 1990s because of its educational activities (Ludwig 1996, 227; Chande 1998, 161). MSAUD also edits the most influential Muslim paper in Tanganyika, *an-Nuur*.

4. The Union of Muslim Preachers of Equivalent Religions (Umoja wa Wahubiri wa Kiislamu wa Mlingano wa Dini), established in 1990, is based at the Mtoro mosque in Dar es Salaam. This association is led by Shaykh Musa Husayn, a scholar born in Ujiji in 1918 who was closely affiliated with the South African *da'i* (preacher) Ahmad Deedat as well as Shaykh Saidi Musa (Lacunza Balda 1993, 229; Ahmed 2005).[21] In recent times, the pro-Iranian leanings of leading members of and sympathizers with the Umoja led to a split. A new organization, "al-MALLID" (al-Markaz al-Islami li-tanbih al-ghafilin 'an al-din; Kituo cha kuwazindua walio ghafilika katika Din, The Islamic Center for the Awakening of Those Who Have Become Negligent in Religion), rejects the pro-Iranian positions of the Umoja and tends to cultivate positions which are closer to Wahhabist interpretations of Islam (Ahmed 2005, 3). At the same time, al-MALLID seems to stress *da'wa* among Muslims more than the struggle against Christian missions.

5. The Fiysabilil-lah (Arabic, Fi-sabil Allah) Tabligh Markaz (On the Path of Allah Propagation Center), the Tanganyikan branch of the Tablighi Jama'at, is based in Gongo la Mboto, Dar es Salaam. It also maintains a number of schools and Islamic centers in Dar es Salaam and other urban centers such as Morogoro (see Constantin 1995; Lacunza Balda 1997; Grandin 1998).

6. The Shura ya Maimamu (Council of Imams) has strong *ansar al-sunna* (radical, activist) tendencies (see later). In 2004, al-Hajj Shaykh Musa Kundecha was the council's amir (see Njozi 2003, 71).

7. The Jumuiya ya Uamsho (Society of Revival, "Awakening") is the most important of the *ansar al-sunna* groups.[22]

8. The Umoja wa Vijana wa Kiislamu Tanzania (UVIKITA, the Tanzanian Muslim Youth Union) was formed by a group of University of Medina graduates in the late 1970s. They later joined Warsha (see earlier) and were finally registered as an independent reformist (Wahhabist) group (Ansar al-Sunna Youth) in 1988 (Chande 1998, 222).

9. The Taasisi na Jumuiya za Kiislam Tanzania (The Association of Muslim NGOs of Tanzania) is led by Shaykh Ally Bassalleh.[23]

10. The Consultative Assembly of Dar es Salaam Imams, an organization of the imams of the capital city, was led until 2001 by Shaykh Juma Mbukuzi. Mbukuzi was removed from his position when he chose to support the government (and BAKWATA) in the Dibagula case (Njozi 2003, 27; for the Dibagula case, see later).[24]

11. The Islamic Propagation Center is based in Ubungo, Dar es Salaam. It maintains a large school and tries to advance Islamic education; it is affiliated with MSAUD.

Patterns of Dispute

Although Christian–Muslim disputes seem to have dominated public debates in Tanzania since the 1980s, it has to be stressed that the 1980s and 1990s were equally characterized by rivalries and disputes among Muslims. At the same time, radical and activist Muslim groups, often called *ansar al-sunna*, have become much more visible, not only in the big cities such as Dar es Salaam, Tanga, Kigoma, Bukoba, and Mwanza, but also in small towns such as Bagamoyo, Ujiji, Tabora, and Morogoro. In Ujiji in 1988, for instance, *ansar al-sunna* groups introduced a new form of Islamic funeral which was characterized by its speed and the omission of locally established rites and festivities. They also established a new mosque, in which women were allocated a place for prayer (Lacunza Balda 1989, 281); this triggered a curious response from a Qadiri scholar, Muhammad Nassor, who claimed in a pamphlet that women were not allowed to pray in mosques. Religious conflicts thus occurred not only between Muslims and Christians but also among Muslims, as activist groups were reluctant to accept the *irshad* (guidance) of established authorities for the sake of unity among Muslims and tried instead to establish their own ideas of "true Islam." BAKWATA was a frequent topic of dispute. A letter published in *an-Nuur* warned that the group would "cause the humiliation of Islam" (*Bakwata hii ni kuudhalilisha Uislamu*) through its collaboration with the government and its alleged support for the "sell-out of Tanzania to foreigners in a free-for-all policy" (July 18, 2003). Muslims close to BAKWATA were called "Bakwata Muslims" by the *ansar al-sunna* groups (van de Bruinhorst 2005, 12) and accused of hypocrisy (*unafiki*). BAKWATA has also been accused of creating *fitna* (chaos, strife) among Muslims, as Muslim claims have been torpedoed repeatedly by BAKWATA functionaries, such as in the case of the al-Furqaan school (see later). In that case, as in many others, BAKWATA was accused of contributing to the disputes among Muslims instead of working for Muslim unity.[25]

Tanzania's recent political development has also been influenced, since the early 1980s, by a number of crises that led to further deterioration in Muslim–Christian relationships. Tensions between Muslims and Christians were accentuated by the development of a new type of public preaching, the so-called *mihadhara* sermons (Njozi 2000, 80), around 1984. Also around that time, Muslims began to employ references to the Bible, a strategy which was probably influenced by a visit of Ahmad Deedat in 1981, who had been invited by the Muslim Students Association of the University of Dar es Salaam (Njozi 2000, 11).[26] The *mihadhara* movement should be seen, however, as a reaction to the rise of the Pentecostal churches in Tanzania, which had originated this type of public preaching.[27] Although the Tanzanian government

banned preaching outside places of worship in 1992, because it often involved polemical attacks on the other religion using misquotations of the other's scriptures and consequently triggered disputes, *mihadhara* preaching continued to be legal inside
churches or mosques. One such dispute occurred on March 16, 2000, when Hamisi
Rajab Dibagula, a Muslim from Morogoro, was arrested for stating that Jesus was not
the son of God, that anyone who said that he was the son of God must be an "unbe-
liever," and that Jesus had not been crucified. In the subsequent trial (*Republic of
Tanzania v. H. R. Dibagula*), Dibagula was found guilty by the Morogoro District
Court and was sentenced to a prison term of eighteen months on July 31, 2001 (Njozi
2003, 22–23). The Dibagula case spurred Muslim mobilization throughout Tanzania,
although the Tanzania High Court reviewed the verdict and released him in August
2001. However, the court confirmed that "slandering religion" had correctly been
identified as a criminal offense by the Morogoro District Court. The statement "Jesus
is not God" has since become a major bone of contention, as Muslim *wahadhiri*
(preachers) seem to quote it deliberately to incite Christian reactions.

Despite the interdiction of public preaching, *mihadhara* preaching continued
outside places of worship after 1992 (Ahmed 2005, 5). In fact, announcements of
public *mihadhara* meetings appear frequently in the Muslim press. On July 16, 2004,
for instance, *an-Nuur* announced that the Zanzibari *ansar al-sunna* leader Shaykh
Nassor Abdallah Bachu[28] would give a lecture in Moshi later that month, as part
of an East African *ansar* rally organized by the Markaz Ansar of Moshi. Other
wahadhiri from Mwanza, Mombasa, Nairobi, Tanga, Arusha, and Dodoma were
invited as well. In another example, on September 3, 2004, *an-Nuur* carried an
announcement that a *mihadhara* would be held on the following day, organized by
the Jumuiya ya Maendeleo ya Wanawake wa Kiislamu ya Salafiyya (Society for the
Development of Salafi Muslim Women) and taking place in the Mskiti Answaar
Sunna in Kinondoni in Dar es Salaam, with a number of *wahadhiri* preaching.

Christians tend to object, of course, to Muslim preaching that counterposes the
religions, arguing that "religious lectures will cause war" (*mihadhara ya dini itazua
vita*; Njozi 2000, 81), although radical Christian groups have practiced this kind of
public preaching as well (Adam Shafi, personal communication, April 2, 2005).
Consequently, a number of conflicts have erupted from *mihadhara* meetings. In April
1993, Muslims attacked three butcheries in Dar es Salaam (in the Magomeni and
Manzese neighborhoods) which had allegedly sold pork to Muslims. In the aftermath
of these riots, thirty-eight Muslims were imprisoned. Shaykh Yahya Hussein, the
leader of BALUKTA, who publicly declared that he had been the driving force
behind the riot, was subsequently taken to court and BALUKTA was dissolved in
June 1993 (Ludwig 1996, 219). In another incident, the so-called Mwembechai
killings, on February 13, 1998, four Muslims were killed by Field Force units outside
a mosque in Mwembechai, Dar es Salaam, after a priest told police that Muslims had
insulted Jesus Christ in a *mihadhara* sermon (Njozi 2000, 5).[29] The Mwembechai
killings took place in the context of rising religious tensions; in January 1998
President Benjamin Mkapa, in office since 1995, had declared war "on people who
go about distributing cassettes, booklets, and convening meetings, where they
insulted and ridiculed other religions" (Njozi 2000, 31). The killings have become a
historical marker for radical Muslim groups, who have revived their memory every

year since. For instance, Muslim groups and organizations used the 'Id al-Fitr celebrations of January 1999 to complain about the treatment of Muslims by the government of Tanzania, including the way Muslims were treated in the Mwembechai incident. In 2001, *ansar al-sunna* groups tried to transform the celebrations on the *yawm al-Arafat* into demonstrations of Muslim unity and to again use the Mwembechai killings as a "historical marker"; *an-Nuur* proclaimed that Muslims would "stand upright" in Jangwani that Sunday (*Waislam kusimama Jangwani jumapili*, March 2, 2001). With the phrase "standing upright in Jangwani" the *ansar al-sunna* allude to a central religious feature of the hajj, the "standing [*wuquf*] at Arafat," translating it into a form of political protest and thus linking a major religious ritual with local politics (van de Bruinhorst 2005, 1).

A number of topics have emerged as central to Muslim public discourse in the Muslim–Christian disputes. These topics are activated again and again when a specific context allows their citation. Areas of confrontation, even if only symbolic, are manifold, such as a dispute about the shifting of graves in Ilala, Dar es Salaam, in 2003, to allow construction. The *ansar al-sunna* pointed to a fatwa (legal opinion) by Shaykh Hassan b. Ameir against such shifting of graves ("Asikanyage mtu kufukua kaburi," *an-Nuur*, August 15, 2003). Also, almost every week the Muslim press carries a story of police storming a mosque, or Muslims being accused of slandering Christianity. Disputes between Muslims and Christians, between Muslims and the state, and among Muslims themselves thus have changing local, regional, and national dimensions and may correspondingly change character quickly.

Muslim–Christian and Muslim–state conflicts acquired an additional twist in 1988, when Sofia Kawawa, then leader of the UWT, urged the CCM to abrogate the Islamic Marriage Act because it discriminated against women, a demand which has resurfaced since then.[30] This request triggered riots in Zanzibar in May 1988, led by Shaykh Nassor Bachu, Saleh Juma of Forodhani, and Shaykh Ali Hemed Jadir (Lacunza Balda 1989, 328), who had become, by that time, Zanzibar's most prominent *ansar al-sunna* leaders. When President Mwinyi defended Kawawa, he was attacked in the magazine *Sauti ya Zanzibar Huru* for giving Christians too much consideration: "The leaders of the Zanzibari government dare to join forces with the great enemy of Islam and to persecute the Shaykhs. Today, Christian preachers are left free to preach and spread Christianity in Zanzibar while the Shaykhs of Islam are squeezed to make them restless. Where do these things come from? How is it that Christians have no obstacles?" (quoted in Lacunza Balda 1989, 304–305). Muslim anxieties were confirmed in 1987 when Professor Kigoma Malima (1938–95) became the first Muslim minister of education and publicly declared that Muslims had been disadvantaged by the Tanzanian system of education in the past and that they should now be preferentially selected for secondary school education. This statement incited Christian groups, which claimed, in 1989 at a conference of the Christian Council of Tanzania in Dodoma, that Muslims in the government were pushing to prepare Tanzania for a "jihad" (Ludwig 1996, 217). The dispute over issues of education acquired a new dimension in February 1992, when the government decided to hand back to its former owners (i.e., mostly Christian churches) the hospitals and schools that had been nationalized in 1972. Muslims immediately complained that missions and churches would benefit most from this return (Ludwig 1996, 218).

Twelve years later, in 2004, Shaykh Ally Bassalleh, the leader of the Taasisi na Jumuiya za Kiislam Tanzania, commented, despite a 1992 parliamentary inquiry as well as a report by the Catholic Church and a memorandum of understanding between the churches and the state, which had acknowledged structural imbalances in politics and education between Muslims and Christians (Lodhi and Westerlund 1999, 107),[31] that nothing had changed: Muslims were still marginalized, as they had been marginalized since 1961, and Muslims remained underrepresented in schools. For example, only 20 percent of secondary-school students in Dar es Salaam were Muslim, although Muslims made up 80 percent of the city's population. Among his complaints, Shaykh Ally Bassalleh enumerated instances of discrimination against Muslims, such as the dissolution of the EAMWS in 1968, until he arrived at the most recent case of "government marginalization of Muslims," namely the closure of the al-Furqaan Islamic Primary School in Buguruni/Ilala, Dar es Salaam. Not only had the school been closed, but its accounts at the Akiba Commercial Bank had been closed in July as well, at the demand of the Bank of Tanzania. This action confirmed Muslim anxieties, as the school was considered a showcase, the best Muslim school in Dar es Salaam, one to which even Christian parents sent their children. In a series of articles in July and August in *an-Nuur* and *Nasaha*, the state was accused of having engineered its closure.

The imbalance between Muslims and Christians was not only sensed or polemically presented but could be concretely documented. Muslim students are still underrepresented at the University of Dar es Salaam. A survey reported by the *Guardian* on July 18, 2003, that used students' names to identify their religion showed that of the 2,420 students admitted to the University of Dar es Salaam for the academic year 2003–4 (of whom 24 percent were women), only 304, or 12 percent, were Muslim (see also Chande 1998, 196–201; Chande 1993; and Said 2001). At the same time, churches are proliferating in Dar es Salaam: although the 1995 city map registered a total of 303 places of worship, more than half of them mosques (187 mosques, 112 churches, and 4 Hindu temples), the situation has changed completely today. Driving through Dar es Salaam, not only the center and Kariakoo but, more important, the different Ilala quarters, as well as Kigamboni, Temeke, Tandika, Kinondoni, Mwenge, and the new neighborhoods on the major roads leading to Bagamoyo and Morogoro, one sees more church buildings than mosques, and these buildings, especially the Pentecostal churches, are of surprising size.

The relative numerical strength of the different religious groups was another topic of dispute in the 1980s and 1990s. Relying on the 1957 census, which showed Muslims outnumbering Christians three to two, Muslims maintained that they constitute the majority of the population. Christians, however, referred to the 1967 census, which put Christians at 32 percent of the population, Muslims at 30 percent, and African "traditional" religions at 37 percent, and claimed that they were the largest single religious group. Tanzania's most recent census of 2002, by contrast, is silent on the issue of religion (Tanzania Government 2002). The different census data gave rise to an ongoing debate about the respective strength of each group and these debates continue to disturb public discourses. Ali Kettani, for instance, claimed that in 1978 Tanzania's population was about 55 percent Muslim (10.2 million out of a total population of 18.57 million; Kettani 1982), while Christians such as Reverend

Curthwell Omari claim that by the mid-1980s Christians constituted 44 percent of the population, Muslims 32 percent, and adherents of African "traditional" religions 22 percent (Omari 1984, 373; for discussion see Ludwig 1999, 229). By contrast, Chande's discussion of numbers and statistics, based on a critical analysis of the different sources, supports the impression that Muslims are still Tanzania's largest religious group, even though estimates of their number vary wildly (from 34 percent to 60 percent), and Christians are the second largest group, although more visible (Chande 1998, 7).

Another bone of contention in Muslim–Christian disputes is the role of Muslims in the national struggle for independence. Muslim authors such as Muhammad Said claim that Christians deliberately deemphasized the importance of Muslims and overemphasized their own. Tanzania's history after Independence is consequently seen as a history of the increasing marginalization of Muslims in many respects. Instances such as the 1964 dissolution of AMNUT (All Muslims National Union of Tanganyika) and the failure to build an Islamic university in Dar es Salaam; the 1968 dissolution of the EAMWS and its replacement by BAKWATA; the constant underrepresentation of Muslims in government, administration, and education; and the union government's intervention to prevent Zanzibar from joining the Organization of the Islamic Conference (OIC) in 1993[32] are constant reminders of these policies of marginalization.[33]

It has to be mentioned, however, that Muslims often fail to realize that Christians may equally argue that Muslims are, at least formally, overrepresented in a number of institutions, because of the strong position of (Muslim) Zanzibar in union institutions and Parliament, even though radical Muslims do not usually consider the Zanzibari Members of Parliament who are, at the same time, members of the CCM to be "proper" Muslims.[34] The current parliament of Tanzania has 50 members from Zanzibar, whereas 182 represent the mainland. Also, the mainland has twenty-one administrative regions, and Zanzibar has five, plus a House of Representatives of its own; the mainland has no such institution. Muslim Zanzibar, in addition, receives 4.5 percent of all foreign aid allocations, though it has only 3 percent of the Tanzanian population (Hofmeier and Hirschler 2004, 40). Christians see radical Muslims as a threat to Tanzania's political development and picture them as such to the public, particularly after the 1998 embassy bombing in Dar es Salaam and the capture of the first Tanzanian al-Qaeda suspect in Pakistan in 2004.

Conclusion

Attacking the government and its branches, such as BAKWATA, and accusing them of protecting "the Christians" while suppressing Muslims became a favorite strategy of the *ansar al-sunna* in the late 1980s. Such attacks appeared continually in Muslim papers like *an-Nuur*, in articles titled, for instance, "There is total war against Islam and Muslims" [Vita kamili dhidi ya Uislamu na Waislamu], *an-Nuur*, August 13, 2004. These perceptions of marginalization have been linked with discourses of "Othering": Muslims feel that somebody has to be blamed for historical failures. But when we consider the historical relationships between Muslims, Christians, and the state in German East Africa, Tanganyika, and Tanzania, we see that Muslim perceptions of marginalization should not be accepted at face value. Muslims had a rather privi-leged role in the German colonial period and also in the Tanganyikan independence movement of the 1940s and 1950s. Also, it cannot be said that the British colonial administration deliberately discriminated against Muslims. However, the German as well as the British administration did support the activities of the Christian churches and their respective missions, and in the 1950s and 1960s mission-educated Christian Tanganyikans gradually acquired paramount importance as administrative cadres. At the same time, Muslims largely failed to develop modern systems of education which could have graduated a comparable number of Muslims. When Tanganyika became independent in 1961, therefore, Muslims were still in an advan-tageous political position but lacked a modern, educated elite which would have been able to translate this political prominence into structural advantages. And even when Muslims had a second chance at this in the 1970s, they were unable to do so. As a consequence, the educated class, those who could administer a modern state, hospi-tals, schools, companies, and so on, became even more Christian in the 1980s and 1990s, to the chagrin of many Muslims, who increasingly came to see the time since Independence as a time of "missed chances." In order to explain their failure, Muslims have recourse to scenarios of intrigue—and are, at least sometimes, right, as a number of post-Independence events indeed evidence the deliberate marginalization of Muslims.

However, Muslim "litanies of complaint" do not necessarily support the assump-tion that every Muslim failure in Tanzania is due to Christian intrigues. Some Muslims have started to challenge established interpretations of Muslim failures. These Muslims are no longer waiting for state intervention but have started to imple-ment their ideas and to establish, for instance, modern Islamic schools, often against the resistance of BAKWATA-oriented scholars. The many conflicts among Muslims in Tanzania are thus caused not only by Muslim opposition to the state but also by Muslim activist opposition to established Muslim cadres in the government: the state is seen as being controlled not only by Christians but also by corrupt Muslims who collude with Christians. And because, since the 1980s, activist Muslims have blamed Muslim failure not only on the state and on Christian intrigues but also on the inactivity of two generations of Muslim functionaries, disputes among Muslims are probably as virulent today as are polemics between activist Muslims and activist Christians. For this reason, conflicts among Muslims in Tanzania strikingly resemble a conflict of generations. In this conflict of generations, young radical Muslims gain legitimacy by referring to old and comparatively conservative scholars who can point to similar experiences of marginalization in the early years of the Nyerere administra-tion. Shaykh Hassan b. Ameir, for instance, is seen today, despite his *tariqa* affiliation, as a representative of a "decent" form of political Islam, not yet corrupted and, at the same time, independent of government concepts of development.

The history of Tanzania, particularly of Muslim–state relations, thus shows that religion (Islam) has been used and understood as a function of politics. Islam and Islamic codes and symbols have been instrumentalized to attack and to delegitimize political decisions. In the context of strategies of legitimization and delegitimization of politics, religion has also become a tool, a platform to present political demands. This political perception of religion was confirmed by Muslim as well as non-Muslim representations of Islam as a political code, a "theology of liberation," or, conversely, an ideology condoning terror. Each of these essentialistic representations of Islam, as a positive or a negative force in politics, has triggered apologetic reactions that sought to defend the respective construction of "political Islam." Apologetic constructions of religion have again entrenched the notion that Islam is primarily a political ideology. Such an essentialistic reduction of Islam has to be viewed, however, as an "orientalist trap" that leads Muslims in a self-defeating dialectic to ultimately confirm Western notions of political Islam, even if they are presented in more sympathetic terms. A political reading of Islam not only denies the nonpolitical dimensions of religion but also turns religion into a factor in a political equation which may be manipulated and instrumentalized at will. The instrumentalization of religion for political purposes thus renders religion as quotidian as the political context and ultimately destroys the legitimatory force of religion as an ethical superstructure. Religion is transformed into a platform for conflict negotiation and becomes as disputable and negotiable as all other factors in a given context. In order to overcome constructions of conflict based on religious argumentation and the cultivation of Muslim and Christian complexes of discrimination which may easily develop into complex-ridden perceptions of reality, as well as to develop strategies for the amelioration of interreligious tensions in Tanzania, it will be necessary to desacralize public political debates.

Turning back to our initial discussion of the structural differences between different categories of Muslim countries in Africa, we can now compare Tanzania with Nigeria and try to find an answer to the question as to why religion has over and over again been a destabilizing force in Nigeria and why it has so far not acquired this role in Tanzania: Nigeria and Tanzania, after all, were both colonized by the British, became independent in the early 1960s, are of equal geographic size (although Nigeria's population is four times Tanzania's), and are characterized by extreme ethnic diversity, with several hundred linguistic groups in each country. In addition, the countries have similar ratios of Muslims, Christians, and adherents of African "traditional" religions. Yet whereas Nigeria's postcolonial history is marked by an endless succession of coups and military governments, a vicious civil war in Biafra, and numerous local and regional armed conflicts involving an ever-changing mix of ethnic, economic, historical, religious, political, and social motivations, as well as virulent regional antagonisms between the north, the south, the east, and the "Middle Belt," Tanzania may point to a rather harmonious postcolonial history dominated by a teacher-president, a peaceful transition to multiparty parliamentarianism, a victorious war against Uganda, a long tradition of nation building, the emergence of Kiswahili as a truly national language, and the fading away of particularistic ethnic traditions. And even if Tanzania's politicians have built their own record of mismanagement, corruption, and arbitrary execution of power, particularly during the *ujamaa* period of the 1970s, they compare rather well with Nigeria's maze of corruption and record of bad government, especially during General Abacha's rule in the 1990s. Despite being well endowed with natural resources, particularly oil, Nigeria has also never managed to develop a cohesive program of national development but has been torn by bitter struggles over the allocation of these resources. Tanzania, by contrast, never had to think much about the distribution of wealth but still managed to build one of the most ambitious programs of national education and public health in

Africa. In short, it may be said that Tanzania has managed to develop into a nation since Independence, whereas Nigeria has been torn apart by unending wars of positioning and the maneuvering of regional political factions.

Although religion is a strong mobilizing force in both countries, both Islam and Christian denominations have been much more significant as markers of identity, as political players, and as legitimizing references in local, regional, and national politics in Nigeria than in Tanzania, where both Islam and Christian denominations have been much more integrated into national development and, consequently, are less identifiable as independent political players. Whereas the political realm has always controlled the expression of religion in Tanzania (to the chagrin of some radical groups), religious players have managed, by contrast, to hijack politics in Nigeria. Nigerian politicians, as a consequence, have repeatedly become hostage to religious radicals, most visibly in the recurrent sharia debates. As a result, two different religio-political cultures have developed in Nigeria and Tanzania: whereas public debates in Nigeria are often heated, and in many cases turn violent, public debates in Tanzania are characterized by a general desire to reach a consensus, even at the cost of suppressing historical truth and justifiable (even if particularistic) aspirations. I became witness to Tanzanian ways of dealing with the past, for instance, when taking part in a conference in Britain on the Muslim–Christian dialogue in Africa. One of the speakers started to praise the achievements of Julius Nyerere, and all Tanzanians in the audience, their different religious and political orientations notwithstanding, joined his eulogy. When I asked an outspoken Muslim radical why he had not protested, as he was well aware of Nyerere's rather anti-Muslim policies, he responded that of course he knew the legacy of the Nyerere era, but it was still "too early" to talk about it in public. "It would hurt too much. If we wait twenty years, we can talk about it in peace."

Notes

1. In 1933, Tanganyika had twenty-one different missions (Mbilinyi 1980).
2. For a more extensive presentation of the development of education in British Tanganyika, see Buchert 1994, Mbilinyi 1980, and Wright 1971.
3. Approximately two-thirds of the Christian population is Catholic today (Mbogoni 2004). This was also the case in the late 1950s. According to the 1957 census, 31 percent of the population was Christian, and two-thirds of the Christians were Catholic (Ludwig 1999, 30).
4. Both President Julius Nyerere (1961–85) and President Benjamin Mkapa (1995–2005) were Catholic, whereas President Ali Hassan Mwinyi (1985–95) was Muslim. Other Christian national politicians include Oscar Kambona, Job Lusinde, and Paul Bomani (Ludwig 1999, 32–33).
5. The TAA was established in 1928–29 by Abdallah Kleist Sykes (1894–1949) and later led by his son, Abd al-Wahid Sykes (1924–68; Said 1998, 40–44.).
6. The MAT was established in 1933 by Abdallah Kleist Sykes, who was a member of the *mawlid* committee in Dar es Salaam, which was responsible for organizing the *mawlid al-nabi* celebrations (the celebrations of the birthday of the Prophet Muhammad); it was later led by Shaykh Hassan b. Ameir.
7. Bibi Titi Muhammad was born in 1926 in Dar es Salaam and died on November 6, 2000. For her life and struggle in TANU, see Geiger 1997, Askew 2002, and Said 1998, 182.

8. Shaykh Hassan b. Ameir ash-Shirazi was born in 1880 in Makunduchi, Unguja, and died October 8, 1979. In the 1940s and 1950s, he became the foremost leader of Tanganyika's Muslims. For his biography, see DUMT 2004.

9. Chaurembo was a member of the Zaramo people and local leader of the Shadhiliyya in Dar es Salaam. He studied with Shaykh Hassan b. Ameir until 1961, when he broke away from him (Said 1998, 269). In the 1960s, he became the chairman of the *mawlid* committee as well as a member of the TANU central committee.

10. The number of Muslim ministers in the new union government actually increased to ten, whereas fourteen were Christians. All ministers from mainland Tanzania were Christian (Ludwig 1999, 70; Said 1998, 275).

11. In 2004, an Islamic university was finally opened in Morogoro.

12. Oscar Kambona had been a major ally of Nyerere and actually saved his regime in 1964 during the mutiny in Dar es Salaam. Later, however, Nyerere came to see him as a competitor and removed him from important government and party positions. In 1968, Kambona fled to Kenya (Geiger 1997; Said 1998).

13. Only in 1984 did Nyerere publicly rehabilitate her. According to many, Bibi Titi Muhammad was one of the few TANU politicians other than Nyerere who was known throughout the country in 1961, at the time of Independence. Like most leading TANU women of the 1950s and early 1960s in the UWT, she was Muslim. In the mid-1960s, Christian women were still a minority in the UWT (Geiger 1997).

14. Fundikira was a leading TANU member and an opponent of Nyerere (see Chande 1994; Nimtz 1980, 164; and Lodhi and Westerlund 1999, 102).

15. One group of Muslims in Bukoba claimed that the two *raka'at* prescribed for the Friday noon prayers (*zuhr*) should be added to the usual daily four *raka'at*. Their opponents, led by a Muslim teacher from Bukoba, Adam Nasibu, insisted that Friday prayers superseded the normal routine and that the number of *raka'at* for the Friday *zuhr* prayers was only two and not the cumulative six. On account of this issue, the *jum'a-zuhuri* group, which was strongly supported by the Indian Muslim population of Bukoba, finally split off and established the Tanzania Muslim Education Union (TMEU), while Adam Nasibu remained in command of the Bukoba branch of the EAMWS (Chande 1998, 136).

16. Chaurembo had broken with Shaykh Hassan b. Ameir in 1961. See the series of articles on the "EAMWS dispute" (*mgogoro* EAMWS) of 1968 in *an-Nuur*, August 9, 2002, September 6, 2002, and August 16, 2003.

17. BAKWATA seems to have been dominated in the 1970s and 1980s by scholars affiliated with the Qadiriyya Sufi order (see Lodhi and Westerlund 1999, 103).

18. Shaykh Saidi Musa was born in Simbom near Ugweno in Northern Pare in 1943. In 1962 he moved to Zanzibar, where he was a student of Shaykh Abdallah Salih al-Farsi until 1967, when al-Farsi left Zanzibar. In 1968, Musa left Zanzibar as well and settled in Kariakoo, Dar es Salaam, where he worked from 1968 to 1992 for the Tanzania Shoe Factory. At the same time, he started his *da'wa* activities, published numerous writings (including a biography of al-Farsi), and became an outspoken representative of the "radical" reformist movement in Tanzania. In the late 1970s, he started to publicly support the Iranian revolution. Every Friday, he gave a sermon in the Manyema mosque (est. 1912) or the Qiblatayn mosque. Although Musa has been very active in *da'wa* and influenced a considerable number of radical Muslims in Tanzania in the 1970s and 1980s, he never founded or led an official organization, though he did influence the Union of Muslim Preachers of Equivalent Religions.

19. Shaykh Nur al-Din Husayn (born 1924 or 1925 in Kilwa) has become the foremost leader of the Shadhiliyya in contemporary Tanzania (Ahmed 2005). He studied not only with local shaykhs in Tanzania but also at al-Azhar University in Egypt, before settling in Lindi in the early 1950s. In Lindi, he opened a madrasa and worked at various jobs before he started his own business as a trader of dried fish. In 1965, he was put under arrest for allegedly plotting against Nyerere and spent eight months in prison in Mtwara. After his

release from prison, he settled in Tanga and resumed trading and teaching and was invited to establish a new madrasa nearby in Korogwe. In 1980, he moved to Dar es Salaam and established another madrasa in Kariakoo. In 1992, he set up the Hajj Trust, a private company which organized Tanzanian pilgrims (annually about three to five thousand), although this task technically remained BAKWATA's prerogative until 1995. Through the Hajj Trust, Shaykh Nur al-Din became a household name in Tanzania. In addition, he has gained national importance as the leader of the Baraza Kuu la Jumuiya na Taasisi za Kiislamu. The Baraza Kuu has assumed control over the Tanzania Islamic Centre in Magomeni and was involved in an initiative (supported by some *ansar al-sunna* groups) to "hijack" (according to CCM-BAKWATA reports) BAKWATA-controlled mosques in Dar es Salaam (Sören Gilsaa, personal communication, April 21, 2005; Adam Shafi Adam, personal communication, April 2, 2005; see also Lodhi and Westerlund 1999, 107).

20. In 1993, Shaykh Yahya Hussein was involved in riots in the Magomeni and Manzese neighborhoods and was arrested (Njozi 2000, 2003).

21. In a recent paper, Chanfi Ahmed quotes a Tanzanian author, Muhammad Said, who claims that the Umoja wa Wahubiri wa Kiislamu originated in Kigoma in the colonial period as a reaction to the activities of a Jew in this region. Ahmed himself thinks that it was established in reaction to the first activities of the Ahmadiyya movement in this region in 1934 (Ahmed 2005, 2).

22. Oppositional activists such as the *ansar al-sunna* groups have established an array of seemingly independent organizations (such as Uamsho, the Shura ya Maimamu, and others) to escape repression (especially in Zanzibar) and to confuse observers. The *ansar al-sunna* in mainland Tanzania are organized in several semi-independent groups, based in Dar es Salaam, Tanga, Mwanza, and other urban centers. At the same time, individual members of oppositional groups may be employed by the government (Sören Gilsaa, personal communication, July 1, 2005).

23. Shaykh Ally Bassalleh writes for both *an-Nuur* and *Nasaha*. He was born in 1946 in Zanzibar and has become one of the best-known *mhadhiri* preachers in Tanzania. He attended the Zanzibar Teacher Training College and has taught at primary as well as secondary schools in Zanzibar and mainland Tanzania. In November 2001, he was imprisoned by the police for having declared that Jesus was not God.

24. Until then, Shaykh Mbukuzi had been an outspoken opponent of BAKWATA (Njozi 2003, 71).

25. See "Baada ya al-Furqaan waislamu kaeni chonjo" (Muslims continue to quarrel), *an-Nuur*, August 13, 2004.

26. Ahmad Deedat (b. 1918), who founded the South African Islamic Propagation Centre in 1957, died in August 2005.

27. The first Pentecostal church in Tanzania was founded in Mbeya in 1959. Since the early 1980s, Pentecostal activities have exploded, and, in the late 1990s, about 1 million Tanzanians were members of Pentecostal churches. For the growth of Pentecostal churches as well as changes in church strategies in the 1980s and 1990s, see Ludwig 1996, 222–23; Ludwig 1999, 183, 186.

28. Nassor Bachu (or Pachu, or Bachoo), a Zanzibari, is a major spokesman and leader of the *ansar al-sunna* movement. He is presently the imam of the Kikwajuni Juu mosque in Zanzibar. He has written a 165-page treatise on the sighting of the moon (*ufafunzi*).

29. Hamza Njozi's book on the Mwembechai incident (Njozi 2000) was banned in August 2000 by President Benjamin Mkapa. This was immediately seen by *an-Nuur* as another case of discrimination against Muslims (Wijsen 2002, 235–36).

30. Sofia Kawawa's statement may have been linked with BAKWATA's demand, in 1987, that the Islamic courts be reinstated. They had been abolished in 1971 in the context of the unification of Tanzanian laws and the integration of sharia personal law into the secular system of law (Lodhi and Westerlund 1999, 104). For the development of the Tanzanian civil law and the separation of church and civil marriage, see Ludwig 1999, 145.

31. This memorandum of understanding aroused considerable protest among Muslims, who saw it as providing state funding for Christian institutions, particularly hospitals and schools (see the Baraza Kuu's note of protest of October 9, 2000, in Njozi 2003, 189).

32. Zanzibar's effort to join the OIC triggered corresponding church complaints of "Muslim insults" (Ludwig 1999, 213).

33. In 1993, Tanzania had 8 Muslim district commissioners, as compared to 113 Christian ones (Njozi 2000, 90; see Lodhi 1994 for further data); and, in 1970, the Tanzanian House of Parliament had 23 Muslim members, whereas 80 were Christians (56 Catholic) and 5 were "traditionals" (Njozi 2000, 4).

34. Since October 2005, Mrisho Kikwete, CCM, a Muslim politician from Bagamoyo, north of Dar es Salaam has been Tanzania's president, having succeeded Benjamin Mkapa. His nomination for the presidency of the CCM constituted a break with an unwritten rule of Tanzanian politics, namely, that a Christian president from the mainland is followed by a Muslim president from Zanzibar.

References

Ahmed, Chanfi. 2005. The Muslim Bible Preachers (Wahubiri wa Kiislamu) in East Africa. Paper presented at "Conversion in Africa," conference of the Centre of Modern Oriental Studies, Berlin, November 25–26.

Askew, Kelly. 2002. *Performing the nation: Swahili music and cultural politics in Tanzania.* Chicago: University of Chicago Press.

Buchert, Lene. 1994. *Education in the development of Tanzania, 1919–90.* London: James Currey.

Chande, Abdin N. 1993. Muslims and modern education in Tanzania. *Journal of Muslim Minority Affairs* 14 (1–2): 1–16.

———. 1994. Ulamaa and religious competition in a Mrima town. *Islam et sociétés au sud du Sahara* 8: 43–51.

———. 1998. *Islam, ulamaa and community development in Tanzania: A case study of religious currents in East Africa.* San Francisco: Austin and Winfield.

Constantin, François. 1995. The attempts to create Muslim national organizations in Tanzania, Uganda and Kenya. In *Religion and politics in East Africa: The period since independence*, ed. Holger Bernt Hansen and Michael Twaddle, 19–31. London: James Currey.

DUMT (Dar es Salaam University Muslim Trusteeship). 2004. *Tusikubali Kubaguliwa Kielimu: Nasaha za Shaykh Hasan bin Ameir (1880–1979).* Dar es Salaam: Dar es Salaam University Muslim Trusteeship.

Forster, Peter G. 1997. Religion and the state in Tanzania and Malawi. *Journal of African and Asian Studies* 32 (3–4): 163–84.

Geiger, Susan. 1997. *TANU women: Gender and culture in the making of Tanganyikan nationalism, 1955–1965.* Portsmouth, N.H.: Heinemann.

Grandin, Nicole. 1998. Les confréries soufi à Zanzibar: Passé et présent. In *Zanzibar aujourd'hui*, ed. Colette La Cour Grandmaison and Ariel Crozon, 321–40. Paris: Karthala.

Hofmeier, Rolf, and Hirschler, Kurt. 2004. Kurzdarstellung Tansania/Tansania im Jahre 2003. In *Nigeria-Tanzania-Djibouti: Sonderdruck aus Anlaß der Afrika-Reise des deutschen Bundespräsidenten Johannes Rau im März 2004*, 31–42. Hamburg: Afrika-Institut.

Iliffe, John. 1969. *Tanganyika under German rule, 1905–12.* Cambridge: Cambridge University Press.

———. 1979. *A modern history of Tanganyika.* Cambridge: Cambridge University Press.

Kettani, Ali. 1982. Muslim East Africa: An overview. *Journal of Muslim Minority Affairs* 4 (2): 104–19.

Koponen, Juhani. 1994. *Development for exploitation: German colonial policies in Mainland Tanzania, 1884–1914.* Hamburg: Lit Verlag.

Lacunza Balda, Justo. 1989. An investigation into some concepts and ideas found in Swahili Islamic writings. Ph.D. diss., School of Oriental and African Studies, London.

———. 1993. The role of Kiswahili in East African Islam. In *Muslim identity and social change in sub-Saharan Africa*, ed. Louis Brenner, 226–38. London: C. Hurst.

———. 1997. Translations of the Qur'an into Swahili, and contemporary Islamic revival in East Africa. In *African Islam and Islam in Africa: Encounters between Sufis and Islamists*, ed. Eva Evers Rosander and David Westerlund, 95–126. London: C. Hurst.

Lodhi, Abdulaziz Y. 1994. Muslims in Eastern Africa: Their Past and Present. *Nordic Journal of African Studies* 3 (1): 88–99.

Lodhi, Abdulaziz, and David Westerlund. 1999. Tanzania. In *Islam outside the Arab world*, ed. David Westerlund and Ingvar Svanberg, 97–111. Richmond, Surrey: Curzon.

Ludwig, Frieder. 1996. After ujamaa: Is religious rivalism a threat to Tanzania's stability? In *Questioning the secular state: The worldwide resurgence of religion in politics*, ed. David Westerlund, 216–36. London: C. Hurst.

———. 1999. *Church and state in Tanzania: Aspects of a changing relationship, 1961–94.* Leiden: Brill.

Mbilinyi, Marjorie J. 1980. African education during the British colonial period, 1919–61. In *Tanzania under colonial rule*, ed. M. H. Y. Kaniki, 236–75. London: Longman.

Mbogoni, Lawrence E. Y. 2004. *The cross versus the crescent: Religion and politics in Tanzania from the 1880s to the 1990s.* Dar es Salaam: Mkuki na Nyota.

Nimtz, A. H. 1980. *Islam and politics in East Africa.* Minneapolis: University of Minnesota Press.

Njozi, Hamza Mustafa. 2000. *Mwembechai killings and the political future of Tanzania.* Ottawa: Globalink Communications.

———. 2003. *Muslims and the state in Tanzania.* Dar es Salaam: Dar es Salaam University Muslim Trusteeship.

Omari, Cuthbert K. 1984. Christian-Muslim relations in Tanzania: The socio-political dimension. *Journal of Muslim Minority Affairs* 5 (2): 373–90.

Said, Muhammad. 1998. *The life and times of Abdulwahid Sykes (1924–1968): The untold story of the Muslim struggle against British colonialism in Tanganyika.* London: Minerva Press.

———. 2001. Intricacies and intrigues in Tanzania: The question of Muslim stagnation in education. http://www.islamtz.org/nyaraka/Elimu2.html.

Sivalon, John C. 1992. *Kanisa Katoliki na Siasa ya Tanzania Bara, 1953–1985.* Ndanda-Peramiho: Benedictine Publications.

Tanzania Government. 2002. Population and Housing Census. http://www.tanzania.go.tz/census/.

van de Bruinhorst, Gerard. 2005. Siku ya Arafa and the Idd el-Hajj: Textual knowledge, ritual practice and social protest in Tanzania. Seminar paper, 6th Swahili workshop, Oslo, March 31–April 2.

Wijsen, Frans. 2002. When two elephants fight, the grass gets hurt, Muslim-Christian relationships in upcountry Tanzania. *Church and Theology in Context*, 40 (1): 235–48.

Wright, Marcia. 1971. *German missions in Tanganyika, 1891–1941: Lutherans and Moravians in the southern highlands.* Oxford: Oxford University Press.

CHAPTER 8

KENYAN MUSLIMS, THE AFTERMATH OF 9/11, AND THE "WAR ON TERROR"

Rüdiger Seesemann

Introduction

Much has been said about 9/11, but relatively little attention has been paid so far to the impact the events of that day had on Africa—at least if one discounts studies that focus on the rising U.S. security concerns in the aftermath of the attacks on the World Trade Center and the Pentagon.[1] In contrast to most previous analyses, my approach to the matter attempts to highlight how Africans—in this case, Kenyan Muslims—view the effects of 9/11 on their communities and the challenges they face in the post-9/11 world.

In several respects, the post-9/11 era has dramatically brought to a head earlier trends connected with the "age of neoliberalism." Democracy and capitalist market economy, the two basic ingredients of "Western civilization" (which has been gaining ground all over the world since the collapse of the Soviet empire), suddenly appeared to be under a serious threat. To some observers, the events of 9/11 suggested that the deprived might no longer be willing to accept the gap between the rich and the poor as a matter of destiny (see Mamdani 2004). Moreover, the attacks made it clear that a group of radicals was ready to fight "the West" with all available means—up to and including weapons of mass destruction. In short, the world seemed to be on the edge of the often-invoked "clash of civilizations."[2]

In this chapter, I propose to explore some of the myths and realities of the "clash of civilizations" by looking at the impact of 9/11 and the "war on terror" on Muslim communities in East Africa, with a particular focus on Kenya and occasional reference to Tanzania, Kenya's southern neighbor.[3] Questions I will address include how Muslims perceive the "war on terror," and how the changing configuration of geopolitics in the aftermath of 9/11 has affected their lives, their attitudes, and the course of political events in the region. The perspective taken here differs from previous works on 9/11 and Africa (e.g., Nielinger 2002; Glickman 2003; Kraxberger 2005; Carmody 2005) insofar as my focus is on African perceptions of the aftermath of 9/11, rather than on American or European perceptions. The chapter addresses several areas of public life where 9/11 has left its imprint in Kenya, a country of about

30 million inhabitants where Muslims constitute between 20 and 25 percent of the population.[4] I will pay particular attention to the recent debates about the role of Islamic law in the Kenyan constitution and the repercussions of the proposed Suppression of Terrorism Bill for the Muslim community. Both controversies help to illustrate the extent to which most Kenyan Muslims feel under siege in the aftermath of 9/11. In the concluding section I argue that the strong Muslim reactions to the two great national debates (on the Kadhis' Courts and the antiterrorism bill) reflect the increasing tendency among Muslims to perceive themselves as a vulnerable minority.

The chapter also demonstrates that the long-term impact of 9/11 on East Africa will depend less on global issues or on U.S. policy than on political and religious developments at the national and local levels. Rather than being a potential front line in the "clash of civilizations," Kenya is an arena where a Muslim minority tries to define and negotiate its status within a secular state at a moment of heightened religio-political tensions not only in East Africa but also in many other parts of Africa and the world; and these tensions are presently reinforced by an increasing awareness of religious identity among both the Christian and the Muslim communities in the country.

Reactions to 9/11 in Kenya and Beyond

In late September 2001, several American and European TV stations aired a documentary film, originally produced by PBS, focusing on the global Islamic terrorist network (Smith 2001). One of the longer portions of the film examined the attack on the U.S. embassy in Nairobi on August 7, 1998, which claimed 256 lives, including 12 Americans, and injured almost 5,000 people.[5] At almost the same time, a bomb was detonated in front of the U.S. embassy in Dar es Salaam, killing thirteen people. Statements by Osama bin Laden, released later, led to the conclusion that al-Qaeda was responsible for the strikes. The documentary's authors diligently gathered considerable information on the history leading up to the Nairobi attack, information that was based on CIA research. With the exception of one Palestinian, who was married to a Kenyan and had lived in Kenya for an extended period of time, all the men involved in the planning and execution of the attack hailed from Arab countries, and none had personal ties in Kenya.[6]

Toward the end, the documentary featured a short interview with Ali Shee, an Islamic preacher from Mombasa. When asked what Kenyan Muslims thought of Osama bin Laden, Shee responded, "He is a hero." Since the 1980s, Ali Shee had been one of the most vocal critics of the Kenyan regime and an outspoken advocate of a radical interpretation of Islam (see Bakari 1995), and in the interview he came across as the personification of an anti-American propaganda campaign, drawing African Muslims into this stream. When we consider that pictures of Osama bin Laden on t-shirts, posters, and bumper stickers have been highly popular in East Africa and elsewhere on the continent since September 11, 2001, one is tempted to conclude that bin Laden is viewed as the leader of a global Islamic fight for the liberation of Muslims, a man the people enthusiastically want to follow. If this assessment is accurate, then the attacks in Nairobi and Dar es Salaam could be seen as the tip of an Islamist, militant, and anti-American iceberg, and the 9/11 attacks would have triggered a feeling of satisfaction among Muslims in East Africa.

However, that impression is misleading.[7] Bin Laden may have garnered admiration in Tanzania and Kenya, but he has not won the sympathy of Muslims. Like former Iraqi dictator Saddam Hussein, who was hardly a man with Islamist ambitions, bin Laden symbolizes for East African Muslims resistance against the global political and economic hegemony of the U.S. Bin Laden is considered someone who has dared to stand up on his own against the world's no. 1 superpower. The people praise his courage, but they do not condone his actions. They admire him as a pop icon but not as a "holy warrior." How strongly bin Laden's Islamic legitimization of terror is rejected in the East African region is reflected in the fact that many Kenyan and Tanzanian Muslims continue to argue that the true perpetrators of the World Trade Center attack cannot have been Muslims, as Islam prohibits such violence.

In fact, the reactions of Kenyan Muslims to 9/11 were similar to their reactions to the earlier attack on the U.S. embassy in Nairobi. On August 7, 1999, the first anniversary of the devastating strike, the Supreme Council of Kenyan Muslims (SUPKEM), an umbrella organization run by professionals rather than religious scholars that claims to speak for the community of Muslims and defend their interests vis-à-vis the government (see Constantin 1995), had a statement read in all mosques around the country: "What would be the reason for planting bombs in Nairobi and Dar es Salaam if not to disrupt the spread of Islam in East Africa, which has been enhanced by the existing peaceful atmosphere?" In Nairobi's Jamia Mosque, Kenya's largest, SUPKEM chairman Abdulghafur Busaidy gave a speech summarizing the painful experiences of Kenyan Muslims since the attack: sweeping suspicions of Muslims as terrorists; public defamation of Islam by the media, politicians, and church representatives; and the banning of six Islamic nongovernmental organizations (NGOs) which allegedly threatened domestic security; as well as confiscation of files and computer drives from the offices of Islamic organizations (*Daily Nation* [Nairobi], August 7, 1999).

Such statements reveal two basic features of how Muslims view the current situation. First, they reflect an interpretation of the events as part of a global fight led by the U.S., or even "the West" as a whole, against Islam. On the other hand, they show that Muslims in Kenya and Tanzania are, from their own experiences, fully aware of the negative impact that such terrorist attacks have when they are carried out in the name of Islam. For many, this reason is sufficient to condemn and reject such violent action. Therefore, 9/11 and the subsequent "war on terror" did not mobilize East African Muslims. Instead, they revived memories of the August 7, 1998, attack, which was much more traumatic for Kenyans than the attacks on the World Trade Center and the Pentagon.

From a Kenyan perspective, the claim that "the world changed on 9/11" is inaccurate. If there was a crucial date, then as far as Kenya is concerned it was 8/7. In several respects, the developments after 9/11 were a repetition of what Kenyans had experienced three years earlier: More NGOs were banned (for instance, the Saudi-financed al-Haramain), public statements against Islam were made again, and, perhaps more than before, Muslims became the target of security and intelligence services. Positioning itself as a loyal U.S. ally in the "war on terror," the Kenyan government allowed foreign intelligence organizations, including the FBI, the CIA, and Mossad, to operate in Kenya (see Amnesty International 2005), and Mombasa's port served as a base from which European and U.S. naval vessels could monitor the shipping traffic on the Horn of Africa.

The Prospects of "Indigenous African Terrorism" in Kenya

Still, the question remains whether the aftermath of 9/11 could, in the long term, lead to the emergence of Islamic terrorism in East Africa. Stefan Mair, a German political analyst, has recently argued that the anti-American attitudes of African Muslims might develop into an "indigenous African terrorism" if there were leaders able to incite the Muslim public (Mair 2002). This opinion is matched by the assessment in American intelligence circles that Muslim hatred of the U.S. could lead to organized violence against American citizens and institutions.[8]

However, a look at confrontations involving Kenyan and Tanzanian Muslims over the past few years shows that violence usually only occurred when Muslims were the victims of repressive government measures. One example is the suppression of the Islamic Party of Kenya (IPK), which was banned in the early 1990s and excluded from participating in parliamentary and presidential elections (see Oded 2000). The massive and occasionally violent police action against IPK followers triggered an extraordinary—and unrepeated—mobilization and solidarity among Kenyan Muslims. Similarly, the so-called Mwembechai killings, in which Tanzanian security forces entered a mosque in a suburb of Dar es Salaam and killed several Muslims on February 12, 1998, had local causes.[9]

In recent years, U.S. Middle East policy repeatedly angered Muslims in Kenya and Tanzania. Still, that anger never led to escalations comparable to those that occurred during the IPK ban in Mombasa or during the violent confrontations between Tanzanian Muslims and security forces in Dar es Salaam or Zanzibar. Especially since the second Intifada in the Israeli-occupied Palestinian territories, there have been frequent anti-Israeli and anti-American demonstrations in Nairobi and Mombasa (see Hamadouche 2002). However, apart from occasional clashes with police forces, the demonstrations did not lead to widespread violence. In mid-2002, a call to boycott U.S. goods in Kenya was largely ignored. Lists of specific goods to avoid were distributed in many mosques, but nothing resulted beyond some discussion.

On November 28, 2002, terrorists carried out two more attacks, this time near Mombasa. On the property of the Paradise Hotel at Kikambala, which is primarily visited by Israelis, explosives hidden inside a car went off, claiming eighteen lives, including those of the three perpetrators and three Israeli tourists. Almost simultaneously, two SAM-7 missiles were fired at an Israeli charter plane carrying 261 passengers just after its takeoff from the Mombasa airport, and they narrowly missed their target. Although a report came in from Beirut saying the previously unknown Army of Palestine had claimed responsibility for that attack in a letter, a government spokesman in Washington suggested that the Somali organization al-Ittihad al-Islami, which is linked to al-Qaeda, could be behind the two attacks (*IslamOnline.net* 2002a).[10] As in August 1998, Kenyan Muslim officials again spoke up, condemning terrorist attacks. An official SUPKEM statement read,

> whoever planned and executed the bombing is definitely the number one enemy of Islam and Muslims of Kenya. . . . the Muslims of Kenya will continue to co-exist with Kenyans of other faiths as they have always done. (*IslamOnline.net* 2002b)

A few days later, al-Qaeda claimed responsibility for the attacks (Amnesty International 2005, 3).[11] Nevertheless, according to the general opinion among East African Muslims, terrorism in Kenya and Tanzania cannot be blamed on Islam and is even less the fault of Muslims in the area. Instead, they view it as a security problem for the state, which is in charge of protecting the national borders against external attackers. For that precise reason, the population of Zanzibar—more than 90 percent of which is Muslim—reacted with disgruntlement when the U.S. State Department issued a terror warning for Zanzibar in January 2003, with many European governments following suit. Most Zanzibaris simply ruled out the possibility of an attack being carried out on "their" island, and some locals working in the tourism industry suggested that the warning was the result of a conspiracy by interested parties attempting to ruin Zanzibar's booming business with foreign visitors. Considering the widespread rejection of terrorist attacks among East African Muslims, the concern in U.S. intelligence circles—that Muslim rage could turn into organized anti-American violence on a large scale—is just as exaggerated as Mair's thesis of an "indigenous African terrorism."[12]

Since September 11, 2001, the U.S. government has pursued a two-dimensional strategy in Africa to tackle the problem of mounting anti-Americanism. On the one hand, it has intensified its intelligence efforts in many sub-Saharan states.[13] On the other hand, it has sought ways to counter the negative image that Muslims have of America. This strategy is based on the assumption that the tensions were merely due to an "image problem" which could be solved with a public relations campaign. The U.S. embassy in Nairobi assumed a leading role in these efforts. Members of the Public Affairs Section developed an Internet site providing regular updates on the "war on terror." At the same time, the website stresses that the measures it reports target not Islam but terrorist groups that unjustly use and cite Islam for their purposes. The site also describes the peaceful coexistence of different confessional groups in the U.S., and attributes it to the U.S. government's friendship toward Islam.[14] The Public Affairs Section also distributes a journal in Kiswahili under the title *Maisha Amerika—Uislamu Amerika*, which features articles similar to those on the website.[15] In a related effort, the United States Agency for International Development (USAID) tried to establish contacts with Islamic schools and Muslim charity organizations in order to explore the possibility of cooperation to enhance education and provide support for needy Muslims (Hamadouche 2002).[16]

Yet, with few exceptions, the U.S. measures described here did not yield tangible results. It seems unlikely that the causes of anti-Americanism among Muslims in Kenya, any more than its causes elsewhere in the Islamic world, can be addressed by an image campaign, especially where the activities of the secret services continue to fuel the mistrust of the population. Several of my Muslim respondents who receive *Maisha Amerika—Uislamu Amerika* as unsolicited mail from the U.S. embassy told me that they don't even look at it, leaving no doubt that they regard these materials as shallow propaganda and junk mail.

To some extent, the anti-American mood among Kenyan Muslims seems to support the notion of a global confrontation between Islam and "the West." One of the major effects of 9/11 has been the growing awareness among Muslims in East Africa of belonging to the *umma* (i.e., the worldwide community of Muslims). They closely follow the Israeli–Palestinian conflict and the course of events in Iraq and Afghanistan. "Solidarity with Muslim brothers and sisters" has occupied an important place in religious discourse, both formal (such as in sermons and Islamic newspapers) and informal. When Muslims all over the world expressed their outrage at the publication of cartoons depicting the Prophet Muhammad in Danish and other European news-papers in early 2006, Kenyan Muslims quickly joined the ranks of the protesters and organized demonstrations in Nairobi and several smaller cities. However, it would be wrong to portray Kenya or East Africa as a new front in a presumed global con-frontation, where the decisive developments are those that occur at the international level. Although it is certainly true that the heightened awareness of global events has changed the general outlook of Muslims on matters pertaining to their religion, there is ample evidence to suggest that local and national matters, rather than global issues, will determine the future of the Muslim minority in Kenya.

Representatives of organizations such as SUPKEM and the Council of Imams and Preachers of Kenya (CIPK) regularly lament the discrimination against Muslims in the educational system, as well as the conversion campaigns by Christian missionar-ies, which are sometimes aggressive and are usually tolerated by the government.[17] Unlike SUPKEM, which is based in Nairobi and sees itself primarily as a link between the Muslim community and agencies of the state, the CIPK has been fairly outspoken in its criticism of government policies. Led by the charismatic Shaykh Mohammad Dor, this Mombasa-based organization has repeatedly issued statements on political matters about which SUPKEM officials preferred to keep silent, thus lay-ing claim to both spiritual and political leadership of the Sunni Muslim community in the country. However, whereas the political positions taken by CIPK officials frequently appear to reflect Muslim popular opinion, the religious positions taken by individual scholars have not always garnered universal approval.

In fact, apart from the general complaints directed against "the Christians" or "the West," other pressing issues are debated solely among Muslims. The unity Kenyan Muslims display in matters concerning the global *umma* or in issues relating to their status as a minority in the country does not stand the test when it comes to questions pertaining to the position of women, correct religious practice, matters of ritual, or whether certain beliefs and practices are reprehensible "innovations" (Kiswahili, *bidaa;* from Arabic, *bid'a*); the latter is one of the major themes in reformist discourse. Perhaps the best example of the limits of Muslim unity is the recurrent dis-pute about the correct dates of the religious festivals at the end of Ramadan and at the time of the pilgrimage to Mecca, which habitually divides the community into two groups that perform the festivities on different days. Such debates continue to raise the tempers of Muslims in local contexts, even if, from an outsider's perspective, they appear to be overshadowed by larger questions that concern the Muslim community as a whole. There seems to be a particular dialectic at play here, in which the orienta-tion toward global matters enhances unity, whereas focusing on the local produces division. At the same time, local and global issues are closely intertwined and do at times influence each other.

In the following, I will explore this dialectic further by discussing the two topics that have dominated the religio-political field in Kenya since 2003: the position of the so-called Kadhis' Courts in the proposed Kenyan constitution and the Suppression of Terrorism Bill. Both matters can be said to be of crucial importance for the future development of the Muslim community in the country, and both cases show how the larger impact of 9/11 has affected the debates about the status of the Muslim community within the Kenyan state.

The Controversy over the Kadhis' Courts

Muslim religious courts have existed along the Swahili coast for centuries. After the British established their protectorate in 1895, they retained the Kadhis' Courts but limited their jurisdiction to personal status law. This policy followed that of other British colonies with a significant Muslim population. The British also created the office of Chief Kadhi, with the rank (and salary) of a government official (see Mwakimako 2006)—a measure that allowed the colonial administration to enhance its control of Muslim subjects. When Kenya became independent in 1963, the Kadhis' Courts were entrenched in Section 66 of the constitution, granting Muslims who lived in the regions of the former Protectorate (i.e., the coastal strip) the right to resolve matters of personal status (marriage, divorce, inheritance) according to Islamic law, to be administered by qualified Muslim judges under the supervision of the Chief Kadhi. The Kadhis' Courts Act, promulgated in 1967, extended the jurisdiction of the courts to all national provinces, provided that all parties involved in the case professed Islam. An appeal from a Kadhis' Court went to the Chief Kadhi or to the High Court; the latter, however, might determine the matter without reference to Islamic personal law.

The importance of the Kadhis' Courts to Kenyan Muslims goes far beyond the partial administration of justice according to Islamic law.[18] Most Muslims, in Kenya and elsewhere, perceive the sharia as the expression of the divine will. As such, sharia law is hardly open to question, though different views may be held with regard to its interpretation. From a normative Islamic perspective, compliance with the injunctions of the sharia becomes the yardstick for proper religious practice. Although Islamic legal theory confines the application of Islamic penal law to Muslims living in an Islamic state, it regards Islamic personal status law as indispensable no matter where Muslims live. For many Muslims, being able to marry and divorce, to bequeath and inherit according to the sharia, therefore forms an essential part of what it means to live as a good Muslim. Moreover, given the history of this institution in the Kenyan context, the Kadhis' Courts in effect symbolize the official recognition of the Muslim minority in the country. In the eyes of most Kenyan Muslims, changing the institutional arrangement made at the time of the British Protectorate would amount to changing the terms under which the coastal strip, with its predominantly Muslim population, became a part of what later emerged as the independent state of Kenya. This explains why any attempt at revising the national laws governing marriage, divorce, and succession was met with fierce resistance from the Muslim community.[19] Thus, in addition to their legal purpose, the Kadhis' Courts perform functions that are crucial for Islamic identity in Kenya: they help Muslims to handle personal status matters in accordance with their religion, and they define the status of Muslims as an officially recognized religious minority.

The latest and biggest row over the Kadhis' Courts began in September 2002, when the Constitution of Kenya Review Commission (CKRC), led by the law professor Yash Pal Ghai, published the first draft of a new constitution. The commission had received its mandate during the rule of former president Daniel Arap Moi and was originally supposed to complete its work before the December 27, 2002, elections. However, Moi did not appear to be particularly committed to concluding the process before the elections, as the new constitution was expected to curtail the powers of the president. After the victory of the National Rainbow Coalition (NARC), the new president, Mwai Kibaki, promised that Kenya would have a new constitution within one hundred days—a timetable that quickly turned out to be unrealistic. During the prelude to the National Constitutional Conference in May 2003, where six hundred delegates were supposed to discuss the CKRC draft, public debates evolved around two main issues: the power balance between the president and the proposed prime minister, and the status of the Kadhis' Courts. As a result of extensive consultations with representatives of the civil society and Muslim organizations, the CKRC suggested a considerable expansion of the Kadhis' Courts system. In Section 199 of the draft, the courts were given a mandate to determine not only personal status matters but also questions pertaining to civil and commercial disputes in cases where both parties were Muslim. In Section 200 the draft also suggested the creation of a three-tier system of district, provincial, and national Kadhis' Courts, with a Supreme Court of Appeal at the top of the hierarchy.

The CKRC's decision to include these suggestions in the draft seems to have been guided by a general concern to enshrine the rights of minorities in the constitution. Whatever the case, it was not prompted by a large-scale Muslim campaign to strengthen the status of sharia law. The move to expand the jurisdiction of the Kadhis' Courts and to introduce appeals courts primarily came in response to low-profile consultations and not to popular demands. Prior to the consultations, the role of the Kadhis' Courts and the sharia did not figure prominently in Muslim discourse. Only in a few isolated cases have Kenyan Muslims publicly pushed to expand the role of the sharia beyond personal status law, whereas in some other countries in sub-Saharan Africa, such as Nigeria and Sudan, application of the sharia is at the top of the Islamist agenda and the matter of fierce public controversies. Likewise, secular Muslim voices, which represent the other side of the spectrum in sharia debates elsewhere, did not feature at all in the Kenyan debate. A possible explanation for the lack of such voices lies in the fact that, even though two Muslim parties may turn to a kadhi to contract a marriage or to solve their personal status disputes, they are also free to choose the "secular" option as provided in the Family Code and to opt out of the provisions of Islamic law.

Although Muslims in Kenya were familiar with the "sharia controversies" in Nigeria and Sudan, they were also aware that their situation was rather different: being a minority in a predominantly Christian country, they could not realistically demand a substantial expansion of sharia law. It was therefore not until the publication of the CKRC plans with regard to the Kadhis' Courts that the Kenyan version of the "sharia controversy" started. The release of the draft constitution sparked an intense and prolonged public debate on the sharia and the kadhis' jurisdiction among politicians, church leaders, and representatives of the Muslim community.

Significantly, the bone of contention was not the modest upgrading of the Kadhis' Court system but rather the more fundamental question of whether such courts should be allowed to exist at all in the country.

In early 2003, several members of Mwai Kibaki's government pointed out that the CKRC suggestions undermined the separation between religion and state. Christian officials raised the concern that the constitution would not be treating all religions equally if it granted recognition to the Kadhis' Courts (*Daily Nation* 2003b). Christian and Hindu members of the so-called Ufungamano ("Alliance") Initiative, a group composed of representatives of all religions with the aim of promoting interfaith dialogue, also made public statements rejecting the clause on Kadhis' Courts, implying that the proposed steps would amount to officially endorsing sharia law. This stance aroused the anger of the Muslim members of Ufungamano, who had joined the initiative as representatives of SUPKEM and the Muslim Consultative Council (MCC). They accused Ufungamano of having "abandoned the principle of mutual respect between faiths" and decided to withdraw collectively from the forum, describing the criticism of the Kadhis' Courts as a "painful stab in the back" for Kenyan Muslims (*Daily Nation* 2003a).

Whereas the delegates at the National Constitutional Conference managed to conduct a relatively calm if controversial debate about the issue, the wider public soon appeared to be deeply divided. A confederation of forty-three evangelical churches, known as the Kenya Church, launched a campaign calling for Christianity to be declared "the official state religion" unless all reference to religion was deleted from the draft constitution.[20] Evangelical leaders repeatedly warned of the great danger of enshrining the Kadhis' Courts in the constitution, describing the courts as the first step toward the introduction of full-fledged sharia law in Kenya. They continually downplayed the number of Muslims in Kenya, thus giving the impression that a tiny minority (Christian estimates of the Muslim population usually range from 6 to 8 percent of the total population, whereas Muslim sources speak of 30 or even 35 percent) was about to take over the judiciary in a country overwhelmingly Christian. Church representatives also tended to omit reference to the fact that the Kadhis' Courts only have jurisdiction where both parties profess Islam. Muslims, on the other hand, argued that no Christian would be affected if personal status matters or commercial disputes that involve only Muslim parties were resolved according to Islamic law. However, this argument has failed to defuse the growing tension. In a move that has been dubbed "the 9/11 syndrome" by some observers (*Daily Nation* 2005b), evangelicals continue to portray the Kadhis' Courts as an attempt to impose sharia law, and ultimately a radical Islamic agenda, on all non-Muslims. Built on the assumption that sharia is equivalent to stoning and cutting off limbs, this scenario plays on widespread prejudices against Islam that have thrived in the aftermath of 9/11.

Yet opposition to the Kadhis' Courts was not limited to the evangelicals. Leading representatives of the Anglican, Methodist, Lutheran, and Catholic Churches rejected the establishment of a parallel court system for Muslims, emphasizing that the provision would privilege Islam over other religions. By March 2004, when the final version of the constitution was due, the CKRC had made some concessions to Christian demands: rather than extending the jurisdiction of the Kadhis' Courts and establishing a Supreme Court of Appeal, the document now retained the courts in almost the same form they were given in Section 66 of the previous constitution. Most Muslim leaders seemed resigned to this solution, even though they had failed to achieve what they had been hoping for. Christians, however, were dissatisfied with the compromise. Evangelicals vowed that they would not support the document as long as it contained any reference to the Kadhis' Courts. A group of Christians even staged a demonstration outside the venue of the Constitutional Conference, where a leader of the Redeemed Gospel Church condemned the draft constitution as "creating a way for the country to be ruled by Islam. . . . If the government yields to this, it is selling this country into chaos and I'm not ashamed to say they will take blame for the bloodshed" (Mulama 2004).

The long delay in the constitution-making process was only partly related to the row over the Kadhis' Courts. The biggest bone of contention was the creation of a prime minister, who would share power with the president. Although the CKRC draft provided for a strong prime minister, Mwai Kibaki and his allies insisted that executive powers should remain vested in the president. Several ministers in Kibaki's government disagreed with the presidential model, quoting the "Memorandum of Understanding" adopted by the National Rainbow Coalition before the 2002 elections, which had clearly stated that a NARC-led government would ensure that the new constitution transferred power from the president to the prime minister.

As a result, support of or opposition to the CKRC draft was determined more by adherence to one of the rival factions within NARC than by what the constitution actually said. According to the procedure defined in the Constitutional Review Act, the next step was for Parliament to revise and adopt the draft. The attorney general would revise it further, and the final version would be submitted to a popular vote. Even before Parliament began debating the draft in July 2005, a number of church leaders announced that they would campaign for a "no" vote in the referendum because of the contentious Kadhis' Courts clause. In Parliament, the Kibaki faction used its majority to curtail the powers provided to the prime minister. The version that went to the attorney general stipulated a strong presidency, with a prime minister who simply followed the president's orders. Appalled by Kibaki's move to retain his power, several members of the government joined the "no" camp.

On August 23, 2005, the attorney general published the final version of the constitution and announced that the referendum would be held on November 21, 2005. Although he had not touched the sections concerned with the presidency, he was still able to come up with a major surprise. Instead of removing the Kadhis' Courts provision, as some of the die-hard evangelicals had still hoped for, the attorney general's version allowed for the creation of "religious courts" for Muslims, Christians, and Hindus. This was obviously an attempt to invalidate the claim that the constitution gave precedence to one religion over others, and it ultimately aimed at overcoming Christian resistance to the Kadhis' Courts without losing the support of Muslims.

Both Christian and Muslim reactions to the new model have been ambivalent. In fact, in the run-up to the November 21, 2005, referendum, confusion reigned in both camps. Whereas the evangelicals under the umbrella of the Kenya Church, together with some Protestant churches, presented the referendum as nothing less than a battle to stop the forced Islamization of Kenya, mainstream churches such as the National Council of Churches of Kenya (the umbrella grouping for the main

Protestant denominations), the Catholics, and most Anglicans finally advised their congregations to vote according to their "individual conscience." The Ufungamano Initiative issued a similar statement. This neutral stance is certainly not related to Christian enthusiasm for religious courts—in fact, most church leaders have publicly declared that they have not asked for such courts and that they do not need them. Rather, it seems to have been the result of intense lobbying by Kibaki's supporters in the government, who were well aware that they could not afford to lose the votes of mainstream Christians if they wanted the new constitution to become a reality. Thus the churches' decision not to issue a guideline to their congregations appears to have been based on political considerations rather than on rejection or endorsement of the religious courts clause.

Muslims also appeared divided over the religious courts. SUPKEM and other organizations did not respond for two weeks, and the public statements they eventually issued often contradicted each other. Some leaders asked Muslims to support the new constitution, whereas others urged them to join the "no" camp. A third group followed the example of the mainstream churches in telling their followers to vote according to their conscience. Some Muslims planned to vote "yes" because they were satisfied with the religious courts provision or because they saw the proposed constitution as an improvement over the current one; others intended to reject the constitution because they believed that the religious courts provision did not grant sufficient constitutional protection to Kadhis' Courts. Yet, overall, as in the case of the Christians, the dividing line between the supporters and the opponents of the new constitution seems to have been determined by political rather than by religious considerations. The question of whether executive powers should remain with the president (Mwai Kibaki's position) or whether the president should share some of his power with an executive prime minister (the argument of the "rebel" faction within NARC) has thus overshadowed previous debates about the Kadhis' Courts.

The referendum ended with a crushing defeat for the government. The vote was either "yes" or "no," and, in order to facilitate participation for illiterate voters, the government decided to give the voters a choice between two symbols: a banana representing "yes," and an orange representing "no." The "orange team," which tried to entice voters with the prospect of an "orange revolution" against the "banana republic," achieved a comfortable victory when 58 percent of the participating electorate voted "no."[21] The Kibaki government conceded its defeat and attributed the result to its failure to communicate its agenda to the voters, whereas the leaders of the "Orange Democratic Movement," as the antigovernment alliance referred to itself after the referendum, interpreted the rejection of the draft constitution as a vote of no confidence against the president. Kibaki reacted by reshuffling his government, eliminating the six ministers who had opposed the draft constitution, and the ensuing public debates shifted away from the constitution and the Kadhis' Courts, focusing instead on the usual political bickering and, more recently, on corruption.

Compared to the tense atmosphere and the acrimonious exchange of accusations at the beginning of the Kadhis' Courts debate, this development appears almost as a relief. Already ahead of the referendum, Muslims had realized that they did not have much to lose. If the draft constitution were rejected, Section 66 of the old constitution would remain in force; if the draft were adopted as the new constitution, the

Kadhis' Courts would continue to exist, under the religious courts provision. Apart from a few Muslim hardliners, only the evangelicals continued to view the referendum as a vote for or against the Kadhis' Courts. Two months ahead of the referendum, Bishop Margaret Wanjiru of the "Jesus Is Alive Ministries," who speaks on behalf of the Kenya Church, insisted that "the matter is this simple, as long as the sharia courts are spelled out in the constitution, the Christians will ultimately reject the proposed constitution" (*Daily News* 2005). Yet it is intriguing that this position is the exact opposite of what the Kenya Church had pushed for during the earlier National Constitutional Conference. Back in 2003, the Kenya Church had conceded that the Kadhis' Courts "may be retained as they are in the draft constitution, provided that the word 'Khadi' [*sic*] be replaced with the word 'religious arbitrator' wherever it appears. . . . This will allow . . . all recognized religious groups and Christian denominations to set up Religious Arbitration Courts."[22] The fact that the Kenya Church still opposed the Kadhis' Courts even after their demands had been met illustrates the continuing potency of the "9/11 syndrome." It is likely that tempers will flare up again once the government delivers on its promise to restart the constitution project afresh. However, given the present political deadlock, this is not likely to happen in the near future, even though President Kibaki appointed a committee of experts in February 2006 to reexamine the controversial matters.

The Kenyan Version of the "War on Terror"

Although public attention moved away from the Kadhis' Courts in the course of the constitution debate and practically ceased in the wake of the referendum, there is another area where 9/11 has also left visible traces: the antiterrorism policy of the Kenyan government. It was already mentioned that the August 1998 bombing of the U.S. embassy in Nairobi had a painful aftermath for Muslims. The attacks of September 11, 2001, came at a time when interreligious tensions in Kenya had ebbed. However, 9/11 brought East Africa in general and Kenya in particular back into the spotlight. President Moi used the opportunity to improve Kenya's strained relations with the U.S. and Great Britain (which were mainly due to his autocratic ruling style and the government's involvement in large-scale corruption) by offering full cooperation in the "war on terror" during state visits to New York and London in November 2001. At the same time, a wave of arbitrary arrests swept through Mombasa and other coastal towns in Kenya. More than fifty Muslims were arrested on suspicion of terror links and kept in detention without charge. Some detainees were released after a few days, but others were held for interrogation, occasionally involving the FBI.[23] In most cases, their only "crime" was that they had received money from Arab countries—a rather common occurrence in a country where many people maintain business relations with the Middle East or have relatives who live there as migrant workers and send remittances to their families back home.

Reacting to what they saw as the unwarranted intimidation of Muslims, leading representatives of the Muslim community warned the government that its action would fuel political tension and might even give rise to internal conflict. Criticism of the arbitrary arrests and the unlawful detentions came not only from Muslims. Mwai Kibaki, the leader of an opposition party at the time, demanded the release of those imprisoned and asked the Moi government to "fully explain to Kenyans what plans we as a country have put in place for the fight against terrorism" (Rowan 2001).

Yet, once in power, the same Mwai Kibaki followed the policy of his predecessor and took a number of measures that reveal the long-term impact of 9/11 on Muslims in Kenya. The event that triggered the new dimension in the Kenyan "war on terror" was the November 2002 suicide bombing of the Paradise Hotel at Kikambala, with the almost simultaneous attempt to shoot down an Israeli charter plane near Mombasa, just a few weeks before the elections that brought the National Rainbow Coalition to power. In the meantime, the U.S. administration had started to put pressure on African governments to take new legislative steps in the fight against terrorism, similar to the Patriot Act implemented in the U.S. after 9/11.[24] Responding to this campaign, the Kibaki government began to draft antiterrorism legislation, an exercise that was completed in April 2003. Although their primary purpose was to fill a gap in Kenya's law, which at the time did not consider connections with terrorist organizations a criminal offense, the new measures far exceeded the original objective, as they essentially sanctioned the measures that were already in place: arrest of suspects without evidence of involvement in terrorist acts; holding detainees incommunicado; prolonged detention without charge or trial. Yet in July 2003, when the government made a bid to rush the so-called Suppression of Terrorism Bill through Parliament before the summer retreat, several members of parliament raised serious concerns and succeeded in delaying the vote on the bill.

It was only after the government failed to quickly enact the new legislation that the wider public took notice of its plans. Strong opposition from human rights groups and other civil institutions, including several church representatives, prompted the government to withdraw the first version of the bill. The amended version, drafted in close consultation with the Law Society of Kenya and presented to the public in 2004,[25] failed to silence the critics, and the enactment of the laws has since been put on hold. As several organizations, particularly Amnesty International, have highlighted, the bill fails to clearly define terrorism; it grants extensive powers to the police and customs officers to stop, search and seize, and detain and arrest; it permits incommunicado detention and denies suspects the right to legal representation during interrogation; it makes detention the rule and bail the exception, thus limiting the right to personal liberty; it grants state officials immunity from prosecution or civil suits under the bill; it curtails the freedoms of association and expression; it contains only vague definitions of the crime of "incitement to commit a terrorist act" wholly or partly outside Kenya; and, finally, it does not provide for safeguards and due process in decisions to extradite suspects to foreign countries (see Amnesty International 2005).

Kenyan Muslims rejected the Suppression of Terrorism Bill as strongly as did human rights groups. Public statements from Muslims for Human Rights (MUHURI), an organization working under the umbrella of the Kenya Human Rights Commission, argued that the legislation violated the international human rights standard. Representatives of other major Muslim organizations issued declarations that echoed the general resentment among the Muslim community. Thus, officials speaking on behalf of SUPKEM and the CIPK claimed that the suggested measures specifically targeted Muslims. Mohamed Hyder, the chairman of the Mombasa-based

Muslim Civic Education Trust, heavily criticized the antiterrorism investigations of the Kenyan government as "singl[ing] out one community for condemnation, intimidation and harassment," adding that "the Suppression of Terrorism Bill makes us even more worried because all the illegal things that the Government is doing at the moment are permissible under the said Bill" (Hyder 2003).[26]

Indeed, seen from a human rights perspective, the Kenyan version of the "war on terror" gives rise to great concern, even if one does not share the view, widespread among Muslims in Kenya and elsewhere, that the "war on terror" is actually a "war on Islam." Amnesty International's report *Kenya: The Impact of "Anti-terrorism" Operations on Human Rights* documents cases of ill-treatment during detention, including torture and other physical abuse; the detention of suspects without charge in undisclosed locations and without access to a lawyer or relatives; the holding of suspects in degrading and unsanitary conditions without access to medical care when needed; the harassment of family members and the arbitrary detention of relatives to put pressure on suspects to turn themselves in; and the failure of police to show warrants when arresting individuals or conducting searches of property (Amnesty International 2005).

Although the number of Muslims who have undergone arbitrary arrest, incommunicado detention, interrogation by foreign agents, and mistreatment has probably reached several hundred, so far only one case has made it to court. In June 2004, after fourteen months in prison, four individuals suspected of involvement in the preparation of the car-bomb attack on the Paradise Hotel at Kikambala on November 28, 2002, faced charges on fifteen counts of murder before the High Court in Nairobi. The long-awaited verdict came on June 9, 2005: the court ruled that all defendants were to be acquitted, as "it is a general principle of criminal law that a person may not be convicted of a crime unless the persecution [*sic*] have proved by [*sic*] any reasonable doubt that he caused a certain event or that responsibility is to be attributed to him" (*Daily Nation* 2005a). In the opinion of the court, the prosecutors had failed to produce sufficient evidence showing that the accused had a hand in the killings at the Paradise Hotel. Even though there was evidence connecting the defendants to the house in which the bomb used in the attack was built, and evidence that they communicated with an alleged coordinator of the al-Qaeda network in Kenya, the prosecution was unable to establish that they had prior knowledge of the suicide bombers' plans.

Muslim organizations saw the judgment as a confirmation of their critical stance toward the "war on terror," as most of those detained in the aftermaths of 9/11 and 11/28 were held on the basis of evidence even scantier than that in the case that went to trial. For the Kenyan government, however, the judgment was a major blow. The government now appears to be under renewed pressure from the U.S. and the Israeli administrations to enact the Suppression of Terrorism Bill (Mulama 2005). Had the bill been in place at the time of the trial, it would have allowed the court to convict the defendants of being connected to terrorist networks, however loosely, rather than conducting lengthy proceedings in which the prosecutors failed to substantiate difficult murder charges. Given the bill's vague definition of terrorism, its imminent enactment is likely to lead to an even larger number of arbitrary arrests and, ultimately, to a further alienation of Kenya's Muslim population.

Conclusion: Integration or Exclusion?

What lessons can we learn from the aftermath of 9/11 in Kenya? Perhaps the most obvious lesson is that the "war on terror" cannot be won *against* the Muslims. The steps taken by the Kenyan government in its attempt to suppress terrorism have so far yielded contradictory results. Sweeping accusations against Islam, in combination with violations of human rights, have alienated Muslims in Kenya as well as in other regions of East Africa and other parts of the world.

As Alex De Waal and A. H. Abdel Salam have pointed out in a recent study on the Horn of Africa, Islamism, and the "war on terror," the labels "terrorist" and "jihad" have become "common currency, often with little reference to political realities, and with the intent of closing down the prospects for political dialogue and compromise" (De Waal and Abdel Salam 2004, 247). To caution against the unreflective use of such terms does not mean to underestimate the possible dangers of radical ideologies or to advocate toleration of religious violence. Yet the case of Kenya suggests that it is misleading and probably equally dangerous to employ labels like "Islamists" in a generalizing manner and to build a whole "war on terror" policy on such a shaky foundation. To assert that "Islamism in Kenya is steadily advancing, disrupting political, social and economic order and progress," as a recent study by the Washington-based Center for Security Policy does, distorts the present state of affairs in the country, as does the claim that "the instability being fomented there by Islamists has the potential to unleash chaos in an already deeply troubled region" (McCormack 2005, 15).

Instead of integrating Muslims and "winning their hearts and minds," as some Western politicians nowadays like to put it, a policy based on such problematic assumptions is likely to add to Muslims' feelings of marginalization, already so pronounced in present-day Kenya. The row over the Kadhis' Courts is a case in point: from Muslims' perspective, what is at stake in this debate is no less than their recognition as a religious minority within the Kenyan state. The twists and turns in this debate, as well as in the recent controversy over the antiterrorism legislation, reveal a common pattern: the more marginalized Muslims believe themselves to be, the more they tend to perceive themselves as participants in a worldwide confrontation between "Islam" and "the West." In other words, the degree of identification with the global *umma* appears to increase in direct proportion with the sense of being subject to discrimination in the national context. Seen from this perspective, the answer to the "clash of civilizations," if there were any such clash, would lie in the integration of Muslims into the political process. It thus seems plausible that a successful integration on the local and national levels could effectively reduce the appeal of "global" ideologies that promote a worldwide confrontation between "Islam" and "the West." Muslims would probably continue to disapprove of what they consider injustice committed against fellow Muslims by the U.S. and Israel elsewhere in the world, but identification with the global *umma* would arguably lose some of its local significance.

In the present political situation, Kenya is at the crossroads. The pattern of the relationship between the Muslim community and the Kenyan state as analyzed in this chapter suggests that the mounting tensions can be contained when Muslims feel assured that their official recognition as a respected minority is not in question. However, if the 9/11 syndrome persists and the "war on terror" targets the wider Muslim community, the Kenyan government, in conjunction with some of the evangelical churches, risks producing the radicals whom they claim to be fighting. What is at stake here is not a "clash of civilizations" but rather a process of negotiation involving questions of inclusion and exclusion, religious tolerance, and political participation.

Notes

Different versions of this chapter have been presented on various occasions, the latest being the annual meeting of the African Studies Association in New Orleans, November 10–14, 2004, and the lecture series "Africa in the World" at the African Studies Centre, Leiden, December 4, 2004. My field research was sponsored by the German Research Foundation (Deutsche Forschungsgemeinschaft, DFG) through the Collaborative Research Project "Local Agency in Africa in the Context of Global Influences," based at Bayreuth University, Germany. I gratefully acknowledge the financial support I received from the DFG, and the comments and suggestions made by the participants at the ASA meeting and the Leiden lecture series.

1. Among the few studies that do address 9/11 from an African perspective are Nielinger 2002 and Souley 2002. A recent issue of *Africa Today* features contributions that focus on U.S.-African relations after 9/11; see Kraxberger 2005 and Carmody 2005. Glickman 2003 offers a typical example of the standard approach, which is almost exclusively informed by a Western perspective. Other authors are more critical of U.S. policy; see for instance Adebajo 2003 and De Waal and Abdel Salam 2004.
2. The phrase "clash of civilizations" is usually attributed to Samuel Huntington (see Huntington 1993, 1996). However, the first author to popularize the idea with reference to the Muslim world was Bernard Lewis (see Lewis 1990).
3. I will draw on field research conducted during five visits to Kenya between 2001 and 2005, and three short research trips to Zanzibar and Dar es Salaam between 2002 and 2004.
4. There are no reliable statistics on the numerical strength of religions in Kenya. See the discussion of the problem in Cruise O'Brien 1995, 201, on which my estimate is based.
5. Estimates of deaths in the Nairobi bomb attack vary between 213 and 291.
6. In October 2001, four defendants (one Jordanian, one Saudi citizen, one American born in Lebanon, and a Tanzanian) were sentenced to life imprisonment for their participation in the attacks in Nairobi and Dar es Salaam (*IslamOnline.net* 2001).
7. The following paragraph is based on interviews and informal discussions I conducted with imams, religious scholars, and Muslim activists during field trips to Nairobi, Mombasa, Malindi, and Zanzibar in August 2002, February and August 2003, and July and August 2004.
8. On anti-Americanism in sub-Saharan Africa, see Seesemann 2006.
9. See the account in Ndjozi 2000; this book is banned in Tanzania.
10. Another report deals with the relatively strong Israeli presence in Kenya; see Hanafi 2002. Al-Ittihad al-Islami is on the list of terrorist groups drawn up by the U.S. government after 9/11, which includes all organizations viewed as potential targets in the "war on terror." For one of the latest versions of this list, see U.S. Department of State 2005, 92–129.
11. It is striking that, to this day, nothing has been revealed about the identity of the suicide bombers. The only names mentioned in the media or by official investigators are those of the alleged planners and supporters of the attack, the suspected mastermind being Fazul

Abdullah Mohammed from the Comoro Islands, who is also wanted in connection with the August 7, 1998, bombings. Another suspected member of the same al-Qaeda cell, Suleiman Abdalla Salim Hemed, is a Tanzanian citizen of Yemeni origin and was arrested in Mogadishu in March 2003. He was later brought to Kenya, and the Kenyan government handed him over to U.S. authorities.

12. A more recent but equally misleading scenario has been advanced in a publication on the "Islamist danger" in Africa by the Washington-based Center for Security Policy. The author of this report lumps together a wide range of Islamic organizations and movements and labels them "Islamist," claiming that they are, in Kenya, "only one degree removed from violence" (McCormack 2005, 14). However, the hard evidence provided for this claim is rather scant.

13. In Kenya, the CIA worked closely with the national intelligence services (see Hamadouche 2002). On FBI involvement, see Mason 2001. A recent Amnesty International report (2005) lists several incidents involving foreign agents in the country. Nowadays, U.S. diplomatic missions in sub-Saharan Africa systematically gather information on Islam in the respective countries.

14. See http://usembassy.state.gov/nairobi/wwwhtoc.html (retrieved December 3, 2002, and October 16, 2005).

15. By June 2005, twenty issues of *Maisha Amerika—Uislamu Amerika* had appeared.

16. The Public Affairs Section of the U.S. embassy also tried to initiate cooperation with the Nairobi-based Islamic radio station Iqra FM, obviously without much success. However, it has established a good working relationship with the Muslim Civic Education Trust in Mombasa.

17. This situation has not changed much since it was described in 1993 by Ali Mazrui, one of the country's most widely known Muslim intellectuals. See Mazrui 1993.

18. For studies of different aspects of the Kadhis' Courts and legal practice in Kenya, see Brown 1993, Hirsch 1998, Stockreiter 2002, and Swartz 1979.

19. Examples are the prolonged debates about proposed reforms of marriage law (from the late 1960s to 1979; see Anderson 1969 and Cotran 1969) and succession law (in the 1980s; see Kameri-Mbote 1995). See also Constantin 1989 and, for a comparative perspective on Islamic personal status law in East Africa, Hashim 2006.

20. See, for instance, the advertisement in the *East African Standard*, May 23, 2003.

21. Out of 11 million voters, about 6 million cast their vote, with more than 3.5 million rejecting the draft constitution.

22. See the full-page advertisement in the *East African Standard*, May 23, 2003.

23. See Rowan 2001. The same report mentions that local "Special Crimes Prevention Units" have acted upon a list, provided by the FBI, of two hundred suspects with possible links to 9/11.

24. See the State Department *Country Reports on Terrorism*, especially the section on the U.S. East Africa Counterterrorism Initiative (U.S. Department of State 2005, 29). Uganda and Tanzania enacted their antiterrorism bills in 2002.

25. The amended version is available on the Law Society of Kenya's website: http://www.lsk.or.ke/downloads/publications/lskterrorism.pdf (retrieved July 12, 2005). The Kenyan government's failure to enact the bill is one of the reasons why the U.S. State Department report notes that it "registered only slow progress towards the overall strengthening of its capabilities to combat terrorism, prosecute terror suspects, or respond to emergency situations" (U.S. Department of State 2005, 30).

26. Ironically, the Muslims were joined in their criticism of the government's antiterrorism campaign by the oppositional Kenya African National Union (KANU), the party of former president Moi, which had followed a similar policy when in power, while Kibaki, then in the opposition, had questioned Moi's measures against terrorism. See *East African Standard* 2003.

References

Adebajo, Adekeye. 2003. Africa and America in an age of terror. *Journal of Asian and African Studies* 38 (2–3): 175–91.

Amnesty International. 2005. *Kenya: The impact of "anti-terrorism" operations on human rights.* AI Index AFR 32/002/2005. http://www.web.amnesty.org/library/Index/ENGAFR320022005?open&of=ENG-2AF (accessed July 12, 2005).

Anderson, James Norman D. 1969. Comments (on Kenya Commission Reports) with reference to the Muslim community. *East African Law Journal* 5 (1–2): 5–20.

Bakari, Mohamed. 1995. The new 'ulama in Kenya. In *Islam in Kenya: Proceedings of the National Seminar in Contemporary Islam in Kenya*, ed. Mohamed Bakari and Saad S. Yahya. Nairobi: MEWA Publications.

Brown, Beverly B. 1993. Islamic law, Qadhi's Courts and women's legal status: The case of Kenya. *Journal of the Institute of Muslim Minority Affairs* 14: 94–101.

Carmody, Pádraig. 2005. Transforming globalization and security: Africa and America post-9/11. *Africa Today* 52 (1): 97–120.

Constantin, François. 1989. Loi de l'Islam contre loi de l'état: Petite chronique d'un été Kenyan. *Islam et Sociétés au Sud du Sahara* 3: 207–23.

———. 1995. The attempts to create Muslim national organizations in Tanzania, Uganda and Kenya. In *Religion and politics in East Africa: The period since independence*, ed. Holger Bernt Hansen and Michael Twaddle, 19–31. London: James Currey.

Cotran, Eugene. 1969. Marriage and divorce: A new look for the law in Kenya? *East Africa Law Journal* 5: 107–40.

Cruise O'Brien, Donal B. 1995. Coping with the Christians: The Muslim predicament in Kenya. In *Religion and politics in East Africa: The period since independence*, ed. Holger Bernt Hansen and Michael Twaddle. London: James Currey.

Daily Nation (Nairobi). 2003a. Muslims quit faiths team over Kadhi row. April 23.

———. 2003b. Sharia warning in Kadhis' Courts row. April 24.

———. 2005a. Insufficient proof in terrorism case. July 18.

———. 2005b. Suffering from the 9/11 syndrome. September 2.

Daily News (Durban). 2005. Ministers flee violent crowds: Kenya split over proposed constitution calling for sharia courts. September 23. http://www.dailynews.co.za/index.php?fSectionId=500&fArticleId=2888667 (accessed October 16, 2005).

De Waal, Alex, and A. H. Abdel Salam. 2004. Africa, Islamism, and America's "War on Terror" after September 11. In *Islamism and its enemies in the Horn of Africa*, ed. Alex De Waal. London: Hurst.

East African Standard. 2003. Kanu, Muslims attack government. June 30.

Glickman, Harvey. 2003. Africa in the war on terrorism. *Journal of Asian and African Studies* 38 (2–3): 162–74.

Hamadouche, Louisa Aït. 2002. L'image de l'Islam en Afrique s'obscurcit, le Kenya trouble la lutte américaine antiterroriste. *La tribune* (Algiers), December 1.

Hanafi, Khaled. 2002. Mombasa a Strong Message to Mossad in Africa. *IslamOnline*, November 29. http://www.islamonline.net/english/news/2002-11/29/article33.shtml (accessed December 3, 2002).

Hashim, Abdulkadir. 2006. Unity within diversity: Unification and codification of Muslim law of personal status in East Africa. In *Interaction and interrelation in Africa: Academic conference research papers*, ed. African Universities Congress, 329–49. Khartoum: International African University.

Hirsch, Susan F. 1998. *Pronouncing and persevering: Gender and the discourses of disputing in an African Islamic court.* Chicago: University of Chicago Press.

Huntington, Samuel P. 1993. The clash of civilizations? *Foreign Affairs* 72 (3): 23–49.

———. 1996. *The clash of civilizations and the remaking of world order.* New York: Simon and Schuster.

Hyder, Mohamed. 2003. Muslims and the Suppression of Terrorism Bill 2003. http://www.mcetworld.com/profhyder.htm (accessed October 16, 2005).

IslamOnline.net. 2001. Four bin Laden aides jailed for life over Africa embassy bombings. October 18. http://www.islamonline.net/english/news/2001-10/19/article5.shtml (accessed December 3, 2002).

———. 2002a. Kenya attacks suspects hunted, U.S. blames Somali group. November 30. http://www.islamonline.net/english/news/2002-11/30/article53.shtml (accessed December 3, 2002).

———. 2002b. Kenya's main Muslim group condemns Mombasa bombing. November 29. http://www.islamonline.net/english/news/2002-11/30/article40.shtml (accessed December 3, 2002).

Kameri-Mbote, Patricia. 1995. *The law of succession in Kenya: Gender perspectives in property management and control.* Nairobi: Women and Law in East Africa.

Kraxberger, Brennan M. 2005. The United States and Africa: Shifting geopolitics in an "Age of Terror." *Africa Today* 52 (1): 47–68.

Lewis, Bernard. 1990. The roots of Muslim rage. *Atlantic Monthly* 266 (3): 47–60.

Mair, Stefan. 2002. Terrorismus und Afrika: Zur Gefahr weiterer Anschläge in Afrika südlich der Sahara. *SWP-Aktuell* 54 (December). http://www.swp-berlin.org/common/get_document.php?id=398 (accessed February 22, 2003).

Mamdani, Mahmood. 2004. *Good Muslim, bad Muslim: America, the cold war, and the roots of terror.* New York: Pantheon Books.

Mason, Barry. 2001. FBI send agents to Kenya. *WSWS News and Analysis*, October 3. http://www.wsws.org/articles/2001/oct2001/ken-o03.shtml (accessed July 12, 2005).

Mazrui, Ali A. 1993. The black Intifadah? Religion and rage at the Kenyan coast. *Journal of Asian and African Affairs* 4: 87–93.

McCormack, David. 2005. *An African vortex: Islamism in sub-Saharan Africa.* Occasional Papers Series, no. 4. Washington D.C.: The Center for Security Policy. http://www.centerforsecuritypolicy.org/Af_Vortex.pdf (accessed July 12, 2005).

Mulama, Joyce. 2004. Constitutional endorsement of Muslim courts provokes anger. *Inter Press Service News Agency*, March 13. http://www.ipsnews.net/interna.asp?idnews=22842 (accessed October 16, 2005).

———. 2005. Give rights precedence over realpolitik—NGOs. *Inter Press Service News Agency*, September 6. http://www.ipsnews.net/news.asp?idnews=30159 (accessed October 16, 2005).

Mwakimako, Hassan. 2006. The *'ulamâ'* and the colonial state in the Protectorate of Kenya. In *The global worlds of the Swahili: Interfaces of Islam, identity and space in 19th- and 20th-century East Africa*, ed. Roman Loimeier and Rüdiger Seesemann. Hamburg: LIT Verlag.

Ndjozi, Hamza Mustafa. 2000. *Mwembechai killings and the political future of Tanzania.* Ottawa: Globalink Communications.

Nielinger, Olaf. 2002. Afrika und der 11. September 2001. *Afrika im Blickpunkt* (Institut für Afrika-Kunde Hamburg) 2: 1–10.

Oded, Arye. 2000. *Islam and politics in Kenya.* Boulder, Colo.: L. Rienner.

Rowan, David. 2001. Arbitrary arrests of Muslims in Kenya. *WSWS News and Analysis*, November 21. http://www.wsws.org/articles/2001/nov2001/keny-n21.shtml (accessed July 12, 2005).

Seesemann, Rüdiger. 2006. Sub-Saharan Africa. In *Anti-Americanism in the Islamic world*, ed. Sigrid Faath. London: Hurst.

Smith, Martin, dir. 2001. *In search of bin Laden.* Public Broadcasting System, video. Updated version of a film originally aired in 1999 as an episode of *Frontline.*

Souley, Hassan. 2002. La presse africaine et les événements du 11 septembre. *Islam et Sociétés au Sud du Sahara* 16: 121–32.

Stockreiter, Elke. 2002. Islamisches Recht und sozialer Wandel: Die Kadhi-Gerichte von Malindi, Kenia und Sansibar, Tanzania. *Stichproben: Wiener Zeitschrift für kritische Afrikastudien* 2: 35–61.

Swartz, Marc J. 1979. Religious courts, community and ethnicity among the Swahili of Mombasa: An historical study of social boundaries. *Africa* 49: 29–41.

U.S. Department of State, Office of the Coordinator for Counterterrorism. 2005. *Country reports on terrorism 2004*. Department of State Publication 11248. http://www.state.gov/documents/organization/45313.pdf (accessed October 27, 2005).

Chapter 9
Politics and Sharia in Northern Nigeria

Sanusi Lamido Sanusi

Introduction

The election of civilian governments in the Federal Republic of Nigeria in 1999 was preceded by a political campaign in which ethnic and religious identities and differences were a major component. For a substantial part of the nation's history, and particularly during the long periods of military rule, the leadership of the federal government had been in the hands of Muslim officers from the north of the country. By 1998, therefore, when General Abdul Salami Abubakar took over (after the death in office of General Abacha) and declared his intention to hand over power to an elected government in 1999, there was a strong campaign in the south for what was then called a "power shift" away from the north. Politicians reached a consensus after much acrimony, and northern politicians, with one or two notable exceptions,[1] decided not to seek their parties' nomination for the presidency but, rather, to endorse and support Christian candidates from the south.

In May 1999, Olusegun Obasanjo, a Christian retired general and former head of state (1976–79) from the southwest of the country, was elected president. Less than one year later, Sani Yerima, governor of the northwestern state of Zamfara, declared full implementation of Islamic penal laws, and this declaration was followed by similar ones in eleven other predominantly Muslim states in the north. In many of these states the implementation of sharia was a result, at least outwardly, of mass popular demand for it, led by mainly young and educated Muslims associated with Muslim activism and supported by Islamic scholars, particularly graduates of Arab universities. The developments since then are well known. In some of the northern states the full implementation of sharia led to the amputation of the hands of some persons convicted of theft. There have been sensational judgments against divorced women in Sokoto and Katsina states who were convicted of bearing children "out of wedlock" and were sentenced to death by stoning. The judgments were overruled by the appeal courts in the sharia circuit. In Jigawa and Kano states, men have been sentenced to death by stoning for sodomy. The sentence of the Jigawa court was set aside when the convict's relatives testified that he had a history of insanity, and the case in Kano is under appeal.

In general, although sharia was ushered in with a flurry of sensational rulings, these have been substantially toned down. There is a general reluctance to implement sentences like death by stoning. It is not very clear how much of this is due to the pressure of the international community and how much to a belated acceptance of the position, long established in Muslim jurisprudence, that these sentences are only rarely carried out, if at all, given the near impossibility of meeting the strict standards of proof set out in the law (Sanusi 2002b). However, the issue remains topical in a world that has seen two wars in Iraq, the U.S. war against Afghanistan, the September 11, 2001 attacks on the U.S., the exacerbation of the Palestinian crisis, and increasing tension between the U.S. government, on the one hand, and the governments of Syria and Iran, on the other. In the context of general interest in Islam and the Muslim world, Nigeria has become a focus of attention.

Some of the contemporary interest in the West in sharia and Islam has been driven by a sense of global insecurity and an attempt to understand, as it were, the underlying psychology of the "terrorist" mind. In other cases, there has been a genuine interest both in improving mutual understanding and respect and in reaching out to "other" cultures and civilizations with a view to fostering world peace and progress. Finally, research has in some ways deepened an ongoing academic project that objectifies Islam for the purpose of academic disciplinary study. This project has approached Muslim society from anthropological, sociological, and historical perspectives. Muslim thought itself has increasingly tended to explore the tensions between traditional Islam and the demands of modern society and attempted to construct a new hermeneutics of Islamic texts that frees received interpretations from the legacy of embodiment in historical context. Among those associated, to a greater or lesser extent, with this last trend are scholars like Abdullahi An-Na'im, Khaled Abou El Fadl, Ebrahim Moosa, Nasr Abu Zayd, Abdulkader Tayob, Aziza El-Hibri, Ali Mazrui, Abdolkarim Soroush, Amina Wadud, Fatima Mernissi, Farid Esack, and many others. Many of these scholars have redefined Islamic studies by applying the results of current work in literary criticism and philosophical hermeneutics, ideology critique, legal theory, social theory, and the whole collage of multivariate perspectives usually gathered under the rubric of "postmodernism." The ideas of subjectivity and embodiment and the need to decenter "Islamic" discourse by deconstructing and isolating its constitutive elements (derived from historical context and cultural pretexts) seem to bring these thinkers together. Some critics have alleged that postmodernist perspectives represent only a pragmatic device to conceal from the West a fundamentalist commitment to the Islamization of society.[2] A few authors are seen as writing from a purely secular perspective, such that their critique of Islamic law is more a secular criticism of religious laws than a contribution from within the Muslim tradition.[3]

In this chapter, I will give an overview of the situation in northern Nigeria and the relationship between the sharia project, as I call it, and global and local politics. In the next section I give a brief history of Islam in the region, particularly in the nineteenth and twentieth centuries. This background serves to explain the strong place of Islam in the construction of identities in the region and the role of the British colonial administration in that regard. I then proceed to a discussion of economics, globalization, and sharia in northern Nigeria and try to highlight the complex elements of local and international politics that play a role in Islamic revival and religious tension in the region. The concluding section discusses future prospects and possibilities for defusing religious tension in this great African nation.

Brief Historical Background

Nigeria is the most populous African country, and the great majority of the people in the north are Muslims, albeit from various ethnic groups. The most widely spoken language in the region is Hausa. Islam came early to northern Nigeria, beginning from the old Kanem-Borno, almost immediately after the death of the Prophet Muhammad. Sources suggest that Islamic influences in the Chad region appeared around the year A.H. 46 (A.D. 666–67) with the arrival of the first group of Muslims under the leadership of Uqbah bin Nafi (A. Kane 1987, 13). The kings of Kanem-Borno, however, did not accept Islam until the eleventh century A.D. Islam came to Hausaland much later, and its entrenchment is usually linked with the reign of one of two kings of Kano, Yaji Dan Tsamiya (1349–84) or Muhammadu Rumfa (1463–99). In any case it is generally agreed that Islam came to Hausaland prior to the fourteenth century (A. Kane 1987, 33).

Between 1804 and 1808, a Fulani scholar, Uthman bin Fudi (Dan Fodio) waged a jihad against Hausa rulers, whom he accused of syncretism and polytheism, and established Muslim emirates founded on a reformed Islamic law.[4] Along with his brother, Abdullahi, and his son, Muhammad Bello, Shaykh Uthman put in place a sociopolitical, economic, and legal system that was modeled after Muslim caliphates of the Abbasid and Ottoman periods. The ethico-legal foundations of the political and economic system in this period have been the subject of much scholarly study, a prime example being the work of Tukur (1999). Shortly after Shaykh Uthman's jihad, a rival scholar in Borno, Shaykh Muhammad Amin El-Kanemi, took over control of the Muslim empire of Kanem-Borno to the east and introduced radical reforms aimed at cleansing the system of innovation and polytheism.[5] As a result of these two events, northern Nigeria, or at least the larger portion of it, remained under the control of two Muslim empires, one led by the Fulani in Hausaland and the other in Borno to the east, for a full century before the British colonial takeover. The Sokoto caliphate was itself made up of component emirates, numbering over three dozen (Abubakar 1977, 1), and its territory extended beyond the borders of contemporary northern Nigeria into neighboring Cameroon, Niger, and Benin. Old Borno's sphere of influence also extended into modern Chad.

The coming together of so many peoples under a single political authority, bound by a common ideology rooted in Islam and sharia, and the endurance of the system for a century, necessarily produced a near-monolithic society in most of northern Nigeria. The political and administrative structures of the emirates more or less mirrored each other. The sharia was the operative law in all emirates, and the school of jurisprudence (*fiqh*) was Maliki. The educational system, which was based on a deep study of key texts of Maliki jurisprudence, Ash'arite theology, mysticism, grammar, rhetoric, and exegesis, remained largely unchanged from the fourteenth century to the present day. The prolific writings of the triumvirate in Sokoto (Uthman, Bello, and Abdullahi) were taken as a source of guidance by the emirs of the caliphate.

Arabic was the official language of the court, and most of the people spoke Hausa and Fulani, even though the caliphate encompassed Muslim populations that spoke such diverse languages as Nupe and Yoruba.

The British decided, after an initial, unsuccessful attempt at imposing direct rule, to accept the policy of indirect rule recommended by Lord Lugard. This policy, ironically, restored the waning power of the emirs and entrenched the precolonial cultural value systems in return for the aristocracy's political loyalty and its acceptance of certain amendments to the system aimed at improving governance and human rights, as well as meeting minimum standards set by the British on the basis of their own normative systems. This seems to have been the expectation of the *wazir* of Sokoto, Muhammad Bukhari, when he signed a peace treaty with the British. It seems clear from his reasoning that he opted to cede political ("worldly") power to the British in return for the preservation of the Muslim faith and Islamic law in the territory under the control of the descendants of the jihadists.[6] Indeed, when in 1900 Lord Lugard proclaimed the Protectorate of Northern Nigeria, he explicitly "pledged not to interfere in the religious affairs of the Muslims" (O. Kane 2003, 35) Lugard did, however, introduce amendments to legislation at the same time that he encouraged emirs to adopt positive law. By encouraging emirs to renounce bodily punishment, Lugard took a first step in a process that culminated in the adoption of the Native Authority Ordinance in 1933. The last remnants of the *hudud*—fixed punishments in Islamic law—were abolished on the eve of Independence (O. Kane 2003, 93).

It is important to note, however, that, as in other parts of the Muslim world, personal law remained Islamic even under colonialism. Also, the penal laws of northern Nigeria were based substantially on Islamic law, with the exception of bodily punishments. Finally, when the emirs had to rule in a manner contravening the dictates of the sharia, they took pains to distance themselves from such rulings. For example, court records of the judicial council of the emir of Kano 'Abbas in 1913–14 reveal that when he had to hand down a ruling, according to the guidelines given by the colonial government, it was invariably classed under the rubric of *hukm zamanina* (the law of our times), a legal innovation reluctantly applied (Kano Judicial Council 1994, esp. 11–17).

In general, the colonial administration entrenched the power of emirs and a class alliance was established between them, the colonial administration, and the trading firms. The power of the emirs was "validated by the religious authority of Islam and institutionalized through complex bureaucratic and judicial administrations" (Diamond 1988, 34). According to Dudley, indirect rule increased the emir's administrative power (by designating him the sole Native Authority in his territory), his economic security (by making him the instrument of colonial tax collection), and his judicial authority (through new powers of appointment and new emirs' courts; Dudley 1968, 16). The result was that indirect rule actually reinforced the emir's power by removing traditional checks on centralized authority. According to one scholar, the colonial government had vested in the emirs "powers . . . that were unknown in the pre-colonial era." However, because the emirs' flexibility in taxation and patronage (through arbitrary largesse) had been curtailed, they were ironically forced to resort to coercion in order to exact compliance with their orders. Thus colonial rule marked a distinct turning point in the relation between the emirs and the people, intensifying class distinctions and strengthening traditional rulers who were able to implement their will through instruments of coercion (Ibrahim 1988, esp. 71–75).

One consequence of the alliance between the British and the emirates was that the integrity of the political and social structures in the north could only be achieved by sealing the region off from Western influences, including from southern Nigeria. In this attempt to insulate the north from modernity, Western education was severely curtailed in order to prevent in the north what Lord Lugard termed the "utter disrespect for British and native ideals alike" that was beginning to emerge in the south (Coleman 1958, 137). By 1947, according to Coleman, the north, with over half of the country's population, accounted for only 2.5 percent of its primary school enrollment (134). At Independence, the north had less than 10 percent of primary school enrollment and less than 5 percent of secondary school enrollment (Dudley 1968, 281). As late as 1951, the 16 million inhabitants of the north "could point to only one of their number who had obtained a full university degree, and he was a Zaria Fulani convert to Christianity" (Coleman 1958, 139).

This situation was a result of deliberate policies aimed at limiting the number of Western-educated northerners. The British were committed to reproducing the social and political structures of colonial northern Nigeria and determined to ensure that the "natives" did not, by obtaining adequate education, begin to think for themselves. Until 1958, northern Nigeria did not possess a single secondary school offering sixth-form education, whereas southern Nigeria had sixteen. As a result, in 1960, the year of Independence, out of 2,290 students enrolled in the two universities in the country only 300 were from the north (Tibenderana 2003, 25). Even where schools were established, their purpose was the development and maintenance of an "inherently inequitable and unjust organization of production and political power" (28). To quote Tibenderana, "the colonial schooling which the British brought to Northern Nigeria was perhaps the meanest and the most futile form of imperialist education" (28).

The principal aims of colonial education in northern Nigeria were set out by a colonial appointee, Hanns Vischer, in July 1908 as the following:

1. developing the national and racial characteristics of the "natives" on lines that would enable them to use their own moral and physical forces to the best advantage;
2. widening their mental horizon without destroying their respect for race and parentage;
3. supplying men for employment under the native administration; and
4. preventing the introduction of the idea that it is more honorable to sit in an office than to do manual labor (Tibenderana 2003, 36).

The children of the poor were not to be taught English. Elite children were to be trained to fulfill Lugard's vision of the northern Muslim elite as "invaluable co-operators with the British administration" (Tibenderana 2003, 28).

The northern region that came into the union we presently know as Nigeria was therefore a more or less homogeneous entity, with the exception of a substantial number of small ethnic groups in the southern part of the region who became Christians under colonial rule. More important, it was educationally backward, politically reactionary, socially hierarchical, and deeply steeped in a dependent mind-set. Its Muslim leaders, although holding on strongly to their religious identity, did not share the vibrant revolutionary fervor of, for example, the more educated and urbane Egyptian Muslim elite of the time. They were staunch supporters of colonialism and in firm control of a large population deprived of education and prospects for upward social mobility.

By the time of Nigeria's Independence, October 1960, there were already some indications of fault lines in the northern polity, between the Christians in what came to be known as the Middle Belt and the people of Borno, on the one hand, and the Fulani-dominated Sokoto caliphate, on the other.[7] However, religious crises in the form of violent conflicts between Christians and Muslims are a relatively recent phenomenon, with roots in the failure of the Nigerian state and the emergence of Pentecostal Christian and extreme Islamist groups. Matthew Hasan Kukah (1993) and Ousmane Kane (2003) have both studied at length the politics of Muslim–Christian confrontation in northern Nigeria.

The point here, however, is that Islam and sharia were entrenched in the history and culture of the region, and the Muslims of northern Nigeria have internalized a religious identity that suppressed ethnic and tribal identities. This internalization was actively supported—and, one must add, controlled—by imperialist Britain. Unlike many of the groups in southern Nigeria, among whom ethnic and tribal identities outweigh all others (the Yoruba, Ibo, Bini, Ijaw, and Itsekiri, to give a few examples), the Hausa, Fulani, Nupe, Kanuri, and other Muslim peoples in northern Nigeria have, since the nineteenth century, seen themselves primarily as Muslim. In response, the non-Muslim groups who populate the so-called Middle Belt have also constructed an opposite, mainly Christian, identity, complete with its own mythology of historical oppression and marginalization by the Muslim "Hausa-Fulani." Religion therefore plays a more exaggerated role in the politics of the region than in other parts of the country, and it is against this background, among other things, that one must read contemporary events.

Disengagement of the State, Globalization, and Sharia in Northern Nigeria

A number of studies have attempted to show the link between the failure of the Nigerian political elite and the emergence of religious politics, or, put in another way, to argue the thesis that religious politics have secular roots in the struggle for economic and political space.[8] The "oil boom" of the mid-1970s seems to have coincided with the rise of religiously charged politics in northern Nigeria. Ever since the late 1970s, northern Nigeria has witnessed many religious riots and conflicts. Initially, these seem to have been restricted to conflicts within the Muslim community itself, between emergent dissident groups who challenged the traditional interpretation and practice of Islam in Nigeria—notably between both reformist (so-called Wahhabist) groups like the Society for the Removal of Innovation and Reinstatement of Tradition (popularly known as 'Yan Izala) and violent millenarian groups like 'Yan Tatsine, which set Kano on fire in December 1980, on the one hand,

and the general populace, on the other. At roughly the same time there were conflicts between the Muslim Brothers, an Islamist group inspired by the Iranian revolution and seeking the establishment of an Islamic state in Nigeria, and government forces. The final stage is represented by the interreligious violence between Muslims and Christians.

Some may argue that religious crises should not be linked with the discourse on sharia. This argument rests on a somewhat naive attempt to ignore, at the very least, evidence of a strong diachronic correlation between the two. The elections of 1979 were preceded by a bitter constitutional debate over the role of sharia in the constitution. Questions like Nigeria's membership in the Organization of the Islamic Conference and the distribution of political appointments among adherents of different faiths have been central points of controversy over the years. Finally, the implementation of sharia in the Muslim states of the north has been accompanied by its own problems. In states with large non-Muslim populations, the prospect of implementation led to serious conflicts and bloodshed. This was the case in Kaduna state, for instance, which has a long history of interreligious violence, such as the Kafanchan riots (1987) and the Zangon-Kataf riots (1992).

Ousmane Kane's study of interreligious tension in Nigeria (2003, 204–5) traces the root of the phenomenon to what we may condense into three main sources. First, northern Christian minorities who had been educated by the colonialists became politically aware and determined to change the existing social order, which they felt was dominated by Muslims. Second, the leadership of the Christian Association of Nigeria (CAN) and the Jamaatu Nasril Islam (JNI), the umbrella bodies for Nigerian Christians and Muslims, respectively, became politicized. This politicization was personified in Archbishop (now Cardinal) Olubunmi Okogie and the late Shaykh Abubakar Gumi. Finally, as Ruth Marshall (1995) argues (see also Hackett 1999), Pentecostals began aggressively proselytizing, demonizing Islam and thus fueling the rise of Islamic fundamentalism.

Much of Kane's detailed discussion points to the general sense of economic deprivation felt by the people of the southern part of the Middle Belt as the source of tension. But this is only half of the story. In reality, poverty and deprivation in the north are the lot of both Muslims and Christians, and the widespread frustration has been a major reason for conflicts. A number of Muslim scholars have, for instance, questioned the sincerity of Muslim politicians who claim to be implementing sharia in an environment of abject poverty, illiteracy, and unequal distribution of income.[9] The structural adjustment program imposed on Nigeria by its external creditors, and the reliance on market forces for resource allocation in the age of globalization and unbridled bourgeoisification, have both taken a major toll on the Nigerian economy. The currency has been devalued, small-scale industries have collapsed, terms of trade have worsened, and inflation has increased. The period since 1986 has seen increased impoverishment of the population, with more than 90 percent of Nigerians living below the poverty line.[10] The general economic situation is therefore a major factor contributing to religious crisis.

There are also external influences. The Iranian revolution in the late 1970s led to a new wave of Islamism across the Muslim world. In addition, the oil wealth of Saudi Arabia meant that the desert kingdom now had the resources to set up institutions for indoctrinating Africans who would spread the ideology of Wahhabism.[11] Many of the scholars at the forefront of the project to establish sharia in Nigeria today—understood as the implementation of penal laws—are of a strict Wahhabist orientation, though many who have ties to Sufi orders also supported the sharia project. Many of the scholars come from poor social backgrounds; they tend to have little Western education, to be settlers in their host communities, and generally to use Wahhabism as a vehicle for social mobility and a challenge to the establishment.[12]

But perhaps the most appropriate perspective is one that places the sharia debate within the context of an ongoing struggle among various factions of the political elite for ascendancy. No analysis of contemporary Nigerian politics can ignore the nature of the Nigerian state, an oil-rich state that is the arena for intense struggle among the political elite, notorious as one of the most corrupt in the world. The power wielded by the state continues to make it attractive to the establishment. As Gaetano Mosca noted, so long as "all moral and material advantages depend on those who hold power, there is no baseness that will not be resorted to in order to please them; just as there is no act of chicanery or violence that will not be resorted to in order to attain power, in other words, to belong to the number of those who hand out the cake rather than to the larger number of those who have to rest content with the slices that are doled out to them" (1939, 144).

The foregoing analysis seeks to highlight the complex and dialectical interplay between theological and secular materialist elements in generating religious tension in Nigeria. The failure of the Nigerian political elite to forge a true national consciousness, the corruption and the absence of a social safety net for the poor, historical identities and the search for authenticity, the struggles between and within religions are all contributory factors. It is also important to recall that these factors all play out in an international environment in which Islam and the West are presented as two mutually antagonistic forces and every conflict or catastrophe, from the Palestinian struggle to the war in Iran to September 11, is seen primarily as an unfolding of one more phase of this confrontation.[13] At the same time, one must stress that the discourse of sharia, even among its protagonists, is not univocal. Different individuals and groups adopt different approaches to its implementation, and it would be a mistake to consider all twelve states implementing sharia as being in complete, or even substantial, agreement on what it means. It is also far from certain that all those who announced the implementation of sharia are indeed committed to it in any important respect. On the contrary, the state governors have shown varying degrees of commitment—and in some cases a patent lack thereof.

Conclusion: The Way Forward

When the northern Nigerian state of Zamfara started the implementation of sharia in full in 2000, observers were deeply concerned about the consequences of the act for the continued existence of Nigeria as one nation. The natural tensions between a liberal constitution and laws unique to a specific religion in a pluralistic society accounted for these concerns. The history of interreligious conflicts in the region, coupled with religious and ethnic violence not just in Africa and the Middle East but also in central and eastern Europe, added to this fear. Within Nigeria itself, violence erupted between Muslims and Christians in Kaduna, Kano, and Plateau states. Although this violence was not always linked to the implementation of sharia, it was nonetheless one of the consequences of an intense politics of religious identity in the region.

The initial implementation of sharia had mass popular support. The people of the north were generally dissatisfied with their lot; they had just been forced out of political power and felt generally insecure, and, like other Nigerians, they were victims of a corrupt and mismanaged system that led to widespread poverty and apathy. Religion offered a sense of hope and an opportunity to improve their pathetic circumstances. In addition, the international environment was such that Muslims in general considered themselves to be under siege, with the U.S. administration under George W. Bush in particular seen as employing double standards in world conflicts and pursuing a thinly disguised anti-Islamic agenda. The presence of a new breed of scholars committed to Christian and Muslim extremism served to compound the situation and aggravate tension in the region.

Over a period of four years, the euphoria seems to have fizzled out. After the initial sensational sentences of amputation, caning, and even stoning to death (which was not carried out) the people have come to realize that nothing in reality has changed and that the poor seem to be the only ones facing the wrath of the law.[14] There is now a focus on the real problems facing the people, and questions are being asked about good governance, competence, and genuine commitment to the welfare of the people.

The dialogue between Muslims and other Nigerians, as well as among Muslims themselves, is ongoing. At the theoretical and practical levels, a number of questions need to be resolved. The role and limits of religion and religious laws in a liberal state must be defined. The relation between the secular liberal state and religion continues to pose problems in all societies. Political liberalism, to quote Habermas in this context, "understands itself as a non-religious and post-metaphysical justification of the normative foundations of a democratic constitutional state" (Habermas 2005, 340). A state that is obligated to "world-view neutrality" finds itself at odds with any presumption of dependence on autochthonous religious traditions, or any collectively binding ethical traditions, for that matter (339). In the case of the debates within Islam, this argument has been put up by one spectrum of scholars. Abdullahi An-Na'im argues that the sharia, as it is understood by Nigerian and other Islamists as a public law, has always been a secular law because of its mediation by human agents. He argues that the very idea of an Islamic state is "conceptually incoherent, and practically very dangerous for the integrity of the religious experience of Muslims themselves" (An-Na'im 2005, 341). A major issue for An-Na'im, therefore, is that the Muslims of northern Nigeria have not sufficiently clarified for themselves what they want, nor have they understood the real implications of their demands in a pluralistic state that is supposed to be religiously neutral. Although An-Na'im's thesis continues to generate controversy, it is important to recognize that he is not the only scholar to take this position. Wael Hallaq, in an insightful critique of the call for restoration of the sharia, traces the "demise" of the law to its codification, a process that is "not an inherently neutral form of law, nor is it an innocent tool of legal practice, devoid of political and other goals" (Hallaq 2004, 23). Hallaq contends, in forceful terms, that "this pervasive and dominating discourse misses the crucial point that the Shari'ah is no longer a tenable reality, that it has met its demise nearly a century ago, and that this sort of discourse is lodging itself in an irredeemable state of denial" (22).

On the other hand, there are Muslim intellectuals who believe in the possibility of implementing sharia, but who insist on opening up space for its reinterpretation by different societies at different times. Usually these scholars rely on traditional sources of law and popularize views and interpretations that had been suppressed or marginalized by dominant cultural and political discourses. Others seek to interpret the law according to ontologies of freedom, equality, and justice that are decidedly modern. Still others question the authority of particular legal sources, such as individual jurists, schools, or traditions.

It seems to me that the increasing airing of these viewpoints and free and unfettered conversation will lead to a new consensus among Muslims and between Muslims and others on the place of sharia in Nigeria. The reality of the world in which we live, the demands of women for greater freedom, the requirements of good governance, and increased awareness of the capacity of religious demagogues for mischief will all push the debate toward more secular areas and reduce the religious tension. Ultimately, improvements in Muslims' understanding not just of the law but also of the meaning of citizenship and the importance of personal liberty, are crucial to the future of this debate. Only then will it become difficult to use religion as a divisive tool for the attainment of political ends.

Notes

I am grateful to the African Studies Centre (ASC), Leiden, and Centre d'études d'Afrique noire (CEAN), Bordeaux, for the invitation to participate in the conference in Paris, May 12–13, 2005. All views expressed in this chapter are personal and do not necessarily reflect the views of the First Bank of Nigeria or its board or management.

1. I have in mind here Alhaji Abubakar Rimi, civilian governor of Kano state (1979–83) and later a federal minister. In both 1999 and 2003 he insisted that zoning was reactionary and remained in the race almost until the party primaries. He did not have the support of his party. A second example is Alhaji Umaru Shinkafi, former deputy inspector-general of police and director-general of the Nigerian Security Organisation, who comes from the northwest. In 1999, he remained a candidate for the presidency until the last minute, when he agreed to be the running mate of Chief Olu Falae on the joint ticket of the All Nigeria Peoples' Party and Alliance for Democracy. They lost to Olusegun Obasanjo and Abubakar Atiku.

2. This is, for instance, the view of Caroline Fourest in her scathing critique of the oeuvre of Tariq Ramadan, *Frère Tariq* (Fourest 2004). Personally, I think that many of the judgments made in the book reflect unsubstantiated logical leaps. But this is not the point here.

3. This would seem to be the view of, for example, Fatima Mernissi, Abdullahi An-Na'im, and Nasr Abu Zayd. It is, in my view, a bit simplistic but not entirely unfounded.

4. For a history of the jihad, see Last 1977.

5. On the debates between the leaders of the Sokoto jihad and El-Kanemi, see A. Kane 1987, 87–106; Brenner 1992.

6. For the *wazir*'s self-defense and his justification for signing the peace treaty with the British, see his epistle titled "Risala ila Ahl al-'Ilm wal-Tadbir," published in full in Galadanci 1982, 264–67.

7. This tension was appropriated by politicians, leading to the formation of the United Middle Belt Congress, led by Joseph Tarka, and the Borno Youth Movement, led by Ibrahim Imam.
8. These include Kukah 1993 and Usman 1987.
9. For an excellent example of this, see Mohamed, Adamu, and Abba 1999.
10. For a detailed and critical review of Nigerian economic policy over the period and its impact, see Sanusi 2005a.
11. For an analysis of Wahhabism and how it breeds intolerance, as well as the secular roots of extremism, see Sanusi 2004.
12. For a study of the social base of Wahhabist scholars in Kano, see O. Kane 2003, chapter 4, esp. 104–10.
13. I have elsewhere reviewed this intercultural dialogue and made concrete proposals for improving our understanding; see Sanusi 2005b.
14. A number of works have covered this and other dimensions of the project. See, for example, Sanusi 2002a and Ibrahim 2004.

References

Abubakar, Saad. 1977. *The lamibe of Fombina: A political history of Adamawa, 1809–1901*. Zaria, Nigeria: Ahmadu Bello University Press.

An-Na'im, Abdullahi Ahmed. 2005. The future of shari'ah and the debate in Northern Nigeria. In *Comparative perspectives on shari'ah in Nigeria*, ed. Philip Ostien, Jamila M. Nasir, and Franz Kogelmann, 327–57. Ibadan, Nigeria: Spectrum Books, in association with Safari Books.

Brenner, Louis. 1992. The jihad debate between Sokoto and Borno: Historical analysis of Islamic political discourse in Nigeria. In *People and empires in African history*, ed. J. F. Ade Ajayi and J. D. Y. Peel, 21–43. London: Longman.

Coleman, James S. 1958. *Nigeria: Background to nationalism*. Berkeley: University of California Press. Quoted in Diamond 1988.

Diamond, Larry. 1988. *Class, ethnicity and democracy in Nigeria: The failure of the First Republic*. Syracuse: Syracuse University Press.

Dudley, B. J. 1968. *Parties and politics in northern Nigeria*. London: Frank Cass.

Fourest, Caroline. 2004. *Frère Tariq: Discours, stratégie et méthode de Tariq Ramadan*. Paris: Bernard Grasset.

Galandaci, S. A. S. 1982. *Harakat al-Lugha al-'Arabiyya fi Nigeria*. Cairo: Dar al-Ma'arif.

Habermas, Jürgen. 2005. On the relation between the secular liberal state and religion. In *The Frankfurt School on religion: Key writings by the major thinkers*, ed. Eduardo Mendieta, 339–50. New York: Routledge.

Hackett, Rosalind I. J. 1999. Radical Christian revivalism in Nigeria and Ghana: Recent patterns of conflict and intolerance. In *Proselytization and communal self-determination in Africa*, ed. Abdullahi Ahmed An-Na'im, 246–67. Maryknoll, NY: Orbis.

Hallaq, Wael B. 2004. Can the Shari'a be restored? In *Islamic law and the challenges of modernity*, ed. Yvonne Yazbeck Haddad and Barbara Freyer Stowasser, 21–53. Walnut Creek, Calif.: AltaMira Press.

Ibrahim, J., ed. 2004. *Sharia penal and family laws in Nigeria and in the Muslim world: Rights-based approach*. [Abuja]: Global Rights.

Ibrahim, Omar Farouk. 1988. The fabric of rule: A study of the position of traditional ruling families in the politics of Kano State, Nigeria, 1960–1983. Ph.D. diss., Rutgers, the State University of New Jersey.

Kane, Ahmad Muhammad. 1987. *Al-Jihad al-Islami fi Gharb Ifriqiya (Waraqah Thaqafiyyah no. 7)*. Madinat Nasr, Cairo: Al-Zahra' li al-I'lam al-'Arabi.

Kane, Ousmane. 2003. *Muslim modernity in postcolonial Nigeria: A study of the Society for the Removal of Innovation and Reinstatement of Tradition*. Boston: Brill.

Kano Judicial Council. 1994. *Thus ruled Emir Abbas: Selected cases from the records of the Emir of Kano's Judicial Council,* ed. Allan Christelow. East Lansing: Michigan State University Press.

Kukah, M. H. 1993. *Religion, politics and power in Northern Nigeria.* Ibadan, Nigeria: Spectrum Books.

Last, Murray. 1977. *The Sokoto caliphate.* London: Longman.

Marshall, Ruth. 1995. "God is not a Democrat": Pentecostalism and democratisation in Nigeria. In *The Christian churches and the democratisation of Nigeria,* ed. P. Gifford, 239–60. Leiden: Brill.

Mohamed, Abubakar Siddique, Sa'idu Hassan Adamu, and Alkasum Abba. 1999. Human living conditions and reforms of legal systems: The Talakawa and the issue of the shari'ah in contemporary Nigeria. Paper presented at "The Shari'ah and The Constitutional Process," a conference held in Zaria, Nigeria, November 17–18. The paper was later published as a pamphlet by the Centre for Democratic Development Research and Training. http://www.ceddert.com/detail.htm.

Mosca, Gaetano. 1939. *The ruling class (Elementi di scienze politica),* ed. and rev. Arthur Livingston. Trans. Hannah D. Kahn. New York: McGraw-Hill.

Sanusi, Sanusi L. 2002a. Class, gender, and a political economy of "sharia." In *Islamization in secular Nigeria: Implications for women's rights,* Women Living under Muslim Laws, 53–59. Readers and Compilations Series. London: Women Living under Muslim Laws.

———. 2002b. The *hudood* punishments in the northern Nigeria: A Muslim criticism. http://www.gamji.com/sanusi/sanusi30.htm.

———. 2004. Islam and religious tolerance: From theology to social science. Paper presented at "Religion in the Public Sphere: Challenges and Opportunities," the 11th Annual International Law and Religion Symposium, Brigham Young University, Provo, Utah, October 4.

———. 2005a. Reforming the Nigerian economy—Which model? A critical review of Nigerian economic policy from 1986–2004. Presentation at the 2nd Annual Trust Dialogue organized by Media Trust Limited, Ladi Kwali Hall, Abuja Sheraton Hotels and Towers, January 13.

———. 2005b. The West and the rest: Reflections on the intercultural dialogue about shari'ah. In *Comparative perspectives on shari'ah in Nigeria,* ed. Philip Ostien, Jamila M. Nasir, and Franz Kogelmann, 251–72. Ibadan, Nigeria: Spectrum Books, in association with Safari Books.

Tibenderana, Peter K. 2003. *Education and cultural change in Northern Nigeria, 1906–1966: A study in the creation of a dependent culture.* Kampala: Fountain Publishers.

Tukur, Mahmud. 1999. *Leadership and governance in Nigeria: The relevance of values.* London: Hudahuda/Hodder & Stoughton.

Usman, Yusufu Bala. 1987. *The manipulation of religion in Nigeria, 1977–1987.* Kaduna, Nigeria: Vanguard.

CHAPTER 10

POLITICAL ISLAM IN SUDAN: ISLAMISTS AND THE CHALLENGE OF STATE POWER (1989–2004)

Einas Ahmed

Before the recent elections of Hamas in Palestine, Sudan was the only example of Islamist rule in Africa or in the Sunni Arabo-Muslim world. In light of the problematic of Islamist currents and political power, this country has followed a relatively distinctive path which merits close attention and analysis. In 1989, the National Islamic Front (NIF), the Sudanese Islamist party, worried that its project of restoring sharia law would fail, organized a coup d'état and overthrew the multiparty system that had been in power since 1985.[1] This revealed several elements of the preferences, if not the political culture, of this group at that time, notably its rejection of any political order other than its own. In 1998, the Islamist regime adopted a new constitution and declared the restoration of the multiparty system, which it had originally opposed so vehemently. In January 2005, in Naivasha, Kenya, the government signed a peace accord with its sworn enemy, the southern rebel Sudan People's Liberation Movement (SPLM), which had struggled specifically against an Islamist hegemony.[2] This treaty entails the abandonment of the project of establishing a nationwide Islamic political order. What do these events mean? Is it possible to speak of a real political opening or a transformation of the mentality of Sudanese Islamists? And what about political Islam in Sudan nowadays? These are the questions that I will attempt to answer in this study.

The analysis of political Islam, especially the evolution of the relationship between religion and the state, is all the more urgent for Sudan because of two recent and related events in that country: a new configuration of Islamist leadership in power, and the signing of the peace agreement.[3] Negotiated under international pressure, notably from the U.S., this agreement stipulates and institutionalizes the sharing of power and of wealth between these two groups from opposite ends of the Sudanese political spectrum. It thus brings a reevaluation of the relationship between religion and the state. These developments will significantly affect the balance of power in the country.

These important events have, on one hand, led Sudanese Islamist leaders to "de-ideologize" their discourse and thus to reevaluate their insistence on the linkage of the state and Islam (the very foundation of their party and their political discourse), as is also demonstrated by certain clauses of the peace agreement. On the other hand, they inaugurate the beginnings of a post-Islamist phase in Sudan which largely takes the form of a change in the morphology of political Islam. For example, certain fundamentalist and neofundamentalist Muslim groups that had heretofore been not only apolitical but also anti-Islamist are now entering the political arena. Today, they participate in the regime. But at the same time, there has emerged an Islamist faction that, in disagreement with the government, advocates self-criticism and reform, calling for a return to the original message and discourse of the Sudanese branch of the Muslim Brotherhood (MB). Last of all, an extremist movement led by a prominent Islamist figure has emerged, calling for the secession of the northern region to protect "the Arab and Muslim identity of the country."

Post-Islamism in Sudan is also characterized by the accentuation of ethnicity and of centrifugal tendencies which menace national unity more than ever. Today, the regime and indeed the state are weakened from within by armed regionalist movements and threatened from without by growing pressure from the international community. These developments could signal the beginning of the end of northern hegemony.[4] In this chapter, I will attempt to uncover the underlying logic of this change by analyzing the internal dynamics of the regime that has been in power since 1989.

The Interpenetration of the Religious and Political Fields and the Constitutional Question

A striking characteristic of the Sudanese political field is the powerful influence of religion. Most Sudanese are Muslims, and Islam is the principal base of legitimacy for the major political parties and their principal instrument of domination, but it is also the instrument of their rivalry.

This relationship between religion and politics creates a problem, because there is an important minority of non-Muslims who are not part of the Arabo-Muslim culture with which the majority of northern Sudanese, especially the state and its ruling elite, identify. The situation is all the more complicated because, in the collective imaginary of this important minority, Islam has been associated, ever since Ottoman colonization, with slavery and hegemony. The importation of religion into the political sphere and the identification of the Sudanese state with Islam have only complicated the relationship between them and the ensuing political conflicts by adding a religious dimension.

It follows that the political field is essentially characterized by the confrontation between, on one hand, the partisans of a secularist order represented by various left-wing parties, principally the Sudanese Communist Party (SCP) and African groups, and on the other, the partisans of an Islamic order that includes the ensemble of politico-religious parties, the Umma Party (UP), the Democratic Unionist Party (DUP), and the NIF. However, it is important to relativize this dichotomy between a religious and a secular order, in that the religious field is heterogeneous (including as it does Sufism, Islamism, and neofundamentalism), which entails a split among the very defenders of an Islamic order. Sufism managed to dominate the political scene after Independence: the two dominant political parties, the UP and the DUP, issued from the Mahdiyya and the Khatmiyya orders, respectively. This strong religious influence explains the ease with which the Islamist faction in Sudan has integrated itself into the political field, distinguishing it from similar movements in the Muslim world and in sub-Saharan Africa. In reality, the Islamist elite are part of the establishment that has socially, politically, and economically dominated the country since Independence. With the exception of the short-lived military regime of the Free Officers, that governed in the name of Arab socialism between 1969 and 1972, secularist groups have not been able to achieve political dominance.

This problematic relationship between the state and religion is apparent in three respects: the constitutional crisis, which the country has endured since Independence; the politics of law; and what is commonly known as the North–South conflict. These three are obviously interrelated. The history of constitutional debates in Sudan since Independence is the history of attempts to institutionalize and officialize the relationship between the state and Islam and of the confrontation between conservative and secularizing forces. Ultraconservatives went so far as to insist in 1968 that the constitution explicitly stipulate that "Islam is the official religion of the state" and that the president be a member of the Muslim community.

The questions of an Islamic constitution and the Islamization of the legal system reached their peak during the early 1980s, when President Nimeiry, in power since 1969, decided to adopt "the Islamic way."[5] Only the Islamists accepted this initiative and integrated themselves into political institutions. But in reality, they were not the cause of the adoption of sharia in 1983. As they were in disagreement with the president, they had already been shunted off.[6] This was the Sufi phase of the head of state's new religiosity; he surrounded himself with Sufi personalities and legal counselors, and they were the true architects of the September 1983 promulgation and adoption of the sharia.[7] This version of sharia became territorial law. Although this policy of Islamization was not the direct cause of the southerners' resumption of armed struggle in 1983, it was nonetheless at the heart of the conflict, especially the negotiation between the government and the rebels, particularly after Nimeiry's deposition in 1985.

Essentially, throughout the period of the multiparty regime (1985–89), the laws of 1983 divided political forces between partisans and opponents of this legislation. Even when the laws were suspended by the transitional government (1985–86), the matter was the principal cause of political instability.

It is important to note the position of the Islamists, who were an emerging political force within the National Islamic Front at the head of the parliamentary opposition. Their proposals were elaborated in a document called the "Sudan Charter" (National Islamic Front 1987), in which the relationship between the religious group (*milla*) and the fatherland, as well as citizenship, was spelled out. Although this charter was less categorical than the Islamists' 1968 constitutional project, in that it confirmed the principle of equality of access to the state for all Sudanese, it nevertheless included measures which made the priority of Islam and Muslims in this domain quite clear.

> Muslims are a majority in Sudan. Their religiosity is founded on oneness [*tawhid*].
> Secularism, that is to say politics without religion, is rejected. . . . Muslims, by virtue of

their democratic preponderance and of natural justice, have the right to opt for their religion and to apply it at the personal, familial, and state level.

The sociological concept of a majority is thus used to give priority to Islam at the state level. As for non-Muslims, "they have religious expression at the personal, familial, and social levels." Islam is the primary source of legislation, "as it is the expression of the democratic majority and because it equally contains the values of the other monotheistic religions." The charter envisages the decentralization of law: regions with a non-Muslim majority have the right to establish their own legal system. In 1988, the NIF entered into a coalition with the UP, and its leader was named attorney general and minister of justice, charged with responsibility for drawing up laws to succeed those of 1983. He proposed the Sudan Charter, but with an addition: the crime of apostasy. The acceptance of these new laws by the Council of Ministers and by the Parliament on second reading provoked a lively reaction from secularist forces, a minority in this institution. This crisis was worsened by general discontent, especially in the army, which obliged the prime minister, Sadiq al-Mahdi (UP), to break up the coalition with the Islamists in favor of a more national government. Marginalized, the NIF reacted by staging a coup d'état, bringing Islamists to power.

The Evolution of Political Organization

The first two phases of the new regime were those of revolutionary legitimacy (1989–96) and constitutional legitimacy (1996–98). These years were characterized by vehement ideological discourse identifying the state and the nation with Islam. But in 1998 a third phase began, that of post-Islamism, during which leaders' discourse and positions softened and the loci of power were reorganized. In 2000, intensive negotiations reopened with the SPLM, which led to the 2005 peace agreement. These changes followed the ideological and political shifts of the regime.

It is important to remember that the regime was the product of a coup d'état organized by an essentially political group in the name of a religious project. Although its principal declared goal was the establishment of an Islamic state, there was from the outset a clear separation between political power and religious power. We are consequently far from Khomeini's *velayat-e faqih* in Iran, where religious authority, in the person of *al-murshid*, the guide, also represents political authority.[8] Hasan al-Turabi, the regime's *éminence grise*, was above all a politician, whose charisma was based not just on his religious knowledge but also and above all on his political acumen. He was invariably elected party leader. Iran and Sudan share a significant characteristic, as we shall see below: politics always trumps religion.

The Period of Revolutionary Legitimacy (1989–96)

Following the coup d'état, the Revolutionary Command Council (RCC) was established. The new regime was baptized a "revolution of salvation." At its head was General Umar al-Bashir. The 1985 transitional constitution was annulled and all political parties, including the NIF, suspended. All political leaders, including al-Turabi, were immediately imprisoned. Until its dissolution in October 1993, the

RCC officially constituted the supreme political authority. But the country was governed de facto by a shadowy group, *al-tanzim*, a secret nucleus of hard-line militants (civilian and military) of the Islamist organization.

The new regime was preoccupied with finding "an alternative formula to a multi-party state" in order to "forge a new Sudanese society."[9] It adopted a model of popular congresses. According to the regime's ideologues, the pyramidal structure of this system, rising from local congresses to the National Assembly, guaranteed "fuller popular participation." The new order was simultaneously founded on divine legitimacy (*al-hakmiyya li-llah*, "sovereignty is only God's") and temporal legitimacy, "the sovereignty of the people" (National Congress Party General Secretariat 1991).[10] In 1991, as a corollary of the ideology of "popular democracy," the regime opted for federalism.

In the legal sphere, a strategic domain for the Islamists, the sharia was officially reestablished and a new penal code adopted in 1991. Nonetheless, because the federal system delegated the power to legislate to each state, the southern states, where a majority of inhabitants were not Muslim, were exempted from Islamic law, according to the principle of the territoriality of laws. The link between religion and the state was politically confirmed by constitutional decree: "Islam and the sharia are the fundamental authority of the Sudanese state and the foundation of its laws, of its organization, and of politics." The goal of the regime's civilizational project is "the Islamization of society and the state." A multitude of official bodies were created to "oversee" this objective, such as the Supreme Committee for the Verification of the Legal Conformity of the Banking System; the post of presidential counselor for matters of authentication (*al-ta'sil*), whose task was to encourage "the return to the sources"; and a fund to subsidize the application of sharia.

The new Islamist government was nevertheless aware of the weak reach of its ideology in society at large and of the influence of the Sufi orders. So in order to control all Islamic activities outside the Islamist orbit and to mobilize Sufi support for the Islamist agenda, it created the Council of Remembrance and Those Who Remember God (*Majlis al-dhikr wa-l-dhakirin*), which included representatives not just of the Sufi orders but also of Qur'anic schools, ulama, and charitable groups. This body was under the aegis of the newly created and crucial Ministry of Social Planning. Its secretary-general and its ninety members were appointed by the president. In this way, the state controlled the religious field.

As well as establishing these institutional, political, and legal measures, the government was determined to maintain control over, and surveillance of, society as a whole.[11] Everything was done in the name of Islam and of a civilizational project which, according to its architects, "is a response to the decline and the decadence of the great Arab and Muslim community."[12] The principle of "prescribing the good and prohibiting evil" (*al-amr bi-l-ma'ruf wa-l-nahy 'an al-munkar*), an argument and instrument of control used by all Islamist movements, was promulgated to justify the appropriation of public space and a policy of repression. In its spirit, the Law of Public Order (*al-nizam al-'amm*) created the sort of popular committees typical of totalitarian regimes. Among those most affected by this control were women, who were obligated to adopt the *hijab*. However, that was the only restriction imposed on women by the Islamists.

Everywhere, the exterior signs of a "re-Islamization" were visible: signs bearing Qur'anic verses, others with the image of veiled women; new mosques everywhere, even within ministerial buildings; the names of historic Muslim heroes given to streets, to units of Muslim troops stationed in the South, and to humanitarian convoys destined for fighters. The dinar replaced the Sudanese pound and the term *wilaya* designated regional administrative units. Military service was required in the name of jihad, the ideology of martyrdom was pushed to extremes, and committees for popular defense were created to assist regular troops. Television was the principal means of diffusing these ideas; every evening, images and stories of young soldiers "headed for Paradise" (killed in the civil war) were broadcast. The Ministry of Social Planning was created in 1992 and staffed with hard-line Islamists, with the same aim of controlling the society.

During this early phase, repressive measures typical of a police state were at their peak. Security was prioritized, reflecting the Islamist conception of the state: "In the end, the modern state is the apparatus of security or more precisely the institution which monopolizes and controls all information" (El-Affendi 1995, 42). Thus, hard-line militants, who were scarcely known to the general public, led institutions responsible for security and for the army. Massive purges were carried out not only in the army (the first institution affected by these measures) but also in government administration and in university circles, in the name of "public interest" (*al-salih al-'amm*). Anyone suspected, rightly or wrongly, of constituting a menace was shunted off and replaced by sympathizers. This iron-fisted policy was progressively replaced by a less "revolutionary" and more flexible one, as a result of several internal factors and the effects of globalization.

The Period of Constitutional Legitimacy (1996–98)

In 1995, the National Congress (NC, *al-Mu'tamar al-watani*), now the sole political organization of the country, was fully constituted. The regime's architects pronounced, "Henceforth, the National Congress, and not party pluralism, will guarantee ideological pluralism" (Sudan National Assembly 1995, 29). Al-Turabi was elected secretary-general of the new party.

An Islamist university faculty member explained this: "The idea was to cause the Islamist movement to spontaneously dissolve into the body of a large party which would govern and win all future elections, thanks to the support of its large popular base" (al-Abdeen 1999). It was a heterogeneous assemblage and included non-Muslims. In reality, its goal was to conceive of a system in which everyone "could participate," but only if they approved of the regime's nonnegotiable principles (*thawabit*): the unity of the nation and sharia. Approving them implicitly meant accepting the presence of Islamists and their program at the heart and head of the system. The participation of non-Muslims had its limits and was only fictive, but the dissolution of the Islamist party was designed to marginalize the old guard in favor of al-Turabi and a restricted entourage of second-generation Islamists.

In 1996, elections were organized for a new National Assembly to replace the provisional Parliament, which had been in place since 1992. Al-Turabi was also president of the Assembly. In this way, the organic relationship between *al-tanzim* and

Parliament guaranteed the concentration of both political and legislative power in the hands of the regime's *éminence grise*.

In the same year, President al-Bashir was "elected" by universal suffrage as president of the Republic of Sudan. This was claimed to mark the end of the period of "revolutionary legitimacy" and the beginning of that of "constitutional legitimacy." Decisions and political measures taken in every domain were announced by constitutional decrees in the president's name. But real power lay elsewhere, with al-Turabi and his very small entourage. Until the end of 1999, he was the de facto ruler of the country.[13]

The powers granted the regime's ideologue were immense. The general conference of the party elected him secretary-general and president of the Leadership Council (*Majlis al-qiyadi*). He was responsible for naming the members of the General Secretariat (the party's executive and the nexus of power) and his two adjuncts (the first was required to be an Islamist, and the second a southerner). This power was reinforced by the fact that members of the Secretariat had to be selected from members of the Leadership Council. This organic link consecrated and reinforced the leader's personal control over the key institutions of the party. Al-Turabi was thus the uncontested master of all branches of leadership: the party, the Assembly, and the executive branch. Officially, ministers were nominated in the name of the president, but unofficially it was al-Turabi and his small circle that appointed and removed them. Nonetheless, al-Turabi's personal power would soon be contested and challenged.

What was the army's position within this power structure? This question invites an examination of, on one hand, the relationship between the military as an institution and the Islamist movement, and on the other, the origin of the coup d'état: was it the work of the army, backed by the Islamists, or was it the work of Islamists with the help of their military wing? In reality, the putsch was decided by what is called *al-tanzim*, a secret organization comprised of hardcore civilian and military members of the movement. However, there were only a few militant officers in the army, and they were also a minority within *al-tanzim*. In fact, it was not easy for the Islamist movement to penetrate the army. It began in the 1970s and 1980s by co-opting and training officers during sessions organized by the African Islamic Center (now the International University of Africa). It also profited from discontent within the army during the years of multiparty rule, 1986–89, and by organizing campaigns to mobilize support for the army. This effectively demonstrates that Islamists saw the military as a way of gaining power.[14]

Although there were few Islamist army officers at the time of the coup, they were still well placed within the army hierarchy. Their organization and the secrecy of their activities, especially the coordination of their actions with supporting politicians, were exemplary and allowed the coup to succeed. The support of certain conservative and apolitical officers was also important. Indeed, the fifteen members of the RCC were not all Islamists. Eight were either officers with a conservative reputation or those who shared interests with the regime. Non-Arab representatives were chosen to camouflage the political identity of the putschists in order to present an image of a national team. The widespread purges suffered by the army were intended to guarantee total subordination to *al-tanzim*.

After the dissolution of the RCC in 1993, al-Bashir became president of the Republic and of the Council of Ministers, but I must point out that he was not a member of *al-tanzim*. The army was also represented in every cabinet. In fact, strategic ministries (Defense and Interior) were systematically placed under the aegis of Islamist officers. Similarly, army officers were also, for the most part, charged with the government of large problematic regions such as Darfur and Kordofan. The security apparatus played a central role in the functioning of the regime.

Power seems to have been equitably shared between the army, which controlled the executive (especially all branches concerned with security), and the politicians, who, in their turn, dominated the party and the legislature. However, the army as an institution, in charge of strategic positions, did not monopolize one sector of power. In fact, it governed in the name of *al-tanzim*. These officers had belonged to the Islamist movement ever since secondary school, and they were guardians of the Islamist order. Remember that the slogan of the armed forces was "God is great, and there is no God but God" and that the national mission of the army became the jihad. Because of this, the involvement of military men can be better explained by political affiliation with the Islamists than by their position in the army. Within this network of power, no division existed between a military identity and a political one. The country was governed by a nucleus composed of officers and politicians, "the super *tanzim*," some of whom were unknown to the public at large but truly controlled the state.

The Constitution of 1998

In accordance with its discourse on democracy, in 1997 the regime began to envisage bestowing a permanent constitution on the nation. Islamist leaders and intellectuals progressively articulated an argument for political pluralism and a return to a multiparty regime, reneging on their original firm opposition to a multiparty state.[15] Henceforth, the watchword was consensus (*wifaq*) with all opposing political groups. This corresponded with a certain detente (at the social and political levels) and a relative relaxation of coercive policies. It was in this context, for example, that the government signed the Khartoum Peace Agreement with dissident factions of the SPLM.

Beyond this constitutional event and the political opening which it seemed to inaugurate, lively debates and contestation accompanied the drafting of the constitution. They not only demonstrated the authoritarian nature of the regime and its tendency to personalize power but revealed the old politico-ideological and pedagogical quarrels between the Islamists and the MB.[16] Nevertheless, since the separation of the Islamists from the MB in the 1960s, there had never been a public confrontation between them. The debate over the constitution signaled the break-up of the Islamist movement in Sudan and a new phase in its political trajectory.

The Debate over the Constitution

The task of drafting the constitution was officially confided to a national commission composed of experts in jurisprudence. But the final version (which was "ratified" by a referendum in 1998) included important modifications which bore al-Turabi's fingerprints. This provoked serious reaction from members of the commission as well as from numerous intellectuals but above all from conservative circles. The regime had always tried to co-opt religious conservatives. In general, Sufi groups were in favor of the regime's Islamic orientation, and, with the exception of the Ansars, the MB, and the neofundamentalist group of the Ansar al-Sunna, none of them was really critical of the government. Different groups in the political opposition considered the clauses dealing with multiparty rule ambiguous. In particular, the term *al-tawali*, used to designate the right to form political organizations, was the source of much confusion, as it lends itself to differing interpretations.

The liveliest criticisms came from the MB, which held that the constitution was insufficiently Islamic. This organization, whose members belonged for the most part to the generation which witnessed Independence, represented a relatively important pressure group in public opinion. Many of its members were noteworthy intellectuals who did not hesitate to denounce the regime in public. The MB (whose political importance remains slight) itself was ambivalent, hovering between approval and disapproval, and its disapproval was made public only recently. Members of the Brotherhood see the regime's Islamic project as "an Islam of complaisance," because, in their eyes, it concedes too much to the southerners, as the group's leader explains:

> The members of the NIF . . . once they were in power, their experiment proved to be harmful for the trajectory of the application of Islam in Sudan. . . . Today the National Congress includes Muslims and non-Muslims and I doubt that this party will apply Islam in Sudan. It is to the detriment of this religion.[17]

The new constitution was judged secular because "it doesn't clearly affirm the Muslim, Arab, and African identity of Sudan"[18] and "does not stipulate that the President must belong to the Muslim community, thus giving a non-Muslim the right to lead the nation," which the Muslim Brothers considered contrary to Islamic jurisprudence "because Muslims should be governed only by a Muslim."[19] They discuss measures to be taken to resolve the conflict with the South in terms of Muslims and non-Muslims:

> The constitution does not envisage a proper solution concerning the relationship between the Muslim community and other citizens. Those who wrote the constitution attempted, beyond what religion allows concerning the constitutional principles relative to minorities and majorities, to attribute to non-Muslims the same religious rights as to Muslims.[20]

This sociological conception of the political majority and minority is the argument they systematically used to contest the submission of "the laws of God" to a referendum.

In fact, the constitution makes no explicit reference to an Islamic state, an important deviation from what the Islamists originally clamored for. The principle that citizenship confers all rights is expressed thus:

> Sudanese are equal in rights and duties as regards to functions of public life, and there shall be no discrimination only by reason of race, sex or religion creed. They are equal in eligibility for public posts and offices not being discriminated on the basis of wealth. (art. 21)

In the same spirit, article 37 makes no reference to religious affiliation as a condition of eligibility for the office of head of state, a point on which the Islamists had been adamant in the 1960s.

What does this retreat from the intransigent political and ideological positions adopted at the outset mean? The Islamist leaders' answers to these criticisms reveal the shift of Islamism toward pragmatism. Mustafa Osman, later minister of foreign affairs, explained,

> the government sought an intermediate solution. In this way, Sudan (in this constitu-
> tion) is defined with respect to its geographical characteristics as a multireligious and
> multicultural state with diverse customs, and not as a religious state. Sudan is neither a
> religious state in the Western sense nor a secular state.[21]

Such a statement shows how ideology has retreated in favor of politics. The reality is that, once in power, the Islamists faced the exigencies of leading a state and of con-crete political practice. They thus became pragmatic and realistic and realized the limits of their discourse and of the Islamist program as well as of their hegemonic project, particularly in a society like Sudan. This easing of their policies and ideolo-gies also revealed another important facet of the Islamists: they didn't hesitate to submit religion to reasons of state and sometimes to their own particular interests. The affair of the Chinese loan, which precipitated a good deal of debate and espe-cially provoked the MB, is an example. Ever since the official adoption of sharia in 1983, the bank system has been Islamized in principle. But in 1999, the body in charge of verifying the conformity of banking systems and financial transactions with sharia allowed the government to accept a loan on which interest was to be paid, to finance the construction of a dam. To justify its decision, this agency invoked *fiqh al-darura*, jurisprudence of necessity, an Islamic legal principle which permits the sus-pension of prohibitions under certain circumstances, in this case "the unavailability of funds to undertake a project of vital public importance."[22]

Paradoxically, the constitutional phase of the regime coincided with the beginnings of a split within *al-tanzim*.

Toward a New Configuration of Political Islam

The adoption of a new constitution did not guarantee respect for democratic princi-ples, such as the separation of powers. Thus, al-Turabi's tendency to dominate the executive branch and to place it under the control of the party, or, more precisely, to institutionalize his personal influence, led to the first open crisis, when ten members of the Consultative Council issued a memorandum in December 1998 protesting the preponderant power of the secretary-general. This incident initiated the division within the leadership between al-Turabi's partisans and adversaries. The confronta-tion reached a peak in late 1999, when al-Bashir declared a state of emergency, dis-solving the Assembly in order "to preserve national unity and the cohesiveness of leadership menaced by the dual center of power." These measures were well received by most members of the government.

This crisis initiated the displacement of loci of power and the reconfiguration of relationships between groups within the religious field. Although the quarrel was initially resolved by a compromise which redistributed functions within the party in favor of al-Bashir, events did not stop here, because al-Turabi reacted to his marginalization by founding his own party, the Popular Congress, in June 2000. The crisis showed that the Islamist movement in Sudan was essentially political in spite of its discourse and its putatively meta-political religious pretensions. It confirmed, above all, its factional nature. It was never in any way a question of ideological or even inter-generational disagreement, nor a confrontation between the army and the politicians. In fact, although the military members of *al-tanzim* supported the memorandum of protest, its authors were politicians. The factionalism which characterized all Sudanese political parties had finally reached the Islamist movement. The political events which followed these new alliances within different conservative groups inaugurated a new configuration of political Islam in Sudan.

Post-Islamism: The End of Northern Hegemony?

In search of a new but still Islamic basis of legitimacy, the government appealed to the enemy of its enemy: the MB. Thus, in July 2000, it organized a large conference for "the reconstruction of the Islamic movement" in which representatives of all religious groups—the Brotherhood, the Sufi orders, and the neofundamentalist group Ansar al-Sunna—participated. The MB, representing the majority, declared that the goal of this initiative was "to protect the Islamic project in Sudan, menaced by discord within the NC."[23] It is interesting that the Brotherhood's leadership emphatically confirmed the regime's conformity with sharia. Henceforth, the movement would adopt a favorable attitude toward the regime.[24]

Although the movement's organizers emphasized its social aspects, their intentions were not unambiguous, because, at the same time, they declared that "the NC is the expression of their project in society and the state" and that this new entity would be "the reference [*marji'iyya*] for all decisions and policies relating to nonnegotiable principles such as the constitution, the protection of the Islamic projects and its state, Sudan."[25] The movement's new, apparently political, direction was also evident in its leadership. Its Shura Council included several members of the regime, and the president of the executive bureau was none other than the president of the Shura Council of the NC, the government party. Henceforth, these new groups, formerly apolitical, would be co-opted into the executive branch.[26] Today, it is a faction of Islamists who govern, this time with the open support of most religious movements (with the exception of the Ansars).

As for the government, its strategy is to confirm the Islamic nature of the regime and its party without al-Turabi by co-opting actors in the religious field. Unlike other cases of Islamism, the scenario which played out in Sudan largely consolidated the association of two fields, religious and political. For the MB, long marginalized, it offered the chance to make up for its earlier silence concerning al-Turabi's ambitions and political objectives.[27] This new alliance should thus be interpreted in the light of factional struggles within the Islamist movement on one hand, and between al-Turabi and the MB on the other.[28]

At the same time, the government attempted to rally all the other political groups. The regime's watchword was always *wifaq*, that is, consensus. Thus, it met on multiple occasions with the main political parties. The leaders of the UP and the DUP refused to answer the appeals of a regime that they did not acknowledge as legitimate. But the two parties themselves suffered from factionalism, and some of their members played along with the claim of a multiparty regime by creating their own parties, to the benefit of the Islamists, whose strategy was always to take advantage of divisions within the ranks of their opponents.

All told, can this be called a true multiparty regime, and can the government's actions be seen as a real effort to open it up to other movements? What are the political consequences of this new Islamo-Islamist alliance: a real effort of conservatives to reach out or a superficial pragmatism? Granted, 1996–97 saw a relative detente, and most of the politicians from the two major parties (and even Sudanese professionals and intellectuals) who were in exile returned home. But once again, the alliance was in fact an attempt to construct an order centered on *al-tanzim*. Pluralism was envisaged only among Islamist groups, as the declarations of an Islamist intellectual suggest:

> The Islamic movement dominates the army and the economy . . . and also is in possession of military means. Why should it be afraid of pluralism and the organization of free elections? In fact, within the very heart of the Islamic movement there are several trends and schools, which can create different political parties capable of filling the political vacuum which Sudanese society now exhibits. In this way, pluralism guarantees the renewal of the Islamic movement in Sudan. (Makki 1997)

The idea was not only to dominate the state and the political field but also to homogenize the latter to the benefit of conservative groups. No real national elections could be organized and the NC, or more precisely *al-tanzim*, continued to govern the country. The representation of other political parties at the executive level and in the government is in fact only symbolic.

The arrival of the Muslim Brotherhood and the Ansar al-Sunna onto the political scene is an important new development. We have seen that the reconciliation with the Islamists is implicated in factional politics. The support afforded by these groups is also, for the regime, an important element in the appropriation of so-called Islamic legitimacy and works to attenuate challenges from the conservatives. Still, the reconciliation is more than a simple political alliance; it represents an important change in the morphology of political Islam in Sudan. The organizational and ideological boundaries between fundamentalists, Salafis, and Islamists have softened. By allying themselves politically with the government, this means that they are willing to align themselves as well with its new conception of ideologically sensitive questions: the relationship of religion to the state, and the southern question. Thus not only do the fundamentalists and the Sudanese Salafis enter the political arena but they become less conservative and more collaborative as they learn to play the political game. This differentiates them from most of their counterparts in the Muslim world, which are increasingly distancing themselves from politics and the state. Today, the Sudanese MB even adopts a more conciliatory discourse and admits the importance of taking into account "the modern form of the state." We hear as well of "the necessity and the possibility of renewing Islamic discourse and jurisprudence pertaining to the economy, politics, and international relations, as well as the importance of adapting to modern times while remaining faithful to the original message, *al-asl*."[29]

The Ansar al-Sunna is no longer a current of opinion but a well-organized group with its own organization, the Peace Forum. It has begun to take part in political life. For instance, its members tour the different regions to invite its followers to participate in coming elections and to coordinate their actions with those of the NC. In this way, they help to mobilize Sudanese in favor of the Peace Agreement. We must bear in mind that this agreement inaugurates a new order quite inconsistent with the Islamic order as these groups originally envisaged it. In fact, this new approach is an attempt to use the state to achieve a religious objective (the propagation of Islam), a strategy shared by the MB. On one regional tour, a member of the government explained the benefits of the agreement to the faithful: "Peace is the means of spreading our message; most of all, we will be present in the regions of the South. . . . We will be able to preach among non-Muslims."[30] Unlike other cases, in Sudan the state thus figures at the heart of the re-Islamization (or Islamization) of post-Islamism. Here, the ultraconservatives' strategy resembles that of the government.[31] The first paradox is that the southern rebels obtained a maximum of concessions from the most conservative political groups. Even Nimeiry's socialist regime, which concluded the first peace agreement in 1972, didn't concede as much. Sudanese post-Islamism is thus characterized by a new pragmatism, not only among conservative religious groups but even among the ultraconservatives.

The Naivasha Agreement represents a new development in the history of the conflict, providing for a real restructuring of the Sudanese state, to the detriment of an Islamic political order. The principal demand of the SPLM, which struggles in the name of "all the marginalized regions," is the construction of a "new secular Sudan." The agreement's protocol governing the sharing of political power includes the right to self-rule, which had long been denied to southerners. After a transitional period of six years, a referendum will be organized allowing southerners to opt either for separation or for unity. In the meantime, if the elected president is a northerner, the vice president will be a southerner, and vice versa.[32] The MB's and the Ansar al-Sunna's acceptance of this measure represents a departure from their original rejection of the principle that a non-Muslim might accede to power.[33] In this vein, they invoke the distinction made by certain Islamic thinkers between *al-wilaya al-kubra*, the greater investiture of power—the imamate over Muslims—and *al-wilaya al-sughra*, the lesser investiture.[34] Thus, they distinguish between service ministries (those which merely execute decisions), in which non-Muslims may participate, and ministries of delegation (those with authority to make decisions), which are reserved for Muslims.[35]

Similarly, the status of Khartoum, the capital, was among the most disputed issues. Concessions on all sides allowed an agreement to be reached, as it was in the case of the new judicial system; under it the religious majority in each federated state will determine which legal system to adopt, Islamic or secular. In this way, sharia will be maintained in the states of the North, whose majority is Muslim, and the states of the South will be exempted. But Khartoum, simultaneously the capital and a state in the federation, will have a special status which will, in my opinion, be a source of ambiguity and perhaps conflict in the years to come: the status of non-Muslims will be governed for the most part by principles and instructions rather than by obligatory measures. According to the agreement, non-Muslims will not be subject to Islamic law. In issuing their decisions, judges are called upon to consider the inapplicability of sharia to non-Muslims, tolerance, indulgence, respect for personal liberty, the legal principle that gives the accused party the benefit of the doubt, and reduced penalties.[36] Once again, the fact that conservatives resigned themselves to this personalization of law within the capital, rather than insisting on uniform application, represents an important concession. Under the circumstances, the Islamo-Islamist alliance demonstrates the realism of conservative groups' attitude toward political order in a multireligious society like Sudan.[37] It benefits the Islamist faction in power and, paradoxically, the SPLM.

Nonetheless, is this realism an expression of nationalism? Does it constitute acceptance of a definition of Sudan which takes all of its religious components into account? It does not seem so to me; indeed, it is hardly conceivable, given that the MB remains intransigent on the citizenship question and the religion of the president: "We continue to oppose citizenship as it is defined in the Naivasha agreement," the leader of the MB assured me. Why then did it support an agreement and accept participation in (and indeed the legitimation of) a government that might be led by a non-Muslim? "Because it is an opportunity to work from within and not to deprive all Muslims of hearing the true word [kalima al-haqq], and we will work for the concrete application of sharia in the states of the North."[38] These contradictions in the positions and remarks of different MB leaders (and sometimes in the comments of one individual) express the difficulty of becoming a political group, and they also reveal the organization's internal divisions. Only the trials of sharing power, decision making, and perhaps wealth with the new secular partner, the SPLM, together with the collaboration with the Islamists, will determine the future of the group and of the alliance.

Still, if the government has found new allies who can reinforce the regime's position with respect to its adversaries, it has at the same time provoked the emergence of two dissident Islamist tendencies, one reformist and one separatist. Islamists have not unanimously supported this peace agreement and method of government, and some are its most critical opponents. These new reformers call for the "resurrection of national Islamic action."[39] They want to reform the Islamist movement, to rehabilitate its role in society, and above all to reconsider its relationship to the state. They recognize the failure of the "revolution of salvation," given "its shift from a movement to a government," and admit that the regime's credibility has been damaged by the factional squabbling for power. Hence they acknowledge the necessity "of an objective and sincere self-criticism in order to rehabilitate the group's image . . . and the importance of reconsidering the definition of the Islamist movement, and of its legal and moral status, its ideas and its sources." And to remedy the "absence of Islamic action in society," they call for "a reinforcement of the movement's role in society . . . and for its imposition as a reference for the state and for political action." This is why reformers insist on ameliorating the relation between the state and the movement: "the strength of one should not signal the weakness of the other. . . . on the contrary, the strength of each should reinforce the other." From this, we can conclude that the movement expresses, first, regret at the dissolution of the Islamist movement incarnated by the sole party, and at its loss of identity and independence in relation to the state and al-tanzim. It is almost a critique of the total politicization of the Islamist project, or "the overvaluing of the state and the undervaluing of religion." Second, like the 1999 crisis that led to the emergence of the Popular Congress, it expresses discontent with the failure of the regime's leadership to consult with the movement, which is why it also clamors for "the reform of the party and the state in order to break up the monopoly on political decision making."[40] But the most fundamental aspect of this call for reform, notably the emphasis on ties between the state and the movement, is opposition to the peace agreement and the Islamists' concern over the future of political Islam in the new national context. Although the reformers do not openly criticize the agreement with the SPLM, their discourse reflects reservations about, if not suspicion of, the measures, which in their opinion threaten the unity of the nation.[41] This is why the reformist project insists that "the fate of the movement and that of national unity" are linked. It is highly significant that almost all factions of the Islamist movement have enthusiastically backed this new appeal for "the resurrection of Islamic action." The distinctiveness of Sudanese post-Islamism lies in the Islamist intellectuals' own acknowledgment of the failure of their political project.

Nonetheless, if certain Islamists have opted for self-criticism and "resurrection" and for a "more national" project, others have chosen to form their own forum, the Forum for a Just Peace, to call for a more radical solution: separation from the South.[42] This group, the most extreme of the Islamist and Islamic spectrum as concerns the southern question, considers the peace agreement "detrimental to northern communities" and holds that the "new Sudan" is a "racist project which threatens and harms the Arab and Muslim identity of the nation." Its members take their argument for separation to the limit:

> What unites northern Sudanese and other neighboring peoples is far stronger than what unites them with the southerners. . . . Only Arab, African, and Muslim identity can express the diversity of our society . . . and only separation can safeguard the civilizational identity of the northern population (Mustapha 2004).[43]

They believe that citizenship should be founded on religious community: "There is only one eternal religion . . . so, for the Muslim, nation comes after religion" (Mustapha 2004).[44]

Until now, and unlike separatist voices in southern circles, the Forum has had no influence either with the populace or on the decisions of the government, which does not hesitate to denounce it. Its founders are aware of this fact. The group also includes members who do not belong to any religious organization. But the Forum could eventually become an important and even dangerous pressure group. In fact, in response to the riots which broke out after John Garang's death in August 2005, it successfully incited northern communities to violence.

Nonetheless, it should be noted that the lines separating these Islamist groups are far from clear, because in spite of all their positions (moderate, complaisant, or extreme and hostile), all remain members of the NC and some among them have positions within the executive branch. In fact, these two groups do not yet present themselves as movements protesting the regime.

In lieu of a conclusion, I can report that the leadership of the state and the exercise of power have called into question the cohesion not only of the Islamists but also of the nation as a whole. The government's "civilizational project" has failed in its attempt to replace splits and ethnic particularism with an Islamic identity which would hold centrifugal tendencies in check and guarantee national unity, in the name of which Islamists seized power in the first place. The recent appearance of armed regionalist movements (the Darfur conflict in the west, the return of regionalism among the Beja in the east, and its emergence among the Rashaida) is the result of the state's failures in these regions and of the northern leadership elite's characteristic use of the politics of ethnic exclusion.[45]

All economic development projects have been concentrated in the center of the country, and goods and services have always been poorly distributed in other regions. Political power has remained centralized despite the adoption of federalism. At the local level, although native administration has been reestablished, the structure of power in most regions has not been respected. The regime has been preoccupied with creating a parallel leadership allied with it.[46] This economic and political deprivation has accentuated ethnicity and consequently spurred confrontation with the state.

At the same time, the regime has continued the long northern tradition of exclusivist recruitment: the Islamist leadership, that is to say, *al-tanzim*, essentially consists of members of northern ethnic communities. The appointment of non-northerners remains only symbolic. Not a single person from the western or eastern communities, not even those with a long history of militancy within the movement, occupies a strategic position or is a member of the core leadership. Often such people are entrusted with marginal ministries or the position of governor, generally of a quiet state within the federation. The emergence of groups such as the Justice and Equality Movement (JEM) and the Sudan Liberation Movement (SLM) in Darfur is the result of social and economic injustice as well as exclusion from political leadership, not only in the state but also in the party. Indeed, Ibrahim Khalil, the founder and leader of the JEM, was an Islamist from the non-Arabic Fur group in the west of the country and had even waged jihad in the south. Granted, Darfurian regionalism existed before the present regime came into power, but this is the first time it has taken the form of an armed movement with strength sufficient to call national sovereignty into question.

To return to the questions I posed at the beginning of this chapter, in many respects political Islam in Sudan resembles and follows the same trajectory as other cases of political Islam. Thus, we note the "de-ideologization" of discourse, a more pragmatic approach to politics (national and international), and a very liberal economic policy. Similarly, we note the "rapprochement" between Islamism and nationalism as we have defined them, and not only among the religious majority. This is confirmed by the signing of the peace agreement and the acceptance of a real restructuring of the state (and consequently of power) according to principles other than sharia (in its Islamist version): the fair and democratic sharing of power and resources with non-Muslims. However, the Sudanese case is distinguished from others by the accession of new actors, fundamentalist and neofundamentalist groups, to the political arena, which transforms the morphology of political Islam in Sudan. These new elements (along with regional and international pressures) will have consequences for the post-Naivasha political order. For the time being, two outcomes seem very probable: the restructuring of the political game will reduce the influence of the religious question, and northern hegemony over political life will progressively end.

Notes

1. In June 1989, the Islamists, the third-largest force on the political scene and partners in the coalition cabinet, were brushed aside by a coalition of all the political forces, northern and southern, civilian and military.
2. The civil war had been going on since 1955. After a ten-year lull in hostilities (1972–83), a first peace accord was negotiated. Fighting resumed in 1983 with the emergence of the SPLM under a Sudanese army colonel from the South.
3. Unlike the first separatist movement, Anya-Nya (1955–72), the SPLM claimed to be a movement with national aspirations, fighting in the name of all marginalized regions.
4. Since its Independence, Sudan has been socially, politically, and economically dominated by the elite from the riverine center, where economic development and social progress have been concentrated, to the detriment of other regions.
5. This decision was above all political: searching for a new basis of legitimacy for a regime that had been in crisis for several years, the president decided upon national reconciliation with opposition parties and a turn toward conservatism.
6. The process began in 1978 with the naming of a committee to revise the laws in conformity with sharia. The committee was presided over by al-Turabi, then minister of justice and attorney general, whose propositions were not accepted by the Popular Assembly (Parliament).
7. Although excluded from the government, the Islamists hailed the new laws.
8. The model of *velayat-e faqih* was notably applied during Khomeini's time. After his death, the accumulation of religious and political power ceased, and a sort of "secularization" of political power emerged. See Abdo 2001 and Roy 1999.
9. "Liberal pluralism as practiced in the West is inappropriate for Sudanese society. . . . Poverty, the fragility of the economy, particularist leanings, and the illiteracy from which society suffers prevent the freedom of choice. . . . Sudanese parties are not really political parties. They are only the political expressions of a Sufi order legacy whose objective is to monopolize power" (National Congress Party General Secretariat 1994, 9–10).
10. This stance is consistent with the thought of Muslim reformers such as Hasan al-Banna and Mawdudi. The philosophical foundation of the new order was also developed in the regime's program, *Comprehensive national strategy: 1992–2002* (Center for Strategic Studies, 1994).
11. According to Al-Turabi, "The legal aspect of the sharia is relatively secondary. What is important is to infuse a spiritual energy to build the country, to mobilize in favor of economic development, to reinforce cohesion and national unity and to instigate a moral order" (al-Tourabi 1993, 119).
12. Omer insists, "This is a project of renewal [*tajdid*] and not of modernization, since modernity [*hadatha*] signifies a rupture with the past and any idea of rupture is rejected by our heritage and Islamic methodology, while renewal signifies continuity with them." Modernization is related to "the colonizing project of the West, seeking the annexation and submission of the Muslim world," whose incarnation is "the Westernized secular elite of the Muslim world, breaking with its religion" (Omer 1995, 23–24).
13. More than once, decisions taken and announced by the president were curiously annulled immediately afterward.
14. "The strategy of popular mobilization (the non-revolutionary revolution) adopted by the NIF in 1986 was aimed not so much at overthrowing the established order as at creating and preparing an environment open to changes to come. The Islamist tendency always rejected and discouraged spontaneous popular explosions for fear of their consequences" (El-Affendi 1995, 19). One figure within the movement explained to me that one of the members of *al-tanzim* had declared, "Our party will remain a party of salons if we don't have a presence within the army" (interview, Khartoum, 2003).
15. Even the return of the Sudanese Communist Party was accepted.

16. The Brotherhood criticized the Islamist leader's theological interpretations and less than orthodox, even liberal, positions on certain major social and political issues; some even considered them heretical.

17. *Akhbar al-'Ayam* (Khartoum), January 27, 1999. At the same time, he explained that the movement could not fail to support a regime which wanted to guarantee the application of sharia (interview, Khartoum, 2005).

18. *Akhbar al-'Ayam* (Khartoum), February 22–24, 1998.

19. Declaration of the Muslim Brothers, *Al-Wifaq* (Khartoum), May 2, 1998. On the subject of the group's refusal to countenance the rule of the country by a southerner, one Muslim Brother warned of "the possibility that a Muslim nation like Sudan, whose constitution ought to be the Qur'an, might be led by a product of missionary education, issued from the depths of the jungle and bearing a cross"—an obvious allusion to southerners (*Akhbar al-'Ayam* [Khartoum], February 5, 1999).

20. Communiqué of the Muslim Brotherhood, *Al-Wifaq* (Khartoum), May 2, 1999.

21. *Al-Wifaq* (Khartoum) May 8, 1998. Al-Turabi's answer was very clever: "The questions of the name and identity of the Sudanese state are of no importance, since we are well known and there is no need to identify and define us as Muslim" (*Akhbar al-'Ayam* [Khartoum], February 22, 1998).

22. Communication from the committee in charge of verifying that the banking system and financial system are in compliance with sharia, July 2005.

23. *Al-Wifaq* (Khartoum), July 5, 2000.

24. Conference president al-Karori declared, "We cannot deny that the achievements of the Revolution for salvation and the great national alliance that the NC represents are gains for the nation, for Islam, and for Islamic movements" (*Al-Wifaq* [Khartoum], August 26, 2000).

25. *Al- Wifaq* (Khartoum), August 27, 2000.

26. The Ministry of Religious Affairs was immediately awarded to the MB and the Ministry of Education to the Ansar al-Sunna. Unlike their counterparts in other countries, the Sudanese Ansar al-Sunna thus participated in politics. Today they also have seats in the national committee for drafting the constitution. Although certain individuals within the MB disapprove of the government's politics, the organization approves of any initiative which can reunify Islamic movements within the country.

27. The Brotherhood's goal of integration into the political field is echoed by one of its members, Dr. Issam al-Bashir: "The decision to reorganize the movement has as its goal the reactivation and resuscitation of its spiritual, intellectual, and pedagogical role in society after this period of silence" (*Al-Ra' al-'Amm* [Khartoum], July 25, 2000). Nonetheless, the Brotherhood, concerned with preserving the movement's independence, turned down a government proposition to fuse their two movements.

28. A Muslim Brother also declares that "the movement is worth much without al-Turabi" (*Al-Ra' al-'Amm* [Khartoum], August 10, 2000).

29. Remarks of the minister of religious affairs in a Sudanese television program, March 2005.

30. *Al-Sahafa* (Khartoum), July 7, 2004.

31. The leader of the MB explained to me that "the government gave us this little opportunity—two political positions, one in the government and one in a parliamentary commission—which we decided to accept" (interview, July 2005).

32. Legislative and presidential elections will be organized in 2008.

33. A member of the movement declared that this apparent departure from the MB's original categorical position "does not constitute a contradiction. It involves a change from a position in favor of war to one in favor of peace" (*Akhbar al-'Ayam* [Khartoum], April 6, 2004). He also confirmed that if the MB were invited to participate in the new political alliance of the NC and the SPLM, it would accept, and that it would not oppose the eventual accession of John Garang, leader of the SPLM, to the presidency. Nonetheless, this position contradicted the remarks of the MB leader who confirmed the organization's

opposition to such an accession. It also contradicted its conception of citizenship as based essentially on religion, which was made public in the constitutional committee.

34. Remarks of the minister of religious affairs during a conference entitled "The jurisprudence of minorities," Khartoum, February 21, 2005.

35. This is the theory of government developed by the Islamic thinker al-Mawardi (c. A.H. 450). However, it can be used to argue both in favor of non-Muslims' participation in government and for a limit to this participation.

36. However, the greatest problem is the definition of a reprehensible act and of the limits of individual liberty. In addition, the creation of the Commission for the Protection of the Rights of Non-Muslims to oversee the application of these measures may invite conflict with judicial bodies, and this duality in the judicial system will differentiate between citizens. These difficulties may lead to confusion, if not chaos.

37. The material dimension is not absent from this new alliance. This is above all true for the MB and the Ansar al-Sunna, certain of whose activities now receive financial support from the government.

38. Interview, Khartoum, July 2005.

39. On the initiative of Dr. Ghazi S. El-Din, former counselor to the president for questions of peace, and of several Islamist and Islamic figures, a large meeting was organized in March 2004 involving members of the NC and of the larger Islamic movement, in order to discuss the new project. All of the quotations in this paragraph are from Ghazi S. El-Din 2004.

40. The majority of Islamists are aware of the lack of democracy within the leadership.

41. Ghazi, the project's initiator, was excluded from negotiations with the SPLM because of his intransigence. Ghazi believes that the agreement consecrates the confederal system, to the detriment of the nation's unity, and that "the southerners obtained more than they deserve" (*Akhbar al-'Ayam* [Khartoum], June 22, 2004). Nonetheless, he explains that he disagrees with the government more over "methodology than over goals."

42. The Forum was created on the initiative of al-Tayeb Mustapha, a former member of the government.

43. See also Mustapha's "Before the invasion of Khartoum by the new Sudanese Hulagu: Beware the Trojan horse" (*Al-Sahafa* [Khartoum], July 17, 2004). Hulagu, a descendant of the Tatars, invaded Baghdad in the thirteenth century and carried out the massacres that ended the Abbasid dynasty.

44. *Al-Sahafa* (Khartoum), July 22, 2004.

45. The Beja are the largest ethnic group in the east of the country, followed by the Rashaida, nomads originally from the Arabian Peninsula who came to Sudan at the end of the nineteenth century. Beja regionalism dates back to the 1960s, whereas that of the Rashaida (the Free Lions Movement) is very recent (appearing in 2004).

46. Bear in mind that Sudanese Islamism is urban and has no support at the rural level.

References

Al-Abdeen, T. Zein. 1999. The coup d'état within the Shura Council. *Al-Ra' al-'Aam* (Khartoum), January 7.

Abdo, G. 2001. Rethinking the Islamic republic: A conversation with Ayatollah al-Hossein "Ali al-Montazeri." *Middle East Journal* 55 (1): 9–24.

Center for Strategic Studies. 1994. *The National Comprehensive Strategy, 1992–2002.* Khartoum: Center for Strategic Studies.

El-Affendi, A. 1995. *Al-thawra wa al-islah fi al-Sudan* [Revolution and political reform in Sudan]. London: Muntada Ibn Rushd.

Ghazi S. El-Din. 2004. A call to revive the Islamic national action [Arabic]. *Al-Sahafa* 4234 (March 18), 4235 (March 19).

Makki, H. 1997. Interview in *Al-Mustaqilla* (London, published by Dar al-Mustaqilla), December 22.

Mustapha, al-Tayeb. 2004. Under the ashes I see the spark. *Al-Sahafa* (Khartoum), October 20.

National Congress Party. General secretariat. 1991. The national charter for political action. Khartoum: National Congress Party.

————. 1994. *Nahj al-Siyasa al-Sudaniyya: Bayn al-Tatbiq wa-l-'Usisal-Falsafiyya* [Sudanese political discourse: Philosophical foundations and application]. Khartoum: National Congress Party.

National Islamic Front. 1987. Sudan Charter. Khartoum: National Islamic Front.

Omer, A. H. 1995. *Ru'ya li-al-Nahda al-Hadariyya al-'alamiyya* [A vision of the universal renaissance of civilization]. In *Al-mashru' al-islami fi al-Sudan: Qira'a fi al-fikr wa al-mumarasa* [The Islamic project in Sudan: A reading of ideology and practice], ed. M. Haroun et al., 23–38. Khartoum: Institute of Research and Social Studies.

Roy, O. 1999. The crisis of religious legitimacy in Iran. *Middle East Journal* 53 (2): 201–16.

Sudan National Assembly. 1995. *The political system in Sudan.* Khartoum: National Assembly.

Al-Tourabi [al-Turabi], H. 1993. Entretien avec Hassan al-Tourabi. By M. Duteil. *Monde Arabe: Maghreb-Machrek* 137: 119.

Al-Wifaq (Khartoum). 1998. Declaration of the Muslim Brothers. May 2.

————. 1999. Communiqué of the Muslim Brotherhood. May 2.

Part III
New Ways of Being Muslim

CHAPTER 11

ISLAM IN MALI IN THE NEOLIBERAL ERA

Benjamin F. Soares

At the end of the twentieth century, Mali—one of the world's poorest countries—had become one of the top recipients of foreign aid in the world. In the post–cold war era, the U.S., European donor countries, and multilateral lending agencies have all regularly praised Mali as a model for the transition to democracy, the implementation of economic reforms, and liberalization. For more than a decade, Mali has tended to meet International Monetary Fund and World Bank targets and timetables for structural adjustment programs, privatization schemes, and reductions in state budget deficits. One recent U.S. Agency for International Development (USAID) publication (2002, 11) has even called Mali—without any apparent irony—a "poster child" for such reforms. It would seem that Mali's compliance, which lenders and donors often link to "good governance," has helped to keep massive loans and other aid flowing into the country.

The geopolitical and strategic interests and objectives of some of Mali's major donors are usually hidden from view beneath streams of data and oft-repeated arguments about the necessities and benefits of Washington Consensus reforms of Mali's economy. Yet it remains clear that at least since the early 1990s both U.S. and EU policymakers have seen Mali, with its long borders with Mauritania and Algeria, "as a bulwark against radical Islam in Africa," in the words of the Economist Intelligence Unit (2002, 47). Mali received praise on the international stage as a model of toleration and for its commitment to *laïcité* or secularism, and, after September 11, 2001, was held up as "the sole exemplar of freedom in a majority-Muslim country" in the world (Muravchik 2001); but this changed shortly thereafter. Official U.S. government publications have begun to warn that Mali is "a potential breeding ground for Islamic fundamentalists" (U.S. Agency for International Development 2002, 18),[1] and official U.S. policy of "outreach" to Muslims has been intensified in Mali and elsewhere. In the time leading up to the 2002 presidential elections in Mali, certain commentators—policymakers and journalists in particular—seemed genuinely surprised that Muslim religious leaders in Mali were "suddenly" complaining vocally about "how Mali's secular state was [being] run" (Baxter 2002; Colombant 2002).

Some of Mali's Muslim religious leaders had specific political demands and even openly supported political candidates and parties, which many have interpreted as evidence of rising "political Islam" and even a rampant and dangerous "Islamism" in the country.[2] But the so-called complaints of Muslim religious leaders in Mali were neither sudden nor new. As I will suggest, they relate to longstanding and ongoing debates about Islam, laïcité or secularism, and politics in Mali. What was new by 2002 was the way in which certain Muslim religious leaders and activists articulated their complaints and criticisms. In this age of neoliberalism and governance "from afar" (Ferguson and Gupta 2002), new forms of associational life, increased transnational and global interconnections, and the use of new media technologies have helped to change the terms and conditions of debate. A consideration of some of the recent debates about Islam, secularism, and politics in Mali forces us to rethink some of the assumptions many have made about the prospects for "civil society"—one of the much vaunted panaceas for the world's problems—in Muslim-majority countries in particular and in postcolonial societies more generally.[3]

Juxtapositions

I want to begin by emphasizing the importance of understanding Mali as a place of many contradictions and often jarring juxtapositions and syntheses. Although such a statement might seem utterly banal, possibly even an anthropological fantasy, such juxtapositions include Islam, on the one hand, and what we might call "fetishism," "animism," "paganism," or African "traditional" religion on the other; Muslim and non-Muslim; African and Western. If it has become almost de rigueur for social scientists to identify various kinds of cultural hybridities in the societies we study, such an analytical frame is inadequate to the task of helping us to make sense of contemporary Mali and its history.

Mali is a place where Islam has been practiced for at least a millennium. Islam is incredibly important here, which is not to say that all Malians are Muslims. Although Mali is overwhelmingly Muslim, there is no uniform way of being Muslim. However, Islam has a central place in the social and historical imaginary in Mali. Malians regularly make reference to such renowned centers of Islamic learning in the country as Timbuktu and Djenné—to cite only those known outside of Mali. Malians also regularly invoke Muslim rulers of various precolonial states and empires and past Muslim clerics, saints, and miracle-workers from the distant and more recent colonial and postcolonial past.[4] Such past historical and mythical figures have complex relations to both anticolonial and nationalist discourses, as well as regional inflections, to which I can only allude. At the same time, Mali is a place where what purportedly lies outside of Islam—that is, the un-Islamic or the non-Islamic (which is not to say "Western")—figures very prominently. In fact, Malians regularly invoke a range of historical and mythical non-Muslim figures, sometimes alongside Muslim figures. Similarly, allegedly un-Islamic centers, capitals, and spaces dot the landscape and are also part of the imaginary. Who gets to decide what is or is not Islam or Islamic—"orthodoxy," if you will—and how such orthodoxy might change over time are, of course, crucial questions.[5]

One does not have to travel away from the main metropolitan areas in Mali to get a sense of such juxtapositions. Although anthropologists have recently drawn on fieldwork in far-flung places and among seemingly marginal groups to emphasize their "modernity" and long involvement in globalized worlds,[6] I prefer to focus on Bamako, the colonial city that became the capital of postcolonial Mali. The most populous city in Mali, Bamako is also the country's most important center of economic activity, politics, education, cultural activity, and international assistance, as Mali, on the French model, remains a highly centralized state. Readily available for sale at the back of the large, imposing, modern Friday mosque located in the heart of central Bamako in a congested part of the city are ingredients for what was called "fetishism" in the colonial lexicon, and is now usually called "traditional" African religion or "medicine." Such objects as dried and cured animal parts (horns, skulls, hands, and quills of bush animals) are being bought and sold alongside copper vessels used in writing "magical" and therapeutic texts and a wide array of plant medicines, some of which are now being marketed like Western pharmaceuticals. Although it is usually very difficult for many scholars working in Muslim West Africa not to home in on the exotic, my description of what might seem the contents of a curiosity cabinet has a purpose other than the narrowly exoticizing. All of these "traditional" objects are for sale in a space more or less separate from where other vendors sell more unambiguously Muslim objects, indeed, "modern" Islamic religious commodities— copies of the Qur'an, prayer beads, printed material about Islam, and recordings of sermons by the country's most popular Muslim preachers (Starrett 1995).

Just a few steps away from these markets are the offices of Radio islamique, the Islamic radio station, housed in a building in the mosque complex. Since 1994, Radio islamique has aired regular radio programming in which Muslim preachers (mostly reformist Muslims, though in some cases prominent members of the country's main Sufi orders) exhort Malians in often moralistic language about how to conduct themselves as proper modern Muslims. The presumably correct way of being Muslim involves a standardized set of ritual norms—regular ritual daily prayer, fasting during the month of Ramadan, and almsgiving—that have become much more widespread among Malian Muslims regardless of social distinctions (hereditary or otherwise) over the past few decades.[7] The way of being Muslim espoused on the radio also involves the shaping of moral subjects in contemporary Malian society. Most notably, this is said to entail giving up and avoiding "fetishism," including the kind for which ingredients are sold just steps away, as well as eschewing a wide array of other allegedly un-Islamic objects and practices, some judged more reprehensible than others.

A recurrent motif in the discourse of many Malian Muslim preachers (and laypersons) is that a number of reprehensible things have been more readily available to Malians since the 1991 coup that replaced the authoritarian regime of President Moussa Traoré with a transitional government, eventually leading to multiparty elections in 1992. Not far from Radio islamique, there are kiosks—as there are throughout the city—where one can place bets on French horse races through the French gambling corporation, the Pari mutuel urbain du Mali (PMU). This is the gambling for the masses that arrived shortly after the multiparty elections and the accelerated implementation of neoliberal reforms. On Thursday evenings, one can find out the betting results on Malian national television less than an hour before a program called *Magazine islamique* airs. This weekly program, which sometimes features preachers whose sermons are played on Radio islamique, is broadcast in anticipation of the weekly communal prayers that many Malian Muslims perform on Fridays. Earlier in the evening one might catch a South American telenovela dubbed in French, a program highlighting Mali's cultural heritage, or maybe even an African beauty pageant.[8] The many Malians without access to television can catch the betting results on Malian national radio before the long-running radio program *Les règles de l'Islam* (The Rules of Islam), which features some of the same preachers involved in Radio islamique. It is my contention that one cannot begin to understand contemporary Mali without making sense of some of these juxtapositions, about which there has been much debate and discussion in Mali.

In the Postcolony

Just steps away from the two markets for diverse "modern" and "traditional" religious commodities, the offices of Radio islamique, and the main Friday mosque is the building of the Malian National Assembly, where elected deputies meet. As I have noted, the first multiparty elections were held in 1992, and, ten years later, Mali had the distinction of becoming one of the first African countries to have two successive democratically elected presidents. One of the many things the postcolonial Malian state inherited from France and the colonial state is the idea that the state is to be *laïc* or secular.[9] Following the French model, religion is understood as private and confessional. In such a conception of religion as privatized belief, the state is expected not to intervene in religious matters. But secularism is arguably a derivative discourse in postcolonial Mali in ways similar to how nationalism is a derivative discourse in India and other postcolonial societies (Chatterjee 1993). Since Independence in 1960, every Malian government from the first postcolonial socialist regime to the most recent democratically elected one has sought to associate itself with Islam and with certain public expressions of Islam. Although the ostensibly secular colonial state also actively sought to associate itself with Islam, the difference is that every postcolonial Malian ruler has been Muslim and has endeavored to present himself publicly as such. Much like its colonial predecessor, the secular postcolonial Malian state has also made some rather conspicuous interventions in realms deemed religious.

Secularism in practice in Mali has quite often been fraught with contradictions, as the following examples suggest. Radio islamique in Bamako was actually founded in 1994 by prominent members of AMUPI, the Association malienne pour l'unité et le progrès de l'Islam (Malian Association for the Unity and Progress of Islam), which the Malian government launched in 1980 as the country's sole officially authorized Islamic association. Founded as it was in the wake of the Iranian revolution, AMUPI was explicitly designed to manage conflict and tensions between reformist Muslims and those affiliated with Sufi orders, with whom they often disagree about Islamic religious practice and leadership of the Muslim community. AMUPI was also officially responsible for coordinating the considerable financial assistance from Muslim countries such as Saudi Arabia, Libya, Iran, and the Gulf states for mosques, education, and Islamic cultural centers. Given the state's new commitment to freedom of association after 1991, Malians founded many new Islamic associations, and AMUPI was no longer the country's only officially recognized one. In the past few years, the

Malian government has promoted—again on the French model—a "High Islamic Council" (Haut conseil islamique). Much like the Conseil français du culte musulman (CFCM) recently initiated by the French government, the Haut conseil islamique will presumably represent all Muslims and act as the "official and unique interlocutor of political authorities for all questions relative to the practice of Islam" (Diarra 2002). Such initiatives clearly relate to the state's ongoing efforts to regulate and monitor the activities of Muslim religious specialists and Muslims more generally. At the same time, they must be understood in relation to the history of colonialism (from the late nineteenth century until 1960) and the postcolonial period. One of the truly striking continuities from the colonial period until the present age of neoliberalism is how Islam and Muslims are almost invariably assumed to be among the most significant potential problems for governance.

During the colonial period, the French colonial administration generally sought to restrict Muslim religious specialists' activities to the narrowly religious and educational spheres, such as prayer, life cycle rituals, Qur'anic education, and the running of Sufi orders. "There were always important exceptions, such as . . . [those members] of the 'loyal' Muslim establishment, whose interventions in politics, religion and public policy were integral to the colonial administration's policies toward Islam and Muslims" (Soares 2005a, 212; see also Robinson 2000; Robinson and Triaud 1997). Similarly, certain Muslim religious leaders—various leaders of Sufi orders and living Muslim saints, often referred to as *marabouts*—have had close ties with high-ranking officials of the postcolonial state, including those in recent democratically elected governments.

Although the Malian state uses European-derived codes of law, Muslims in Mali regularly apply Islamic legal principles derived from *fiqh* (Arabic, jurisprudence), and the Maliki school of jurisprudence in particular, in the conduct of their personal lives and affairs.[10] For example, Muslim merchants often rely upon and make reference to such principles in the conduct of commerce, including the prohibition on interest as well as on auctions. Many Muslims in Mali also ordinarily apply Islamic legal principles in areas of so-called family law, including marriage, divorce, and inheritance.[11] This is the case even though such principles sometimes conflict with postcolonial Malian law. Many ordinary Muslim religious specialists in the country regularly advise people on how to conform to Islamic legal principles. For example, one recently deceased Malian Muslim scholar, Ahmad Uthman Bah, who was known for some of his written work (Bah 1992), had an even more widespread reputation for his expertise in matters of inheritance. Many people throughout the country sought him out for his authoritative Islamic jurisprudential knowledge, either to resolve disputes over inheritance or to prevent them from arising. In sermons and in published works, many other Muslims give more general instruction on how to conduct oneself as a Muslim.[12] The sermons on audio and video cassettes (and more recently on DVDs) of Muslim preachers, including those of the country's most important Muslim media star, Chérif Ousmane Madani Haïdara, can be included here.[13] In the secular postcolonial state, such instruction or advice is of course not compulsory. However, the progressive marginalization of Islamic jurisprudence and Muslim religious specialists during the colonial period and after in Mali has paradoxically not led to the kinds of intense debates about sharia witnessed recently in other countries, such as Nigeria.

Although most Muslim religious leaders in Mali regularly invoke sharia, there are relatively few Malians arguing that sharia should be made into state law.

If education and French-language secular schooling were particularly central to the colonial project in West Africa, such education has been no less important in postcolonial Mali. The bureaucrats, civil servants, technical and administrative experts, and other personnel involved in the running of the affairs of the so-called modern sectors of the economy and state have been educated for the most part in the French-language schools the state has promoted. This has helped to marginalize most Muslim religious specialists, including modernist and reformist Muslims, along with proponents of Sufi orders, with their expert religious knowledge premised on literacy in Arabic. Moreover, many of those who have completed French-language secular schooling see Muslim religious specialists and their knowledge, including the Islamic jurisprudence many continue to study and teach, as outmoded, if not explicitly reactionary.

Over the past several decades, many Malian Muslims, including religious specialists, have been active in areas beyond their restricted "traditional" religious and educational activities. Many have been involved as founders, financial backers, and teachers in the new private Islamic educational institutions called madrasas in Mali, where fee-paying students receive a modern education in Arabic along with an Islamic religious education (Brenner 2001). Although some madrasas provide limited instruction in French, many do not. The spread of these private schools relates to the educational and financial ties with the Arab Middle East that have intensified since the 1970s. A considerable number of madrasa graduates have gone on for advanced Islamic religious education abroad, particularly to Egypt and Saudi Arabia. Upon return, many graduates, with their expert religious knowledge and education in Arabic, have had difficulties entering those sectors of the economy where literacy in French is a prerequisite.

After the 1991 coup, the new Malian constitution reaffirmed the principle of secularism and religiously based political parties were not permitted. Given the state's greater commitment to freedom of association and expression, there has been a proliferation of new associations and organizations as well as newspapers and radio stations in the country. Mali, like many other places, is now teeming with all sorts of new nongovernmental organizations (NGOs) and associations—some of the alleged building blocks of civil society. Organizations that have diverse transnational connections for funding, personnel, and support focus on health, education, women's issues, human rights, and development. Some of these NGOs thus operate in areas where the state's involvement has been cut back in accordance with neoliberal prescriptions.

Some of these new associations and NGOs are specifically Islamic in orientation, and, for this reason, Western donors largely ignored them prior to September 11, 2001. There are many dozens of new Islamic associations in Mali, most of which are not only urban-based but usually restricted to Bamako and other urban centers in the country. They include Muslim youth, women's, and reformist associations, as well as Islamic associations promoting development. If some are Islamic NGOs with complex transnational connections, many more are trying to raise funds for the construction of mosques, schools, and development projects from local wealthy donors or from overseas, often without much success. Most of the founders, leaders, and activists in these Islamic associations are madrasa graduates or those with a more "traditional" Islamic education. Many are Muslim intellectuals who are members of a new, highly educated, postcolonial Muslim elite with complex transnational ties and sometimes affiliations (cf. Roy 1994, 2004). Many members of this elite actively foster a standardized set of ritual norms, including regular ritual daily prayer, and they often focus explicitly on the shaping of moral subjects in the broader public sphere. Indeed, many of them are concerned with a very public, deprivatized Islam (Salvatore 2000), whereby modern Muslim subjects eschew the allegedly un-Islamic—whether it be "African" or from "the West." Although this new Muslim elite includes members of Sufi orders and their reformist Muslim critics, it is striking how few members of this elite have large constituencies. The one exception is the Muslim media star Chérif Haïdara, who, despite being a modern preacher and the head of a large modern Islamic association, Ançar Dine, nonetheless tends to comport himself much like a conventional leader of a Sufi order, a living Muslim saint, or a *marabout*.[14] Aside from this one religious leader, no other member of the new Muslim elite has been able to supplant the country's Sufi leaders, Muslim saints, and *marabouts*, who live in certain Islamic religious centers outside the capital. In spite of sustained efforts and bids to represent ordinary Muslims or speak on their behalf since the 1990s, most members of the new Bamako-based Muslim elite lack religious authority and consequently do not have many followers.

Public Debates

In the early 1990s, after the coup, the mood in Mali was quite optimistic. Rapid economic growth, investment in infrastructure, a construction boom, the flourishing of new political parties and associations, and the development of a very lively press and private radio stations fueled the optimism. With ongoing student strikes, disruption of state schools, the Tuareg/Arab uprising in parts of the country, intense political infighting, segmentation, and electoral chaos, the mood became much more somber. The early 1994 devaluation of the CFA-franc currency by 50 percent—in accordance with neoliberal prescriptions—and the subsequent economic decline many Malians experienced only made matters worse. But even before the general optimism had dissipated, some Malians had a number of specific concerns, complaints, and dissatisfactions, which they sometimes articulated in relation to Islam, Muslim values, morality, and so forth. In fact, various Muslim activists and Islamic associations have played a central role in articulating some of these concerns in a series of important and sometimes acrimonious debates, the most important of which I shall briefly discuss.

Shortly after the 1991 coup, certain prominent Muslim religious leaders in Mali made public statements expressing concern that everything now seemed to be permitted in the society.[15] During fieldwork in the 1990s, I frequently heard ordinary Malians discuss and lament the general climate of permissiveness, lax morals, and moral corruption, which seemed to accompany the much-welcomed removal of the authoritarian regime of Moussa Traoré. In a direct reversal of the Traoré regime's policy of closing bars and nightclubs during the month of Ramadan, such establishments were permitted to remain open. Many Malians were very unhappy about this, and there was considerable discussion of the change in policy. Malian secularists argued that closing bars and nightclubs during Ramadan had been a violation of the principle of secularism; to allow them to remain open was to uphold this inviolable principle. But I heard some Malian Muslims say such an argument was disingenuous because bars and nightclubs had more to do with the tourist industry the Malian state was attempting to promote through economic liberalization policies. After all, one cannot hope to attract tourists, especially Western tourists, without bars and nightclubs. With economic liberalization, all sorts of entrepreneurs were relatively free to open places of business, and bars, large and small, suddenly appeared throughout the capital.

Many Malians were alarmed and angry that the new openness in the society meant that pornographic films were being screened in cinemas open to all. In the early 1990s, some Malians actually made threats of violence against those cinemas showing such films. In 1992, a handwritten sign in French pasted on a cinema in central Bamako warned,

> In the name of God, the Compassionate, the Merciful. NOTICE. We ask the management . . . to stop the advertising [and] the screening of pornographic films. If not, we are going to ransack the cinema. *Inshallah*. Thank you.[16]

Although most of the cinemas in Bamako and elsewhere in the country ceased to operate shortly thereafter, this seems to have been due to the proliferation of the videocassette recorder (VCR) rather than to any such threats. As the VCR was starting to become more widely available, pornographic films could be watched in the privacy of one's home. Indeed, with the spread of the VCR, the debate about the public screening of pornographic films ended, though related debates about new alleged threats to morality continued apace. Indeed, a main target of criticism was one area in which there has been massive investment and growth in the era of economic liberalization: the *maison de passe* (as it is called in Mali), where people, usually unmarried couples, can rent rooms by the hour. Hotel and bar owners and other investors had opened such establishments throughout the city, and some, including several catering to the wealthy, were now operating quite openly in close proximity to mosques and madrasas. Some of these entrepreneurs were apparently turning a handsome profit and making additional investments in this and the related hotel sector.

Another highly contentious issue has been gambling. Although Muslim religious leaders in Mali have universally denounced the gambling for the masses of the PMU and condemned it as forbidden according to the precepts of Islam, this does not mean that ordinary Malian Muslims do not gamble. On the contrary, I know many men who, while fasting during the month of Ramadan, spend a good part of the day deciding which horses to bet on. However, many Malian Muslims saw the opening of the country's first casino—a gambling venue presumably for the well-heeled—in central Bamako as a further outrage. If ordinary Malians place their bets on horses at the ubiquitous PMU kiosks in urban public spaces, casino-goers get to place their own bets outside the view of inquiring eyes in the concealed private space of the casino, with its alleged European underworld connections.

If Muslim debate and dissatisfaction had initially been somewhat dispersed, focused on the general laxness of morals or climate of permissiveness and sometimes specifically on pornography or gambling, this changed in the mid-1990s when Islamic associations took center stage in debates about various women's issues. After the United Nations' Fourth World Conference on Women in Beijing in 1995, in which Malians had enthusiastically participated, Malian Islamic associations organized large public meetings where Muslim men and women gathered. Invoking "Islamic values," they issued public statements in which they objected to the Beijing women's conference's "Declaration and Platform for Action" for women's rights as Muslims in ways that were not entirely unpredictable.[17] Indeed, some of their objections accorded with those advanced by Muslim-majority countries such as Iran. The Malian Islamic associations specifically criticized the Malian women's secular NGOs that had participated in the UN conference and had supported the Platform for Action for trying to advance what they considered a Western secular agenda and Western values more generally.

Another issue that has also generated much debate in Mali is excision, or female circumcision. Since the 1994 UN Population and Development Conference in Cairo, when individual countries were urged to eliminate excision, UN agencies, the Catholic Church, various bilateral donors, and Malian NGOs have been involved in campaigns against excision in Mali.[18] One of the most prominent Malian women's rights activists, Fatoumata Siré Diakité, a former schoolteacher, union activist, head of the Malian Association pour la promotion et la défense des droits de la femme (Association for the Promotion and Defense of Women's Rights), and recipient of France's Légion d'honneur, has been in the forefront of the anti-excision campaigns in Mali. In fact, Diakité has been the most vocal person in Mali calling for an outright ban on excision. Along with other Malian women's rights activists and prominent Malian secularists, she has also tried to advance the argument that excision—unlike male circumcision—is not part of Islam (Dembélé 2001). However, many Malian Muslims think the exact opposite is true. In the debates about excision, Muslim religious leaders and activists from different Islamic associations have claimed that excision, just like male circumcision, is actually an Islamic religious practice, which can and should eventually be "medicalized" (Sylla 2001; Kimbiri 2001a, 2001b). Some Malian Muslims have reacted angrily to the organized campaigns against excision in the country, which have relied upon Malian NGOs like Diakité's and have used theater, music, and the mass media to spread their messages against excision. Many have denounced those involved in anti-excision campaigns as advocating the imposition of Western values on Malian Muslims. On several occasions, Islamic associations in Mali have publicly accused Western-funded NGOs of meddling in Mali's internal affairs. One leader of an Islamic association in Mali has even decried what he calls "the crusade" of "immoral Westerners" working with hypocritical Malians "who . . . are [basically] swindling NGOs out of their money [d'escroquer l'argent des ONG] in anti-excision campaigns" (Le politicien musulman 2002). Another Islamic association that has been very active in countering the anti-excision campaigns has had its members hand out leaflets at mosques that say (in French), "Any law against excision, [which is] a practice of the Sunna [that is, the authoritative practice of the Prophet Muhammad], is an attack on the freedom of religion" and "blasphemy."[19]

By the late 1990s, there was much talk of how Muslim values were not being respected and the dangers of the onslaught of Western values. For example, prominent members of the government-initiated AMUPI protested against what they called "the general manner in which Islam suffered from attack" in the country (Keita 1998a). However, AMUPI was not alone in voicing such concerns. Various individual Muslim activists and spokespersons from Islamic associations openly blamed the Malian government for what they saw as a deplorable state of affairs. On a number of occasions in the late 1990s, certain Muslim activists openly protested to the government. In 1998, prominent Muslim intellectuals and Islamic associations called for a boycott of the beauty pageant for Miss CEDEAO (Communauté économique des États de l'Afrique de l'Ouest, the Economic Community of West African States). With Mali hosting the beauty pageant, Malian president Alpha Oumar Konaré and his wife, Adam Ba, a well-known historian, were to have official roles in the event. Some Muslim activists denounced the pageant, with some presenting the Islamic feminist case against beauty pageants for their objectification of women (Kimbiri 1998; Keita 1998b). Interestingly, the preacher Chérif Haïdara accused those calling for the boycott of being hypocrites since they had never condemned beauty pageants staged in Mali in the past. Toward the end of 1999, there was also protest from Islamic associations and even alleged threats of violence after unconfirmed reports that a previously unheard-of organization was to hold a meeting of homosexuals—Le congrès des homosexuels—in Bamako in 2000 (Sow 1999). Many saw such Western values as the social acceptance of homosexuality as repugnant, as they also did the active promotion of the use of condoms against HIV/AIDS and family planning, more generally, by the Malian government, (including President Konaré), Western donors, international organizations, and local NGOs.[20]

As Talal Asad has argued, from "the point of view of secularism, religion has the option either of confining itself to private belief and worship or of engaging in public talk that makes no demand on life" (1999, 191). This is, indeed, one of the conundrums some Malian Muslims face. A related conundrum is that they often risk being denounced as "fundamentalists" or "Islamists" when they do speak publicly. Some Malian Muslims are quite aware of this. It is useful to quote Mahmoud Dicko, the imam of a reformist mosque in Bamako, who has served as an official in AMUPI and as director of Radio islamique, and was elected to the Haut conseil islamique. In 2000, Dicko stated in an interview,

> Fundamentalism is not only religious. Fundamentalism exists in all domains. Even what we are living today is from fundamentalism; it is in part intolerance. No leader has the freedom to govern his country as he wants. They impose ways of doing things on us. Good governance is not from us, they impose it on us, and, if we refuse, they cut off credits, they cut off aid, they cut off everything, they punish you through the media, they make you into a monster. Therefore, this is all in reality a certain kind of fundamentalism, intolerance. (Traoré 2000)

On behalf of an umbrella organization of Islamic associations, the Collectif des associations islamiques du Mali, which eventually entered national politics by endorsing a presidential candidate, the seemingly omnipresent Mahmoud Dicko offered a searing critique of Malian society and its politicians. Dicko wrote that the Collectif condemned "politicians who during the last decade have made no effort to fight against or even simply to condemn the degrading, pleasure-seeking permissiveness [*permissivités ludiques dégradantes*] which gains ground in our country, and also and even more the sociocultural mimicry [*mimétisme socioculturel*] that drains the reference points for our identity" (Dicko 2001b; see also Dicko 2001a and Diawara 2001). It is worth noting that the "sociocultural mimicry" Dicko deplores is perhaps not entirely different from the playful and potentially subversive "mimicry" and "hybridities" Michael Taussig (1993), Homi Bhabha (1994), and their imitators like to celebrate.

In 2001, many Muslims in Mali were preparing for the meeting of the Organization of the Islamic Conference (OIC), to be held in Bamako, where there was the usual heightened sense of the *umma*, the global Islamic community, focusing the attention of Muslims on Muslim issues, particularly the plight of Muslims in various places in the world, most notably in Palestine and Iraq.[21] With preparations for the OIC meeting under way, the Malian government hosted a meeting of traditional West African hunters whose practices are closely identified with the un-Islamic.[22] Many Malian Muslims found it deeply offensive that the state seemed to be celebrating and thereby endorsing the hunters' un-Islamic traditions. Not only did the minister of culture address the conferees in full hunter's garb while sporting the requisite "fetishes" but also the Malian government proceeded to build a monument to the ostensibly non-Muslim hunters in the capital—just one part of a larger project to build national monuments in the country.

Perhaps the most explosive tensions centered on government plans to reform the laws about the family, usually referred to as the *code de la famille* (Family Code) in Mali. In 2001, after lengthy discussion and debate over a number of years, the government announced specific proposals for reform in marriage and inheritance law: raising the age of marriage for girls, making the husband and wife equal in marriage, and giving men and women equal inheritance rights.[23] All of these changes were to be in accordance with the 1995 Beijing Conference Platform for Action and the subsequent follow-up conference in 2000, which the Malian government, Malian women's rights activists, and secular NGOs had advocated and endorsed. For several years, some of Mali's major donors and various NGOs operating in the country have emphasized the importance of such social reforms, which they have sometimes explicitly linked to the other economic and political reforms—democratization and liberalization. However, most leaders of Islamic associations charged that the government's proposed changes were in contradiction with the rules of Islamic jurisprudence upon which Malian Muslims ordinarily rely (Fall 2001; Tamboura 2001).

In 2002, President Konaré formally presented bills to reform the Family Code and to outlaw the practice of excision. Less than three weeks later, they were withdrawn in the face of considerable criticism. If the secular Malian press quickly reported that this was the "last victory of the Islamists" over the outgoing president (Sylla 2002), the government seems to have seriously misjudged the opposition to such reforms. It is unclear to what extent the Malian government took into account neighboring Senegal's experience of reforming the *code de la famille* in the 1970s, which also generated widespread opposition from Muslim religious leaders (Coulon 1981). In Mali, the imam of the main Friday mosque in Bamako was just one of the most high profile and outspoken of the many Muslim religious leaders who objected to the proposed changes, which, they stated, clearly and unambiguously violated Islamic precepts (Daou 2002).

Prior to the 2002 presidential elections, outside observers continued to hail Mali as a place where neoliberal reforms and democracy were working. Despite all the praise, many ordinary Malians talked about the more than ten years of crisis—economic, political, social, even moral—and were openly cynical about democracy and reform (cf. Bratton, Coulibaly, and Machado 2002; Bratton, Mattes, and Gyimah-Boadi 2005). During those years of crisis, certain Muslim actors, mostly officials, activists, and spokespersons from the new Islamic associations, were incredibly busy mobilizing to advance an agenda that did not always sit comfortably with the agenda of President Konaré. After almost ten years of active engagement with the print and audio-visual media, some of them had become rather media savvy. They gave interviews, held press conferences, released public statements and policy prescriptions, perfected their sermon-giving, wrote opinion pieces for newspapers, and appeared on national TV and public and private radio to discuss and debate Islam, Muslim values, morality, and sometimes even politics. At the same time, some of them organized meetings, built coalitions, fundraised, networked, and lobbied the government. In the end, some of them met with politicians and officials in political parties, endorsed a particular presidential candidate, and encouraged people to vote for him, although he was not elected. Despite their moralizing discourses and critiques of the current state of affairs in Mali, the overwhelming majority of these Malian Muslims seem firmly committed to the idea of democracy. Moreover, they frequently invoke their rights to freedom of expression and association as well as their rights as citizens to engage in discussion and debate about religion *and* politics.

Muslim activists' attempts to speak on behalf of other Muslims notwithstanding, it is difficult to say this new Muslim elite is representative of Malian Muslims in all their diversity. With the possible exception of Haïdara's association, Ançar Dine, none of the new Islamic associations in Mali could be considered grassroots organizations. None of the new Muslim religious leaders—again with the exception of Haïdara—even have much popular legitimacy. They nevertheless do seem to speak, at least sometimes, to the concerns of some ordinary Malians. This is not to assert any sort of primordialist Muslim identity here, or a crude instrumentalism on the part of Malian Muslims—or all Muslim activists, for that matter. Rather, some Muslim activists seem better able to articulate some of the concerns of many ordinary Malian Muslims, who face the contradictions of living as modern Muslim citizens in a modernizing and secularizing state where the "un-Islamic" seems to be always just around the corner in this age of neoliberal governmentality. Most observers would be reluctant to consider such forms of Muslim activism, which range from efforts at moral reform and discipline to possible challenges to the state's legitimacy, as evidence of the expansion of civil society in Mali. Many Malian secularists and outside observers find such activism alarming and warn of the dangers of political Islam here and further afield. As I have suggested, rather than simply labeling (or denouncing) this as fundamentalism or Islamism, one must understand such developments in Mali in their complex genesis and equally complex transnational connections in this age of neoliberal reforms.

Notes

I am grateful to Moussa Djiré, Barbara Lewis, Marie Miran, and especially Mark LeVine and Armando Salvatore for invaluable comments and suggestions.

1. Such sentiments were also expressed in journalistic accounts published shortly after September 11, 2001. See, for example, Farah 2001; and Konaté 2001.
2. These included various Western and Malian media outlets.
3. For critical perspectives on the fashionable civil-society approach to "good governance" in Africa, see Comaroff and Comaroff 1999; and Hibou and Banégas 2000.
4. For example, Sunjata, the mythical founder of the medieval Malian empire; Mansa Musa; the Muslim rulers of Macina (r. nineteenth century); al-Hajj Umar Tall (d. nineteenth century); the Kunta shaykhs of the Timbuktu region; and Shaykh Hamallah (d. twentieth century); to name only some of the most prominent.
5. See Soares 1999 and 2005a.
6. Two studies that have received quite a bit of attention are Tsing 1993 and Piot 1999.
7. On these developments, see Launay and Soares 1999; Soares 2004; and Soares 2005a.
8. Malians with access to satellite television have a wider array of choices, which are hard to quantify.
9. Some of the themes in this section are treated at greater length in my book *Islam and the prayer economy* (Soares 2005a).
10. Many Malians also regularly apply diverse principles from "custom," which is often referred to as *laada* (from the Arabic) in the region's vernaculars.
11. For one example, see Soares 2000.
12. See, for example, Tall 1995–96.
13. On Haïdara and his career, see Soares 2004, 2005a. Cf. Schulz 2003a, which contains numerous errors of fact about the history of Islam and its contemporary practice.
14. For a discussion of Haïdara and his association's relation to Sufism and Sufi orders, see Soares 2005a.
15. This was also a topic of discussion in some print media. See, for example, Diombana 1993.
16. I am grateful to Roman Loimeier for making his copy of this sign available to me.
17. See, for example, *La roue* 1996.
18. For a discussion of some of the controversy around excision, see Shell-Duncan and Hernlund 2000. For campaigns against excision in Mali, see Gosselin 2000; Sanou 2000; Camara 2001; and Sissok 2001.
19. Leaflets produced and distributed by AISLAM (Association islamique du salut) in my possession.
20. However, some prominent Muslim religious leaders, most notably Chérif Haïdara, would eventually take positions in support of condom use (Soares 2005b).
21. On this heightened sense, see Eickelman and Piscatori 1996. For Malian press coverage of the OIC meeting, see, for example, *Liberté* 2001.
22. See the extensive coverage of the meeting in a special edition of *Le continent*, February 2, 2001.
23. For a discussion of some of the proposed reforms and specific controversies, cf. Soares forthcoming and Schulz 2003b. Aside from its serious errors of fact, this latter article betrays the author's unfamiliarity with the region's Islamic textual traditions, presenting as it does a deeply flawed understanding of the history of and contemporary discourse about Islamic jurisprudence and "customary" law.

References

Asad, Talal. 1999. Religion, nation-state, secularism. In *Nation and religion: Perspectives on Europe and Asia*, ed. Peter van der Veer and Hartmut Lehmann, 178–96. Princeton: Princeton University Press.

Bah, Ahmad Uthman. 1992. *Diya' al-ghasaq manzuma nasihat al-shabab.* Casablanca: Matba'at al-najah al-jadida.

Baxter, Joan. 2002. Challenging tradition. *BBC Focus on Africa Magazine,* January–March, pp. 48–50.

Bhabha, Homi. 1994. Of mimicry and man. In *The location of culture,* 85–92. New York: Routledge.

Bratton, Michael, Massa Coulibaly, and Fabiana Machado. 2002. Popular views of the legitimacy of the state in Mali. *Canadian Journal of African Studies* 36 (2): 197–238.

Bratton, Michael, Robert Mattes, and E. Gyimah-Boadi. 2005. *Public opinion, democracy and market reform in Africa.* Cambridge: Cambridge University Press.

Brenner, Louis. 2001. *Controlling knowledge: Religion, power and schooling in a West African Muslim society.* Bloomington: Indiana University Press.

Camara, Yousouf. 2001. Réligion et excision. *Le tambour,* June 22, p. 3.

Chatterjee, Partha. 1993. *The nation and its fragments.* Princeton: Princeton University Press.

Colombant, Nicolas. 2002. Mali's Muslims steer back to spiritual roots. *Christian Science Monitor,* February 26, p. 8.

Comaroff, John L., and Jean Comaroff, ed. 1999. *Civil society and the political imagination in Africa.* Chicago: University of Chicago Press.

Coulon, Christian. 1981. *Le marabout et le prince: Islam et pouvoir au Sénégal.* Paris: Pédone.

Daou, Boukary. 2002. Code de la famille et excision: Les musulmans disent non à Alpha. *Le républicain,* June 5, p. 1.

Dembélé, Mady M. 2001. L'excision est un poids des traditions, elle n'a rien de religieux. *Les echos,* July 18, p. 5.

Diarra, Seydina Oumar. 2002. Haut conseil islamique du Mali. *Info-matin,* January 18, p. 5.

Diawara, Amara Diapy. 2001. Meeting du Collectif des associations musulmanes du Mali. *Info-matin,* February 13, pp. 4–5.

Dicko, El Hadj Mahmoud. 2001a. Déclaration. *Le républicain,* May 4, p. 7.

———. 2001b. Declaration du Collectif des associations islamiques du Mali. *Info-matin,* May 7, p. 7.

Diombana, Cheick Sidya. 1993. La jeunesse et la foi en l'Islam. *La roue,* October 25–November 3, p. 5.

Economist Intelligence Unit. 2002. *EIU country report: Mali, March 2002.* London: Economist Intelligence Unit.

Eickelman, Dale F., and James Piscatori. 1996. *Muslim politics.* Princeton: Princeton University Press.

Fall, Birama. 2001. Islam et politique: La colère des islamistes contre le pouvoir. *Le républicain,* April 23, p. 1.

Farah, Douglas. 2001. Mali's Muslim clerics send troubling message: Fragile democracy seen as vulnerable to extremism. *Washington Post,* September 30, p. A24.

Ferguson, James, and Akhil Gupta. 2002. Spatializing states: Toward an ethnography of neoliberal governmentality. *American Ethnologist* 29 (4): 981–1002.

Gosselin, Claudie. 2000. Handing over the knife: Numu women and the campaign against excision in Mali. In *Female "circumcision" in Africa: Culture, controversy, and change,* ed. Bettina Shell-Duncan and Ylva Hernlund, 193–214. Boulder: Lynne Rienner.

Hibou, Béatrice, and Richard Banégas. 2000. Civil society and the public space in Africa. *CODESRIA Bulletin* 1: 39–47.

Keïta, Mamadou. 1998a. Les imams à l'affût des jouisseurs. *Nouvel horizon,* November 23, p. 4.

———. 1998b. Miss Cedeao. *Nouvel horizon,* November 2, p. 5.

Kimbiri, Mohamed. 1998. Boycottons "Miss Cedeao." *Nouvel horizon,* October 16.

———. 2001a. Interdire l'excision est une atteinte grave. *Le républicain,* January 31, p. 5.

———. 2001b. L'excision au Mali: La position des musulmans. *Nouvel horizon,* January 30, p. 5.

Konaté, Kader. 2001. Mali: Le danger islamiste. *Le continent,* September 14, p. 1.

Launay, Robert, and Benjamin F. Soares. 1999. The formation of an "Islamic sphere" in French colonial West Africa. *Economy and Society* 28 (4): 497–519.

Liberté. 2001. Organisation de la Conférence islamique: Le monde musulman. July 3, p. 4.

Muravchik, Joshua. 2001. Freedom and the Arab world. *Weekly Standard*, December 31.

Piot, Charles. 1999. *Remotely global: Village modernity in West Africa*. Chicago: University of Chicago Press.

Le politicien musulman. 2002. Brèves. March 18–April 18, p. 8.

Robinson, David. 2000. *Paths of accommodation: Muslim societies and French colonial authorities in Senegal and Mauritania, 1880–1920*. Athens: Ohio University Press.

Robinson, David, and Jean-Louis Triaud, ed. 1997. *Le temps des marabouts: Itinéraires et stratégies islamiques en Afrique occidentale française, v. 1880–1960*. Paris: Karthala.

La roue. 1996. Déclaration finale des associations islamiques du Mali concernant les valeurs islamiques et à propos du programme d'action de Beijing rélatif aux droits des femmes. January 22–31, pp. 3–5.

Roy, Olivier. 1994. *The failure of political Islam*. Trans. C. Volk. Cambridge, Mass.: Harvard University Press.

———. 2004. *Globalized Islam: The search for a new ummah*. New York: Columbia University Press.

Salvatore, Armando. 2000. Social differentiation, moral authority and public Islam in Egypt: The case of Mustafa Mahmud. *Anthropology Today* 6 (2): 12–15.

Sanou, Jean. 2000. Lutte contre les mutilations génitales feminines. *Le Soudanais*, November 22, p. 3.

Schulz, Dorothea E. 2003a. "Charisma and Brotherhood" revisited. *Journal of Religion in Africa* 33: 146–71.

———. 2003b. Political factions, ideological fictions: The controversy over family law reform in democratic Mali. *Islamic Law and Society* 10 (1): 132–64.

Shell-Duncan, Bettina, and Ylva Hernlund, eds. 2000. *Female "circumcision" in Africa: Culture, controversy, and change*. Boulder: Lynne Rienner.

Sissok, Mamadou Blodin. 2001. Religion et excision: Quand les chrétiens s'engagent contre les mutilations génitales féminines. *Info-matin*, June 29, p. 8.

Soares, Benjamin F. 1999. Muslim proselytization as purification: Religious pluralism and conflict in contemporary Mali. In *Proselytization and communal self-determination in Africa*, ed. Abdullahi Ahmed An-Na'im, 228–45. Maryknoll: Orbis.

———. 2000. Notes on the anthropological study of Islam and Muslim societies in Africa. *Culture and Religion* 1 (2): 277–85.

———. 2004. Islam and public piety in Mali. In *Public Islam and the common good*, ed. Armando Salvatore and Dale F. Eickelman, 205–26. Leiden: Brill.

———. 2005a. *Islam and the prayer economy: History and authority in a Malian town*. Edinburgh: Edinburgh University Press; Ann Arbor: University of Michigan Press.

———. 2005b. Mali: Im Visier der Islamismus-Fahnder. *INAMO* 41: 16–18.

———. Forthcoming. The attempt to reform family law in Mali. In *Gender and Islam in Africa*, ed. Margot Badran. Leiden: Brill.

Sow, Yoro. 1999. Incertitudes pour la tenue du Congrès des homosexuels. *Sud info*, December 8, p. 4.

Starrett, Gregory. 1995. The political economy of religious commodities in Cairo. *American Anthropologist* 97 (1): 51–68.

Sylla, C. H. 2001. Interview exclusive: Le président du Collectif des islamistes parle. *Le républicain*, May 16, pp. 1, 4–5.

———. 2002. Code de la famille et excision: La dernière victoire des islamistes sur Alpha. *Le républicain*, June 10, p. 5.

Tall, Amadou. 1995–96. *Dimensions de l'Islam*. Beirut: Dar El Fikr.

Tamboura, Belco. 2001. Le front religieux, un front de plus pour Konaré. *L'observateur*, June 14, p. 6.

Taussig, Michael. 1993. *Mimesis and alterity.* New York: Routledge.

Traoré, Djibril. 2000. El Hadji Mahmoud Dicko. *Le national,* October 2, p. 5.

Tsing, Anna L. 1993. *In the realm of the diamond queen: Marginality in an out-of-the-way place.* Princeton: Princeton University Press.

U.S. Agency for International Development. 2002. *USAID Mali: Country strategic plan, 2003–2012.* Bamako: USAID, July.

CHAPTER 12

ISLAMIC ASSOCIATIONS IN CAMEROON: BETWEEN THE *UMMA* AND THE STATE

Hamadou Adama

Islam, insofar as it is a totalizing religion which does not distinctly separate the political from the private sphere, makes it possible for us to gauge the modalities of its relationship with state power and to envisage a future beyond national frontiers. Seen in this light, the gradual movement of Muslim agents, literati, and intellectuals into the political sphere, using associational structures qualified sometimes as religious and sometimes as cultural, demonstrates that these actors are no longer content to restrict themselves to the traditional roles of teacher and preacher. They are seeking to participate more actively in the political arena, hoping, if not to change the state, at least to establish a process of negotiation short of instituting a system of administration inspired by Islamic texts. Thus, denunciations of the betrayal of Islamic values and the political and professional marginalization suffered by Muslim intellectuals are at the center of their political discourse.[1]

From this point of view, the Islamic associations which have emerged in the place of Sufi orders as forums for political speech constitute privileged terrain for the regrouping, training, and recycling of arabophone intellectuals. Similarly, the networks of relationships within a globalized Islam, the international exchanges, and the development of communications supply the necessary energy for the functioning of Islamic associations and the globalization of Islam in Cameroon.

However, since the liberalization and democratization of the political field began in the early 1990s, a period characterized in particular by the state's progressive disengagement from such key sectors of social life as education and health, numerous religious and cultural associations have appeared in public life alongside nongovernmental organizations (NGOs). If some of them have simply become NGOs in order—according to their promoters—to attempt to ameliorate the withdrawal of the state from social life, all of them have adopted, at least in the wording of their official documents, an altruistic stance, oriented toward charitable activities and the support of endogenous development efforts. As well as assisting the population in the areas of education and health care, the Islamic associations act in a context of religious competition. By mobilizing the international Islamic community on behalf of Cameroonian Muslims, they imitate initiatives in these domains undertaken by Catholic and Protestant organizations. The vacuum left by the state's incapacity to assume such social responsibilities opens up a field which now extends beyond national frontiers to operate on an even larger scale, capable of attracting international financial resources.

To illustrate this interaction between the local and the global, I have chosen four Islamic associations. Their respective structures, personnel, goals, and sectors of activity will readily demonstrate their character. First, I will chronologically and analytically examine the relationship between these Islamic organizations and the Cameroonian state and discuss the spirit of certain decisions taken by the government when these associations were established. We can thus understand the impact of these political measures on the development of the associations' activities in civil society. Second, I will examine the implications of the vacuum left by the state's withdrawal from social welfare and the different initiatives with which Islamic associations have attempted to appropriate this vacant field by integrating transnational structures into the financing of their local actions.

It goes without saying that the presence of the state as well as its withdrawal from fields of social activity entails attitudes, behaviors, actions, and reactions that this modest contribution cannot describe exhaustively.

The Genesis of Islamic Associations in Historical Context

In a general way, Cameroonian Islamic organizations, whether they are state-sponsored, like the ACIC (Association culturelle islamique du Cameroun, Islamic Cultural Association of Cameroon), or stem from a desire for emancipation from state power, like the CAMSU (Cameroon Muslim Students' Union), are all products of a reaction to or contestation of situations or behaviors judged to be contrary to Islamic norms. The births of some of them are rooted in the colonial era, in the period of French rule.

It is by now an established fact that the French administration was responsible for the institutionalization of Islam in Cameroon, first of all by organizing and controlling the flow of pilgrims who traveled annually to Saudi Arabia, and second by supervising the visits of eminent religious personalities whose travels to Cameroon were transformed into de facto official visits. Illustrations of this institutionalization of Islam "from above" are legion (Bah and Taguem Fah 1993). The organization of the pilgrimage of Sultan Seidou Njimoluh Njoya of Bamum exemplifies this appropriation of the formalization of exchanges between Cameroonian Muslims and their foreign coreligionists (Abwa 2003). Similarly, the Algerian Tijani Shaykh Sidi Benamor was accompanied by colonial officials during a tour of Cameroon in 1949, during which he initiated the Bamum aristocracy into the Tijaniyya (Bah 1996).

Immediately following the colonial era, under the regime of the first president of Cameroon, Ahmadou Ahidjo (1960–82), the "domestication" of Islam took shape with the creation and legalization of a certain number of Islamic associations, including the ACIC. The ACIC was administered at that time by individuals close to the president, for the most part former members of his administration or diplomats who had formerly been posted to Arab countries, such as Aminou Oumarou, Moussa Yaya, and Adamou Ndam Njoya. Cameroon thus inaugurated, through the medium of individuals knowledgeable in Arabic and highly placed in the ACIC, a new era of official relations with Arabic-speaking countries.

With the accession of Paul Biya to power in 1982 and especially with the advent of political pluralism in the 1990s, religious associations were progressively "deinstitutionalized" in public life. An attempted coup d'état in 1984 by elements in the army considered close to Ahidjo, Ahidjo's consequent condemnation to death in absentia, and above all the reestablishment of diplomatic relations between Cameroon and Israel in 1986 considerably weakened the privileged position of what had been until then the most influential Islamic association in Cameroon, the ACIC. The 1990s, which saw the beginnings of democratization in most of the former French colonies in Africa, were also a period of economic crisis combined with a loss of confidence in the institutions embodied by those who had heretofore been regarded as the "fathers of the nation." In the face of these developments, bilateral and multilateral sources of funding reoriented their modes of intervention, bypassing governmental agencies they considered corrupt or bureaucratic in order to collaborate directly with NGOs, which they judged more credible and which were, above all, in permanent contact with the eventual beneficiaries of the development projects those funding sources supported. In this context of budgetary rigor and structural crisis, the country of Cameroon was placed under the de facto supervision of international financial institutions proposing various forms of structural adjustment.

The disengagement of the state from certain economic activities, in the face of its budget deficits and its dependence on international supervision, was extended into the religious domain. Subsidies formerly given to religious schools or to religiously run clinics and hospitals became scarcer and more irregular. Such disengagement was far from total or irreversible. It was, rather, strategic and selective, because the Ministry of Territorial Administration continued to oversee religious organizations and enterprises, although its room to maneuver shrank considerably with the atomization of the religious field and the emergence of private, informal links between Cameroonian Muslims and the Arabo-Muslim world.

This privatization of relations of exchange between Cameroonian Muslims and their foreign coreligionists remains noticeable at the governmental level. Although an Arab policy may be formulated by relying on the experience and knowledge of those familiar with Arabic language and Arab society in order to simultaneously influence the national Islamic community and enhance its diplomatic presence in the international arena, authorities monitor such "Muslim politics" to make sure that the interests of the Cameroonian state are privileged over any other religious, political, or economic considerations. The dispositions which made possible this privatization of Islamic actors lead at the same time, paradoxically, to a desire to affirm a transcendent identity, beyond national frontiers and local cultural specificities. A retrospective and prospective analysis of the internal mutations of several Islamic associations, as well as their changing relationships to the political domain, can not only show how they act in civil society but also give a synthetic idea of their room for maneuver, given their capacity to mobilize people and resources.

The birth of Islamic associations can be dated to 1963, when the ACIC, the first such association in Cameroon, emerged. Until 1992, the ACIC remained the only Islamic association legalized by presidential decree, but with the passage of time, and above all following changes in the conceptualization of Muslim identity, numerous Islamic associations of the so-called second generation emerged in turn. These are, notably, the ASSOVIC (Association solidaire pour la vocation islamique du Cameroun, Solidarity Association for the Islamic Vocation of Cameroon) and the UIC (Union islamique du Cameroun, Cameroon Islamic Union).[2] These two associations disrupted, by their very existence and above all by the notoriety of their respective promoters, the ACIC's monopoly. In particular, they contested its status as official spokesman for the Muslim community of Cameroon.

Beginning in 1992, the field of Muslim associations underwent a major transformation. Law 90/053 of December 19, 1990, liberalized political and associational life in Cameroon and redefined the institutional framework for creating and managing an apolitical association. Under its aegis, numerous associations emerged in civil society. Some adapted themselves to the new legislation by circumscribing their activities within the limits of the regulatory framework, whereas others adopted an administrative structure closer to those of nongovernmental organizations. This law also allowed the emergence within civil society of Islamic associations of the so-called third generation. They were new in being managed almost exclusively by university students[3] or by women.[4] These latter associations, of a type previously unknown in Cameroon, revolutionized Islamic dynamics in the socioreligious field and in the process revitalized the controversy over the place of Muslim women in public life.

Association culturelle islamique du Cameroun

The ACIC seems to have been created in response to the central authorities' attempt to undercut the initiatives of a Tijani shaykh (or *marabout*) of Mauritanian origin, Mahmoud Bah, whose ambition it was to establish an Islamic structure that could reunite all the Muslims of Yaounde, irrespective of their particular origins. The reaction of the authorities resulted in the unilateral creation of the ACIC, which was entrusted to persons known to be unaffiliated with the Tijaniyya. Ahidjo was suspicious of the order,[5] which, through repression and intimidation, he drove into hiding. The Tijaniyya was perceived as a heretical sect and its practices of reciting special litanies of prayers were equated with fostering disturbances and insecurity. Beyond his explicit hostility to the Tijaniyya, Ahmadou Ahidjo's stance betrayed a will to isolate the Cameroonian Muslim community from all Nigerian influence in order that he embody, in their eyes, the defense of true Islam.

Authorized to operate in 1963, the ACIC was officially recognized in 1967 (under law number 67/LF/19 of June 12, 1967) in order to serve as an interface between the state and the Muslim community and as a spokesperson in case of controversy. In practice, the ACIC was supposed to assure the loyalty of the Muslim community and to inform the state hierarchy of any attempt to "threaten or disturb public order." It was hardly a coincidence that its first president, Aminou Oumarou, was a former member of the government who emerged from the ranks of the single party, the UNC (Union national camerounaise, the National Union of Cameroon), and had served as a diplomat in the Arab world since 1986. The ACIC's top-down creation, as well as the struggles for power between individuals and regional interests[6] (because the organization had strategic importance in the disbursal of funds to Franco-Arabic schools), handicapped its success in the socioeducational field for a long time.

In 1988, after twenty-five years of stagnation, the ACIC finally set out to redefine its focus, having revised its foundational texts. All of its energies were hereafter oriented toward the promotion of Islamic doctrine and, in the words of its statutes, the "reinforcement of ties of solidarity, peace, tolerance, and fraternity between Muslim believers." The ACIC positioned itself as the only authoritative interpreter of religious texts and manager of research, reflection, and scientific activities or techniques which could contribute to the realization of Islamic principles. It also sought to be a center for discussion, documentation, orientation, and contacts. It was accorded the right of *ijtihad*,[7] in principle in the hope that it would remain independent of foreign Islamist currents.

Among the preeminent goals of the ACIC are the development of Islamic teaching and education in Cameroon, the promotion of Islamic cultural activities, and the management and financing of modern teaching establishments as well as of traditional Qur'anic schools. These are noble and ambitious goals, whose realization depends on the establishment of adequate infrastructures, staffing, and instructional material. To achieve them, the association has renovated its administrative structures. The general assembly, the administrative council, the steering committee, and the Council of Ulama for Doctrinal, Pedagogical, Scientific, and Technical Affairs now operate under the direction of experienced *arabisants* (that is, those educated in Arabic, who frequently express themselves in that language and promote its use). The general assembly is the supreme branch, the administrative council represents executive power, the steering committee assumes permanent secretarial functions, and the Council of Ulama coordinates activities external to the ACIC in conjunction with its regional representatives.

The ACIC is funded exclusively through government subsidies and bilateral international agreements negotiated at the governmental level with the Arabo-Muslim world. It has on several occasions attempted to diversify its sources of funds, for example by selling memberships, with limited success. The lack of transparency in the management of public funds allocated to the ACIC, notably for financing the operations of schools throughout the country, has long tarnished its image among the Muslim population. The successes achieved in social and educational fields by various competing Islamic associations are due, in part, to the immobility of the governing structures of the ACIC.

The arrival, at the end of the 1990s, of a new team (consisting of Muslim intellectuals trained in the West, and coordinated by Doubla Avaly, an academic) represented a new hope that the ACIC might be pulled from its long period of lethargy by renewing ties with its educational partners and the Muslim community as a whole. The team has concentrated on this task, within the framework of the OESPI (Organisation des établissements scolaires privés islamiques, Organization of Private Islamic Scholarly Establishments), which is independent of the ACIC.

Such disaffection with the ACIC stems primarily from its internal struggles for leadership and its administration's submissiveness to political power. In order to counterbalance the growing influence of Islam on public life, Ahidjo relied primarily on the fidelity of arabophone intellectuals to discredit traditional religious leaders (or *marabouts*), allies of Muslim theocracies, which were rapidly becoming relics of a feudal past, and which were never favorable to him. He expected the arabophone intellectuals, invested in his view with Islamic legitimacy by virtue of their mastery of the Arabic language and Islamic learning, to implacably condemn the Tijaniyya order. By awarding the ACIC the exclusive authority to interpret Islamic texts and define Islamic norms in Cameroon, he effectively transformed this organization into an unpopular institution, which thereafter crystallized all the opposition to his regime. Within the ACIC, there thus flourished a current of opinion which one might characterize as fundamentalist, because it espoused for the most part the ideas of the Wahhabiyya (Kaba 1974; Otayek 1993; Kane and Triaud 1998), calling for prayer and ritual practices to be re-Islamized in order to strip them of inappropriate features and remove them from a compromising proximity to local particularisms. In opposition to this Islam, that was seen as imported by *arabisants* subordinated to the state by their nomination to leadership positions in the ACIC, another line of thought began to emerge that contested the interference of the state in the management of Muslim affairs. The partisans of this latter opinion were recruited among young Cameroonians trained in Western universities who, disillusioned with an administration reluctant to employ them once their studies were completed, adopted another reading of the Wahhabiyya, one that stressed the re-Islamization of behavior through the education of society. Thus, their contestation of the omnipresence of the state and its reluctance to incorporate them into public administration led an important cadre of *arabisants* to create informal Arabo-Islamic schools with the generous aid of foreign donors concerned with the propagation of Muslim *da'wa*.[8] This tendency, beginning in the late 1970s, would increase among young urban Muslims and would, in the course of the 1990s, have an impact even in university circles.

The Cameroon Muslim Students' Union

The structure and administrative organization of the CAMSU (Cameroon Muslim Students' Union) is of interest for two reasons. Not only is the CAMSU a sounding board for ideas that were formerly developed outside the framework of Cameroonian higher education and that some would—rightly or wrongly—qualify as Salafi, but also—and this is in my opinion its most interesting aspect—it provides a more "scientific" face to Islamic reformism. Although the overwhelming majority of the *arabisants* possessed an uncontested and ultimately uncontestable superiority in Islamic learning, they nonetheless experienced real difficulties in transmitting this knowledge in the official languages of Cameroon, French and English. This handicap, a product of their illiteracy in European languages, was hardly an obstacle for members of the CAMSU. They easily combine—and this is their principal strength— Islamic learning and competence in the expression, formulation, and articulation of the Islamic corpus in official as well as local languages.

Their skills can be partly explained by their education and their participation in associations in the context of the search for meaning in the face of economic difficulties as well as the religious effervescence characterizing the 1990s. A retrospective look at the birth of the CAMSU allows us to make several pertinent observations.

Most of the CAMSU's leaders came out of older Islamic associations created on university campuses. The first attempts to create such associations date back to the late 1980s. In 1988, the YUMSCA (Yaounde University Muslim Students' Cultural Association) was created. Several years later, dissident former members of the YUMSCA established a new association named the ASEMUC (Associations des étudiants musulmans du Cameroun, Muslim Students' Association of Cameroon). These two associations included both anglophone and francophone students, and their creation reflected their founders' commitment to establishing a representative structure, reflecting ethnic and regional diversity, which could manage problems specifically linked to the observation of Islamic principles within the institutional framework of universities. The first campaigns to promote awareness among university administrators focused on practical problems, such as a proper place of worship, information about the meat served in university cafeterias, cafeteria hours, and food aid to Muslim students during Ramadan, and so on.

The administration of the University of Yaounde turned out to be receptive to such demands, and the majority of complaints were resolved. But, like all associations during this turbulent period of Cameroon's history, the ASEMUC and the YUMSCA were undermined by internal struggles for leadership. They were also, like the entire country, rife with identity politics, stoked by political discourses and torn between regional (if not ethnic) loyalties and a commitment to the Islamic community as a whole.

The experiment that these two associations incarnated ended after a period of five years. The ideas formulated and proposed had done their work. In 1988, a new association, the CAMSU, was created through the initiative of Abdu Kamfom Bornou and Mohammadou Saoudi, in the course of a seminar jointly organized in Yaounde by the WAMY (World Assembly of Muslim Youth) and a local nongovernmental association called ADF (African Development Foundation). This association conceived of its actions in the spirit of the Qur'anic text (10:49), at the same time affirming the principle of republican secularism guaranteed by Cameroonian law.

It is interesting to note that this position seems to explicitly prioritize the logic of the state and of the nation over the logic of the *umma*. The Salafi vision of the CAMSU is in this way watered down, and the association articulates its discourse around deculturation, a sort of rejection of traditional cultures that it judges anachronistic and incapable of promoting a modernity which is precisely fostered, in their eyes, by the reformist Islam of members of the CAMSU.

Its program for action is summarized in its motto, "Faith, knowledge, success," and it seeks to reinforce the spirit of Muslim fraternity and solidarity, promote "proper Islamic behavior" on and off campus, gain and diffuse learning, and train students. Above all, the CAMSU emphasizes the Islamic education of students and their mastery of English and of new technologies.

To put its objectives into practice, it has simplified its organizational structure by reinforcing the operational units it opened in each of the six universities of Cameroon. The women's units are particularly active. They are in general better infused with Islamic principles and play a central role in the religious education of their sisters. The women also organize the celebration of the fast during the month of Ramadan on campus. The breaking of the fast each evening (*iftar*) is thus transformed into a fraternal communion to which all students are invited, including non-Muslims and nonpracticing Muslims.

Alongside its activities oriented toward realizing a spirit of tolerance, of Muslim fraternity, and of Islamic solidarity in the midst of the student community of Cameroonian universities, the CAMSU annually coordinates a tour of volunteer doctors who come from Saudi Arabia with medicine and equipment to provide free health care to the populations of the northern regions of Cameroon. Every year since the middle of the 1990s, about ten surgeons, dentists, and ophthalmologists have been eagerly awaited by these peoples, to whom they bring a medical expertise sadly lacking in the Cameroonian savanna. These projects by Saudi doctors in North Cameroon, with logistical support from public hospitals, perfectly illustrate the interaction of the logics of the state and of the *umma* in a context of globalization and religious competition.

Similarly, the CAMSU's contribution to religious activity in state universities has won it the respect of university administrators. In Ngaoundere in 1998, in Dschang in 2000, and in Douala in 2002, not only did the CAMSU obtain permission to hold its meetings on campus but leading members of the universities' administrations participated in its activities. It should be noted here that the themes developed in the course of conferences that the CAMSU organizes alongside its congress speak directly to the entire university community.[9] In a sociopolitical climate characterized by an undercurrent of interreligious suspicion and competition, it has been able to stake out a space of encounter and of openness toward other religions, a framework of dialogue with university administrators, and thus demonstrate considerable political maturity.

Its funding depends on contributions by active student members and by honorary members who are either alumni or sympathetic Muslims, Cameroonians as well as foreigners. The "old boys' network" of the YUMSCA, the ASEMUC, and the CAMSU manages to guarantee the CAMSU a certain financial autonomy, which assures its national respectability. Other organizations, such as the WAMY (based in Djeddah, Saudi Arabia, and represented in Cameroon by Shaykh Abdoulkarim Abbo) and the ADF of Shaykh Ali participate to a modest extent in financing the cultural activities of the CAMSU.

Compared to other associations in the Cameroonian Islamic landscape, the CAMSU operates as a modern association, with agendas for its meetings circulated in advance, minutes, audited books, reports of its activities in the public and private media in the official languages of Cameroon, and so on. Such initiatives set a precedent for Cameroonian public opinion and incontestably deserve respect.

For the moment, the CAMSU defines itself as an apolitical Islamic association. Its members are careful to avoid public political pronouncements which would earn them the enmity of the powers that be. Its actions are explicitly social and religious.

One thing is nonetheless certain: the CAMSU includes people capable of presenting, in French as well as in English, the Islamic point of view in any controversial debate in the media or in the context of scientific or cultural activities. The quality and the training of its members, its representation on every university campus, and its audience among Muslim intellectuals constitute a political force that the political authorities have begun to take into account.

The CAMSU has been able to espouse the Salafi ideas that the *arabisants* brought home from years of advanced study in Arabia while refraining from contesting (at least openly) the preeminence of state logic. Even while adopting such ideas, the CAMSU has adapted Islamic reformism to local realities by taking into account the balance of power. Obviously, the CAMSU militates for such values as family, proper morals, and faith in God. Its program takes politics into account without calling into question the structure of the state, its prevalence, or its national interest. In this way, we might say that the CAMSU has managed to give Islam in Cameroon a more human face. It has fostered increasing sensitivity to context in Islamic discourse and practice by reconciling the transnational pretensions and emphasis on the *umma* of the first generation of *arabisants* with the administrative preoccupations of the City of Man. Its highly organized student support network allows the association to plan for the future while strategically calculating its initiatives toward other religions and working to promote a dialogue with its environment.

The CAMSU remains the source from which the other experimental associations that dot the Cameroonian sociopolitical landscape take their roots. Some of these newer associations have transformed themselves into cultural associations or NGOs. The LMPDS (Ligue musulmane pour la paix, le dialogue et la solidarité, Muslim League for Peace, Dialogue, and Solidarity) and the OFIF (Organisation de la femme pour l'Islam sans frontières, Women's Organization for Islam without Borders), to cite just two, are part of this new wave of associations founded by former members of the CAMSU that devote themselves, with greater or lesser success, to the education and consciousness-raising of Muslims in cosmopolitan and multireligious urban settings, such as the agglomerations of Yaounde and Douala.

Ligue musulmane pour la paix, le dialogue et la solidarité (Muslim League for Peace, Dialogue, and Solidarity)

The LMPDS, or more simply the League, is an Islamic association that belongs to what I called the third generation, because it owes its existence to the promulgation in December 1990 of the law granting freedom of association, simultaneously legalizing and simplifying the formation of an association; it could now be done simply by submitting a declaration to the authorities of any prefecture. The new constitution adopted in January 1996 expanded freedom of association by eliminating penalties for publishing texts critical of the regime, marking in this way a real rupture with the former monolithic policies. It was in this sociopolitical context that the League was created in 2000, under the leadership of a group of friends who had met as members of the CAMSU of the University of Yaounde I. This group included Souleymane Bouba, Issa Bikoe, Oumarou Malam Djibring, Ismael Djakité, El Hajj Muhammed, and Yacouba. Other members from different regions and belonging to different ethnic groups joined these founders.

The League was initially known as the CIRC (Cercle islamique pour la recherche et la culture, Islamic Circle for Research and Culture), and changed its name in

April 2004. Souleymane Bouba, its founder, justified the change as a response to new challenges which now faced the Cameroonian Muslim community and to which it had to adjust in order to meet them efficiently.

The League aims to promote peace, interfaith and intercultural dialogue, and education and training. To achieve these goals, Souleymane Bouba surrounded himself with Muslim intellectuals who had backgrounds like his own (he was a Muslim activist at the University of Yaounde) and who were members of different Cameroonian ethnic groups. Issa Bikoe (Beti) is a qualified teacher, Monchamo Abdoulaye (Bamoum) is an agronomist, and Yamata Ismael (Bamileke) is an automobile technician. All of them met as students at the University of Yaounde and all are animated with the same will to bypass ethnic barriers by stressing teamwork. To learn to work together in order to learn to live together beyond all sectarian divisions: this is the philosophy at the base of the League.

The League encourages the Cameroonian Muslim community to be open to other religious communities, engaging in dialogue with them and attempting to close the communication gap that fosters anti-Islamic prejudices. To do this, the League must have recourse to persons who are trained in Islamic sciences as a result of their experiences in CAMSU and who are skilled in the official languages as well as in new information and communication technologies.

The League's funding comes from the contributions of active members (many of whom are former CAMSU compatriots now employed in different sectors of the economy), sympathizers, and honorary members, including the U.S. ambassador to Cameroon, as well as from the sales of items in the course of the association's activities and money solicited through private radio and television programming.

Similarly, with the aim of efficiently facing the new challenges that confront the Muslim community, the League is working to create a federation of Islamic associations within Cameroonian public space that would permit the formation of a transparent platform of collaboration and reflection. The ultimate goal is to establish enough credibility within civil society to direct collective energies toward social domains such as health, education, professional training, and interfaith dialogue. The League is counting on the academic and socioprofessional profiles of its prominent members to accomplish these goals and to make visible the contribution of Muslim elites to the project of endogenous development in Cameroon. It particularly focuses on Islamic education and training, with systematic recourse to new media aids such as literature, theater, radio, and television. Such an initiative would never have seen the light of day without the adoption in January 1996, in accordance with the new constitution, of legislation that decriminalized criticism by the press. Political liberalization and the democratization of the audio-visual landscape spurred the expression of discordant voices in public life, as long as the authors and publishers refrained from libeling public personalities. Thus, members of the League found an opportunity to disseminate their ideas.

In the literary domain, Souleymane Bouba published two works. *Letter of a Muslim to a Christian friend* (*Lettre d'un musulman à un ami chrétien*, Bouba 2001), published in 2001, is a popular exposition of Islamic faith, and *The fast of Ramadan in 100 questions and answers* (*Le jeûne de Ramadan en 100 questions et réponses*, Bouba 2002c), published in 2002, is an invitation to interfaith dialogue between Islam and

Christianity. Both were placed in bookstores and sold well, thanks to the efficient manner in which word was spread throughout the Muslim community, as well as the fact that the author is something of a media celebrity.

Alongside his professional teaching career[10] and his writing, Souleymane Bouba moderates radio broadcasts on "perspectives on Islam" on a private radio station[11] in the town of Yaounde and collaborates on a weekly Islamic program called *Knowledge of Islam* on the national television station, CRTV (Cameroon Radio and Television). He is in addition a producer of bilingual French and Arabic audio cassettes and compact discs on the themes of the nocturnal journey and ascension of the Prophet Muhammad (*Mihraj*) and based on Sa'id al-Qahtani's book of prayers and supplications, *The Muslim Fortress*.

In 2001, the directors of the League (still called the CIRC at that time) launched a contest in the Islamic media for the best Islamic sketch. A national jury was put together to select the winner and reward original works. To facilitate their production, the League founded a publishing house called el-Hikma. Souleymane Bouba published his three plays through el-Hikma, all of which were popular successes.

The play *Islam, our choice* (*Islam, notre choix*, Bouba 2002b) portrays with considerable humor the problems of young converts in adapting to and familiarizing themselves with Islamic principles. It stresses the incomprehension of the young convert's parents, his Muslim coreligionists, and his professional colleagues. The play *The shaykh and the DG* (*Le cheikh et le DG*, Bouba 2002a) satirizes the problems of "nouveaux riches" Muslims who abandon their religious practices once they are promoted to the rank of director general. Through the meeting of two characters, the religious leader and the secularized Muslim, Bouba denounces both corruption and male infidelity. The phenomenon of the *deuxième bureau*, an allusion to a kept mistress, is stigmatized with both humor and seriousness. It is a tender and rich comedy, full of twists and surprises. The play also alludes to contemporary events to underscore through comical situations the shock of cultures incarnated on one hand in Osama bin Laden and the Taliban, and on the other in Rambo the American. *The shaykh and the DG* is well written, with appropriate attention given to gestures and visual effects. The third play, entitled *Scie-Da* (Bouba 2002d), is a fantastic representation through which the author draws attention to the AIDS epidemic and, in the process, the Islamic solution—abstinence and fidelity—as a way of life, counterbalancing the government's campaign, which is focused on the use of condoms as the only solution to the crisis.

From this brief presentation, it should be clear that there is a manifest will to express the fact that Muslim elites are in no way indifferent to social problems. The interconnections of the *umma* and the state are implicitly articulated. The weak involvement of the state in the management of social problems leaves room for the expression of Muslim sensibilities, responding to events on the international stage and manifesting transnational solidarity with the Muslim community, but expressed in terms of lived experience at the local, national, and state levels. The ascension of a new generation has not only led to a redefinition of what it means to be Muslim in a Cameroonian context but also called into question the proper role of an Islamic association in an international climate of anti-Muslim prejudice.

In this respect, the League seems to be becoming an NGO whose actions are deliberately separate from those of public power but which still operates in a space governed by patriotic logic. Adhesion to the *umma*, in this case, would be theoretical, symbolic, even mythical, but necessary in order to mobilize resources that can fund local initiatives while maintaining independence from state authorities. The League positions itself at the forefront of Islamic associations, leaving itself room for maneuver between the necessary adherence to the *umma* and the need to conform to local realities. Literature and theater, the pen and the stage, constitute appropriate means of expression and denunciation for urban Muslim youth, aware that they need to maintain this equilibrium in order to ensure their presence and visibility on the national media scene.

Organisation de la femme pour l'Islam sans frontières (Women's Organization for Islam without Borders)

Muslim women's associations in Cameroonian civil society date from only 1995, the year in which the very first association of this type was born. The appearance of an association led by a woman revolutionized the Islamic associational landscape, characterized until then by a preponderance of males. Space has traditionally been reserved for Muslim women's expression in the context of associations managed by men. Generally, cells are specifically dedicated to treating issues that men judge important to the well-being of Muslim women.

The year 1995 saw a rupture with the past in this regard. Several militant Muslim women in the town of Yaounde began to dissociate themselves from associations managed by men in order to create their own structures. Their "concern for autonomy" (Djenabou 1993) led to the creation, on July 20, 1995, of the very first Islamic association with a woman at its head: the OFIF (Organisation de la femme pour l'Islam sans frontières). This association, led by its founder, Madame Youenyouen Halima, has its headquarters in Mimboman, a suburb of Yaounde.

The OFIF is administered by a general assembly, an administrative council, a surveillance committee, an executive bureau, and a secretariat consisting of six departments (production, health, informal education, Islamic education, social affairs, and cultural affairs). As well as expressing a legitimate desire for independence, its creation exposed underlying tensions between the sexes and demonstrated a critical stance toward male management of associations. The fact that the OFIF rapidly drew many members from other organizations was a patent signal that criticism was brewing and that gender issues had assumed much greater importance. The stimulus came from Madame Youenyouen Halima, considered by her supporters to be an inspiration, a *pasionaria*, a liberator.

Globally, and regardless of the sex of their leaders, Islamic associations aim to promote Islamic values and the well-being of Muslims. The promotion of Islamic values implies knowledge of religion and of religious practices aimed at benefiting from divine grace. It also involves promoting Islamic solidarity and representing Islam to non-Muslims in order to establish a constructive and respectful dialogue whose final objective is the exclusive worship of God in accordance with the Qur'an. Each association specifies particular goals and objectives in its statutes, choosing them as a function of its means (human, financial, political, etc.), of the preoccupations of its political or sociocultural environment, or simply of its understanding of the problems that face the Muslim community and its ability to resolve them.

The OFIF's objectives are the promotion of Islamic values, the education of women (with a focus on literacy among young girls), the struggle against HIV/AIDS, the prevention of adolescent and unwanted pregnancies, aid to the underprivileged, and interfaith dialogue. These ambitious goals leave an important place for Muslim women, perceived as partners of men and as subjects conscious of their role in society. It still remains to translate such pious wishes into concrete acts, which is far from easy to accomplish.

Compared to other Muslim women's associations, the OFIF constitutes an enviable model of activity. It possesses its own buildings, financed with French help, including a primary school that opened in the academic year 2000–2001. The OFIF also provides professional training; another of its buildings is dedicated to teaching crafts appropriate to social and familial economy, such as sewing, embroidery, weaving, cooking, and child care. The association has also been accredited by the Ministry of Public Health to open a health center and is in the process of building an Islamic complex which will include a place of worship, a library, and a conference room.

The OFIF is, to my knowledge, the only officially recognized Islamic association that attempts to free Muslim women from the traditional roles to which they have been confined by several centuries of custom, conveniently Islamized. Behind the black clothes, which disguise a body that has become the object of so many interdictions, new forms of expression and demands are developing, aiming at the recognition of women as equal partners to men. It is no accident that the OFIF's members particularly criticize subjugation of women through ignorance and illiteracy. They see Islamic and Western forms of education as complementary, and as necessary in order for Muslim women to be accorded full freedom in a modern urban context and an increasingly globalized world.

Alongside those Islamic associations that I have briefly described, several other NGOs are working in rural zones to train farmers, organize medical treatment for rural dwellers, and provide Arabic education.

Conclusion

To summarize, three principal phases, not rigorously distinct but with different characteristics, allow us to apprehend the nature of the relations between Islamic associations and the state on one hand, and the global Muslim community on the other.

First of all, if, during the colonial period, the political authorities sought to circumscribe in one way or another the hegemonic pretensions of Muslims, it goes without saying that after colonization there existed a real desire to incorporate traditional authorities, regrouped into Islamic associations faithful to the regime, into the construction of a modern state. Their self-exclusion, stemming from their rejection of Western schooling, contributed to their marginalization on the political stage. Afterward, the establishment of an administration hostile to the *arabisants* limited them to religious roles emptied of substance and influence. The alternative chosen by the *arabisants*—to bypass Western schooling in order to set up a distinct or hybrid school system, in the hope of eventually promoting their participation in the local political arena—was stymied by the ever-increasing emphasis placed on Western values as a path to social mobility and professional promotion. Nevertheless, their mastery of the Arabic language and their knowledge of the terrain would favor a connection with global Islam, with which, through the construction of associational networks, they would be the only viable intermediaries. Eventually, in the mid-1990s, Muslim elites, university-trained in French, English, or Arabic, could distinguish themselves from the two prior types of leadership, traditional religious leaders (or *marabouts*) on one hand and arabophone ulama on the other. Their aim was to modernize Islamic associational structures from the inside in order to furnish them with the tools of modernity. Such initiatives occasionally led to the creation of Islamic NGOs, whose energies were incontestable but whose funding, coming for the most part from outside Cameroon, excited the state's suspicion. Playing on the victimization and marginalization of Muslims in the interior of Cameroon, the Islamic NGOs were able to to exclude the state from the management of their affairs by activating ties of solidarity with Muslims abroad.

The financial circuit linking global to local Islam may have been closely monitored ever since September 11, 2001, but the circulation of people and ideas has not. On the other hand, even if the pure Islam promoted by Islamic NGOs evades state control and supervision, it is nonetheless hardly compatible with a popular Islam imbued with customary beliefs and practices. It remains true that this political Islam, which they are attempting to promote through associational links, is in the process of transforming itself into a counterculture, one that is poorly defined for the moment but that serves as a sounding board for every form of discontent.

Notes

1. In itself, the actual speech of Islamic leaders is never blatantly political, given that associations, in compliance with the law and according to their own charters, declare themselves apolitical. However, such speech contains unstated political implications.
2. The ASSOVIC and the UIC were authorized by the president on February 22, 1992, and November 13, 1992, respectively. After this date, Islamic associations were authorized either by the Ministry of Territorial Administration and Decentralization or at the prefectural level.
3. I have in mind the CAMSU (Cameroon Muslim Students' Union), discussed later.
4. The first Islamic association run by a woman was the OFIF (Organisation de la femme pour l'Islam sans frontières, Women's Organization for Islam without Borders), discussed later.
5. The Tijaniyya in this instance was specifically the branch of the Senegalese shaykh Ibrahima Niasse. See Triaud and Robinson 2000.
6. For details of the struggle between Fulani and Hausa for control of places of worship and schools run by the ACIC in Yaounde, see Moussa 1987.
7. *Ijtihad* is an effort at independent reasoning, intended to solve a practical problem in the application of Islamic law.
8. Christian Coulon's study of the training of new Muslim elites in northern Nigeria parallels, in many respects, the resurgence of Islam in North Cameroon (Coulon 1993).
9. These themes are principally Islamo-Christian dialogue, religious ethics and morality, the importance of education, national integration, human rights, and respect for the common values of all Cameroonians of every ethnicity.

10. Bouba has a diploma from the École normale supérieure of Yaounde. He teaches history in a public secondary school and is simultaneously preparing a Ph.D. thesis on Islam in the Mbam region.
11. Radio Magic FM, 100.1 MHz, Fridays from 4:00 to 5:00 p.m.

References

Abwa, D. 2003. Njimoluh Seidou: Un modèle de souverain traditionnel dans un environnement politique hostile. In *Le retour des rois*, ed. C.-H. Perrot and F.-X. Fauvelle-Aymar, 289–305. Paris: Karthala.

Bouba, Souleymane. 2001. *Lettre d'un musulman à un ami chrétien*. Yaounde: Éditions du CIRC.

———. 2002a. *Le cheikh et le DG*. Yaounde: el-Hikma.

———. 2002b. *Islam, notre choix*. Yaounde: el-Hikma.

———. 2002c. *Le jeûne de Ramadan en 100 questions et réponses*. Yaoundé: Éditions du CIRC

———. 2002d. *Scie-Da*. Yaounde: el-Hikma.

Bah, T. M. 1996. Cheikhs et marabouts maghrébins prédicateurs dans l'Adamawa, 19e–20e. *Ngaoundéré-Anthropos* 1: 7–28.

Bah, T. M., and G. L. Taguem Fah. 1993. Les élites musulmanes et la politique sous administration française, 1945–1960. In *Peuples et cultures de l'Adamaoua*, ed. J. Boutrais, 103–33. Paris: Orstom; Ngaoundéré: Anthropos.

Coulon, C. 1993. Les nouveaux *oulémas* et le renouveau islamique au Nord-Nigéria. In *Le radicalisme islamique au sud du Sahara: Da'wa, arabisation et critique de l'Occident*, ed. R. Otayek, 123–49. Paris: Karthala-MSHA.

Djenabou, Hadja. 1993. Interview by author, Yaoundé, December.

Kaba, L. 1974. *The Wahhabiyya: Islamic reform and politics in French West Africa*. Evanston, Northwestern University Press.

Kane, O., and J.-L. Triaud, eds. 1998. *Islam et islamismes au sud du Sahara*. Paris: Maison des sciences de l'homme.

Moussa, O. 1987. La culture arabo-islamique: Les Hausa du Sud-Cameroun (le cas de Yaoundé) et l'intégration nationale. Ph.D. diss., Université Sorbonne nouvelle-Paris III.

Otayek, R., ed. 1993. *Le radicalisme islamique au sud du Sahara: Da'wa, arabisation et critique de l'Occident*. Paris: Karthala.

Triaud, J.-L., and D. Robinson, eds. 2000. *La Tijaniyya: Une confrérie musulmane à la conquête de l'Afrique*. Paris: Karthala.

CHAPTER 13

NEGOTIATING FUTURES: ISLAM, YOUTH, AND THE STATE IN NIGER

Adeline Masquelier

Dogondoutchi, December 2004. It is Saturday night in this small rural town of southern Niger.[1] On a vast vacant lot where neighborhood boys routinely play impromptu games of football in the late afternoon and where, less frequently, girls in party uniforms dance to welcome political candidates campaigning for votes, a massive crowd of people has assembled around a makeshift podium. Though I spot groups of youthful men as well as women, both young and older, most of the attendees are senior men. Many of them are wearing the local *jaba*—a knee-length tunic worn over pants that has become the standard dress of pious Muslims. Standing on the podium, Malam Shaibou, a local preacher, is angrily denouncing "false" Muslims who worship only halfheartedly. He is a member of Izala, the reformist Islamic association that has organized the two-day proceedings, during which prominent preachers will deliver lectures in rapid succession—a special event whose format and content contrast markedly with the less-flamboyant weekly preaching at a local mosque. "There are people," Malam Shaibou declares accusingly,

> who say that they are Muslim. But [they are Muslim] only in words. Not in their hearts. If it is in dreams that they are Muslims, they should stop pretending. The Day of Judgment will come when God will reveal those who speak the truth and those who are liars!

His words, amplified yet also distorted by the substandard sound system hastily set up for the occasion, carry across the mud walls of nearby compounds to reach even those who do not wish to hear them. "There are people," Malam Shaibou continues,

> when there is a *wa'azi* [sermon], they don't come. But when there is *rawa* [dancing], they go. When there is a card game, they go. They go to bars, they go look for women. These people, God has created their bodies for the hottest hell. There's a *wa'azi* in the mosque, they also do *wa'azi* on television, but these people do not attend the *wa'azi* in the mosque, they do not watch the *wa'azi* on television. They are like wild animals.

A few paces away, behind the walls of an adjacent compound, a much different crowd—composed primarily of jeans-clad youths—is following with rapt attention the performance of a child actor whose spectacular dance-floor routine appears to come straight off MTV. In his tight-fitting white pants, red turtleneck, and black suspenders, the boy bears an uncanny resemblance to the younger Michael Jackson. When he breaks into Jackson's famous "moondance," the youthful audience bursts into applause. Their cheers, combined with the screechy music escaping from a gigantic cassette player, drown further the raspy voice of the preacher berating the masses for their lack of religious commitment. Other skits, some inspired by American hip hop culture, some more obviously rooted in the Nigerien repertoire, follow, while in the adjacent vacant lot, another preacher ascends the podium and starts evoking the tortures of hell to cultivate in his audience a stronger devotion to prophetic ideals. In the end, and despite the noisy interference of each with the other, both events—the sermon marathon held to remind Muslims of their religious duties and the musical show put on by a Nigerien theatrical company to entertain a youthful public—are, by all accounts, great successes.

Surveying the audience at both performances, one might conclude that whereas some people in Dogondoutchi are ostensibly Muslim, others, primarily youths, are not—or are less so. Though it is largely true that many youth neglect the practice of *salla* (prayers, from the Arabic *salat*) and that, as Malam Shaibou unequivocally put it, they would rather go dancing than attend a sermon, I argue that it is nonetheless problematic to state uncritically that youth are "less Muslim." Such a statement implies that because they do not visibly express piety, youth do not concern themselves with Islam. Such a perspective obfuscates rather than clarifies the importance of religion for youth by failing to distinguish religious identity (a sense of belonging to a religious community) from religiosity (the performance of religious acts). As Roy (2004) has recently pointed out, religion and religiosity do not necessarily go hand in hand. Some people may perceive religion to be an integral part of their cultural identity even though they do not regularly engage in acts of religiosity. For others, conversely, religiosity is more important than religion. A significant proportion of the Nigerien youths I will be discussing belong to the former category; that is to say, their self-definition is strongly shaped by a sense of belonging to the *umma* (the global Muslim community) despite the fact that they do not engage in explicitly pious actions (daily prayers, fasts, almsgiving, etc.). As we shall see, this shared sense of Muslim-hood has important implications for the way that young men relate to both the Nigerien state and the West as they struggle to gain a purchase on the newly emerging sociomoral as well as economic realities of the post-9/11 world.

If I evoked a moment ago the simultaneous and proximate unfolding of two events, one religious, the other irreligious—even heretical, in the eyes of some—it was not to suggest a contradiction between two systems of values but rather to highlight how distinct, and at times divergent, forms of religious expression can be shaped by markedly local dynamics of generation. If one were to single out a few young men from among the theatrical show's appreciative audience and ask them if they considered themselves Muslims, the response would undoubtedly be a resounding "yes." And this regardless of the fact that they might attend prayer only sporadically—as did a number of youths I interviewed in December 2004. Upon being further probed, some of them might even point out that being Muslim does not preclude listening to popular music, wearing Western attire, or attending theatrical performances. In this respect, they are often at odds with elders who complain that Nigerien youth should listen to religious sermons instead of rap music and exchange their foreign-made t-shirts and jeans for the less expensive *jaba* of devout Muslims. To such admonitions, unrepentant young men—oblivious as well to the bloodcurdling rhetoric of preachers of all persuasions—generally respond that being Muslim has little to do with one's choice of radio program or wardrobe. As they indulge their passion for popular culture by attending dance parties, watching soap operas, or dressing like rap artists, youths frequently invoke their immaturity in the defense of their lifestyle. They also point to the ways that things have changed, usually for the worse, for the young people of Niger, changes that have forced them to develop new strategies for survival and even to explore alternative careers in crime or in the counterculture of hip hop.[2] Although it is often motivated by a quest for a better, safer, and more ethical life, their embrace of hip hop styles and values is nonetheless lamented by Muslim parents and preachers who fear that core Islamic values are being increasingly threatened by the West.

It is precisely by recognizing the generational basis of emerging disagreements on what Islam might mean that we can begin to appreciate both the pluralistic nature of the Muslim landscape in Niger and the extent to which new forms of Muslim religiosity emerge in tandem with new models of personhood and public life, new modes of production, and new patterns of consumption. This means for our present purposes focusing on youth as a "social shifter" (Durham 2004)—a category that exists independently of the particular environment in which it is used at the same time that it is understood anew in relation to each specific situation in which it is invoked. Summoning the notion of social shifter helps us recognize not just the transitional nature of youth in structural terms but also the ways in which youth as a category is "always in the process of being remade in socio-political practice" (Durham 2004, 601).

Historically, popular and academic representations of youth have been riddled with stereotypes. When they were not seen as rebels, thugs, and perpetrators of physical assault that threatened the fragile fabric of society, youth were inevitably portrayed as powerless creatures, victimized by hunger, violence, and poverty. Whether they were perceived as disruptive agents or as vulnerable victims, they often were primarily understood as "members of a substandard and, ultimately, subservient and subcultural category" (Sharp 2002, 19). To challenge such conventional approaches, anthropologists have begun to focus on children as "social actors in their own right" (Stephens 1995, 23). As the rapidly expanding anthropological literature on youth has shown over the past few years, a focus on youth provides useful perspectives on the dynamics of intergenerational reproduction and change (Cole and Durham 2006; Honwana and de Boeck 2005). By virtue of their structural liminality and through their position as relational beings, young people are uniquely situated to develop new perspectives—"fresh contact," as Mannheim (1952) called it. As such, they can become significant actors in the struggle to define and speak for their generation.

On the African continent, youth has emerged as an especially salient category for addressing issues of authority, agency, and consciousness (Comaroff and Comaroff

1999; Diouf 2003; Reynolds 1995; Richards 1996; Weiss 2004). Nigerien youth, for instance, have much to say about what it means to be Muslim and what such under-standings of "being Muslim" entail for matters of common interest. In what follows, I examine how young Muslims in Dogondoutchi construct their Muslim identities in light of emerging generational debates that center on the notions of piety and prag-matism, the local and the global, and what I have called religion and religiosity. Despite repeated calls by radical Muslims for the eradication of un-Islamic practices that, they say, are ultimately responsible for the troubles of the modern world, being a Muslim has taken on a new sociopolitical, and at times more "secular," meaning for these youths at the beginning of the millennium. They are less insecure about their status as Muslims than their parents and elder siblings were a decade or so ago, less anxious as well to engage in visible displays of piety—though, as I have noted, this hardly means that they no longer define their roles as sons, citizens, husbands, or aspiring musicians through an Islamic system of value.

Islamic Reforms in Late Twentieth-Century Niger

Allow me to backtrack briefly. In the past decade and a half, harangues blaring from strategically placed loudspeakers have become familiar fixtures in Dogondoutchi, a town of some 38,000 people, some 97 percent of whom identify as Muslims. Whether they accuse youth of sexual promiscuity, castigate wives for neglecting their marital duties, or urge tradition-bound Muslims to abandon their "incorrect" prac-tices, the voices of Muslim clerics remonstrating with the faithful are heard in every neighborhood. Throughout Niger, this intensification of sermon delivery in the early nineties coincided with the emergence of an independent anti-Sufi movement, the Jama'at Izalat al-Bid'a wa Iqamat al-Sunna (that is, the Society for the Removal of Innovation and Reinstatement of the Sunna, or Izala for short), in a country that had, until then, been ostensibly oriented toward Sufism (Meunier 1998). Though only a minority of Nigerien Muslims are formally members of any Sufi order (*tariqa*), many are loosely identified as 'Yan Tariqa both because they adhere to certain Sufi practices and because they oppose Izala reformism. Aside from encouraging personal mystical experiences, Sufis approved the use of amulets and the performance of certain rituals (such as the celebration of the Prophet Muhammad's birthday), and promoted, along with the veneration of saintly figures, the redistributive ethos around which much of everyday life is ordered in communities such as Dogondoutchi.[3]

It was to eradicate these allegedly sinful "traditions" that Izala was founded in 1978 in Nigeria. Believing that the ills of the present were a consequence of the fail-ure to follow proper Qur'anic principles, Izala leaders condemned the perceived excesses of Sufi orders and their "corrupt" readings of the Qur'an (Gumi 1992; Kane 1994; Loimeier 1997; Umar 1993). As its name indicates, Izala advocates a return to a "pure" Islam and promotes conservative moral standards.[4] Because they urge those who call themselves Muslims to abandon all heresy, these reform-minded Muslims have been referred to as "fundamentalists" or "Islamists." I use the term "reformist" to describe the particular brand of anti-Sufism that has emerged in Niger. It is more in keeping with the movement's self-designation, which is centered on the suppression of undesirable innovations. Because they routinely invoke tradition to legitimize their

practices and justify their opposition to Izala, I refer to self-described Sufis and followers of particular *mallamai* (Muslim clerics) as "traditionalists." Though opposing
"reformists" and "traditionalists" vastly oversimplifies the fragmented nature of Islam
in Niger, people often understand religious diversity in such terms, and use them to
explain "correct" and "incorrect" Islamic practices.[5]

The Izala movement spread quickly, because of its ability to act as an oppositional
discourse to both the state and "traditionalist" Islam. Although Izala's vision of a lost
Golden Age was fervently embraced by devout Muslim elites, the movement secured
most of its following among the disenchanted (Masquelier 1996, 1999, forthcoming). In Niger, frustrated young men with few prospects welcomed Izala's denunciation of Sufi corruption, social hierarchy, and conspicuous consumption. They agreed
with Izala that Sufi scholars were greedy, questioned fathers' ascendancy over their
sons, and criticized the practices of "unenlightened" Muslims. Overall, the 1990s saw
a significant rise in young Nigerien men's participation in Islamic associations, a
process that produced a key moral discourse by which youth challenged the authority
of both government and elders.[6]

Fast forward to the new millennium. Rather than having recovered from the political instability of the earlier decade, the national economy has taken a deeper plunge.
In 2000, the newly elected government faced a virtually empty treasury, increased
debt, reduced revenue performance, and lower public investment. In a country where
75 percent of the population is under twenty-five years of age, young men are confronted with challenges of unprecedented magnitude in their search for jobs. The
massive reforms brought about by structural adjustment, the retreat of the state from
public life, and the collapse of patronage and other social institutions that had
insured a minimal redistribution of resources have drastically curtailed opportunities
for employment and, with them, access to marriage and full social maturity, as marriage routinely marks the transition to adulthood. Like youths elsewhere on the continent whose hopes of securing something like a future have been seriously curbed,
many young men in Dogondoutchi eke out a precarious living with little certainty of
ever overcoming marginalization. Regardless of their educational achievements, few
can hope to make a living through farming as their fathers did, and yet fewer, among
those who graduate from high school or university, will find permanent employment
as civil servants, unless they emigrate to more prosperous lands. Unable to find work
and to accumulate enough money to marry, a growing number of them spend their
lives as "social cadets" (Argenti 2002).

Dynamics of Inclusion and Exclusion

Although they are increasingly denied full participation in the Nigerien economy and
society, male youths have nonetheless been granted unprecedented emancipation
thanks to the global flows of commodities, information, and images that can now
be accessed with varying degrees of success even in the remotest areas of the Sahel.
The emergence of private radios and televisions—media in which Islam is discussed
outside the direct control of religious authority or the state—has, for instance,
enabled young Nigeriens to participate in debates on what it means to be a Muslim,
a citizen, or simply a youth with moral convictions. It has also encouraged the spread

of youth-oriented forms of musical and political expression.[7] Through the paradox of their structural position—in which "becoming part of the world . . . entail[s] becoming marginal to the world" (Weiss 2004, 8)—youths are well situated to confront problems of power, abuse, violence, and social dislocation, something which they do primarily, though not exclusively, through the medium of rap music. Many of them have also adopted the dress of hip hop artists; baggy pants, oversized t-shirts, ankle-high shoes, and baseball caps are now must-haves for any fashion-conscious young man aspiring to a cosmopolitan look. Predictably, rap music and the clothing trends it has fostered among young men have been condemned as anti-Islamic by Muslim elders. Muslim youths nonetheless justify their adoption of rap musical and sartorial styles by claiming that they are informed by new ethics and motivated by the existence of previously unknown "crises," such as government corruption and the AIDS pandemic—themes that feature prominently in the lyrics of local rap songs.

Countering Muslim clerics' claims that listening to rappers and looking like one are sure ways to experience the fiery tortures of hell—in part because listening to music risks interfering with the timely performance of prayers—young men insist that hip hop is, above all, educational. It is a medium of consciousness-raising and a platform for questioning the status quo in a country where widespread social inequities, corruption, and job scarcity are the norm. "Rap," eighteen-year-old Gabriel told me,

> is a form of awareness and it is also a form of denunciation. It denounces the things that people, like our leaders, are doing. Sometimes in their songs, rappers also try to comment on the values of youth. So, for instance, they'll point out that love is commercialized.

Aside from exposing the problems of youth, such as poverty and unemployment, rap songs, they claim, teach young people how to survive the dangers that they face in today's unforgiving world. More so perhaps than other forms of popular culture that have become ubiquitous in Niger, rap music is both for youth and about youth. This is precisely why, although most parents bemoan their children's choice of entertainment, many of them also leave them to their own devices, hoping that they will eventually move on. On this issue, young men partially agree with their parents. If they justify their immersion in rap culture by claiming that "it is what youth do," they just as quickly point out that when they grow up—that is, when they marry, produce children, and are granted the authority that comes with maturity—they will leave rap culture behind to focus on more "serious" things. Like Islam. "Old people, they don't like music," nineteen-year-old Hamissou pointed out:

> When you grow up, you leave music, you leave all these things. Music, it is the thing of youth [*music abin matasa na*]. Once you grow old, you leave the music so that the younger generation will respect you.

By their own admission, embracing rap is, as some parents suspect, a way for youth to "rebel against tradition by lashing out [at] the old" (Gable 2000, 195). There is, of course, nothing surprising about this. Indeed, the "young" are conventionally perceived as the vectors of modernity and associated with all that is revolutionary, from fashion to technology. Only by flouting the rules during their immature years do individuals learn to respect those rules as they move toward social seniority. Not letting them rebel against tradition has its price. As a local saying has it, "A youth who does not enjoy his youth will make up for it in old age." Because the rebelliousness of youth is perceived as necessary in the pursuit of seniority, some parents do not chastise their children for not following Islam rigorously.[8] But if they consider the "rebelliousness" of their rap-obsessed children normal, they nonetheless worry that rap-centered practices may bring about the collapse of their moral world, as Izala preachers insist will happen if these practices are not promptly abandoned.

Situational Ethics

Youth, on the other hand, are more worried about their material than their spiritual future. As the proportion of educated, underemployed, and unmarried youth grows, the likelihood that they will satisfy the social aspirations that their parents' generation took for granted is shrinking (Masquelier 2005; O'Brien 1996). As awareness of their predicament sinks in, youths look for means to take charge of their future. Hoping to influence future national policies that may directly affect them, some have become involved in politics and did so especially in the months preceding the 2004 presidential and legislative elections. If political engagement is widely seen as a means of enhancing one's chance of securing a future,[9] participation in the promotion of Islam is not. For frustrated young men who see their country's future increasingly imperiled by poverty and chaos, Islam offers limited professional opportunities. A young man whose father was a prominent Sufi cleric put it this way: "There is no opportunity within Islam. Those who study the Qur'an in Qur'anic schools, they don't have jobs either, some have even left for the university." That Islam appears to provide no practical solutions to the problem of youth unemployment is partly due, I suspect, to the widespread suspicion of "traditionalist" Muslim clerics—often described as corrupt cynics who use religion to extort resources from impoverished neighbors. Note that Izala was instrumental in denouncing as unethical the *mallamai* who accepted alms from much poorer household heads than they. Even if they do not affiliate with Izala, many youths have been persuaded by its socialistic ideology of money management. If they do not follow these principles when it comes to acquiring, say, an expensive pair of sneakers, many are nonetheless ready to revisit the ethics of alms to ensure that resources are equitably distributed among the *really* needy.

Although—save for some notable exceptions—Islam no longer provides profitable careers in education or religious leadership, it remains the central means of redefining the terms and boundaries of moral community. Whether or not they pray regularly, fast during Ramadan, and in general conduct themselves in a recognizably Muslim manner, Dogondoutchi youths—except for the small Christian minority and a handful who have opted to participate in *bori* practices of spirit possession—consider themselves Muslims. They see themselves as belonging to a worldwide community whose members are united by their submission to God and their performance of religious duties. For members of Izala, this focus on global Islam implies the emergence of a "new universal community that can bypass and transcend the failure of past models" (Roy 2004, 13) as well as provide an alternative to the morally bankrupt system of Western values. Indeed, for youths who joined Izala in the early 1990s, much of the appeal of the Wahhabist doctrine[10] (focused on the purification of Islamic practices) resided in its universalist conception of an Islam that surpassed local limitations and identified with the wider Muslim world (Brenner 1993). "Traditionalists," too, routinely emphasize Islam's unity rather than its fractious nature, pointing out that all Muslims are inspired by the same Qur'anic message and that Izala is not a new religion (as it was once thought) but simply an association.

That a sense of a common Muslim identity prevails over ritual and doctrinal differences for a growing number of residents is neatly summed up in the comment of a pious sixty-year-old woman: "There are no differences, only disputes"—a probable allusion to the previous conflicts between members of Izala and "traditionalists." Izala members and "traditionalists" now widely agree that they share the same religion. Yet few among the older generation have forgotten the terrible clashes of the 1990s, provoked by Izala's efforts to discredit local Muslim "traditions" (Masquelier 1999). Today in Dogondoutchi, verbal assaults and physical confrontations have given way to more civil interactions and a recognition that people should try to coexist peacefully despite religious differences—though Izala-led riots have broken out in neighboring cities to denounce, for instance, the immorality of Western dress (Masquelier 2002).

Having come of age in a more tolerant time, contemporary youths want nothing to do with the "petty" sectarian disputes that once absorbed their elders' attention. Their own recognition of Islam's transcendental unity is more literal and assertive. In the previous generation, the swift rise of Izala and the concomitant emergence of public debates regarding the authenticity of certain religious practices (such as the celebration of the Prophet's birthday) confused those who were unprepared to question previously immutable Islamic "truths"; but today, youthful Muslims are confident in their identities. The violence that once engulfed Niger is for them a thing of the past, and the criticisms that preachers on both sides still occasionally level at each other are frivolous and of no consequence. "Among the *mallamai* there are problems, but among youths there are none [*babu masala*]," a secondary school student once explained to me. To stress the extent to which divisions have become generational rather than strictly religious, his friend flatly concluded, "it is the elders who have issues, they hate each other." As well as insisting that they had better things to do than argue about praying styles, educated youths periodically reminded me that Niger was a secular state where everyone was free to practice their religion. In Niger, I was repeatedly told, people are tolerant.[11]

What this means, more concretely, is that although they retain a self-conscious sense of doctrine and ritual, the younger generation of Muslims no longer feels the need to legitimize the sectarian roots of their faith as visibly as their parents did a decade or so ago. If the older generation of reform-minded 'Yan Izala has retained their turbans, their ankle-length pants, and their beards, their young successors are less eager to don so visibly the mantle of piety. Few wear a beard and even fewer don turbans. If they wear a *jaba* to pray, so do countless other youths who do not claim to be part of Izala. As a result, it has become difficult to sartorially distinguish a member of Izala from a follower of what I have called "traditionalist" Islam. Youth, in my experience, rarely argue about religious issues. Nor do they challenge each other over, say, the superiority of one style or schedule of prayer over another. Indifferent to the sectarian distinctions that once provoked deep enmity among their elders, they forge friendships, professional ties, and even political alliances across religious affiliations on the basis of their belief that Islam should unite, rather than divide, Muslims. This is not to say, of course, that young members of Izala no longer wish to rally every Muslim to their association or that the most reform-minded among them have stopped condemning listening to music as a sinful, Satan-inspired activity. Rather, mindful of how earlier disagreements over what constituted "proper" Islam tore the town apart, young Dogondoutchi residents are choosing not to focus on what separates them religiously, sartorially, or even socially. For most of those who, regardless of their religious affiliations, have sat next to each other in the classrooms of the local public school and are aware of larger social problems, such as AIDS, poverty, and unemployment, differences in devotional practices do not authorize quarrels among Muslims. As Hassan, an unemployed youth, commented, "I pray, all my friends pray. We talk together regardless of our [religious] differences. When the time of prayer comes, we go to our respective mosques. It's not a problem."

Hassan and his friends acknowledged interrupting their activities to take part in daily prayers, as every "good" Muslim should, but many others are widely suspected of forgetting their religious duties. Indeed, local clerics of the likes of Malam Shaibou routinely berate young men for ignoring the call to prayer when their favorite television shows or musical programs are on. I was often told that if prayer coincided with a popular television series, young people would opt to turn on the television. "It is only after [the show] is over that they remember prayer," a Muslim cleric complained. The issue of the timing of prayer flared up when members of Izala insisted that the "traditional" prayer schedule adopted by local Muslims was incorrect. They created a schedule of their own, in which two of the five daily prayers took place roughly fifteen minutes before "traditionalist" prayers. Arguing that the Prophet had remarked that "praying on time" was the most important obligation of a Muslim, they warned followers and foes alike that exactitude in worship was a good way of ensuring one's place in paradise. In a country where punctuality can allegedly determine one's eternal fate, young men's reluctance to pray on time, or at all, is seen by elders as a distressing sign of their characteristic impiety.

Youth occasionally admit to living with significant compromise. Yet most do not want, for instance, to give up rap music for the sake of looking more "Muslim." They insist that wearing baggy jeans does not prevent one from praying. Several informants described piety to me as an intensely personal attitude that was not motivated by one's appearance—and argued that therefore it did not matter what clothes one wore while praying as long as they were clean—and others told me that as long as they accomplished the five daily prayers, they felt entitled to partake of worldly pleasures. For many of them, adapting to changing socioeconomic realities has meant satisfying their needs and aspirations as consumers—even if such strategies are widely perceived as symptomatic of a lack (or loss) of piety and seriousness. Mindful of the limitations of cultural models that equate consumption with triviality (Miller 1994), I suggest that youths' ostentatious consumption of hip hop culture in an age of economic collapse must be understood as a strategy of identity making that roots consumers in an imaginary, better elsewhere. Like other African youth who have embraced hip hop styles and attitudes in an effort to redefine their relation to the wider world (Weiss 2002), young Nigerien men do not express a prior orientation or identity so much as create it through the performance of a "cultural style" (Ferguson 1999).

This process of identity making is not antithetical to their sense of being Muslim, despite the fact that youths who aspire to a Western lifestyle are often the ones who profess to loathe the West the most—an issue to which I will return. Put differently, young Muslims may be continually engaged in makeshift compromises but they see no contradiction in their casual invocation of different levels of self-identity to justify their actions. As they see it, the world is increasingly devoid of opportunities, so one must be open-minded enough to consider—and occasionally grab—whatever comes one's way, for the sake of survival. Those who are hampered by an excessively dogmatic vision of Islam will not make it in today's world. *Flexibility*, then, is the key to securing the often contradictory and increasingly tenuous promises of the current neoliberal moment when one lives in one of the world's poorest nations. By waiting for their favorite radio shows or soap operas to be over before making their way to the prayer grounds, youths restrict Islamic practices to specific spaces and temporalities, apart from the realm of "secular," Western-inspired practices, and they carefully negotiate their way between these two domains. They have become "pragmatic" Muslims.

For pragmatic Muslims, there is a time to demonstrate one's devotion to God— through prayer—and a time to fulfill other imperatives, such as the mundane concerns of modern existence. From this perspective, ethical behavior is *situational* rather than immutable. I once asked a young man who wore a baseball cap how he felt about local clerics' injunction that youthful Muslims stop wearing these "American" hats because they were anti-Islamic. He first looked offended by the question before answering curtly, "This is my *maganin rana*!" (protection against the sun). Whether he was parodying those who invoke practical rules of pietistic conduct for everything they do or simply stating the truth, what is significant is that he denied any hint of impropriety on his part by resolutely summoning the most pragmatic of reasons for wearing such "wicked" headgear. Muslims routinely invoke their health to justify what might otherwise seem to be a violation of some Qur'anic principle. For instance, breaking one's fast is not a sin if one does it to preserve one's health, and drinking alcohol can similarly be justified if it is done for medicinal purposes. By cleverly invoking the need to protect his head from the sun, the young enthusiast of Western fashion was eschewing any suggestion that the baseball cap he wore could be construed as un-Islamic. His choice of words was not fortuitous: *maganin*, which I translated as "protection against," literally means "medicine for." Like his contemporaries who routinely pointed out to me that the Brazilian and Mexican soap operas they watched on television were more useful than sermons because they were educational (see also Larkin 1997) and more in tune with the concerns of contemporary youth, he eloquently demonstrated how Muslim youths combine piety with pragmatism in their struggle to participate in the definition of Islamic modernity. If he remained unconditionally committed to Islam at one level, at another, more practical level his participation in Islam, like that of many Nigerien youths I met in 2004, was largely situational, informed by a pragmatic knowledge of the exigencies of life on the margins of the Muslim world.

For Islam and Against the West

Among youths who pray regularly, some, rather than remaining faithful to a particular mosque,[12] attend *salla* (prayer) at the mosque that is nearest to where they find themselves when they are summoned by the call to prayer—regardless of whether that mosque is claimed by "traditionalists" or by members of Izala. They generally justify themselves by invoking convenience—it is easier to walk to the nearest mosque. Yet it would be a mistake, I think, not to see this practice as an explicit effort to demonstrate the extent to which the youthful Muslim community has been able to transcend internal divisions. Because the mosque is the place of God, I was often told, it matters little what "affiliation" one has.[13] What is important in the performance of one's religious duty is the actual act of prayer, not the place where that prayer occurs. That youths do not exclude each other on the basis of religious difference, but instead consciously opt to transcend factional boundaries through their choice of prayer sites as well as friends, speaks to the compromises that many have made as they negotiate their participation in what they hope will be a renewed moral order. A significant proportion of young men belong to informal discussion groups known as *fada* that meet regularly at a set location. As members of *fada* with evocative names such as Sa majesté, Internationale des chômeurs, or Bel air, young men listen to popular music, drink tea, and share their concerns, frustrations, and aspirations with one another. Membership in these youth groups cuts across social strata, educational backgrounds, and religious affiliations: secondary school students mingle with their unlettered and sporadically employed counterparts, sons of wealthy households share their resources with less fortunate friends, and all, regardless of their nominal religious affiliations, enjoy each other's company.

For a majority of youths, the notion of a common Muslim identity also means that, whether or not they engage in pious activities, they are "for Islam." More often than not, indeed, they are unconditionally so. Thus, at a time when the Israeli–Palestinian conflict and the invasion of Iraq have crystallized anti-U.S. sentiments among so many Muslim youths, young Nigeriens throughout the country find themselves loudly cheering for Osama bin Laden. After September 11, many celebrated the end of the "evil empire," and t-shirts bearing pictures of the infamous terrorist sold quickly. Boys and girls enthusiastically purchased flip-flops whose upper soles were adorned with a picture of the World Trade Center's burning towers, so that they could stamp on the graphic symbol of America's financial hegemony a thousand times a day. Today, numerous male children born since 9/11 bear the name Osama— ironically enough, a name that, while not in use before, sounds very Hausa. Parents do not, however, want it to be understood that way. After a baby born in December 2004 was named Osama by his father, his mother informally renamed him Osama bin Laden lest there be any ambiguity about whom he was *really* named after.

By providing (through its dual role as the global bully and the victim of retaliation) a blatant confirmation that the world is starkly divided into Muslims and their enemies, the U.S. has emerged as a new focus of Muslim anger—something it was not before the tragic events of 9/11, except in the moralizing discourses of Izala reformists who have long seen the West as a cradle of impiety and decadence. Being "for Islam" sometimes has little to do with faith and religiosity and everything to do with solidarity, as this comment by an eighteen-year-old shows:

> When bin Laden attacked America, all the Muslims of Niger were happy. They think that all Americans are pagans, and since bin Laden is a Muslim, they like him, they like everything he does. They support him.

From this perspective, joining the al-Qaeda movement, even if only in spirit, has become the *duty* of every Muslim, for Muslims must unite against their aggressors. Predictably, youths routinely justified their support of bin Laden by an appeal to Islam. It was all, they said, because of Islam: "Bin Laden is a Muslim. It is because he is a Muslim that he attacked America. And this is why we like him."

In the eyes of many Nigerien youths, 9/11 was the U.S.'s well-deserved punishment for its tyrannical domination of Muslim lands. At the practical level, the jihadist cause promoted by al-Qaeda is largely irrelevant to the struggles of ordinary Muslims for a better life. Yet, as De Waal (2004, 50) notes, jihadism's "failures as a positive political project do not undermine its appeal as a banner of resistance." This is why some youths assured me that if bin Laden ever called on them to fight for the Muslim cause, they would follow him. As one of them put it, "Bin Laden is a big man. If I were over there, I would be with bin Laden. I swear." However, even if bin Laden's spectacular terrorist acts and his "rhetoric that pits the dispossessed Muslim world against America and its puppets" (De Waal 2004, 19) have captured the political imagination of Muslims the world over, they have not, at least in Dogondoutchi, provoked widespread emigration to Afghanistan, Chechnya, or Iraq. Ironically, among the youths I met in 2004, those who most vocally articulated their hatred of the U.S. on the grounds that Americans were "against Muslims" were often the first to express a desire to emigrate to America. How then do we reconcile this manifest loathing for U.S. moral and political values with the widespread aspiration to emigrate to America?

What seems like a contradiction may not be one if we focus once more on the notion of "situational ethics." For young Nigeriens, emigrating to America has nothing to do with moral convictions and everything to do with economic survival. Now that the state can no longer guarantee economic security to its citizens, it behooves them to try to make a future for themselves, even if that means temporarily living in a country of "pagans." For young Muslims who have grown up in the shadows of America's growing dominance over world affairs, such a strategy may require some adjustments, but it should not compromise their moral integrity. Furthermore, if every young man dreams of making it big in the U.S., few have really thought of what such a move might entail at the practical level.

Many youths are profoundly ambivalent about what the West, and the U.S. in particular, has come to represent. While they hope to emigrate to the "land where everyone is rich" and see America as a vital source of cultural capital, they are also keenly aware that, as Muslims, they belong to the *umma*, and must therefore unconditionally oppose the hegemony of the morally bankrupt U.S. In the end, as they consider the choices they must make, practicality prevails. There is a time to express Muslim solidarity and denounce the American oppressors, and then there is a time when economic survival and a chance of earning a social position become more important than moral solidarity.

Muslim Youth and the State

To make sense of the surge of enthusiasm that Osama bin Laden and his attacks on U.S. soil generated among Nigerien youth, one must situate it in the context of youthful discontent with the national policies of a secular government that is widely blamed for the "crisis" in which the younger generation finds itself. Regardless of their religious affiliations, young Nigeriens are thoroughly frustrated with the state's failure to improve the country's troubled educational system and to provide jobs for high school and university graduates; the civil service sector is facing drastic budgetary cuts. They feel particularly victimized by the latest policies implemented by the administration to fight unemployment, and they are angry at the way that the on-going crisis at the University of Niamey has been (mis)handled, resulting in a series of canceled academic years (see Masquelier 2004).

Hoping to influence the political orientation of their country, many Dogondoutchi youths became involved in the presidential campaign of 2004. Youthful members of Izala rallied around Mahamadou Issoufou, the Socialist candidate and leader of the PNDS (Parti nigérien pour la démocratie et le socialisme), whom they saw as more concerned with the predicament of youth.[14] Given Izala's decidedly populist orientation, it is not surprising that so many of its members voted for Issoufou. The PNDS was widely believed to be closely associated with Muslim reformists—so much so, in fact, that many "traditionalist" Muslim elders opted not to vote for Issoufou, despite their approval of his political program, because they feared that a PNDS victory would ultimately mean more power for Izala and perhaps open the door to drastic religious reforms.

If many youthful members of Izala actively participated in Issoufou's presidential campaign, they did so alongside other young Muslims who shared their problems and their preoccupations. Thus, while Izala overwhelmingly supported the PNDS party, nonmembers of Izala, equally worried about their future and eager to do away with a government they perceived as corrupt and irresponsible, also voted for and, in some cases, campaigned for the Socialist candidate. In the end, Issoufou lost the election and the incumbent, Mamadou Tandja of the MNSD (Mouvement national pour la société de développement), was reelected. Despite the defeat of the candidate favored by the younger generation, the election confirmed youths' emergence as social actors in the public sphere. It also demonstrated to what remarkable degree they were united by a common struggle against poverty and unemployment. Though not all of them display, like members of Izala, an overriding concern with revitalizing local Islamic practices by encouraging a stronger commitment to the teaching of the Qur'an, they nonetheless share a vision of a more fiscally responsible, kinder society attentive to the needs of the underprivileged and the younger generation.

A number of youths see being actively engaged in politics not just as a way of contributing to the political life of the country but also as a means of developing themselves—and ultimately of enhancing their chance of escaping poverty. In the context of widespread debates about *l'avenir de la jeunesse* (the future of youth), notions of progress and development are gaining widespread currency, as the following testimony by a university graduate makes clear:

> Youths are implicated in politics because they want to move forward. Those who are not in politics, they remain within their poverty. They cannot move forward. You must participate in politics in order to receive progress.

This desire to be politically active is also motivated by a conviction that the government is misappropriating national resources for its own fraudulent use, and that it must be held in check and its agents punished. Through their scathing critiques of the government, Nigeriens, young and old, provide a moralizing discourse in which corruption is assimilated to a sin perpetrated by "bad" Muslims. As one man explained,

> Muslim clerics, when it does not rain, they say that it's because there is no understanding between people. But when we don't even have millet to sow in our fields, the government does not give us anything. This help that neighboring countries give to the poor people of Niger, it means nothing since we never see it. The government, they are not good Muslims. They do not see the poor and they keep everything [for themselves].

In a post-9/11 world where the experience of poverty and crisis is routinely articulated—most notably by preachers—in terms of Manichaean sentiments, Islam actively shapes the emerging Nigerien public sphere by providing a moral framework for scrutinizing not just social arrangements but also the public conduct of elected officials. "A big man," one member of Izala explained,

> must look behind [to see the little ones who follow him], but the president, he does not look behind him. You must look to see if the little one behind you has eaten. Our president, he does not follow Islam.

Just as it allows disenfranchised youth to feel connected to bin Laden and to sympathize with the cause of jihadists everywhere on the grounds that, because they oppose the U.S., they must be "good" Muslims, Islam also provides a means of assessing the moral worth of public officials—who, as puppets of foreign administrations, rarely do what is best for their constituency. Because the government is widely perceived to flout basic Qur'anic principles, young men feel justified in opposing the state. With the state largely unable to enforce legislation and provide for its citizens, Islam has more than ever become a source of moral order and a mode of social engagement for Nigerien youth.

If Islam shapes their opposition to the corrupt state, it only rarely serves as a justification for its removal. At a time when the issue of whether or not to apply sharia has gained momentum in local debates, youthful critics of the state focus not so much on the deficiencies of the political system as on the depravity of its agents. Though they are aware of the government's inefficiency, they paradoxically still expect the state to "do something" to pull them out of the economic and academic morass in which they find themselves. Even as they admit that the government is unable to institute far-reaching reforms that will benefit young citizens, they still operate on the assumption that the state is empowered to substantially improve their educational and economic prospects. As they see it, if their demands are not met and change is not forthcoming, it is because the government is indifferent to the plight of youth. By acknowledging that the state is incapable of fixing the "crisis" that affects so many of its citizens while paradoxically calling on it to intervene on behalf of the "at risk" generation, Nigerien youths construct the state as both an extremely important and a highly irrelevant feature of their lives.

Conclusion

For Nigerien youths confronted with the state's failure to provide employment and educational services, the quest for a prosperous future has been increasingly imperiled despite Muslim reformists' concerted efforts to purify society of its "wasteful" practices, promote resource conservation, and generate new forms of social services. As they struggle to make something of themselves, some youths end up flouting rules and circumventing conventional circuits of exchange to ensure economic survival whereas others opt for political activism to enhance their economic prospects. Regardless of how they capitalize on new possibilities, many have made significant social and moral compromises, compromises that rarely meet with elders' approval, especially when they are perceived as a threat to Islamic values. Yet, even as they selectively adhere to some tenets of Islam while rejecting others (or ignore most of them altogether), their search for a visible identity is inescapably rooted in a sense of Muslimhood. Besides pointing to the pivotal role of youth in processes of social and religious transformation, these trends illustrate how Islam provides a moral framework for scrutinizing contemporary society. They also show the extent to which, through a process of objectification (Eickelman and Piscatori 1996), "religion" has become an object of individual scrutiny. At a time when the state no longer controls the definition of public interests, and the production of a Nigerien citizenry has become fraught with ambiguity, Islam emerges as a crucial element of identity construction for young Dogondoutchi residents struggling to redefine themselves. Though it offers limited professional opportunities (despite the renewed emphasis on the importance of religious education), it is an important means of claiming moral superiority.

Throughout the Muslim world, Eickelman and Anderson note (1999, 7), "increasingly vocal debates on what it means to be a Muslim and to live a Muslim life frequently translate in highly divergent ways from one context to another." Now that an assertive Muslim identity no longer necessarily hinges on the "discourse of truth and ignorance" (Brenner 2001) that only a decade and a half ago helped fragment the Nigerien religious landscape, "being Muslim" for youth often assumes a less restrictive meaning, and one that has been transformed through its association with entertainment culture (see Abu-Lughod 1998; Vries and Weber 2001; Meyer and Moors 2006). Through their embrace of hip hop style and values, young Nigerien men invoke the right to be different from their elders. Although elders often lament these practices, youths contend that they do not contradict the basic tenets of Islam. What this means, as we focus on the imaginative ways in which young Nigerien avidly "consume" (Appadurai 1996) modernity to reinvent themselves as Muslims, as youth, and as citizens, is that there is no consensus on how to define "Islamic" attire, "Islamic" entertainment, or even "Islamic activity." As Huq (1999) has noted in her discussion of Bangladeshi literature, "Islamic" in this context becomes a volatile signifier, but one that is nonetheless indispensable to the public performance of identity.

When making sense of these new posturings toward Islam, we can no longer ignore the impact of the attack on the World Trade Center on Muslim subjectivities. The events of 9/11 helped focus what had been relatively dispersed recriminations about unemployment, poverty, and marginality. Even youths who maintained no connections to the Izala association, or even professed to be against it, now read their experience of crisis through the lens of 9/11 and the Manichaean world that has emerged in its wake. Their Muslim identity is expressed not by performing prayers but by professing to be on the side of bin Laden and the global Muslim community. Aside from demonstrating that the "very nature of Islam itself as a religion . . . depends as much on 'non-Muslims' as it does on Muslims themselves" (Launay 1992, 76), these strategic positionings point to the need to understand emerging Muslim identities beyond the dichotomy of Sufis (or "traditionalists") versus "reformists" conventionally used to categorize them.

In this chapter, I have tried to do that by focusing on generation and generational change. Demographically, politically, and religiously speaking, youth is a force to contend with in Niger. Battle lines over issues ranging from fashion to education to the performance of piety tend to be generational, with young men's activities being understood by their seniors as un-Islamic and revolutionary. Because youth is techni- cally a stage of life, one is expected to outgrow one's youthful tendencies. Indeed, youths I talked to indicated that their current "impiety" was only temporary and that, come forty, they would become better Muslims, as much to provide proper role mod- els for their future children as to ensure their own salvation. Although this suggests that we should not lose sight of the continuities, it hardly implies that the futures of young Nigeriens are predictable—or, for that matter, viable. In the end, the develop- ment of Islam in Niger is intimately connected to the ways in which and the extent to which youths will be able to shape their future.

Notes

This chapter was written as part of the African Studies Centre, Leiden/Centre d'étude d'Afrique noire, Bordeaux project "Islam, the Disengagement of the State, and Globalization in Sub-Saharan Africa," which was funded by the Netherlands Ministry of Foreign Affairs, The Hague. Research in Niger was carried out in November and December 2004. Special thanks to Benjamin Soares and René Otayek for being the driving force behind the project since its inception. This chapter benefited from their close readings. I also thank Salifou Hamidou for his generous assistance in the field. I am indebted to Shoshanna Green for her editorial assistance. My greatest debt, as always, is to the people of Dogondoutchi for their hospitality, their guidance, and their willingness to share their lives with me.

1. The residents of Dogondoutchi are largely Mawri, a local subgroup of the larger ethnic entity conventionally referred to as Hausa. In this respect, they identify with the

Hausa-speaking Muslim residents of northern Nigeria. In Dogondoutchi, however, the appellation "Hausa" is reserved for northern Nigerians, in contrast to ethnic categories such as Mawri, Gobirawa, Aderawa, which apply to more specifically situated populations of Hausa-speaking Nigeriens.

2. While a great number of Dogondoutchi residents of all ages engage in smuggling to make ends meet, routinely crossing the southern border to bring Nigerian goods into Niger or importing cars or kitchen appliances from Benin, some youths participate in the more lucrative drug trade.

3. The two major orders in Niger are the Tijaniyya and the Qadiriyya. Uthman dan Fodio, founder of the Sokoto caliphate, was a member of the Qadiriyya. Many of the wealthiest merchants of Niger belong to this order. The Tijaniyya order was introduced into Niger later by Tijanis from Nigeria.

4. Common to all fundamentalist and reformist movements, Roy (2004, 11) and others have noted, "is a quest to define a pure religion beyond time and space."

5. See Meunier (1998), who also presents a third category, the "rationalists," composed of mainly French-educated Muslims who consider Islam a personal religion.

6. I do not mean to imply that these are the only two alternatives for Nigeriens in search of a Muslim identity. In Dogondoutchi specifically, a novel form of Sufism has emerged, running officially counter to both "traditionalist" Islam and the reformist movement, that borrows both from conventional Sufi performances of piety and from Izala's concern with frugality and asceticism. Elsewhere in Niger, the religious landscape is similarly divided. On the plurality of Islamic discourses and perspectives and the proliferation of competing Islamic organizations in Niger and Nigeria, see Charlick 2004; Glew 1996; and Umar 2001.

7. The role of media in the dissemination of models of religious reform and counterreform and in the contestation of religious authority has been amply documented elsewhere. See Eickelman and Anderson 1999; Hirschkind 2001a and 2001b; and Meyer and Moors 2006.

8. Predictably, those who insist that their children engage in regular worship are likely to be members of Izala, anxious to foster a strong sense of piety among their progeny.

9. It is difficult, however, to identify the factors that motivate political participation, especially among youths. During the 2004 campaigns, candidates, hoping to gain votes, courted youths with gifts of tea, sugar, and radio-cassette players. Young men told me that they had voted for a particular candidate because, thanks to the gift of a boom box or money for a thatched shelter, they perceived that individual to be particularly aware of their predicament.

10. I use the term "*Wahhabist*" to suggest the ways in which Saudi Arabia has become the model of an Islamic society, which local reformists aim to emulate. Though they do not call themselves Wahhabis, they constantly refer to Saudi Arabia as both the spiritual and geographic center of the *umma* and as the source of "true" Islam. As Soares (2005) notes, however, the term has been misused in West Africa by a French colonial administration frequently suspicious of the threat that "reformists" of all kinds presented to the stability of the colonies.

11. To make their points, informants would often contrast the civility of Nigeriens with the "savagery" of their southern neighbors.

12. Mosques need not be architecturally fancy and can even be humble prayer grounds, delineated by a single row of stones and covered by prayer mats.

13. This issue is all the more significant given that, in 1992, a violent dispute erupted between local members of Izala and "traditionalist" Muslims over the ownership of Dogondoutchi's great mosque, the site of Friday prayers (see Masquelier 1999). Because the mosque is the most visible symbol of a Muslim community, control of a mosque has important political implications. Soon after the brutal confrontation in the mosque, members of Izala started building a large new mosque near the town's Friday market.

14. One member of Izala explained to me:

> We are members of the PNDS because we like this party. Not because we have been given gifts or because we want to receive stuff. We are members of this party because Issoufou has a program, an attractive program which will benefit the people of Niger. Especially youth.

References

Abu-Lughod, Lila. 1998. The marriage of feminism and Islamism in Egypt: Selective repudiation as a dynamic of postcolonial politics. In *Remaking women: Feminism and modernity in the Middle East*, ed. Lila Abu-Lughod, 243–69. Princeton: Princeton University Press.

Appadurai, Arjun. 1996. *Modernity at large: Cultural dimensions of globalization*, Minneapolis: Minnesota University Press.

Argenti, Nicolas. 2002. Youth in Africa: A major resource for change. In *Young Africa: Realizing the rights of children and youth*, ed. Alex De Waal. Lawrenceville: Africa World Press.

Brenner, Louis. 1993. Constructing Muslim identities in Mali. In *Muslim identity and social change in sub-Saharan Africa*, ed. Louis Brenner, 59–78. Bloomington: Indiana University Press.

———. 2001. *Controlling knowledge: Religion, power, and schooling in a West African Muslim society*. Bloomington: Indiana University Press.

Charlick, Robert B. 2004. Niger. *African Studies Review* 47 (2): 97–108.

Cole, Jennifer, and Deborah Durham. 2006. Age, regeneration, and the intimate politics of globalization. In *Generations and globalization: Youth, age, and family in the new world economy*, ed. Jennifer Cole and Deborah Durham. Bloomington: Indiana University Press.

Comaroff, Jean, and John L. Comaroff. 1999. Occult economies and the violence of abstraction: Notes from the South African postcolony. *American Ethnologist* 26 (2): 279–303.

De Waal, Alex, ed. 2004. *Islamism and its enemies in the Horn of Africa*. Bloomington: Indiana University Press.

Diouf, Mamadou. 2003. Engaging postcolonial cultures: African youth and public space. *African Studies Review* 46 (2): 1–12.

Durham, Deborah. 2004. Disappearing youth: Youth as a social shifter in Botswana. *American Ethnologist* 31 (4): 589–605.

Eickelman, Dale F., and John W. Anderson, eds. 1999. *New media in the Muslim world: The emerging public sphere*. Bloomington: Indiana University Press.

Eickelman, Dale F., and James Piscatori. 1996. *Muslim politics*. Princeton: Princeton University Press.

Ferguson, James. 1999. *Expectations of modernity: Myths and meanings of urban life on the Zambian copperbelt*. Berkeley: University of California Press.

Gable, Eric. 2000. The Culture Development Club: Youth, neo-tradition, and the construction of society in Guinea-Bissau. *Anthropology Quarterly* 73 (4): 195–203.

Glew, Robert S. 1996. Islamic associations in Niger. *Islam et sociétés au sud du Sahara* 10: 187–204.

Gumi, Sheikh A. 1992. *Where I stand*. Lagos: Spectrum Books Limited.

Hirschkind, Charles. 2001a. Civic virtue and religious reason: An Islamic counterpublic. *Cultural Anthropology* 16 (1): 3–34.

———. 2001b. The ethics of listening: Cassette-sermon audition in contemporary Egypt. *American Ethnologist* 28 (3): 623–49.

Honwana, Alcinda, and Filip de Boeck, eds. 2005. *Makers and breakers: Children and youth as emergent categories in postcolonial Africa*. London: James Currey.

Huq, Maimuna. 1999. From piety to romance: Islam-oriented texts in Bangladesh. In *New media in the Muslim world: The emerging public sphere*, ed. Dale F. Eickelman and John W. Anderson, 133–61. Bloomington: Indiana University Press.

Kane, Ousmane. 1994. Izala: The rise of Muslim reformism in northern Nigeria. In *Accounting for fundamentalisms*, ed. Martin E. Marty and R. Scott Appleby, 488–510. Chicago: University of Chicago Press.

Larkin, Brian. 1997. Indian films and Nigerian lovers: Media and the creation of parallel modernities. *Africa* 67 (3): 406–39.

Launay, Robert. 1992. *Beyond the stream: Islam and society in a West African town.* Berkeley: University of California Press.

Loimeier, Roman. 1997. Islamic reform and political change: The example of Abubakar Gumi and the 'Yan Izala movement in northern Nigeria. In *African Islam and Islam in Africa: Encounters between Sufis and Islamists*, ed. David Westerlund and Eva Evers Rosander, 286–307. Athens: Ohio University Press.

Mannheim, Karl. 1952. The problem of generations. In *Essays on the sociology of knowledge*, by Karl Mannheim, ed. Paul Kecskemeti, 276–320. London: Routledge and Kegan Paul.

Masquelier, Adeline. 1996. Identity, alterity, and ambiguity in a Nigerien community: Competing definitions of true Islam. In *Postcolonial identities in Africa*, ed. Richard Werbner, 222–44. London: Zed Press.

———. 1999. Debating Muslims, disputed practices: Struggles for the realization of an alternative moral order in Niger. In *Civil society and the political imagination in Africa: Critical perspectives*, ed. John L. Comaroff and Jean Comaroff, 219–50. Chicago: University of Chicago Press.

———. 2002. Of fashion and fission: Intra-Muslim violence in postcolonial Niger. Paper presented at the annual meeting of the Society for the Anthropology of Religion, Cleveland, Ohio, April 5–7.

———. 2004. Youthful reflections on the state: Power, protest, and pedagogical policies in Islamic Niger. Paper presented at "Struggling with the State in Colonial and Postcolonial Africa," a conference at the University of Chicago, May 22–23.

———. 2005. The scorpion's sting: Youth, marriage, and the struggle for social maturity in Niger. *Journal of the Royal Anthropological Institute* (*Man*) 11: 59–83.

———. Forthcoming. Prayer, piety, and pleasure. Contested models of Islamic worship in Dogondoutchi, Niger. In *Religious modernities in West Africa: New moralities in colonial and postcolonial societies*, ed. John Hanson and Rijk van Dijk. Bloomington: Indiana University Press.

Meunier, Olivier. 1998. Marabouts et courants religieux en pays hawsa. *Canadian Journal of African Studies* 32 (3): 521–57.

Meyer, Birgit, and Annelies Moors. 2006. *Religion, media, and the public sphere.* Bloomington: Indiana University Press.

Miller, Daniel. 1994. Style and ontology. In *Consumption and identity*, ed. J. Friedman, 71–96. Chur, Switzerland: Harwood Academic Publishers.

O'Brien, Donald B. C. 1996. A lost generation? Youth identity and state decays in West Africa. In *Postcolonial identities in Africa*, ed. Richard Werbner, 55–74. London: Zed Press.

Reynolds, Pamela. 1995. Youth and the politics of culture in South Africa. In *Children and the politics of culture*, ed. Sharon Stephens, 218–40. Princeton: Princeton University Press.

Richards, Paul. 1996. *Fighting for the rain forest: War, youth, and resources in Sierra Leone.* Oxford: James Currey.

Roy, Olivier. 2004. *Globalized Islam: The search for a new ummah.* New York: Columbia University Press.

Sharp, Lesley A. 2002. *The sacrificed generation: Youth, history, and the colonized mind in Madagascar.* Berkeley: University of California Press.

Soares, Benjamin F. 2005. *Islam and the prayer economy: History and authority in a Malian town.* Ann Arbor: University of Michigan Press.

Stephens, Sharon, ed. 1995. *Children and the politics of culture*. Princeton: Princeton University Press.

Umar, Muhammad S. 1993. Changing Islamic identity in Nigeria from the 1960s to the 1980s: From Sufism to Anti-Sufism. In *Muslim identity and social change in sub-Saharan Africa*, ed. Louis Brenner, 154–78. Bloomington: Indiana University Press.

———. 2001. Education and Islamic trends in Northern Nigeria: 1970s–1990s. *Africa Today* 48 (2): 128–50.

Vries, Hent de, and Samuel Weber, eds. 2001. *Religion and media*. Stanford: Stanford University Press.

Weiss, Brad. 2002. Thug realism: Inhabiting fantasy in urban Tanzania. *Cultural Anthropology* 17 (1): 93–124.

———. 2004. Introduction: Contentious futures: Past and present. In *Producing African futures: Ritual and reproduction in a neoliberal age*, ed. Brad Weiss, 1–20. Leiden: Brill.

LIST OF CONTRIBUTORS

Jan Abbink, a social anthropologist, is a senior researcher at the African Studies Centre, Leiden and a research professor at the Vrije Universiteit, Amsterdam. His main interests are political developments, ethnic relations, and religion in Africa. Among his publications are *Mytho-légendes et histoire: L'énigme de l'ethnogenèse des Beta Esra'el* (1991) and the edited volumes *Meanings of Violence* (2000), and *Vanguard or Vandals: Youth, Politics and Conflict in Africa* (with I. van Kessel, 2004).

Hamadou Adama studied at the University of Bordeaux III–Michel de Montaigne in France. He then worked as an assistant lecturer at the University of Yaoundé I and as a lecturer at the University of Douala, and he is currently an associate professor at the University of Ngaoundéré in northern Cameroon. He has coedited (with Thierno Mouctar Bah) *Un manuscrit arabe sur l'histoire du Royaume de Kontcha dans le Nord-Cameroun (XIXème-XXème siècle)* (2001). His most recent book is *Islam au Cameroun: Entre tradition et modernité* (2004).

Einas Ahmed defended her Ph.D. thesis on the political elite in Sudan at the Centre d'étude d'Afrique noire (CEAN)–Institut d'études politiques de Bordeaux in 2004. She is currently a researcher at the Centre d'études et de documentation economiques et juridiques (CEDEJ) in Khartoum, as well as a research associate at CEAN. She has published several articles on the political and economic situation in Sudan.

Denise Brégand is a researcher for the Centre national de la recherche scientifique at the Centre d'étude d'Afrique noire (CEAN)–Institut d'études politiques de Bordeaux and is studying Islam and Muslim communities in Benin. Her work focused initially on northern Benin, but her present research deals with the new Islamic movements in the coastal towns of Benin. Her most significant publication is *Commerce caravanier et relations sociales au Bénin: Les Wangara du Borgou* (1998).

Mayke Kaag is a social anthropologist at the African Studies Centre, Leiden. She was awarded her Ph.D. in 2001 for research on Senegal and has recently conducted research on transnational Islamic NGOs in Chad. Her present research focuses on the transnational livelihood network of the Senegalese Mouride order, and she is currently engaged in related fieldwork in Italy, the U.S., and Senegal.

Roman Loimeier, a research fellow at the Centre of Modern Oriental Studies in Berlin, has conducted research on Muslim societies in Africa, particularly in Senegal, northern Nigeria, and Tanzania, as well as on Islamic reform movements, the dialectics of Muslims' relations with the state, the development of Islamic education, and the concepts of time and space in Muslim societies. His publications include *Islamic Reform and Political Change in Northern Nigeria* (1997) and *Säkularer Staat und islamische Gesellschaft* (2001).

Adeline Masquelier is a professor of anthropology at Tulane University in New Orleans. She is the author of *Prayer Has Spoiled Everything: Possession, Power, and Identity in an Islamic Town of Niger* (2001) and the editor of *Dirt, Undress, and Difference: Critical Perspectives on the Body's Surface* (2005). She is currently writing a book entitled *Mixed Blessings: Islam, Gender, and Revival in a Nigerien Town*.

René Otayek is director of research in political science at the Centre national de la recherche scientifique. He is also currently the director of the Centre d'étude d'Afrique noire (CEAN)–Institut d'études politiques de Bordeaux. His publications include *Démocratie et société civile* (2002), *Identités et démocratie dans un monde global* (2000), *Dieu dans la cité* (1999), *Le Burkina Faso entre révolution et démocratie (1983–1993)* (1996), and *Le radicalisme islamique au sud du Sahara: Da'wa, arabisation et critique de l'Occident* (1993).

Zekeria Ould Ahmed Salem is a professor of political science in the Faculty of Legal and Economic Sciences at Nouakchott University, Mauritania. He has written on a wide range of topics: Islam in Mauritania, the elections in Mauritania and Senegal, the political economy of fisheries and maritime transport in Senegal and Mauritania, democratization, lawyers, and politics. He recently edited *Les trajectoires d'un État-frontière: Espace, évolution politique et transformations sociales en Mauritanie* (2004).

Marleen Renders is a political scientist in the Law Faculty (subsection for non-Western law) of Ghent University in Belgium and affiliated with the Middle East and North Africa Research Group (MENARG) at the university's Centre for Third World Studies. Her current research focuses on neotraditional leaders and institutions in the reconstruction of war-torn societies. She is the author of various publications on Islam and Islamism in the Arab world and in sub-Saharan Africa.

Samadia Sadouni wrote her doctoral thesis on the Indian Muslim community of South Africa at Montesquieu–Bordeaux IV University. A research associate at the Centre d'étude d'Afrique noire (CEAN) in Bordeaux, she is currently conducting research on humanitarian assistance and citizen participation among Muslim minorities in Southern Africa and transnational Muslim networks linking Africa and India.

Sanusi Lamido Sanusi holds a degree in economics from Ahmadu Bello University, Zaria, Nigeria, and another in sharia and Islamic studies from the International University of Africa, Khartoum, Sudan. After briefly teaching economics at Ahmadu Bello University, he took up a career in banking and is at present the executive director for risk and management control at the First Bank of Nigeria PLC. His interests as a public intellectual are on religion and the state, as well as on the interpretation of Islam in modernity.

Rüdiger Seesemann, a scholar of Islam, is an assistant professor in the Religion Department of Northwestern University. His areas of interest include Islamic mysticism,

Islam and modernity, Islam and politics, Islamism, and Islamic education in the contemporary period, particularly in Sudan, Senegal, and Kenya. His publications include *Ahmadu Bamba und die Entstehung der Muridiya* (1993). He recently completed his habilitation thesis on Sufism in West Africa, *Nach der Flut: Ibrahim Niasse (1900–1975), Sufik und Gesellschaft in Westafrika*, at Bayreuth University.

Benjamin F. Soares, an anthropologist, is a senior researcher at the African Studies Centre, Leiden. He previously taught at the University of Sussex, the University of Chicago, and Northwestern University. He is the author of *Islam and the Prayer Economy: History and Authority in a Malian Town* (2005), the co-editor of *Islam, Transnationalism and the Public Sphere in Western Europe*, a special issue of the *Journal of Ethnic and Migration Studies* (2004), and the editor of *Muslim-Christian Encounters in Africa* (2006).

Index